CONDUCTOR'S WORLD

DAVID WOOLDRIDGE

CONDUCTOR'S WORLD

BARRIE AND ROCKLIFF
THE CRESSET PRESS
LONDON

© 1970 by David Wooldridge
First published by
Barrie & Rockliff, The Cresset Press
2 Clement's Inn, London WC2

SBN 214 66733 2

Printed in Great Britain
by Butler & Tanner Ltd
Frome and London

TO
LANSING HAMMOND

CONTENTS

ILLUSTRATIONS

TABLES AND DIAGRAMS

FOREWORD

Wilhelm Backhaus tells the story of Brahms listening to a performance of his B minor Clarinet Quintet—a performance which clearly delighted him, and he exclaimed to his friends that this was exactly how he had intended it to go. Shortly afterwards there was another performance by different artists, and their reading of the work was entirely different. But far from expressing his dismay, Brahms was equally delighted, and his friends were not unnaturally surprised that he should have felt able to give his unqualified approval to two such disparate interpretations. Brahms explained that both performances had been by first-class players, and that in both cases the artists had put their heart and soul into penetrating and communicating his ideas. Although the two readings were totally unalike, both had conveyed his intentions with equal fidelity.

Backhaus is a pianist for whom I hold a veneration equal to that for Erich Kleiber and Wilhelm Furtwängler as conductors, and his anecdote tells us two things. First, that the greater the music, the more room there is for different and even disparate readings by the great interpretative artist, and the more ridiculous does any question of a "definitive" interpretation become. And secondly, that it is wholly possible to divine the essential characteristics of the music-making of a bygone age on the basis of enlightened musical anecdotes which have come down to us—providing that we are prepared to select certain key figures as our spiritual mentors, and place our implicit faith in them.

This book subscribes to such principles of divination, and although the musical scholar may object to its proliferate surmise, it must be said that it was not written with him primarily in mind. In so far as it touches upon matters which are the legitimate domain of the musicologist, it is hoped that the evidence will be found to be sufficiently well documented, and my only quarrel with the science of musicology—as practised in this country, at all events—is the extent to which it is incapable of the dimension of inspiration, while only too capable of indulging itself in the "ninety-nine per cent hard work". But it is a book with certain pretensions to an other than scholarly seriousness, and is addressed rather to the interested professional music-maker, the enlightened layman, and the intelligent amateur of music.

Much of the writing is based on sets of values which were instilled in me as a child, when I enjoyed the acquaintance of Sergei Rachmaninoff, and between the ages of seven and twelve laboured under the delusion that all concert pianists were expected to play the piano as well as he did. But it established a criterion of judgement which has remained with me ever since. Student years brought me into contact with Erich Kleiber, Wilhelm Furtwängler and Herbert von Karajan in London, years in Vienna and Munich with Clemens Krauss and Hans Knappertsbusch, and years in America with —among others—Charles Munch, Leopold Stokowski, Dimitri Mitropoulos and Georg Szell. Of these experiences, my years in Vienna were perhaps the happiest, and it has been distressing to have had to write uncharitably of a city which was so largely responsible for shaping my musical character. Munich, on the other hand, was an experience which was for me devoid of consolation, yet with the wisdom of years I have come to realise that, for all the arrogance, complacency and provincialism of Bavaria's capital, it bore by far the richer fruit. *Res severa verum gaudium.*

These formative years taught me, not only to examine my own professional shortcomings with ruthless honesty, but to try and define that intangible quality which distinguishes the great conductor—and every great artist— and which Graham Greene, in another context, has called "the capacity for desperation". This does not of course mean the capacity for emotional or material desperation, which are negative qualities, but for what I would call "spiritual desperation", the antithesis of spiritual euphoria. Like all superlative qualities, it is a capacity requiring genius, and it is a species of genius which has been accorded to but few. But it is sufficient to realise that Wagner, Liszt, Bülow, Strauss, Mahler, Nikisch, Furtwängler, Kleiber, Stokowski, Koussevitsky, Munch and Mitropoulos have all been the possessors of it. So have many of the younger generation, but few, I think, are members of the musical profession.

Mention of the younger generation must underline the state of incipient crisis which the conducting profession has experienced since the war. After all, Richard Strauss became general musical director of the Berlin *Staatsoper* at the age of thirty-four, Erich Kleiber at the age of thirty-three, Herbert von Karajan its effective director at the age of twenty-eight. Leopold Stokowski was appointed director of the Philadelphia Orchestra at the age of thirty. It remains an open question whether the younger generation of our own day has been accorded less opportunity or less talent, but it is certain that the postwar musical world no longer has the talent for *listening* to music which it had in pre-war days, and this I think is because their musical palate has become jaded by a surfeit of conventional repertoire. The young conductor of today either defers to managements and impresarios by "playing safe" with established classics, or uses contemporary music as a vehicle to bring him publicity. And in neither case does he exercise the prerogatives—and moral courage—which a conductor of stature should, and must, if the art of music-making is to be kept alive.

There is no greater fallacy than that which supposes that conducting is easy, or that conducting a first-rate orchestra is easier than conducting a fifth-rate one. No one would seriously suggest that it is easier to realise the maximum performance of a Rolls-Royce or a Ferrari than of a Family Ford, though of course it *looks* easier. Anyone who—by virtue of his knowledge of the components and capacity of his car, his ability to secure fine-tuning and smooth synchronisation of the moving parts, and his willingness to effect running repairs and to improvise—can obtain a maximum performance from a Family Ford is certainly a better mechanic (and perhaps a better driver) than the inexpert amateur of the Rolls or the Ferrari, which "drive themselves" to a large extent, once a rudimentary skill in motoring has been acquired. But in driving situations where the Rolls or the Ferrari begin to outstrip the Family Ford with effortless grace, driving has already become potentially dangerous, and both cars are still far below the maximum potential of even their lower gears. It takes inspired talent to realise anything like the maximum potential of a great car, and a skill in diagnosis which enables the expert driver to put his finger on some potentially troublesome symptom and correct it "without the car's knowledge". This is one of the secrets of great conducting, and why it looks so deceptively simple even to the comparatively expert eye of the orchestral player. The conductor should be able to combine something of the *sangfroid* of the Rolls chauffeur with the flair and temperament of the racing-driver. Most conductors drive sports-cars nowadays, but there are significantly few who would look at home behind the wheel of a Rolls-Royce, or would know how to drive one in anything more than a pedestrian fashion.

I have consistently used the word "concertmaster" instead of the "leader" of British vernacular—not only out of deference to the continent of North America, or because "concertmaster" is a literal translation of the word in every other European language, but because it defines more accurately and with greater dignity his function and responsibilities. For metrical values I have used the American nomenclature of "half-note", "quarter-note", "eighth-note", "sixteenth-note", etc. in place of "semibreve", "crotchet", "quaver", "semiquaver", etc., partly because it is the literal translation of the *"halbe"*, *"viertel"*, *"achtel"*, *"sechzehntel"*, etc. of all German-speaking countries—while the British nomenclature shares with the French, Italian and Spanish the anomaly of being incomprehensible to everyone else—and partly

xiii

because of its manifest logic in furnishing a direct relationship with the time-signature. I have used "cor anglais" in place of "English horn" for no very obvious reason save that it is the term in current use in this country, and that the instrument originated, like the hunting-horn, in France. I have retained the word "bar" instead of the American "measure" since it is less specific of the drinking habits of the professional musician.

For permission to quote from copyright works, I am grateful to the following publishers:

Associated Music Publishers Incorporated
Boosey and Hawkes Music Publishers Limited, London
Charles Foley Incorporated, New York City, N.Y.
F. E. C. Leuckart, Munich
Peters Edition
Universal Edition (Alfred Kalmus Limited)

Finally, I would like to thank Miss Madeleine Burnside, for her help and encouragement, and Mr. Robin Golding, for his kindness in reading the proofs.

Musical examples from the first, second and fourth movements of Charles Ives' Fourth Symphony, and from the *Fourth of July*, are used by arrangement with Associated Music Publishers, Inc., publishers and copyright owners.

D. H. M. W.
Elba–London–Geneva 1967–8

CONDUCTOR'S WORLD

INTRODUCTION

The whole miracle of Western art-music owes its clearest manifestation to the emphasis which the Christian Church had laid upon music as a necessary adjunct to her liturgy. From the first, the Church had taken into account the influence of music upon the emotions, and from the earliest times she had employed music to relate her legends and expound her dogma—not merely because this was the only means of reaching a people which could neither read nor write, but also because it instructed them in a way which, far from breeding critical enquiry, was peculiarly capable of being used as a direct stimulus to states of devotion and contrition. The degree and extent of the Church's influence in the science, practice and plain economics of music-making is evident from the vivid account by the monk Wulstan of the great organ installed in Winchester Cathedral *c.*A.D. 965:

> Twice six bellows above are ranged in a row, and fourteen lie below. These, by alternate blasts, supply an immense quantity of wind, and are worked by seventy strong men, labouring with their arms, covered with perspiration, each inciting his companions to drive the wind up with all his strength, that the full-bosom'd box may speak with its four hundred pipes, which the hand of the organist governs. Some when closed he opens, others when open he closes, as the individual nature of the varied sound requires. Two brethren of *concordant spirit* sit at the instrument, and each manages his own *alphabet*. There are moreover hidden holes in the forty tongues, and each has ten pipes in their due order. Some are conducted hither, others thither, each preserving the proper situation for its own note. They strike the seven differences of joyous sounds, adding the music of the lyric *semitone*. Like thunder the iron tones do batter the ear, so that it may receive no sound but that alone. To such an amount does it reverberate, echoing in every direction, that everyone stops with his hand his gaping ears, being in no wise able to draw near and bear the sound which so many combinations produce.[1]

This is cogent testament both to the importance which music had by this time come to enjoy, and to the engineering skills which already existed. With

[1] Wulstan's *Life of Ethelwold, Bishop of Winchester* (963–980), Acta Sanctorum Ordinis Benedict. Saec. V, pp. 631 ff.

the coming of the Christian millennium, musical science was accorded an instance of apocalyptic revelation. The evolution, at the hand of the Benedictine monk Guido of Arezzo, of an effective system of musical notation—first published c.1025 in the musical treatise *Micrologus*—was, during the next few centuries, to translate the language of music into an art medium whose complexity and range of expression fast outpaced the primitive musical refinements of other cultures, and embodied a principle so fundamental that it has remained the basis of our musical speech for nearly a thousand years.

The function which distinguished Guido's discovery was that it allowed, for the first time, a measure of articulate communication between musicians in the act of music-making. Harmony of execution was no longer dependent upon the "concordant spirit" of the religious brethren of whom Wulstan wrote—a spirit fostered by an ecclesiastical learning which, over ten centuries, had devised a mighty organ but nothing more complex, in terms of musical device, than rudimentary *organum*. The first five centuries A.D. had witnessed the matchless refinement of Ambrosian and Gregorian plainchant, which represent the Christian apotheosis of monophony—yet to what extent the organic development of musical speech had been inhibited is clear from the fact that, during the next five centuries, music had not progressed beyond the crude combination of two voices (i.e. *organum*). Now, for the first time, musical ideas could be recorded on paper, could be compounded, assembled and refined, and the progress of a single voice or confluence of voices accurately predetermined and rehearsed. Monophony—the basis of music upon the unison idea—is a characteristic of all other civilizations, from Egypt, Assyria, Greece and Byzantium to the myriad culture of the East, much of whose musical expression remains radically and immutably monophonic after three thousand years. That Oriental music in general has never experienced the need to evolve a fluent system of notation of its own, and has never seriously entertained the adoption of Western notation, must account for the fact that its language, for all its subtlety and intricacy, has never progressed in a creative sense, while its traditional instruments remain unchanged after tens of centuries of usage. And it must suggest that the need for the musician to express himself and to communicate that expression to his colleagues and to his audience in exact terms—a need which had given rise to the system of staff notation—is something peculiar and essential to Messianic culture as a whole. The five centuries following Guido's discovery, which culminated in the full flowering of the Renaissance, were to accomplish for music the transcendant mastery of the Polyphonic era, and an art in the combination of voices in highly organised counterpoint whose perfection and ingenuity must remain forever unsurpassed.

In 1600 the Lutheran chronologer, composer and mathematician Sethus Calvisius published *De Initio et Progressu Musices*, which was the first attempt at tracing the history of music from its origins to his own day. Fifteen years later Michael Praetorius, a prolific composer and the most illustrious German musician of his day, produced the first of a projected four volumes comprising his *Syntagma Musica*, a history of the function and usage of music and its relationship with poetry. Both differed from the famous Catholic treatises of Cerone, Mersenne and Buontempi (who regarded music as a universal manifestation of the divine will based on the immutable principles of divine law) in their suggestion that music was a constantly changing art, progressing by virtue of the accumulated genius of individual men and serving all functions of society, secular as well as sacred. Martin Luther had been no musician, to be sure, but he accidentally laid the foundation-stone of German instrumental music in creating the chorale, for by introducing folk-music into hymnody he united the secular and the sacred, broke down the intricate structure of polyphony, and popularised the major and minor modes which were to become the essential vocabulary of instrumental music and prepare the way to the introduction of equal-temperament.

If the writings of Calvisius and Praetorius reflect the intellectual spirit of the Reformation and the breakaway from the influence and patronage of the Roman Church, another kind of revolution was taking place in those countries over whom the Church of Rome still exercised undivided dominion. Italy had suffered a moral convulsion with the sack of Rome in 1527, and the humiliation of Florence three years later. The Spanish Inquisition was in full sway and the Renaissance shackled, the *Sacra Rappresentazione* and *Commedia dell'Arte*—forerunners of ballet and opera in their combination of song, dance and instrumental music—were banned, even painting was suspect, and the findings of the Council of Trent in 1563 came as an inevitable conclusion, demanding the excision of all profane elements from music which accompanied the liturgy, and an unqualified emphasis upon the clarity and intelligibility of the text in performance. Strictures thus imposed on an art which had become diverse and elaborate to a degree were transcended by the towering genius of the conservative Palestrina, but elsewhere music sought new patrons in the rich merchants of the Renaissance, and the monopoly of Church patronage was broken.

As a predominantly merchant community Venice was the only state in Italy which was enjoying—and which for many generations had been enjoying—internal peace. Astute government, merchant wealth and the physical limitations of the island city combined to imbue the Venetian with a sense of warmth and pageantry, a love of comfort and a refinement of manner which are most immediately perceived in the exquisite formality and tact of the Venetian school of painting. But just as it was in Venice that the first schools of San Giorgio, Santo Stefano, San Giovanni and Sant' Ursula were founded, so was it also in Venice that the first schools of music came into being. And it was to Venice that the Fleming, Orlandus Lassus, was sent in 1567, as Kapellmeister to Duke Albert of Bavaria and one of the first musicians of stature to enjoy private patronage, to engage the services of thirty instrumentalists—one of the first ensembles to approach orchestral proportions. And it was to Venice, in 1613, that Monteverdi came, after a year significantly spent in his native town of Cremona, to assume the post of Master of Music to the Republic of Venice, where for the first time he was to give to music a public orientation. In 1637, the first theatre was opened to the public with a performance of Manelli's *Andromeda* at the Teatro San Cassiano, and when in 1639 Monteverdi's *L'Adone* was produced in the new SS Giovanni e Paolo theatre, opera had moved from the prince's palace into the public domain. During the next sixty years no fewer than seventeen theatres opened their doors in the one city of Venice, all as commercial undertakings dependent for their support upon the immense box-office appeal which the new medium of opera had created among the general public.

It is with Monteverdi that we first see evidence of the composer beginning to think in orchestral terms, and we know that for the first performance of *Orfeo* before his patron, the Duke of Mantua, in 1607, Monteverdi assembled an orchestra of forty musicians—more than were available to Beethoven at any time in his life. *Orfeo* is thought to have been inspired by the performance, seven years earlier, of Jacopo Peri's *Euridice* at the Palazzo Pitti in Florence, on the occasion of the betrothal of Maria de' Medici to Henri IV of France, which had already used the unprecedented "orchestra"—in the secular context—of three recorders, three guitars, clavichord and theorbo, all played by amateurs from among the Court. The employment in Monteverdi's *Orfeo* of clavichord, regal, two positive organs, two lutes, ten *viole da braccio, viola da gamba,* two *pocchetti* (pocket-violins), oboes, *clarini* (trumpets), and about fifteen violins, is therefore historic.[2]

No less important than Monteverdi's contribution to the language of opera and to the growing art of orchestral writing, is the circumstance of his

---

[2] That Monteverdi, as Master of Music to Duke Gonzaga of Mantua, should have chosen to set *Orfeo* may have another origin, for it was in the little Marquisate of Mantua that Angelo Poliziano had written *La Favola di Orfeo*—the musical setting of a text of only 434 lines which anticipates Peri's and Monteverdi's essays by over a century. None of the music remains to us, but it is clear that the principal role was a musical one, that there was some kind of instrumental accompaniment, and that there were choral sections set as *frottole*—an early form of the madrigal. Monteverdi was a prolific composer of madrigals, and his operatic style shows their influence quite as much as it develops the art of orchestral writing.

birth at a time when musical history of quite another nature, and of vital consequence, was being made in his native town of Cremona. Monteverdi had studied the viol under Marc' Antonio Ingegneri at the cathedral school in Cremona, and it was as a viol-player that he first entered the service of the Duke of Mantua in 1583, at the age of sixteen. The instrument which he played was in all probability by Gasparo Bertolotti, a native of Salò who worked in Brescia and was probably the finest maker of viols of his day. It is known that Gasparo experimented with the construction of violins, but it was in Cremona that the violin was already being perfected by the Amati family— from Andrea Amati, born in 1520, to his grandson Nicolò, born in 1596, to whom both Guarneri and Stradivari were later apprenticed. And although some fine instruments had certainly been made before Monteverdi reached adolescence, it is significant that the violin does not appear to have attracted him at this time, and it was not until after his return to Cremona in 1612 and his appointment to Venice the following year that he began to put the instrument to artistic use. Nor is this very surprising, for the violin was regarded at that time as the property of the street-musician and the drinking-house, and exposed to musical abuses akin to the saxophone or the electric-guitar in our own day. Yet this was the family of string instruments which was to revolutionise instrumental-playing, and provide the foundation to the modern orchestra.

The genesis of the idea of the violin is not easy to trace, for although the progress of instrumental music was discovering the limitations of the viol and the larger *viola de braccio* and *viola da gamba*, the instance of Monteverdi shows conclusively that music was not yet clamouring for the extrovert violins, violas and violoncellos of Amati, Stradivari and Guarneri, whose range and richness have remained unchallenged through four centuries of enormous advance in the language and technique of string playing. Just as the prosaic gesture of the "Guidonian hand" was slow to leave its indelible imprint on the course of musical history, so the disreputable violin had to wait a century before it was to be graced with serious musical attention from Arcangelo Corelli. It is irrelevant to enquire whether the idea should be accredited historically to Andrea Amati or Gasparo da Salò, or what were the pressures from composer or performer which brought about its birth. The violin evolved because it was aesthetically necessary that it should do so, and the coincidence of the superlative craftsmanship of the Cremona masters, the geographical location of that city on the hot, dry plains of Lombardy and on the old trade routes to the forests of spruce, pine and maple across the Adriatic, and a moment of musical history which allowed patient and uninterrupted workmanship, combine to have made its evolution inevitable.

There could have been no foreseeing that the instrument would find its supreme justification in the music of Mozart, Beethoven and Alban Berg, no inspired intuition as to the course which music was to take during the next two centuries. Inherent in this very fact is the absolute integrity of the violin family, for great violin-making was largely a question of time, and the secret of the Cremona masters lay in their complete absence of hurry. They could afford to wait for the right wood to arrive, and to let it mature in the sun when it did arrive. They could allow time for the varnish to sink in, and to carry on their work near the Piazza San Domenica undisturbed by the political up-heavals of the day which brought Cremona under siege three times during the ninety-three years of Stradivari's lifetime. We have the wood and the varnish which Amati and Guarneri and Stradivari used, but our violins today are manufactured as pieces of merchandise rather than as works of art.

Meanwhile the accession of Louis XIV to the throne of France had ushered in *le grand siècle*. If an insidious puritanism can descry only vanity and self-indulgence in the monument of Versailles, and a tenuous democracy finds itself at loggerheads with the principle of autocracy, the monument and the principle are yet amply vindicated by the spirit of enlightenment which they fostered and reflected. Art knows no other values than those inherent in the architecture of a Versailles, the tapestry of a Gobelin, or the sovereign qualities of a *roi soleil*. In 1646, the Chevalier de Guise had befriended a young Italian street urchin whom he had found taking part in a minstrel-show at the carnival of Florence, and took him to Paris where he was installed as a scullery-hand in the household of Mlle de Montpensier—a cousin of the young king, famous for the part which she had played in the *Fronde* movement.

Giovanni Battista Lulli had learned the elements of music from a Franciscan friar and had taught himself to play the violin, and when his musical ability was discovered he was promoted to *garçon de chambre* and put in charge of his mistress's small band of *violons*. Six years later Lulli entered the service of the fourteen-year-old King Louis, in the triple capacity of *baladin*, ballet-composer, and violinist in the *Vingt-Quatre Violons du Roi*, under the leadership of Michel Lambert, Lulli's future father-in-law. This remarkable ensemble had been founded by Louis XIII, and although writers —and painters—are notorious for the gaffes which they perennially commit in techno-musical matters, it seems clear from the description by Marin Mersenne in his *Harmonie Universelle* of 1636 that this was indeed a band of the violin family, and not a huge consort of viols. If this is true, the violin must have been imported to Paris by Italian musicians who, in the retinue of Catherine de' Medici, had taken part in the Ballet Comique de la Reine in 1581—by which time many Amati instruments were in general use. But it formed in any case a remarkable string section which was not equalled in size until the nineteenth century. Lulli found favour with the king, and in 1656 was allowed to form a second orchestra of sixteen players—*Les Petits-Violons du Roi*—later increased to twenty-one, in the proportion of ten violins, five violas, five violoncellos, and a *contre-violon*. Under his leadership this ensemble quickly surpassed the older band, for Lulli introduced the practice of playing from individual parts rather than improvising by ear from a basso continuo which had been normal practice until then. It is fair indication of the favour which he enjoyed that when Louis XIV assumed sovereignty in his own right in 1661, he signed letters of naturalisation for Lully (as he now styled himself) which describe him as the son of "Lorenzo Lulli, gentleman of Florence". And when, the following year, he married Madeleine Lambert and succeeded her father as *Maître de Musique à la Famille-Royale*, the marriage-contract was signed by Louis, the Queen and the Queen Mother—a mark of personal interest in music and the musician which it would be hard indeed to find today. Lully's career continued to prosper and his influence to grow. In 1671 he acquired—under circumstances which reek of intrigue—the royal patent for the Academie Royale de Musique (forerunner of the Paris Opèra) and two years later he obtained a royal decree prohibiting any theatre from employing more than two singers or six *violons*, thereby giving Lully a virtual monopoly over all operatic performances throughout France. Paris, not inappropriately, had witnessed the birth of opera-house politics. Lully died in 1687 from an infected wound of his foot, sustained while beating time with his ballet-master's cane during a performance of his *Te Deum*, and must go on record as the only conductor to have lost his life in the direct service of his art. The *Vingt-Quatre Violons du Roi* continued with diminishing lustre until 1761 when, by the *décret du 2 âout*, they were disbanded by Louis XV on the grounds of their expense. But meanwhile an ensemble of subtler dimensions had emerged in 1708 with the chamber orchestra of the Chapelle Royale, comprising six violins, three 'cellos, a contrabass, two flutes, two oboes, and a bassoon.

The violin family had taken more than a century to gain acceptance in any ambience more serious than that of the *ballet du cour*, the new opera house, and the tavern. Slower still to find their orchestral identity were the elements which constitute the woodwind family, and whose employment until the eighteenth century had been haphazard and confined almost exclusively to the recorder (a direct and largely unimproved descendant from the Arabic *naï*) and the oboe family—*oboe, oboe da caccia* and *oboe d'amore*—which had evolved from the Egyptian shawm of 3700 B.C. Both types of instrument, together with the lute, guitar and rebec—forerunner of the viol—had found their way to Europe via the Crusades and the Moorish domination of the

Mediterranean, and the recorder consort, involving sometimes as many as eight different sizes of instrument, and had been used since the sixteenth century to complement the consort of viols. But with the advent of the violin family, their insipid tone was lost, and only the treble recorder survived in ensemble usage—though Bach was quick to replace it with the newly invented "transverse flute" used by Quantz whenever one was available. Similarly, the *oboe da caccia* and *oboe d'amore* possessed a tone too distinctive to blend effectively with the symphonic colour of the new string section and fell into general disuse, while the transverse flute, as a German invention of Baroque implications, did not find much immediate favour until a suitable partner had been found for it in the clarinet. Only the oboe itself persisted in general use, to provide the essential core and temperament of the future woodwind section, and it is for this reason that the first oboist of the symphony orchestra of today occupies a position of especial responsibility in relation to his colleagues and to the orchestra as a whole—a position second only to that of the concertmaster.

The practice of grouping the wind instruments in pairs is based upon an acoustical principle very near to the heart of Austrian music which, with the growing alliance between Schönbrunn and Versailles, culminating in the marriage of Marie-Antoinette to Louis XVI, had begun to inherit the responsibilities of a major activity in the life of the Austrian court. A device which typifies Austrian music from the ländler to the waltz, and from Mozart to Mahler, is the characteristic use of passages of parallel thirds—the duets from *Così fan tutte* and *Der Rosenkavalier* furnish obvious examples. This device has a practical origin in the Austrian Tyrol—and music from the Italian Tyrol shares this same characteristic—where the practice of yodelling as a necessary if revolting expedient of communication from one mountain-top to another had, at some blessed instant of history, stumbled upon the acoustical truth that for two people to yodel in thirds, rather than in unison, was to increase the carrying power of the human voice four-fold. With the movement of music into the ever wider public domain not only of the opera house, but now also of the concert hall, there was an ever-growing need to increase the volume and audibility of instrumental sound in proportion to the number—and expense—of the players available. (Such an acoustical principle had indeed lain behind the combination of voices in the polyphonic music of the Church, and had taken advantage of the natural resonances of its architectural fabric and in turn influenced the study of applied acoustics in giving preference to musical considerations. In the cathedral performance of an orchestral work today, it is the winds which enjoy the advantages of acoustics which tend to blur the string tone.) The function of the new string section had been to adopt and extend the role of the human voice in four-part conjunction, and the inclusion within this framework of a counterpoint of wind instruments whose structure was derived from the principles of poly-phony was in complete harmony with the symphonic idea. To preserve unanimity of tone-colour, the wind instruments were accordingly grouped in pairs—an *a priori* principle already embodied in the Chapelle Royale band of 1708. The urgent need was now to find a satisfactory complement, within the wind family, to the pair of oboes which constituted its basis.

The hunting-horn had evolved as another means of communication, and in another social and geographical context, for in the dense forests of the boar-hunt the human voice, and the silver trumpets which had resounded through the stone palaces of Tutankhamen, were quickly stifled. The hollow animal horn, which gave the musical instrument its name, provided a blander tone with acoustical properties which could penetrate the woods and valleys of hunting terrain, and this primitive instrument continued to serve until, with the hunting predelictions of the Louis, the *cor de chasse* or *cor français* was evolved—a brass tube some eight feet in length, coiled for convenience and carried slung over the shoulder. Lully was probably the first composer to in-troduce the *cor de chasse* into the orchestra in his ballet-comique *La Princesse d'Elide*, performed at Versailles in 1664, and Bach uses two *corni di caccia* in his first Brandenburg Concerto of 1721. The tonal quality of the hunting or "natural" horn provided an ideal complement to that of the oboe, but it was severely inhibited—in common with the "natural" trumpet—in that it had few notes available to it, all directly allied to the tonality of its fundamental note. Yet this very limitation, which in baroque music had confined the activities of the horns and trumpets to their extreme registers where adjacent harmonics lie grouped closely together, was now of major consequence in bringing the symphonic idea to fulfilment: for while the composer could only use horns and trumpets in their "harmonic" register to establish the tonality of a piece at its outset, and to herald the return of that tonality at given moments in the musical discourse, this could now be turned to dramatic advantage in determining and refining the symphonic argument. The use of a pair of horns became universal, and the extent to which the quartet of two oboes and two horns provided the self-sufficient wind section in the early symphony orchestra can be seen from Mozart's earlier symphonies. Before the *Paris* Symphony of 1778 (usually styled as No. 31, though in fact fortieth of a total of more than fifty symphonies by Mozart), no less than nineteen symphonies confine themselves to a wind section of oboes and horns, with the sole addition of two trumpets in a further ten, and of flutes in a further six. Bassoons appear in only three, and clarinets not at all.

After the *Paris* Symphony Mozart's use of the bassoon is consistent, for it provided an agile reinforcement to the bass line and an apt mirror to the oboe at the lower octave, and in passages which would have been wholly alien to the horns. One can only deduce from Mozart's earlier disdain of the bassoon that players were simply unavailable in Salzburg, or that their command of their instruments had left too much to be desired—and indeed, to the present day, both good players and good instruments are hard to come by. The use of clarinets after the *Paris* Symphony is less consistent—as it is in the later symphonies of Haydn—and they only find a permanent place in Beethoven's orchestra. But with their permanent appearance, the hitherto neglected transverse flutes find their justification, and flutes and clarinets become almost inseparable. With the permanent addition of trumpets and drums, traditionally associated in the martial context, the classical orchestra was complete.

Or so it would seem. Yet the fires of revolutionary zeal which were sweeping Europe so much at the instance of the creative artist, held for him consequences not wholly benign. With the growing spirit of republicanism which music had done so much to engender, the patronage system was slowly undermined, the position of the patron compromised, and music addressed itself more and more to the multitudes—not only of its own choice, but because the audiences of the aristocracy which had demanded of it grace and charm, and nurtured its refinement and indulged its *rousseauiste* tendencies, were now preoccupied with their own self-preservation and no longer so readily available. Nor was their liberal if capricious purse. Musicians cost money, and with the coming of the bourgeoisie they cost even more money, for the musician could depend less and less on the security of the Hofkapelle and began to demand his rights like any other good citizen. The symphony orchestra had been born of the experience of a hundred private court orchestras, but it was still in a state of helpless infancy in comparison with the complexity and technical difficulty to which the language of symphony and opera had attained. Under the patronage of Marie-Antoinette, Gluck had been able to insist on six months' rehearsal for the Paris première of *Iphigénie en Aulide*—six months fraught with near-strike conditions, the musicians demanding overtime and impervious to those musical standards which the composer, with little enough insight into orchestral psychology, sought to enforce. Concert halls and concert societies had sprung up all over Europe, the London series instituted by Johann Christian Bach and Friedrich Abel in 1764, the inauguration of the Leipzig Gewandhaus in 1781, the Salomon Concerts in 1786, the St. Petersburg Philharmonic Society in 1802, the London Philharmonic Society in 1811, the Gesellschaft der Musikfreunde in

Vienna in 1813, and the Société des Concerts du Conservatoire in Paris in 1828. An adequate orchestra, with adequate rehearsal, presented a grave expense for the impresario who could no longer benefit from an orchestra and programme amply prepared under princely aegis, and both players and rehearsal time were reduced to a minimum.

When Beethoven's Fifth Symphony first appeared in Vienna, it bore the following dedication on the title-page:

> *Sinfonie pour deux violons, deux violes, violoncelle et contre-violon, deux flûtes, petite flûte, deux hautbois, deux clarinettes, deux bassons, contre-basson, deux cors, deux trompettes et trois trompes: composée et dediée à son Altesse Sérénissime Monseigneur de Prince régnant de Lobkowitz et à son Excellence le comte de Rasumoffsky par Louis van Beethoven.*

It is a normal practice to specify a basic quintet of strings as implying a full string section, and a reference to two violins, viola, 'cello and contrabass would not have been untoward. But Beethoven specifies *deux violes*—two violas—as an integral part of the full formal dedication of his most famous work. The reason for this is not hard to divine, and its significance is conclusive. The viola part divides, in the second, third and final movements, in a way which precludes its being played as a double-stop, and the specification of two violas is therefore a minimal requirement—a requirement which must apply equally to the other elements of the string section, or the simple specification of string-quintet would have been sufficient. In other words, Beethoven is telling us that, in this gigantic testament of faith in mankind, which was to make use for the first time in symphonic history of the massive sound of a trombone section at the start of its finale, a string section of only six players will, *faute de mieux*, suffice.

I do not know if it is of other than academic interest to know whether the Fifth Symphony was ever in fact performed under such conditions, and one may hope that no musicologist will ever demand that it should be so performed in the interest of its composer's declared intentions. What is of interest is the conclusion which may be drawn from this evidence, and which is twofold: that no established norm for the optimum size of a string section operated in Vienna at this time, and that Beethoven was thinking not in terms of posterity, but of practical expediency—an attitude which immediately distinguishes the artist from the dilettante. A concept of orchestral balance which we take for granted in the established symphony orchestras of today was as alien to Beethoven's experience, even as an intuitively conceived absolute, as the playing of Paganini would have been to the self-sufficient craftsmanship of Guarneri who had built Paganini's fiddle one hundred years earlier. What can have been the standards which attended the performance of Beethoven's works during his lifetime, or which were applied by the violin-conductors of his day who can have had no concept at all of an orchestral ensemble of which Beethoven himself was but tentatively aware, must defy the imagination. It is sufficient to know that it was not until 1839 that there was an artistically coherent performance of the Ninth Symphony under Habaeneck, the last of the violin-conductors, and this only after *three years'* rehearsal. Beethoven is sanguine enough, in his letters, on the subject of mediocre standards of playing, but his footnote to the string-cadenza in *Leonora No. 3* is all-revealing: if the whole section can play the passage at all— as the viola, 'cello and bass sections are required to do at their respective entries—then there is no need to confine the entries of the first and second violins to "two or three violins" only. The passage is not technically difficult, and the only reason for such a marking can have been that it is exposed, has no immediately defined metre, and starts abruptly with a new and very fast tempo. In short, it is the classic instance of the need for a real conductor who can transmit a new tempo instantaneously and unambiguously and with a single down-beat, for there is no time to prepare the *Presto* with an up-beat which would have no place or function in the musical context in any case. Such refinements, which were readily understood by individual musicians in Beethoven's time, are hardly understood by many conductors to this day, and it is not surprising that Beethoven, for reasons of expediency, should have added the direction "due o tre violini". For even before he had begun to be plagued by deafness, Beethoven displayed none of the instincts which we now recognise as being those of a substantial conductor. Neither, we may judge, did Mozart. His decision to sit at the piano at the performances of *Entführung* —"for the sake of the ensemble"[3]—his delight at the ensemble of the Mannheim orchestra under Stamitz, his difficulties with his own "rabble of players" at Salzburg,[4] and his concern during his own rehearsals of the *Paris* Symphony which vanished at the first performance under Lahoussaye's direction—these must suggest that the authoritarian element was lacking from Mozart's otherwise transcendental musicianship. Historians still continue to surmise why Haydn was seated at the piano during the performance of his London symphonies when Salomon himself was patently directing their performance from the first desk of violins, and they have gone so far as to suggest that the inclusion of a piano continuo in the performance of Haydn symphonies is *ipso facto* authentic and therefore to be desired. Haydn added instruments and

[3] Mozart's letter of 19 October, 1782.
[4] Ibid. 9 July, 1778.

changed instrumentation according to the availability of musicians at individual performances at Eszterháza[5], and if he added a continuo part in some of his earlier symphonies it was because he considered one necessary for an individual performance. For the London concerts he sat at the piano for reasons of expediency, and to reinforce an ensemble which was weak not by reason of any shortcomings on the part of individual players or of any deficiency in their number, but by very reason of their number and of a shortcoming in the practice of an art of conducting, whose necessity had not yet been realised or understood at all.

It is a commonplace in the history of art that at its very moments of richest creativity it has tended to lose a sense of historical perspective. Mantegna's *Agony in the Garden* derives spiritual and architectural strength from a background of modern-day Rome, and Shakespeare ascribes an awareness of the earth's rotundity to a Macbeth who was assuredly brought up to believe that the world was flat. In the same kind of way the full flowering, predominantly at Mozart's hand, of the genius of symphony and opera evaded for a time its most urgent perspective—that of a central authority who would not only insist upon the accurate reading of the individual parts (which the traditional violin-conductor or concertmaster could do), nor yet only secure a substantial degree of precision in ensemble through the antics of the drillmaster, but one who was able to realise the composer's whole intention.

This even the composer himself was not yet able to do although, as we shall see, the first conductors of stature were in fact composers, and nearly all the great conductors up to the present day have been composers of greater or lesser merit. But the composer, in any case, could not now be present to supervise performances of his own music. His traditional position as Hofkapellmeister had encouraged his art by demanding a regular output of music which it became his automatic duty to perform, and the performance of the music of a colleague from elsewhere had been the exception rather than the rule. But now the giving of public concerts, calling for the first time on the undivided attention of the audience rather than providing incidental entertainment to the social activities of the private court, had become a rapidly expanding enterprise, and programmes had to exhibit variety and initiative. Increasingly effective publishing of orchestral material allowed and occasioned performances far from the composer's own habitat, and some music, for the first time in musical history, was beginning to survive the composer himself in popular esteem—Handel's *Messiah* was an early example of this phenomenon, and Mozart's orchestration from the continuo part afforded him a

---

[5] Flutes and oboes interchange inside the same works, clarinet parts are added quite arbitrarily, e.g. the Salomon symphonies.

much needed income during the last years of his own life[6]. The role of Kapellmeister, which had been more or less synonymous with that of Konzertmeister (Haydn, Mozart, Stamitz and the Toëschi brothers had been fiddlers all), was now becoming too specialised for the violin-conductor whose responsibilities, with the advancing complexities of string writing, were directed more and more towards his own section, while the increasing need for meticulous wind-ensemble required more and more expert attention. It was no longer sufficient for the violin-conductor to direct a rehearsal or a performance from the first-violin part, and it was impracticable for him to do so from the full-score without compromising his duties as leader of his own section. The violin-conductor continued to survive in the opera house where the orchestra traditionally faced the stage with their backs to the audience, and where the independent conductor was indeed at a severe disadvantage—for he was constantly compelled to turn his back on the orchestra in order to concentrate on stage ensemble, and at those very moments when the attention of the orchestra was most needed. It fell to Carl Maria von Weber in 1818, as director of the Dresden Court Theatre, to change this arrangement.

[6] Musical copyright did not then exist, and it was common practice for publishers to pirate one another's works. Music copyists would frequently sell a composer's work without his knowledge, and Mozart himself took the precaution of making a second copy of his own manuscripts—"from memory" in the case of the Sinfonia Concertante for winds, according to his letter of 1 October, 1778, and soon after he had parted with the original. There was probably no authority for the performance of *Messiah*, and it was deemed cheaper to have a new orchestration commissioned from a pirated continuo part than to negotiate for the original set of parts.

Chapter 1

WEBER, BERLIOZ AND WAGNER

One cannot, as a string-player, study a page of Vivaldi, or as a pianist, a page of Liszt, without being impressed by the superlative mastery which each displays of their respective instruments, be the passage one of the most eloquent bravura or of the uttermost simplicity, for there is a sense of un-yielding *tour de force* in even their most unpretentious writing, which is in-extricably bound up with their sovereignty as makers of music. One of the distinguishing features of Weber is that his is pre-eminently conductor's music in the same way that Vivaldi's is violinist's music and Liszt's pianist's music. That Weber was a conductor as no musician before him had been a conductor is evident from the awareness that his music exhibits that every phrase and passage shall respond to expert control—an awareness neither more nor less conscious than that of Liszt and Vivaldi in their own writing—and the evidence becomes overwhelming when one has conducted Weber with any frequency. It is a matter not only, nor even primarily, of the or-chestration, which is in turn magical, brilliant, and—but rarely—sadly mis-judged. The final chord preceding the *Allegro con fuoco* in the overture to *Oberon* is frequently cited as a master-stroke of orchestration—which it is, as much by virtue of its placing in the musical context as by the unusual dis-placement of the instruments. It also appears in most conducting manuals as a *locus classicus* requiring the greatest circumspection, for it is one of the few instances in the symphonic literature where the conductor may be quite sure that every member of the orchestra will be watching him like a hawk. Cer-tainly there are few passages which reveal so cogently or so swiftly whether or not the conductor knows what he is about.

Weber had trained as a pianist, and remained a virtuoso exponent of that instrument throughout his life. This was to establish a new precedent, for although Haydn and Mozart had been pianists *par excellence*, it had been with the violin that they had directed most of their performances, and the tradition of the violin-conductor was still strong. But the breakaway had started. Gluck, who only assumed the duties of a Hofkapellmeister at the age of thirty-eight—first to Prince Sachsen-Hilberghausen and then, two years later, at the head of the Vienna Hofoper—had been a 'cellist, and anticipated another 'cellist-conductor in his intolerance and irascibility. Spontini, for nine years associated with the Théâtre des Italiens in Paris, and for twenty-two at the head of the Royal Opera in Berlin, had been a singer. Ludwig Spohr, an immediate contemporary of Weber, had been a violinist, but forsook the violin for the baton for the first time at a London Philharmonic Society concert on 20 April, 1820, to the widespread consternation of the orchestra. Only Habaeneck, another contemporary of Weber, whom Berlioz greatly admired and Wagner, not unkindly, dismissed as an *"alte Zöpfe"*, survived as the last outstanding violin-conductor. His death in 1849 brought to an end an era which had begun with Johann Wenzel Stamitz in Mannheim in 1744.

The virtue of the pianist-conductor at this stage of music's development was self-apparent. The violin-conductor had provided a vehicle for the symphonists, and in so doing had established an instrumental formula whose capacity now exceeded his artistic grasp. With Mozart's *Zauberflöte* had come the first awakenings of German opera—as opposed to *Singspiel*—which was to be crystallised with Beethoven's *Fidelio* and Weber's *Freischütz*, and through Gluck the opera house had inherited the format of the symphony orchestra. The vertical compass of the piano keyboard and the nature of its literature, with its closer approximation to orchestral sound than any individual orchestral instrument could provide, placed the pianist at an immense advantage. His fluency at the keyboard and ability to transcribe the full score on to the piano for rehearsal purposes gave him a new and immediate contact with his singers inside the opera house, and with the members of his orchestra in the context of chamber-music. If he were socially presentable he could enhance his social prestige by taking part in musical soirées for his patrons and protectors, and rub shoulders with influential members of his public, and this in turn could be used to account in gaining improved musical conditions for his work. As a composer his creative talents had ample outlet, for the emphasis was necessarily still very much on the performance of contemporary music, and this could only reinforce his position. He began to acquire definition as a personality, and as a focus and fulcrum to the musical ambience in which he worked.

It is significant, however, that the two revolutionary figures of the nineteenth century who were to accomplish so much both for the composer's and the conductor's art, and to give to the symphony orchestra an identity which was substantially that which we have inherited today, were neither of them keyboard virtuosi, and that, for this very reason, their struggle for per-

sonal recognition and the recognition of universal artistic standards was prolonged and violent. Berlioz, born in 1803, inherited the culture of a Paris still
infirm from the trauma of the Revolution, hungering for war, politically,
morally and artistically corrupt, yet still the first musical city of a Europe
whose musical standards had reached their nadir. Wagner, born ten years
later, inherited the twin cultures of Leipzig and Dresden, and a yearning for
musical and political identity in a Germany divided and dominated by provincial philistinism.

When, in September 1819, Spontini left Paris to go to Berlin at the
behest of Friedrich Wilhelm III of Prussia, the more than a century-old
battle between the Paris Opéra and the Théâtre des Italiens might seem to
have been at an end. The Italian opera had already been integrated with the
Comédie Française under Spontini's direction in 1810, when the first Paris
performance of Mozart's *Don Giovanni* in the original Italian had been given.
Foreign influences were still strong, as the names of Gluck, Meyerbeer,
Spontini and Cherubini—head of the Paris Conservatoire—bear witness. But
it had been French opera which had conquered them, and not they who had
conquered French opera. Thus Berlioz might have been expected to have
appeared on the Paris scene at a favourable moment. Yet his life is a history of
persistent failure and frustration, only here and there relieved by a brilliant
success. His theatrical style and manner were non-conformist at a time when
a spirit of retrenchment was rife in France, nor was he properly equipped to
conform, for his was a natural genius, imperfectly trained, and he forfeited
the much-needed opportunity of teaching at the Conservatoire because he
could not fulfil the rudimentary requirement of being able to play the
piano.

Berlioz's command of orchestration was legendary, and the *Traité de
l'Instrumentation*—written in the same year as the *Carnaval Romain* overture
and published in 1844 as his Op. 10—is both more comprehensive and displays a musical insight more acute than most more recently published works
on the subject. Like Weber, his command of the orchestra is in turn brilliant
and magical, sometimes awe-inspiring, occasionally ill-judged and even per-
verse. And like Weber, there is in his writing the constant awareness of the
conductor as the moving executive spirit. When one considers that the
Symphonie Fantastique received its first performance only six years after that
of Beethoven's Ninth in Vienna, one must realise the stupendous advance
which had taken place both in the concept of orchestral writing and in that of
orchestral control. The treatise on instrumentation and its appendix, *L'Art du
Chef d'Orchestre*, published twelve years later, give ample evidence of Berlioz's
acute insight into the responsibilities of the conductor, together with valuable

B

commentaries on the practices of established conductors of his time—
Habaeneck in particular. Berlioz had by this time acquired considerable experience as conductor, had met Wagner, Liszt and Bülow and had conducted
in Leipzig, Weimar, Berlin and Vienna, as well as in London. Yet it should be
remembered that Berlioz was twenty-five before he first heard a Beethoven
symphony—under Habaeneck's direction—while the musical examples in his
treatise, which had been written before the experiences mentioned above,
confine themselves to the veriest handful of composers. Nevertheless, the
penetration of these examples is an object-lesson in interpretative musicianship to composer and conductor alike, and speaks well, generally, of the
standards of playing which Berlioz had experienced in Paris. His remarks
with reference to orchestral string-playing are revealing:

> Violins are able, nowadays, to execute whatever they will. They
> play up to the extreme height as easily as in the middle. Passages
> the most rapid, designs the most eccentric, do not dismay them.
> In an orchestra where they are sufficiently numerous, *that which
> one fails to perform is done by the others*: and the result is that,
> without any apparent mistake, the phrase is delivered as the author
> wrote it.

This is followed by a quotation, from the first movement of the *Symphonie
Fantastique*, where the upper strings divide, although such division is today
quite unnecessary.

> In cases, however, where the rapidity, complication, and height
> of a passage make it too hazardous, or if only for the sake of greater
> sureness and neatness of execution, it should be dispersed; that is to
> say, the mass of violins should be divided, and one part of the
> passage given to some, the rest to the others. In this way the music of
> each division is sprinkled with little rests, unperceived by the hearer;
> allowing, as it were, breathing space to the violinists, and affording
> them time to take carefully the *difficult positions*, and thus to obtain
> the necessary firmness for a vigorous attack.

It is evidence of the advance which string-playing has made since Berlioz's
time that, notwithstanding his claim that "passages the most rapid, designs
the most eccentric, do not dismay them", he considered such a passage as
this to be critical:

Ex. 1

Tempo I (Allegro agitato e appassionato assi: $\quad$ = 132)

and then 13 bars later:

(continued overleaf)

Ex. 1 (*continued*)

Its chief difficulty, played *unisoni* as any American orchestra trained by Charles Munch or Pierre Monteux does play it, lies in the length of the passage which must needs go at breakneck speed, and where a sense of sectional articulation can easily be lost. But it is the conductor's rather than the players' responsibility to preserve this articulation. It is interesting to compare Wagner's remarks from *Über das Dirigiren*, published in the *Neue Zeitschrift für Musik* for 1869–70, referring to another famous passage from the first movement of Beethoven's Ninth Symphony (bars 116 *et seq.*), which he declares never to have been played so evenly—*sempre pp*—by even the most distinguished orchestras under his own direction, as he had heard it played, thirty years before, by the Paris Conservatoire Orchestra under Habaeneck:

Ex. 2

Allegro ma non troppo

Wagner goes on to write:

> How was it possible for these Paris musicians to arrive at so infallible a solution to this problem? Firstly, of course, by nothing else that the most conscientious perseverance—a perseverance only to be found among musicians who are not contented with mutual compliments, do not flatter themselves that solutions are self-apparent, but feel awed by the presence of anything which is not directly understood and are prepared to resolve the difficult from the standpoint with which they are most at home, namely the standpoint of technique. The French musician is influenced to such an extent by the Italian school, to which he first and foremost belongs, that music is incomprehensible to him save through the medium of song: to

play an instrument well, in his eyes, is to make it sing. And (as I have already said) this wonderful orchestra truly sang this symphony. To be able to 'sing' it correctly, however, meant finding the *right tempo* for its every beat: and this was the second thing which so impressed me on that occasion. Old Habaeneck possessed no kind of abstract aesthetic animation in relation to the work—he was totally uninspired. *But he found the right tempo, and patiently guided his orchestra into discovering its melos.*

Berlioz's own experiences of Paris conductors had not always been so happy, and one is compelled to remind oneself, when reading his *L'Art du Chef d'Orchestre*, that he was writing of current professional practices and abuses:

> Happy may that composer esteem himself to be when the conductor into whose hands he falls is not at once incapable and inimical. For nothing can resist the pernicious influence of this person. The most admirable orchestra is then paralysed, the most excellent singers perplexed and rendered dull. There is no longer any vigour or unity. Under such direction the noblest daring of the author appears extravagance, enthusiasm beholds its soaring flight checked, inspiration is violently brought down to earth, the angel's wings are broken, the man of genius passes for a madman or an idiot, the divine statue is precipitated from its pedestal and dragged in the mud. And what is more, the public and even auditors endowed with the highest musical intelligence are reduced to the impossibility (if a new work be in question, and they are hearing it for the first time) of recognising the ravages perpetrated by the conductor—of discovering the follies, faults, and crimes which he commits.[1]

It is the perennial complaint of composers, not all of whom are endowed with Berlioz's genius as a composer or his insight into the conductor's art, that conductors ruin their works—if indeed they show them the magnanimity of performing them at all. Present-day ears have become attuned to the sound of good and accurate orchestral-playing, and the general public as well as the musical intelligentsia tend to be far more readily able to recognise the dull or incompetent reading of a new work than the insufferably dull or abused reading of a familiar classic. Wagner also has his tilt at those conductors who butchered his own music, but his aim was surer. He contended that they simply did not know how to conduct in any case, and history proved him right, for they one and all retired from the professional scene to become conservatoire professors or schools' inspectors. The fact of the matter is that no incompetent conductor can be expected to make sense of *any work at all*, and

[1] Hector Berlioz, *L'Art du Chef d'Orchestre*, 1856.

that to make sense of a new work must require the conductor to be a composer himself. Almost every conductor of lasting consequence has been a
capable, if not always a singularly prolific or gifted, composer, and much the
same may be said of solo-performers. An active participation in the processes
of composition is essential to the performer who is to have any creative instinct for his work.

Berlioz continues:

> Fortunately I here attack the exception: for the malevolent
> orchestral-conductor—whether capable or not—is very rare. The
> conductor full of goodwill but incapable is, on the contrary, very
> common. Apart from the innumerable mediocrities who direct
> artists who are frequently much their superiors, the composer might
> scarcely be accused of conspiring against his own works. Yet how
> many are there who, fancying that they are able to conduct, inno-
> cently injure their best scores! Beethoven, it is said, more than once
> ruined the performance of his symphonies, which he would conduct
> even at the time when his deafness had become almost complete[2].
> ... The example of Beethoven leads me at once to say that, if the
> direction of an orchestra appear to me very difficult for a blind man,
> it is indisputably impossible for a deaf one, whatever may have been
> his technical talent before losing his sense of hearing. The or-
> chestral conductor should *see* and *hear*; he should be *active* and
> *vigorous*, should know the *composition*, and the *nature* and *compass* of
> the instruments, should be able to *read the score*, and possess—
> besides the especial talent of which we shall presently endeavour to
> explain the constituent qualities—other almost indefinable gifts,
> without which an invisible link cannot establish itself between him
> and those whom he directs; the faculty of transmitting to them his
> feeling is denied him, and thence power, empire, and guiding
> influence completely fail him. He is then no longer a conductor, a
> director, but a simple beater of time—supposing that he knows
> how to beat it, and divide it, regularly.
>
> The performers should feel that *he* feels, comprehends, and is
> moved. Then his emotion communicates itself to those whom he
> directs, his inward fire warms them, his electric glow animates them,
> his force of impulse excites them. He throws around him the vital
> irradiations of musical art.

There is much here which is still very true to this day. A contempt for
the conductor and a feeling of artistic superiority are still familiar sentiments
among orchestral players whose arrogance—and artistry—are perhaps more
marked than they were in Berlioz's time. And the well-meaning but incapable
conductor is equally common—but this is a perennial hazard which exists to

---

[2] Indeed, entirely so—*vide* the terrible first performance of his Ninth Symphony.

a greater or lesser extent in every specialised profession. The incapable lawyer, the incapable doctor, the incapable business executive—all shelter behind the façade of good intention. What is alarming is to discover that such mediocrity existed in Paris, which Wagner upheld as the shining example, superior to Dresden, which had inherited the legacy of Weber, or London, whose Philharmonic Society had commissioned Beethoven's last symphony. Berlioz goes on to denounce the habit of double-bass players:

> ... to permit themselves, from idleness, or from a dread of being unable to achieve certain difficulties, to simplify their part. *This race of simplifiers, be it said, has existed for forty years*; but it cannot endure any longer.

How, then, did these bass-players negotiate the famous passages from the finale of Beethoven's Fourth Symphony, or the Scherzo of the Fifth, or the recitatives from the Ninth? How did they negotiate them at all in Dresden or London or Vienna? Again:

> Performers playing stringed instruments will rarely give themselves the trouble to play a *tremolo*; they substitute for this very characteristic effect a tame repetition of the note, two, and sometimes three times slower than the one whence results the true *tremolo*. .... The action of the arm necessary for producing a true *tremolo* demands from them too great an effort. This idleness is intolerable.

How then did the famous string *tremolo*, accompanying the solo clarinet entry, sound in the overture to *Freischütz*? How had it sounded under Weber's baton at the Dresden Opera? Again:

> An orchestra, the instruments of which are not in tune individually, is a monstrosity. The conductor, therefore, should take the greatest care that the musicians tune accurately. But this operation should not be performed in the presence of the public. And, moreover, every instrumental noise—every kind of preluding between acts—constitutes a real offence to civilized auditors. The bad training of an orchestra, and its musical mediocrity, is to be inferred from the impertinent noise it makes during the periods of quiet at an opera or concert.

The matter of good intonation is one which is generally well attended to among professional orchestras today, although there are occasional and frightening lapses. The question of orchestral comportment on the concert platform and in the opera house is one which has long been a matter of self-respect among the members of orchestras of international class. I do not know that it is practised to any very great extent in this country, and I have experienced many a silent *fermata* which has been ruined by carelessly shuffling feet, turning of pages—and not always the pages of an instrumental part—or the involuntary movement of a bow-arm. There are fine orchestral players, and even conductors, who are not yet aware of the significance of a *fermata* over the final rest or the final bar-line of an interior movement, and will relax, mop their brows, blow their noses, cough, exchange a word with their partners—all the while encouraging the audience to do likewise—at the very moment when the silent tension inherited from the final notes of one movement should and must be carried over into the next, as an integral part of the work. The Brahms–Haydn Variations are the most frequent victim.

It has been from time to time fashionable to condemn Wagner's prose writing and to remark that a composer's business should be to write music, and not to write about it. It is certainly nobody's business to write about music if he is not a composer or a practising musician of some sort, and such condemnations must issue from those who have never given themselves to serious study of Wagner's literary *œuvre*, or be addressed to those who will assuredly never have the curiosity to examine it for themselves. It is true that his writing reflects his manifold weaknesses—egomania, megalomania, persecution mania, blind spots for Brahms, blind spots for Schumann, blind spots for the Jews, an unquenchable thirst for polemics and a want of charity towards some colleagues which tends to discount that charity which he displays towards those whom he openly admires. Thus much said, it is impossible for the musician to ignore the compulsion of his writing, or the stature of its substance.

Berlioz, in *L'Art du Chef d'Orchestre*, had summed up a host of musical abuses which could be laid directly or indirectly at the door of the conductor of his day, and had presented him with a somewhat didactic table of injunctions, from the manner of beating time under all manner of circumstances, the size and colour of stick which he should use, the nature and purpose of his duties, to the optimum size of the orchestra: a string section of nine first violins, eight second violins, six violas, seven 'cellos and six double-basses for the "Mozart" orchestra, and fifteen first violins, fourteen seconds, ten violas, ten 'cellos and eight double-basses for the "Beethoven" orchestra and the opera house.[3] These, as has been said, hold good to the present day to a very considerable and very alarming extent. But when we come to Wagner's

---

[3] Ibid.

writing on the subject of conducting, and the standard practices of the symphony orchestra and the opera house, both in the famous series of articles *Über das Dirigiren* and on numerous other occasions, we enter another world. Between virulent attacks on provincial standards and dilletantism, are expressed the sentiments and musical understanding which must motivate the art of interpretation, and which indeed distinguish and define the conductor's art as a new dimension of musical expression. Writing of the metamorphosis which takes place in the slow movement of Beethoven's Ninth Symphony—the break into 12/8—Wagner wrote:

> Here we see how the tempo of the *Adagio*, which had seemed to be moving in some cosmic time-scale, has now crystallized, as it were, while the earlier sense of a boundlessly free tonal expression, allowing a subtle gradation of tempo between very fine limits, now acquires a movement precisely determined by the accompanying figuration—a time-scale, by final analysis, common to that of the *Allegro*.

Ex. 3

The affinity between the great *Adagio* and the great *Allegro* was nothing new to music. Its principle was inherent in the music of Bach—in the great D minor Chaconne or the *Agnus Dei* from the B minor Mass, for example—and in the music of Palestrina, and it was to appear again in the 12/32 variation from the *Adagio* of Beethoven's Op. 111. It is inherent, for that matter, in the very opening bars of the Ninth Symphony. What is significant is that Wagner, in his capacity of conductor, should have been the first musician to remark the principle and apply it in his performance of the music of other composers. A few pages later he is speaking of Mozart, and of the difficulties which the latter had experienced in securing a real *Presto* in the performance of the overture to *Le Nozze di Figaro*:

> As I have said that, in the ideal sense, the pure *Adagio* can never be too slow, so the pure, the absolute *Presto* can never be taken fast enough.

It is one of the hallmarks of great artistry that the *Allegro* never loses a sense of repose, and indeed acquires a kind of cosmic pulse at the hands of a great conductor, though it may retain every incidental characteristic of turbulence and high drama. And it is the common experience of the orchestral player, when he has just performed the overture to *Figaro* or the finale to the G minor Symphony K.550 under such a conductor as Erich Kleiber, and at prodigious speed, to find that technical difficulties had vanished, and that the passage of the music had never before seemed to him so clear or so articulate. Wagner confines the secret of this executive phenomenon to the conductor's understanding of the word *melos*—a word of whose meaning, he declares, the German conductor understands nothing:

> I have never met a single German Kapellmeister or musical-director who could really *sing* a melody, be his voice good or bad. No, music to them is an abstraction, a mixture of syntax, arithmetic and gymnastics . ..

The burden of Wagner's complaint was three-fold. Firstly, that conductors in Germany had become the more ignorant and perfunctory as the demands upon the orchestra had become more exacting. As long as these demands did not persist beyond those entailed in a score of Mozart, there still stood at its head the traditional Kapellmeister, sound, reliable, and above all gruff, the "*alte Zöpfe*"—Schneider in Dessau, Guhr in Frankfurt, Joseph Strauss in Karlsruhe, Esser in Vienna—all capable of excellent work of its kind. But with their passing, the demands upon the orchestra had also vastly increased, and the methods of the "*alte Zöpfe*" were wholly inadequate:

> To recognise and remedy that which had escaped those Kapell-meisters of the old school should have been the first duty of the young conductors of the new order. But care was taken that they should not prove an embarrassment to the administration, and that they should not inherit the weight of authority of the sturdy *Zöpfe* of old . . .

Promotion was accomplished by application of the law of inertia, by submission to an ignorant and conceited administration, by a deliberate leniency towards the musicians committed to their charge. The injury done to the artistic growth and well-being of even some of the greatest orchestras and opera houses in the country was inestimable.

Secondly, there had arisen another genre of conductors—*die Flotte Routinier*, as Wagner calls him:

> These are the people who can put on an opera in a fortnight, are dab hands at making cuts, and write their own cadenzas for prima

donnas to interpolate into other people's scores . . . These are our
modern music-bankers, sprung from the school of Mendelssohn,
or recommended to the world under his personal patronage—
musicians not bred within the orchestra or on the stage, but properly educated at the new-fangled conservatories, composers of
oratorios and psalms, auditors at rehearsals of subscription-
concerts. In conducting too they have taken lessons, and crown
the whole with an elegant polish such as no musician ever displayed before . . .

But he goes on to acknowledge:

I honestly believe that these people have exercised an influence
on our orchestras which is much to the good. A great deal of raw-
ness and loutishness has disappeared, and many an elegant detail of
performance has since been paid attention to and stressed. They
were already more at home with the modern orchestra, as it in turn
was indebted in many ways to their master, Mendelssohn.

But Wagner's reservations over the profounder aspects of Mendelssohn's
musicianship are severe and penetrating, and he is unable to avoid identifying
Mendelssohn's Victorian slickness as an interpretative artist as being symptomatic of the musical flair and fluency of the Jewish race as a whole:

I once heard Mendelssohn conduct Beethoven's Eighth Symphony at a concert-rehearsal in Berlin. I noticed that he would pick
out a detail here and there—almost at random—and polish it up with
a certain pertinacity, which did such excellent service for the detail
that I could only wonder why he did not pay the same attention
to other nuances . . . With regard to conducting, he personally told
me that a too slow tempo was the devil, and that for choice he would
rather things were taken too fast. A really good performance was a
rarity at any time, but with a little care one might gloss things over,
and this could best be accomplished by never dawdling, and by
covering the ground at a good, stiff pace . . .

This was the spirit which was to engender Stanford, Parry and Arthur
Sullivan, the choral society and the prancing choirmaster with a Doctorate
of Music in his hand and the ultimate benediction of the Royal College of
Organists to guide his heel and toe. But Mendelssohn had not only been a
bastion of the Philharmonic Society in London: he had held influential posts
in Berlin, Leipzig and Düsseldorf, and had been one of the most sought-after
musicians in Germany. And it was the destiny of German music as a whole
which occasioned Wagner's deepest foreboding.

For Germany, since the Thirty Years War, had suffered political and cultural anonymity. For better or for worse, she was now on the brink of national unity under Bismarck—a unity which Wagner, for better or for worse, had done much to champion and foster. This was no sense of pious nationalism, for he writes:

> My mind has frequently been preoccupied with trying to gain a clear picture of what we really understand by the term *deutsch*. It is the commonplace of the patriot to utter his country's name in blind homage. The greater the nation, however, the less concerned it seems to be with the blazoning of its own name with all this display of reverence. In the everyday life of England and France, people are not constantly harping on "English" and "French" virtues, but the German must be continually appealing to *deutsche Tiefe*, *deutsche Ernst*, *deutsche Treue* and the like . . .[4]

It is rather with the eclipse of German culture that Wagner is concerned, and his convictions find another emphasis than that of nationalism:

> Yet when its native countenance and its very speech was lost, there remained to the spirit of Germany one last, one undreamt-of sanctuary wherein to record the expression of her innermost heart. From the Italians she had adopted music and made it her own, and if anyone would seek a single incomparably vocal image of the amazing individuality, strength and meaning of the German spirit, let his gaze linger at length upon the baffling, well-nigh inexplicable figure of music's master-magician, Sebastian Bach. He is testament enough to the innermost life of the German spirit throughout the cruel century of the utter extinction of the German peoples. Witness that head, absurdly swaddled in French full-bottomed wig. Witness that *Meister*, a wretched organist and cantor, slinking from one Thuringian parish to another, villages whose names we scarcely recognise. Witness him so unregarded that it has taken a full century to drag his works from oblivion. Witness even music itself presenting for him but an effigy of his age, dry, stiff, pedantic, a periwig and pigtail which must be set to music. Then see what an unfathomable world the great Sebastian drew from these elements!

This was the radical spirit which had caused Wagner to flee his post at the Dresden Opera in 1849, to be exiled from the whole of Germany until 1860, which provided ammunition for his political opponents in Bavaria, and deprived Munich of an opera-house and the world of a school of music

---

[4] Richard Wagner: "Was ist deutsch?", sketched in 1865 and first published in the *Bayreuther Blätter*, February 1878.

which would at last have been worthy of the musical profession. (It is fair comment that Munich should have built its Prinzregenten-Theater in 1901 after the model of Bayreuth, and fairer comment that it should have remained that city's second opera house.) Second only to Wagner's dream of a national opera house which should be properly equipped in every way to perform his own and other composers' works, had been his desire to establish a school of music which would subscribe to those musical standards and artistic values for which he so tirelessly fought, and which are everywhere in evidence in his work as a composer, interpreter and writer. In his report to King Ludwig of Bavaria, Wagner wrote:[5]

> In short, in our opera houses we poorly imitate or distort that which is foreign. Though France and Italy are stricken with artistic palsy, their works are still in harmony with their national peculiarities, and their performances stylistically correct. But we, for our everyday entertainment, take these self-same works, mutilate them and perform them incorrectly.
>
> In the face of such evidence as this, what standards of performance, I must ask, has a German conservatorium of music to conserve? I should very probably be answered that, in addition to these foreign products, we also perform Mozart and Gluck, and that our conservative care must remain directed to the works of these masters. And in such a plea, we may discern the root-error in the German way of thinking, for we are obliged to decipher the operas of Gluck and Mozart by the light of the self-same French and Italian peculiarities of style as in other foreign works, and in precisely the same faulty and mutilating way have we made Mozart and Gluck our own . . . and there is no plainer evidence of the shortcomings of our present-day operatic personnel than the utter lifelessness and lack of colour which attend their performances precisely of Mozart and Gluck—for all the hypocritical praises which they accord their music . . .
>
> I will therefore forego a complete catalogue of the countless evils which attend this root-fault in German singing (careless and unclear pronunciation), and for the present accede to being called one-sided when I claim it is a *sine qua non* of the singing-school now about to be constituted that its first aim shall be directed at a solution of the problem of how to bring the art of singing into proper relation with the idiosyncrasies of German speech . . .
>
> It is indispensable that the singer should also be a good musician, and how ill-equipped we are in this respect—for all our vaunted superiority over the foreigner—cannot be loud enough bewailed . . . It will therefore be expedient to begin a thorough general

---

[5] *Bericht an seine Majestät den König Ludwig II von Bayern über eine in München zu er richtende deutsche Musikschule* (1865).

instruction in music simultaneously with specific instruction in
singing. By this I mean a theoretical tuition and practical exercises
in harmony, advancing to the stage in the craft of composition
which closes with an accurate knowledge of the form of a piece
of music, its phrase-structure, the significance and relationship
of its thematic material, and a correct interpretation of its phrasing ...

Many must be the dust-covered copies of Wagner's prose works lodged upon
the shelves of our musical institutions which find this last paragraph under-
lined in the quavering hand of the joyous professor of harmony and counterpoint who thinks to have lighted upon his ultimate vindication. But if he has
read on, his joy will have been short-lived, for two pages later Wagner continues:

> The human voice is the practical foundation of music, and how-
> ever far the latter may progress upon the path of its choice, the
> boldest expressions of the composer or the most daring bravura of
> the instrumental virtuoso must always return to the essence of song
> for its ultimate vindication. Thus I maintain that elementary in-
> struction in singing must be made obligatory for every musician,
> and in the successful organisation of a singing-school upon these
> lines should be found the basis for the intended all-embracing
> school of music. Only then should it extend frontiers which it has
> been seen to reach with the need to instruct the singer in the ele-
> ments of harmony and rudimentary analysis of musical compo-
> sition.
> But here I must emphatically repeat that I abide by the express
> character of our institution as a purely practical school for cultivating
> those standards of performance demanded by the classical and
> German media of music. To want to introduce musical science in
> all its forms into a music-school must divert us from the all-
> important objective—that of instilling perfection into the execu-
> tion of musical works—and can only impede and undermine its
> potential. The expert knowledge needed by the executive musician
> as well as by the composer is best acquired in a practical way, above
> all by his personal involvement with high performance standards and
> by his listening to them and being taught to evaluate them. What lies
> between, namely the study of the rules of theory, is a matter of
> private study, and in none of the larger towns of Germany—least of
> all at the seat of this proposed school of practical music—will
> there be any want of teachers competent for *that*.

Coming to the instrumental department of his Music School, Wagner
is less critical at the outset. He allows that every large town in Germany has

a comparatively good, and sometimes exceptional orchestra, and that there is no lack of excellent wind and string players. But he goes on to say:

> The fault is this. We possess a classical literature, but as yet no class in the way in which we perform it. The works of our great masters have influenced the larger public by virtue of their authority rather than by any genuine impression upon their feeling, and they have therefore no innate feeling for them as yet. And herein—but precisely herein—lies the hypocrisy of our cult of classicism, upon which so much opprobrium has been cast from quarters unworthy of notice. One has only to witness the care and the pains which the Italians and the French have devoted to the performance of the works of their respective cultural epochs. Look, even today, at the wholly admirable diligence whereby French musicians have sought to digest even the most difficult works of Beethoven and to render them capable of aspiring directly to the higher feelings. And we shall be astonished to see how easily we Germans persuade ourselves that everything comes to us as if of its own accord, as though by some miraculous gift of nature. Let anyone name me a school in Germany where the authentic playing of Mozart's music has been established and preserved. Is this something which comes to our orchestras and their duly appointed directors of its own accord? Who then has ever instructed them? . . . Now let us imagine one of the sensitive melodic lines of that Master in whom was ingrained the classic nobility of Italian vocal art of earlier times down to the innermost throb and pulse of its accent, the very soul of its expression, and who toiled to endow the orchestral instrument with this expression as had none before him. Let us imagine this line delivered without inflection, without the smallest hint or shade of accent, without any of those modifications of time and rhythm so imperative to the singer, played smooth and neat with the same expression one might give to a mathematical problem. Let us find the difference between the impression originally intended by the Master and that which we nowadays receive, and we shall be able to judge what kind of piety is observed towards Mozart's music by our "music-conservers" . . . But not content with leaving these nearest problems entirely unsolved as yet, the conservers of our conservatoriums have chased up the works of far remoter masters, and of every age and style, to seek in an aggravation of their task, as it would seem, an apology for solving none of them . . .

Coming on top of Berlioz' comments on Parisian musical standards, which Wagner finds so much in advance of those current in his own country, this does not speak well for the state of European music in the mid-nineteenth century. Certainly we may fairly claim that the great orchestras and the great conductors of the world know something more about the interpretation of

Mozart than was known and practised in Wagner's time. But which school of music anywhere in the world today can claim to establish and preserve the authentic playing of Mozart? Or of Beethoven? Or Brahms, or Berlioz, or Wagner himself? No, their conductors have either patently failed in the professional field as interpreters of just these composers, or are evading the responsibility which rests upon them by exploiting less familiar repertoire for their own professional ends. What kind of Conservatory is this? And if our greatest orchestras may fairly claim to know something about the interpretation of these masters by virtue of the tradition which has been instilled in them since Wagner's day, this does not diminish the atrocities which are committed in the name of music-making by less illustrious ensembles.

To read Wagner's account of a rehearsal with the Vienna Hofkapelle of Weber's overture to *Der Freischütz* is to find heartening reassurance of those values which should inform and enliven the conductor's art, and it instructs us in that art as does no other work—least of all Berlioz's essay with its prim and precise instructions, as they now must seem by comparison, for the beating of seven-in-a-bar and five-in-a-bar and three-against-two-in-a bar, and never a word about the music which lies between the bar-lines. The magic of *Freischütz* is not lost on Berlioz the composer when he talks about the attributes of the clarinet in the body of his treatise on instrumentation, though it would seem to have been lost on Mr. Cecil Forsyth, writing in a book of similar intention[6]: "Then again," says Mr. Forsyth, "there is the abominable circusy effect in the *Freischütz* Overture":

Ex. 4

* Forsyth gives the trombone entry "*pp*"

It seems impossible that a musician educated in the best traditions of the orchestra of the Philharmonic Society, and a pupil of Stanford and Parry, could have so misconstrued the sudden terror of this muffled wolf-snarl from the trombones which invades Agathe's music, and one is impelled to ask if it was not the conductors of Mr. Forsyth's day rather than Weber

[6] Cecil Forsyth: *Orchestration*, London, 1914.

himself who were wont to indulge in "circusy effect[s]": or did Mr. Forsyth's orchestra still play everything—as had been Wagner's own experience—*allegro giocoso, sempre mf?*

Berlioz's *L'Art du Chef d'Orchestre* is invaluable as an historical document, but Wagner's *Über das Dirigiren* has an authority and an urgency which remain for us immediate because he never loses sight of the essential greatness of the music about which he is writing, or of the inherent dignity of the musicians under his command—however impatient he may be about those who seem to him to transgress those standards to which he subscribes. The whole mystery and significance of *Freischütz*—historical as much as dramatic—is resurrected before our eyes, and this is the abiding genius which distinguished Wagner and the other great conductors who followed him. Others may claim passion, vitality, elegance and precision: but the great artist has never lost the sense of communicated wonder, and it is a sense which is not one whit diminished when it is tempered by awareness and understanding.

Chapter 2

MENDELSSOHN, LISZT AND BRAHMS

At Mannheim, during the eighteenth century, the idea of the symphony orchestra had been conceived and had found its birth. Whatever the contribution, in purely aesthetic terms, from the predominantly Italian culture which was to nurture Haydn and Mozart, it was the coincidence of the discovery of a symphonic form and the instrumental means, at the hand of Johann Wenzel Stamitz, which enabled orchestral music to put forth branches from the dry stem of the suite, and in turn to flower into the magnificence of the masterpieces of the Vienna School.

We need not be too sceptical of the standards which attended performances in the late eighteenth century. While Nikolai, writing in 1783[1], shortly after the Mannheim orchestra had moved to Munich under Christian Cannabich, awards to them the palm for the accuracy, unanimity and excitement of their playing which "assuredly has no equal in Germany", he found great merit in the playing in Berlin, Dresden and Vienna, and writes with a rare perception and understanding of orchestral techniques which are still in evidence today. At the court of the Elector of Bavaria, the Mannheim orchestra carried seventeen first and second violins, and a full wind section including clarinets and four horns—as did the Dresden Hofkapelle—while Berlin could boast twenty violins, six violas, eight 'cellos and four basses. Paris, in 1773, had evidently inherited Louis XV's *violons* from Versailles, for the Opéra had no less than twenty-two violins, nine 'cellos, six basses and eight horns, while the orchestra of the *Concerts Spirituels* had twenty-four violins and ten 'cellos. This is beginning to surpass forces employed in the present day, and indeed the famous Dr. Burney, writing of the orchestra of the San Carlo Opera in Naples in 1770, claimed to have witnessed no less than thirty-six violins, divided into two equal sections of eighteen each. This is in savage contrast to Beethoven's pathetic demand, in 1813, for at least four first and four second violins, two 'cellos and two basses, for the first performance of his Seventh Symphony. Even in 1846, the optimum size of the

1 Friedrich Nikolai: *Reise durch Deutschland und die Schweiz im Jahre 1781.*

string section in Vienna was placed at no higher than four firsts, four seconds, two violas, two 'cellos and two basses[2]—numbers which had been current in the smaller Hofkapelle of the eighteenth century.

Such was the price of democracy. The size and vitality of orchestras in Paris is fair comment on a standard of music-making which—on Wagner's evidence—persisted well into the nineteenth century, and his own experiences of that city had been bitter enough for us to feel sure that his judgement was in no way tinged by a sympathetic republicanism. In those cities of Germany whose musical life did not enjoy the protection of the Court, music-making was dependent upon civic enterprise, as it is in America to this day, and while it was slow to gather momentum, the example of the Leipzig Gewandhaus is evidence of what had already been accomplished by the late eighteenth century.

Nevertheless, it was those cities which possessed royal patrons of opera (and the sheer physical expense of the operatic medium made such patronage imperative), who continued to dominate the musical scene—Berlin, Dresden, Munich, and now Weimar. For German opera, under the initial impulse which it had received from Weber, and now enjoying the elemental championship of Richard Wagner, had joined hands with the genius of Mozart and provided the prime stimulus to Germany's musical life, and a unique training ground for the growing art of the conductor. The internal organisation of the opera house was essentially democratic, and by degrees it was learning to allow and to demand that the conductor in embryo learn his job and assume his responsibilities by careful stages, and that he apply a diligence and an industry which would ensure that his talents came quickly to the notice of his colleagues and confirm his position in the eyes of his musical peers, long before he was exposed to the vagaries of public opinion, or that of the Press. Equally, a spurious talent could be ruthlessly exposed and suppressed *in camera*, where ebullience of manner or an elegant profile were of no avail without the addition of professional skill. We can well understand why Wagner fulminated against the "oratorio-conductors" who had never in their lives sullied their hands in the cause of an honest day's music-making, and why he was so perplexed that a genius which could have invented the music to *A Midsummer Night's Dream* or *Fingal's Cave* should have been so deaf to perfection in executive standards. For the conductor on the concert platform could "get away with it"—then as now. Providing that he had a dashing enough manner, and could put on a show, the audience wanted nothing better, and musicians of real ability could be diverted from the soul-searching path of artistic conscience and ride the royal road to success, with never the

---

[2] Ferdinand Gassner: *Dirigent und Ripienist*, Vienna, 1846.

sound of a still, small voice to blind them with its integrity. Wagner knew the proper routine of the opera house as did no other conductor of his day—his letters to Hans Richter are sufficient evidence of this—and he knew that it was only when one has tasted the blood of the battlefield of opera that one has any authority on the parade-ground of the concert hall. Not that the opera house was free of its own abuses and injustices, any more than it is today, for it was the traditional hotbed of politics, of corruption, venality and favour-itism when there was not the benign but despotic and all-seeing hand of the autocrat to guide it—and the autocrat was becoming rare.

There is a famous letter from Wagner, written from Zurich to Franzisca von Bülow, the mother of the pianist and conductor[3]. It is a letter of symphonic proportions and developed with the force and accuracy of a sym-phonic argument, which every aspiring artist who has suffered the intract-ability of his parents, and every parent who has experienced misgiving over his or her child's desire to enter the musical profession, should study—for it requires study—as a supreme example of logic, understanding, fair-minded-ness, and authority. It was followed, eight days later, by a letter from Liszt in Weimar, twenty or so lines long, which combined humanity, directness and a princely courtesy with an astonishingly penetrating appraisal—when we con-sider where Hans von Bülow's talents were eventually to lead him—of the artistic potential of a nineteen-year-old boy. The original letter was in French:

Madame la Baronne,
    Several friends of your son's have spoken to me (unknown to him, as I believe) to beg me respectfully to submit to you a request. Little as I am calculated to serve as a negotiator with you for wishes and hopes—a noble and legitimate ambition—yet I confess that the knowledge of the duty, as well as the sincere affection I bear to your son, will not permit me to put aside entirely the so pressing requests which, I feel sure, are in accordance with your son's vocation. Whatever decision you may come to with regard to the future of his career, pray excuse, Madame, the liberty I am taking in meddling thus with questions of a nature at once so serious and so delicate, and do not impute to this letter any motive contrary to my habits and convictions.
    Hans is clearly gifted with a musical organisation of the rarest kind. His executive talent will easily place him in the front rank of the greatest pianists, and his essays at composition denote quite excep-tional qualities of imagination, of individuality, and of conception. Besides, Hans has taken an antipathy to every career which would

---

[3] Marie von Bülow: *The Early Correspondence of Hans von Bülow*, 1895 (trans. Con-stance Bache, 1896).

sever him from Art. [His mother wished him to finish his law studies.] Permit me, then, to confide to your motherly love the happy solution of the noble struggle between his natural vocation and that destined for him, however bright and alluring it might be; and in view of the sentiments which dictate this letter, pray pardon the intercession I have ventured to make to you today.

I have the honour to be, Madame la Baronne, with deep respect,

Your devoted servant,

Franz Liszt[4].

These letters were written in September 1850, when Wagner was thirty-seven and Liszt thirty-eight, and they provide—together with Hans von Bülow's own letter to his mother of 6 September—an auspicious coincidence, at the very heart of the century, of the three personalities who were to dominate its stage in their influence upon the art of executive musicianship. Liszt had come to Weimar two years earlier, under contract to the young Grand Duke Charles Alexander, to direct the Hofkapelle at Schloss Altenburg during three months of each year, and this marks the beginning of his twelve-year liaison with Princess Carolyne de Sayn-Wittgenstein and of a period of immense activity as a conductor, in which he introduced a vast new repertory of operatic and instrumental works. Weimar became a focal-point in the musical life of Europe, abounding in the names of outstanding artists who gave their services there or who sought Liszt's advice and help, in person or by letter. Sitwell sums up Liszt's character as follows:

> The prodigious gifts with which he was endowed were such as to encourage in him the character of actor or magician. When this is taken into consideration it is surprising how little he was spoiled by adulation. His transformation into a priest was the result of sincere religious feeling. The generosity of his character proved itself in his support of so many younger musicians: Dvořák, Grieg, Borodin, Tchaikowsky[5]. All things considered, Liszt must remain one of the phenomena of music. As a pianist he has never been equalled; he is a great, if neglected, composer; and he ranks with Byron among the most striking figures of the whole Romantic epoch.[6]

One of Liszt's earliest accomplishments at Weimar had been the staging, on 28 August, 1850, of the first performance of Wagner's *Lohengrin*, as the culmination—on Goethe's birthday—of a five-day festival at which Hans von Bülow and his mother had been present. On 20 March, 1852, came the stage

[4] Martie von Bülow: *The Early Correspondence of Hans von Bülow*: 1895 (trans. Constance Bache: 1896).

[5] A study of Liszt's letters reveals that this list may be extended a hundredfold, to include every manner of musician—composers, conductors, singers, instrumentalists and even music-publishers.

[6] Sacheverell Sitwell: *Franz Liszt*, London, 1934.

première of Berlioz's *Benvenuto Cellini*, and on 13 June of the same year—less often remembered—the first of several performances of Schumann's *Manfred*. On 8 June, Liszt had written to Schumann:

> It is with very great pleasure that I am able to announce to you the first performance of *Manfred* for next Sunday, and to invite you to come to it ... The last rehearsal is fixed for Friday afternoon [sic]; perhaps it will be possible for you to be present at it, which would of course be very agreeable to me. Your Leipzig friends [of the *Neue Zeitschrift für Musik*?] will see the announcement of this performance in the papers, and I think you will consider it your duty not to be absent from the performance ...[7]

This letter tells us three things: that Liszt—who by no means enjoyed an unassailable position as an artist, particularly in the eyes of certain sections of the press—was anxious that Schumann be present to give the first performance of *Manfred* his blessing and to spread the gospel of Weimar in Leipzig; that Liszt the interpretative artist would welcome, but did not have to rely upon, the composer's presence at the general rehearsal; and that the standards of music-making at Weimar were high enough and leisurely enough to dictate that the general rehearsal should take place, not on the day of the performance nor even the day before, but *two* full days beforehand, out of deference to the singers and the importance of the occasion, as Liszt saw it. Few opera houses today could afford such a luxury. On 26 June, Liszt wrote to Schumann again:

> My very dear friend,
> I regret extremely that you could not come to the second performance of your *Manfred* [Schumann had failed to appear at the first performance either], and I believe that you would not have been dissatisfied with the musical preparation and performance of that work, which I count among your greatest successes. The whole impression was a thoroughly noble, deep and elevating one, in accordance with my expectations ... With regard to the *mise-en-scène* something might be said, yet it would be unfair not to speak in terms of praise of the merits of the producer, Herr Genast ... One sole remark I permit myself: the introductory music to the Ahriman Chorus is too short. Some sixty to a hundred bars of symphony, such as you understand how to write, would have a decidely good effect here. Think the matter over, and then go fresh to your desk ... Shall I send the manuscript score back? ... I am by no means an autograph-collector, but the score, if you don't require it any longer, would give me pleasure[8].

[7] *The Letters of Franz Liszt*, Vol. I, edited by Walter Bache, 1894.
[8] Ibid.

Once again we have evidence of Liszt's warmth and authority as a musician. He admires the work immensely, and has sufficient respect for the authorship of an almost exact contemporary not only to suggest to him a flaw which had appeared in the structure at performance, but to invite him to correct it forthwith. This is in strange contrast with the remarks of one of Brahms's biographers, and a former critic of the London *Times*:

> Joachim was convinced, *sooner than anyone else*, that Schumann and Brahms were in the royal line of the great composers. This does not seem a very strange position in the present day, but the 'moderns' of that time[9], with Liszt at their head, were never tired of sneering [?] at Schumann, and though they professed to uphold the classics, yet it was clear to everyone that they were working for their own glorification rather than in the cause of legitimate music. It was their assertion that opinion in Germany *was unanimously on their side* which roused Joachim, Brahms and one or two others to make the famous protest which appeared in 1860[10].

It is difficult to see how Joachim, who was only nineteen, and concertmaster of the Weimar orchestra at the time of *Manfred*'s first performance, could have experienced convictions as to Schumann's greatness prior to those which were demonstrably already those of Liszt himself—even though it was a conviction which Liszt could not at that time extend to *Brams*, as Liszt was wont to call him, who was also only nineteen. And it is perfectly clear from Liszt's own correspondence that he never imagined for one moment that opinion in Germany was "unanimously on his side"—in fact Liszt's letters of the late 'fifties became almost piteous in their acceptance of an almost universal hostility towards his music. Germany at this period was experiencing a growing wave of militant Protestantism, and the figure of Liszt—the master-showman, the composer of dazzling transcriptions, the professedly devout Catholic—was held up as an arch-hypocrite with his boundless flow of religiously oriented works from the Weimar period, combined as it was with his co-habitation with a Russian princess of the blood. Here was something to make the tongues of the *petite bourgeoisie* go clack-clack-clack, and the press made capital out of it. Brendel's paper, *Anregungen*, which Liszt actively sponsored, doubtless caused much mischief, but when we read the self-righteous correspondence of the opposing faction, of which Clara Schumann's summons our closest attention, and regard the level of polemics to which the *Neue Zeitschrift für Musik* and the *Wiener Presse* were

[9] The so-called 'New German School'.
[10] J. A. Fuller-Maitland: Preface to *Letters From and To Joseph Joachim*, London, 1914.

prepared to descend, we must reconsider our position in regard to the famous battle.

The dispute is long since dead, and did no credit to those figures who contributed to it. If there is any purpose in resurrecting it for a moment, it is to attempt to bring to the fore some of its more positive aspects, and to examine the musical reasons behind the antipathies which the two parties allegedly felt for one another. That Joachim, at the age of twenty-five, should have written to Liszt to tell him in all candour that he found his music bereft of any musical virtue whatever[11], and should by then have become a devoted admirer of Brahms, tells us nothing whatever of Brahms's attitude to Liszt, which was best expressed by his publication, six years later, of the two books of *Paganini Variations*. In another famous confession, Weber had written to the Swiss composer Nägeli:

> My views differ so radically from those of Beethoven that we can never meet. The brilliant and incredible gift of invention which is his is marked by such confusion of thought that I can really like his first compositions only—his later works are for me nothing but chaos, an incomprehensible effort to find new effects, above which shine a few heavenly sparks of genius, which show how great he might have been if he had been willing to bridle his ever-rich imagination. My nature does not allow me to appreciate Beethoven's genius.

The essential difference between Liszt and Wagner, and Schumann and Brahms, lies not in their compositions, nor in their attitudes to one another's works, but in their attitude towards the orchestra as a living and thriving instrument. Liszt had abandoned his career as a monumental virtuoso of the piano in 1848 to become a conductor and incidentally to promote the music of Wagner and that of a host of lesser composers, among whom he counted himself. As a superlative executive artist, he cannot have been willing to let pass anything less than superlative performance standards, and the names of famous musicians and singers who took part in his performances bear witness to this. Hans von Bülow wrote to his mother in October 1851 of Liszt's return to Weimar after a prolonged absence:

> I was at the station both morning and midday to await his arrival; but the servants, who were sent on ahead, said he would not come till the last train, at ten o'clock. So I went quite unconcernedly to hear *Cortez*—music so full of power and nobility to be-Flotow'd ears. There he appeared suddenly and unexpectedly a few yards before me in the stalls, as though he had sprung from the earth by magic. A

---

[11] Joachim's letter to Liszt of 27 August, 1857 (*The Letters From and To Joseph Joachim*, London, 1914).

whisper ran through the whole house and reached the orchestra, which during his absence had run wild and gone to sleep—and in their terror they played twice as badly, and Liszt got in a rage, and would have liked to seize the baton from his humdrum deputy, and to have made an end to the *gemüthlich* Philistine anarchy with the despotism of his own conducting-genius, had his scruples allowed it . . .

This was after all the orchestra for which, thirty-eight years later, Richard Strauss was to write *Don Juan*—a work of stupendous orchestral virtuosity—and the orchestra which was to give the first performance of Mahler's First Symphony under any other baton than Mahler's. This is not to suggest that Liszt's writing for orchestra was immaculate, in the sense which that of Wagner and Strauss was immaculate, and there is evidence to suggest that he was never a conductor of the stature which Bülow himself was to attain. It is rather that Liszt's orchestral writing is informed with the awareness of the orchestra as a performing instrument in the same way as is his piano-writing, and that his stature as an executive artist was to establish a performing tradition through the vehicle of his own works and those of his colleagues. These were values which had evaded the young Joachim in his decision to abandon a Weimar which had been so valuable to him.

Wagner was a great conductor, who equally demanded superlative standards from his orchestra and his singers. The notes themselves, and the technical difficulties which they embraced—these could be taught, and a solution found. Artistry could not—save through example, divined rather than acquired. This was the compelling power which overwhelmed Wagner's fellow-musicians, and won them to his music and through it provided the essential platform for every great conductor until the present time. To come to grips and to come to terms with the conducting of Wagner is to understand for the first time the essence of the conductor's art which alone will provide a release into the more rarefied air of the performance of Beethoven and Mozart. It is Wagner the *conductor* whom we must strive to rediscover.

Brahms, by contradistinction, was little more than competent as a conductor, while Schumann was totally incapable. And it is significant that the structure of their works is dependent upon intrinsic musical values which are sometimes less apparent or less fastidiously upheld than in the works of Wagner and Liszt. The morning after the catastrophe of the Leipzig performance of Brahms's D minor Concerto, the twenty-five-year-old composer wrote to Joachim:

Dearest friend,
    Although I am quite dazed by the sublime delights with which my

eyes and ears have been assailed for the last few days through the sight and sound of this musical town, I will force this hard and pointed pen of Sahr's[12] to relate to you how it came about that my Concerto has had here a brilliant and decisive—failure. First of all I must say that it was really done very well. I played far better than I did in Hanover[13], and the orchestra was excellent—Cherubini's *Elisa* overture was done, then an *Ave Maria* by him was sung very softly, so that I hoped that Pfundt's[14] drums would make their effect [at the opening of the Concerto]—The failure has made no impression on me whatever, and any feeling of depression which I may have had vanished when I heard Haydn's C major symphony and the *Ruins of Athens* . . . There is nothing more to say about this episode, for not a soul has said a word to me about the work—with the exception of David [the concertmaster], who took a great interest in it, and was very kind and took a lot of trouble about it . . . I asked Sahr a few questions this morning, and was pleased by his frankness . . .

This was Brahms' first orchestral work, and his first experience at firsthand of the orchestra. He could not—and would not have known how to—question the reputation of an orchestra which had achieved international eminence under Mendelssohn's direction. It was not a question of antipathy on the part of the orchestra or the audience of Leipzig to a work whose style must have sounded at serious odds with the remainder of the programme, for not even the most incompetent conductor could today be obtuse enough to sandwich the work between Cherubini and Haydn. The D minor Concerto has one of the most savagely exacting orchestral parts in the symphonic repertoire, and needs immense skill in its accompaniment. It is but rarely, and then only with a first-class orchestra, that it receives more than an adequate performance even today—even then requiring a full-sized string section and doubled woodwinds to contend with the anger of its opening tutti or its gigantic first-movement coda. How could the Leipzig orchestra, with its Haydnesque proportions, have begun even to understand the problems with which it was faced?

But because the grand piano of Brahms' day was slighter than the great concert grand pianos of our own time, this does not mean that the Haydn orchestra of the Leipzig Gewandhaus should have provided a just balance. One could as well suppose that the ceiling of the Sistine Chapel would make its effect equally as well viewed through the wrong end of a telescope. Certainly the instrumental specification of the D minor Concerto—as of its

[12] The assistant-conductor.
[13] The first performance, five days earlier, on 22 January, 1859.
[14] Timpanist of the Leipzig Gewandhaus Orchestra, who later invented the machine-head.

later companion in B flat—is identical with that of a late Haydn symphony, but here all similarity ends. This was an altogether new texture of sound, which had to reach well into the twentieth century before it was to find its fulfilment, while the orchestral accompaniment posed problems of conducting which must have utterly baffled the solid routinier, Julius Rietz, quite as much as they baffle the general practitioners amongst us today on first acquaintance. Brahms's adherents do him a further disservice by insisting that "this is a serious work, which eschews all effect". The American critic, William James Henderson, makes the fatuous observation:

> . . . The pianist has little opportunity to astonish by his mastery of scales, trills, thirds, and double-octaves . . .[15]

The concerto abounds in prolonged and exposed passages of thirds (and fourths, which are more difficult), the finale in the use of immensely rapid scale passages and brilliant broken arpeggios, and the soloist has further to contend with chains of savagely difficult octave trills and the first double-octaves used by any composer save Liszt in his E flat Concerto of a few years earlier. The notorious double-octave passage which begins the development section of the first movement, emerging as it does *subito ff* out of a hushed orchestral *pp*, is among the pianist's worst nightmares—if only because it is wrought of a material of greater musical integrity than analogous passages in Liszt or Tchaikowsky. What then was Brahms seeking if not effect—even as Michelangelo had been? If Brahms can still be so misunderstood by his self-appointed disciples, what opportunity had the orchestra or the conductor or the public of his own time to perceive what he was about? How far could Brahms discern this even for himself?

This is of course analogous to the circumstance of Beethoven, mentioned already, but with a fundamental difference. Beethoven had been compelled to write in the vacuum created by his deafness, but he had been a prodigious pianist in his youth, and was well aware of the virtues of instrumental mastery —the bassoon solo in the finale of his Fourth Symphony, and the horn solo in the slow movement of the Ninth Symphony tell us that. By the time he came to write his First Symphony at the age of thirty, and before deafness had begun seriously to assail him, he had acquired a close working experience of the orchestra as it then was—a motley rabble, to be sure, but with the beginnings of a tradition already established by Haydn and Mozart, and the growing comprehension of a new medium. Nor had Beethoven the musician lost contact with the substance of music, for when the twelve-year-old Liszt was

[15] W. J. Henderson: "Brahms", *International Cyclopaedia of Music and Muscians:* New York, 1938.

taken to meet him by Czerny, it was the music of Bach which he was invited to play—and Bach's music had only recently been rediscovered. The values which Beethoven demanded of executive musicianship were also manifest at that meeting. "Can you transpose that fugue on the spot?" Beethoven had demanded, to which the boy Liszt had replied that "fortunately I could, and the Master was pleased". Brahms also possessed this kind of universal musicianship, and the occasions of his transposition of the piano-score of the *Kreutzer* Sonata at sight, and of Bach's "Forty-Eight" from memory, have become legendary. But he also possessed exceptional technical powers at the keyboard, with an especial facility for certain pianistic problems which are amply exposed in the *Paganini* Variations. If he felt a certain antipathy towards the *Glanz-Periode* of Franz Liszt—yet he became a close friend of Leschetitzky at the end of his life—it was not so much because he eschewed executive brilliance, which is constantly in demand in his writing, but because he fought shy of any public demonstration which might arouse superficial enthusiasms. His own playing has been described by his admirers[16] as having been soft and introspective, and by his detractors as clumsy and unfeeling. Wagner wrote, in 1869:

> Mr. Johannes Brahms was once kind enough to play me a piece of his—a set of serious variations. It told me that he would allow no jokes, and in itself I found it excellent. I also heard him play the works of other composers at a piano-recital, which afforded me less pleasure. Indeed, I could only deem it an impertinence that this gentleman's adherents should ascribe to Liszt and his school a "by all means notable technique" and nothing more, when the woodenness and primness of Mr. Brahms's playing distressed me to the point where I would have given anything to have heard his own technique lubricated with a little of that school's oil—an oil which does not seem to exude from the keyboard itself, but to emanate from a region far more ethereal than that of bare "technique"[17].

Weber's confession about his attitude to Beethoven's later works tells us that it was not so much their inordinate technical difficulty which stood in the way of their comprehension as an interpretative tradition, without which it was impossible to come to grips with the technical problems, and Beethoven the conductor had done nothing to enlighten his musicians here. Weber's confusion was the greater because he himself had been an excellent conductor, and he could not know that there would be an enormous advance in the art of conducting, orchestral-playing and interpretation before Beethoven's later music would find its fulfilment.

[16] The late Adelina de Lara, *inter alia*.
[17] *Über das Dirigiren.*

If Brahms was endowed—as he undoubtedly was—with an extraordinary command of the keyboard, then Wagner's statement must be allowed
as fair, if uncharitable, comment. The experience of the first performance of
the D minor Concerto must, in the light of our evaluation of the work today,
stand in evidence that something was lacking in Brahms' interpretative
equipment. One might suppose that, because his chamber and instrumental
music has orchestral qualities, Brahms would have been entirely at home in
the ambience of the orchestra—yet it was alien to him until later life, and he
had little working contact with it until, in 1872, he succeeded Anton Rubinstein as director of the orchestra of the Gesellschaft der Musikfreunde. There
were musicians in Vienna in 1952 whose colleagues of their youth had played
under Brahms, and had taken part in the Vienna Philharmonic's first performance of the Haydn Variations in 1873. His conducting was severally described as benign, diffident, scholastic and gruff, with a visible show of
annoyance that it could not elucidate the *Vivace* and *Presto* variations at even
a very moderate tempo. The clarinetist, Vlach, who had known Mühlfeld at
Meiningen, said that the orchestra itself seemed able to derive no clear sense
of the music's texture, and that Brahms himself can have had no absolute
conception of this, although the "bare bones" of the music—the elaborate
counterpoint, instrumentation and so forth—were abundantly clear. With
the first performances of the Third and Fourth Symphonies under Hans
Richter, this had been another matter altogether, for the players were by this
time convinced by Brahms's music, and were familiar with its idiom. But the
feeling had persisted that the orchestration—as distinct from the instrumentation—was ill-judged, although they could not perceive in what respect this
might be so. The *melos* of the music evaded them.

If the practice of *rubato* is anathema today in the performance of
Beethoven's orchestral music—although it was common enough in the nineteenth century, and is apparently acceptable today in the performance of his
instrumental music—then nothing is so ludicrous as the absence of *rubato* in
the music of Brahms. But the effective use of *rubato* must come from deep
inner conviction on the part of the interpretative artist—a conviction which,
in the case of the conductor, must be transmitted to and unanimously
accepted by the orchestra, otherwise there is no, or at best a reluctant, ensemble. There is no greater "give-away" than the *ritardando* which meets the
conductor unprepared, and not having made a decision which is in keeping
with the internal logic of the musical context—the orchestra is at once aware,
and if the condition persists through rehearsal to the performance (and this
kind of conductor is the one who never does any homework) the awareness is
transmitted to the audience, and the music suffers. But the immaculately

paced *rubato* which is so essential to the *melos* of Brahms is a thing of infinite subtlety, and it is possible that it had evaded the precise and authoritarian baton of Hans Richter, as it had evidently evaded the composer himself during his three years of office in Vienna. Yet, in 1881, Bülow wrote of Brahms:

As a conductor he took the orchestra by storm, and his benevolent forbearance has inspired us to renew our efforts which are often thankless enough, owing to the paltriness of the conditions here.

Chapter 3

HANS VON BÜLOW

In Hans von Bülow we discover the first great conductor who was to achieve artistic eminence in the eyes of the musical public at large in his own lifetime, and to develop the art of orchestral-playing into something which approaches —and must in some respects have surpassed—the standards of great playing as we know them today. And not the least remarkable feature about his life is that this reputation should have been acquired, and the standards in question established, during the two brief periods of five years each when he held office as a conductor—from 1864 to 1869 in Munich, which included his direction of the first performances of *Tristan und Isolde* and *Die Meistersinger*, and from 1880 to 1885 in Meiningen.

There had, it is true, been the few months which he had spent as a conductor in Switzerland when, after the historic first performance of *Lohengrin* in Weimar, and after the letters of Wagner and Liszt to his mother, he set out on foot, against her express wishes and with a single-minded impetuousness which characterises his personality and his work, on the two-day walk from his father's house in Öltishausen to the theatre in Zürich where Wagner was working. That these few months provided the basis for a lifelong link with Wagner is certain. That they accomplished anything of permanent value for him as a conductor is doubtful, for we see him behaving like a complete amateur—whatever the glowing accounts from his fond parents.

He had heard Wagner conducting during his youth in Dresden, where Wagner occupied the position—from 1843 to 1849—of *erste Kapellmeister* under the musical directorship of Karl Riessiger. In 1847, the seventeen-year-old boy had received this note from Wagner:

> Your compositions, dear Herr von Bülow, have given me great pleasure; I did not want to give them back to your friend Ritter[1] without accompanying them with a cheering word to you. I do not add a criticism to them, for you will possess enough self-criticism without me; and I feel the less disposed to pick out weaknesses and

[1] Alexander Ritter, a lifelong friend of Bülow, and later violinist under him at Meiningen.

other things which did not please me, as I see from all that remains that you will soon be able to criticize your earlier attempts for yourself. Go on trying, and let me see some more . . .

Writing to his mother less than a year later from Leipzig where, despite his extraordinary talents as a musician, he was studying law, Bülow says:

I saw the most wretched performance of *Robert le Diable*—especially by the orchestra. The tempi were much too fast—except for Wagner, I don't know any conductor who does not commit this fault. Berlioz relates that Mendelssohn did it too . . .

Certainly the Leipzig Opera has never possessed the standards or the reputation of the Gewandhaus orchestra, whose roster of conductors goes back to the middle of the eighteenth century—though Wagner writes, in *Über das Dirigiren*:

At the famous Leipzig Gewandhaus concerts in my youth these pieces [Mozart, Beethoven] were simply not conducted at all. They were led off by Matthäi, the concertmaster of those days, somewhat as the overtures and entractes at the playhouse. Hence there was no disturbance by the conductor's personality. Moreover these masterpieces of our classical orchestral music, which presented no great technical difficulties *per se*, were got through regularly every winter. They went quite smoothly and precisely. One saw that the orchestra, knowing them all by heart, was glad to give the annual greeting to its favourites.

Only with Beethoven's Ninth Symphony, things would not go at all . . .

Writing of a Gewandhaus performance of the Ninth Symphony, Bülow continues in the same letter to his mother:

The concert was very full. 824 tickets were sold, and 632 thalers taken. Many people had paid a *louis d'or* for one or two tickets. Uncle[2] had defrayed the expenses—175 thalers—out of his own pocket . . . The concert opened with an overture by Gade *Im Hochland* . . . an aria from *Figaro* was well sung by Fräulein Schwarzbach . . . David [the concertmaster whom Brahms was to mention in his letter to Joachim eleven years later] played some bad variations of his own very cleverly . . . the sextet from *Don Giovanni* was beautifully done . . . Moscheles played a very beautiful *Rondo* of Mendelssohn's with orchestra . . . Livia[3] sang two songs by Rietz which are very pretty and made a perfect *furore* . . . and a little song by Mendelssohn.

[2] Kammerrat Frege, a trustee of the orchestra.
[3] Bülow's cousin by marriage.

c

The Ninth Symphony went very well—I was absolutely and entirely in heaven. Rietz conducted in a praiseworthy manner, as well as he could. The ladies' parts [soprano and contralto solos] were much better done than in Dresden, the rest not so good . . .

Such was the musical company which the Beethoven Ninth was accorded in 1848. In the following May began the riots inspired by the Vaterlands-verein which were to lead to open revolution and, for Wagner in Dresden, fifteen years' exile from his native Germany. Bülow was sent to Weimar where he and his parents were already long-standing acquaintances of the omniscient Liszt. From Weimar, Bülow wrote to his mother in June 1849:

Early yesterday I was with him at the rehearsal of *Fidelio*. I was perfectly carried away by his conducting—admirable, astounding . . . He gave us immense pleasure on Tuesday by his performance (on the piano) of the *Tannhäuser* Overture, which he had paraphrased in a most wonderful manner . . . it does not look so difficult on paper, yet the playing of it was such a strain on him that he was obliged to stop for a moment once near the end [sic], and he very seldom plays it because it exhausts him so much, so that he said to me afterwards: "You can write in your diary today that I have played the *Tann-häuser* Overture for you . . ."

Music occupies the young Bülow's letters to the exclusion of all else, and this should have afforded a measure of warning to his parents, who were now divorced, his father remarried and living at Öltishausen in Switzerland. To the correspondence from Wagner and Liszt he had weakly left the decision to his former wife, Franziska, who was obdurate in insisting that Hans should complete his law studies—already interrupted by the 1849 riots in Leipzig—before all else. Her stubbornness cost the foolish woman much anguish, and Bülow's step-mother wrote later from Öltishausen, where he had gone to stay for a few weeks:

One morning Hans had vanished. He was absent from breakfast, lunch and dinner. All enquiries were unsuccessful. Eduard soon said: "Hans has gone to Wagner in Zürich," and I could not but think the same thing. He took the post at Rossbach—the railway in that part was not yet finished—and went to Zürich. The next day he came back, very much upset and excited. Hans had fallen at his father's feet, and implored him to let him become a musician . . .

In October 1850, Hans von Bülow wrote to his sister Isidore:

We[4] did the trip on foot in two days: firstly to escape any possible pursuit on Papa's side, and also because I wanted to test

[4] Alexander Ritter, also engaged by Wagner, travelled with Bülow.

whether I had the energy to make that journey on foot in the most awful weather, amid ceaseless rain and storm . . . I have already conducted four times in public . . . It is not such an easy task as it seems—it requires a thorough and intensive study, almost to the point of learning the operas by heart, and that is a great strain[5] . . . The singers, who are for a wonder all extremely good, at first intrigued with the orchestra against me, because I am so young and in-experienced, and had not yet commanded sufficient respect . . . The *Bundes Zeitung*, which is the first paper here, said of my conducting in *La Fille du Regiment*: "Herr von Bülow, a pupil of Wagner's, has already shown himself to be a very talented conductor, and the one or two slips that occurred were merely the result of the orchestra not showing enough confidence in the young man . . ."

But two weeks later, in a letter to his father, he wrote:

. . . The third opera I conducted (since you were here) came to grief through the apathy of the public, and the consequent disinclination and reluctance of the singers—that is to say, it did not actually *fail*, but on the stage they intended to make it do so, in order perhaps to throw the blame on me afterwards . . . However, the chief thing is that I should learn conducting, and this I should be able to do, and much else besides I hope, as we have only one month behind us and six still to come. Under the circumstances Ritter cannot take part in the conducting here and must wait until I am thoroughly broken in and all the prejudices overcome . . . Yesterday was *Don Giovanni* under Wagner, with an overflowing house but a most dull, stupid and thankless audience. Wagner had taken the most exceptional trouble, and we had all three been several days and nights correcting errors in the orchestral parts, replacing instruments which were lack-ing, such as trombones, with others. Wagner had translated the Italian recitatives into German—he also simplified the scenery, and had cleverly reduced the everlasting scene-changing to a single one in the first act . . . It has driven me nearly wild when I remember how Wagner used to be accused in Dresden of conducting Mozart's music badly on purpose—how he could not bear his music because he was so eaten up by his own conceit . . .

The prejudices against young Bülow were not overcome, however, and a month later the theatre administration insisted on his dismissal, on the ground that he was causing too much dissension among the musicians. He wrote at once to his father:

As regards my immediate future, chance has interposed so favourably that I might almost be superstitious. Yesterday I received the offer of an engagement as musical director at St. Gall from

[5] This would seem to scotch the myth that Bülow had a photographic memory.

the director, Herbort, who heard that I had broken with Zürich
... I leave on Tuesday morning: Ritter goes with me, and will begin
by being repetiteur under me as conductor ... It is just possible
that, through Wagner, I might get something to do with Liszt at
Weimar ...

The musical conditions in St. Gall were appalling, many of the players
amateurs with no command of their instruments, and the young Bülow's
impatience and abusiveness did not aid him:

> What sort of animals I have to deal with in my orchestra would
> exceed the powers of natural history to describe. If one could only
> get to them somehow—but they understand absolutely nothing.
> I would gladly learn to grunt and to low in order to accomplish
> something, but it would not help matters. In the end there is nothing
> else for it but to laugh—in derision.

His father was clearly perturbed and unsure that this activity would really be
profitable to his son, and wrote secretly to Liszt to secure his advice. In
Liszt's reply, written on 4 January, 1851, he says:

> Allow me to observe, M. le Baron, that the harvest your son will
> reap from a conductor's position similar to that which he now
> occupies might be rather problematic *in the long run*; and that unless
> he found a solid and somewhat more lucrative position, whether
> morally or materially, there would be every reason to advise him to
> give up at once this business of little-enviable luxury ... I may say
> in passing that I entirely agree with your opinion in regard to his
> project of an opera of Jesus Christ. What theatre would produce it?
> What actors would play it? And what public would accept it?
>   The career of a German composer is full of hindrances and diffi-
> culties—Wagner, and some others of far less talent, furnish proofs
> of this every day. The very real interest I take in your son makes me
> hope that circumstances will allow of my being serviceable to him.
> Unfortunately I am unable to offer him any post near me, as you do
> me the honour to wish; and besides, I should have to be clearer
> about his ideas, projects, and the limits of his ambition, to come to
> any decision of that kind ...

The perennial wisdom of Franz Liszt is here again in evidence. He knew that
the career of a conductor in his own day was a thankless one, offering none of
the artistic—or financial—rewards which he felt convinced the talent of the
twenty-one-year-old Bülow should rightly inherit. He knew that he had won
a position of artistic independence for himself, such that he could act the role
of autocrat at Weimar, only by dint of the gruelling musical campaign which
he had fought as a virtuoso-pianist since childhood, and that such a position

was not to be attained lightly by one of Bülow's talent and integrity—a talent and integrity which could, however, well be perverted by over-exposure to mediocre standards. Above all, he was unsure of the boy's ultimate seriousness. He had been surrounded by adulation in his youth, from parents and relations whose contact with the world of professional music-making was only at the most superficial level, and who were the first to express misgivings in the face of any crisis. Liszt was far too discerning an artist to be ready to welcome him unconditionally to Weimar, even had he been empowered to do so, until he was convinced that Hans possessed, behind his extraordinary facility and musicality, a professional stamina which went beyond the desire for trivial success expressed in this letter from Eduard von Bülow to his cousin Ernst:

> Hans is now, as you know, at St. Gall. There he has formed an opera out of almost nothing. I was with him a week ago, when he conducted *Der Freischütz*, which he had studied by himself. The house was full to overflowing, the applause tremendous, and the performance excellent. Hans conducted in every respect like a master, *and without looking at the score*! The most notable men of the place—wealthy merchants, professors, doctors—play in the orchestra, partly for Hans' sake, and in order that the affair may succeed . . . He is invited to the first houses, and my banker had already invited him three times before he knew that it was my son . . .

And again, when the season had ended in May:

> Hans has been with us for the last four weeks, well and bright, for a rest after his veritable musical campaign in St. Gall. His labours there have ended with honour. He has gone through a schooling such as no musician of his age would easily do, and is now in a position to conduct any orchestra . . .

Liszt, however, had written to Wagner that he would allow Hans to come to Weimar as a pupil, and after more than a year's complete estrangement a measure of reconciliation was brought about with his mother, who certainly regarded Liszt as the lesser of two evils, and was prepared to finance her son on condition that he would use the experience to provide a basis for a "solid musical career"—teaching in a conservatory, or some such. When, two years later, he started on his first concert-tour as a pianist, which was to take him to Vienna and Budapest, she wrote to his sister:

> At a quarter to ten on Wednesday night Hans started for Vienna, where I earnestly hope he has safely arrived. *He has six letters from Liszt*—letters such as he rarely gives . . .

But one week later, when Hans had written from Vienna lamenting that
success had been far from instantaneous:

> From Hans I have heard only once, and it was bad news: I am
> hourly hoping for better tidings. Liszt, with whom I am in corres-
> pondence, certainly does not lose hope but, much as I like him, that
> does not comfort me. Everything that I foresaw, when he took that
> unlucky step in the autumn of 1850, has come to pass literally. God
> forgive those who led him to it . . .

This expression of the hysterical divorcée bewailing the cruelty of the big,
wide world to her darling son is a commonplace, and it is only remarkable
that it is an expression which has been and still is shared by parents of more
balanced disposition and by society in general in their estimation of what
constitutes the life of the artist. For them, all success must be immediate, and
if it is not, then far better give the whole thing up, and do something worth-
while. "I comprehend less and less how this artist's life can and does satisfy
him", wrote Franziska von Bülow a year later—though she was swift to bathe
in reflected glory whenever he had a success, and imagined that all would now
be plain sailing[6]. Because those who are not spiritually attuned to the artist's
work can only measure it in terms of their experience of the finished product,
in terms of the degree and frequency of its applause, they do not enquire what
lies behind success, or what lies between success and failure. A Liszt or a
Rubinstein or a Paganini or a Horowitz—these are seen only as glittering
examples of a pinnacle of achievement to be marvelled at or carped at in the
light of their own success or failure to grasp the principle which motivated
these artists' work—that of doing one's task always to the best of one's
ability. Yet who amongst us has not suffered the tortures to which we daily
expose ourselves in our human relationships—or want of them? Should this
not rather persuade us that the compassion which lay behind the vanity of
Liszt the man must have informed his stature and understanding as an
artist? That the theft by Wagner of the wife of his closest friend and greatest
admirer—trivially echoed a thousand times a day in the divorce-courts of our
world—is but the *locus classicus* of an everyday human tragedy brought about
by the need for a spiritual communion which found fulfilment in Wagner's
music? That the sense of resignation and loneliness embodied in the figure of
Brahms, and his renouncement of society as we understand it, was the price
which he was compelled—and prepared—to pay for the overwhelming spirit
of humanity which informs the *Vier ernste Gesänge*?

[6] It must be said in all fairness that Bülow's mother continued to finance him through
his early struggles for recognition.

In writing to Schumann's biographer, Joseph von Wasiliewski, four years later, Liszt was to say this:

> The frequent ill-success of my performances of Schumann's compositions, both in private circles and in public, discouraged me from including and keeping them in the programmes of my concerts which followed so rapidly upon one another—programmes which, partly from want of time and partly from carelessness and satiety of the *Glanz-Periode* of my pianoforte-playing, I seldom, except for the rarest cases, planned myself, but gave them now into this one's hand and now into that one, to choose what they liked. That was a mistake, as I discovered later and deeply regretted, when I had learned to understand that, for the artist who wishes to be worthy of the name of artist, the danger of not pleasing the public is a far less one than that of allowing oneself to be decided by its humours—and to this danger every executive artist is especially exposed, if he does not take courage resolutely and on principle to stand earnestly and consistently by his conviction, and to produce those works which he knows to be best, whether people like them or not . . .

For the moment, in his reply to Franziska von Bülow of March 1853, Liszt wrote:

> . . . Upon the whole, I am far from judging his actual position in Vienna to be as bad as he would seem to have described it to you . . . The only thing necessary is that he must not let himself be discouraged, and that he must preserve a little *sangfroid*, in order to profit by the means, which will continue to offer, of conquering step by step the ground to which he has a right. The bitter and one-sided tone of the newspaper critic ought not to make him in the least uneasy; he must learn to bear his part in these things with calmness, like a man of sense and talent; ill-fortune of this nature must not be regarded as sinister, and has never prevented anyone from winning his rightful place, as our friend Hans will do, be it a little sooner or a little later . . .

It was to be a little later before Hans von Bülow reappeared on the stage as a conductor, and later still before he conquered the world as a solo pianist. In the meantime, he had played in much of Europe with great brilliance and little conclusive success, had fulfilled his mother's secret desires in becoming professor of piano at the Max-Stern Conservatoire in Berlin, and had married Cosima, the eighteen-year-old daughter of Franz Liszt.

The opposition which Bülow had experienced from his own family was something new to music. Handel's father, it is true, had been violently opposed to his son's training as a musician, which obstacle had been removed by his own untimely death. But most other eminent musicians had themselves been born into musical families, and the status of the musician was such that it was a trade which a man's son might follow as well as any other, with perhaps the prospect of advancement if he found favour as some prince's *Kammermusiker*. With the advent of the bourgeoisie, van Beethoven and von Weber had brought prestige to the profession, for they were *Freiherrn*, freemen who, if they had not entirely lost the common touch, had none the less "walked with princes". Wagner was of course a radical, and had very properly been expelled from Germany along with all his kind in the Revolution of 1848, but Liszt—a wonderful pianist to be sure, but not even a serious composer—had not only achieved royal patronage but was, if appearances could be believed, accepted among them on equal terms and had a royal mistress. The bourgeoisie was not quite sure what to think, but could only regard the musical profession with growing admiration and its behaviour, musical and social, with the gravest misgiving. If a member of one's own family were eccentric enough to wish to embark on a musical career, then let him be respectably married—like Hans's cousin Livia—or at least seek a safe position in some reputable conservatoire. What did the commendations of Liszt and Wagner amount to, viewed realistically?

The faith which Wagner had had in Bülow as a conductor had been largely implicit, for before he invited him to come and work under him in Zürich he had already expressed his belief that the young man possessed an extraordinary potential, and it is testament to Wagner's own insight into the art of conducting that he should have been able to divine this, when so few conductors of our own day can claim a distinguished pupil at all. Nor can the brief month in Zürich which culminated in Bülow's dismissal have done much to support Wagner in his convictions. Yet they remained unalterable, and it was to Bülow that he turned when, with his own vast comprehension of the art, he was compelled to abandon the performance of *Tristan* in Vienna after seventy-seven rehearsals, and it was declared unperformable. The foundation for this faith would seem to have been threefold: Bülow's determination, which persisted through the easy exaltations of success and the deep depressions of failure, combined with his acute psychological perception and flair for diagnosis; his executive talent as a pianist, which had already won the endorsement of Liszt; and his awareness as a composer—and it was on this last that Wagner placed the greatest emphasis, for the *unverneinbares Talent* which he had perceived in the compositions of a seventeen-year-old boy were evidence enough, as he implied in the note which he sent to Bülow, of those critical and creative faculties whose combination is essential to the conductor's art.

The emphasis which Wagner placed upon the ability to compose as a necessary adjunct to the art of conducting—and he was a conductor before he became a composer in the fuller sense—has ample justification in the generations of conductors who succeeded him, and for whom a mastery of the art of composition and a perception of the forces which must generate the creative act went hand in hand with their executive work, and the examples of Bülow, Richter, Strauss, Mahler, Nikisch, Weingartner, Furtwängler and a host of other great conductors are sufficient evidence in support of this view. It matters not a whit that the works of all but two of them have long since been forgotten: it is the extent to which their ability to write enhanced their conductor's art which should not be forgotten. Nor, by an ability to compose, did Wagner mean those elegant niceties produced by the dashing young conservatoire conductors about whom he was so scathing. Rather was it an insight into the higher art of composition which could be discerned in the essays of musicians of more critical and less fertile invention—an insight evident in the piano transcription of *Tristan* which Bülow was preparing in Berlin during those years which preceded its ultimate first performance. With the eyes of hindsight we may see how wide was Bülow's tentative ending to the Prelude—which had for the moment evaded Wagner himself—of the mark which its composer later found with such unerring accuracy:

Ex. 5

In the A major 6/4 is an element as totally foreign to the harmonic language of *Tristan* as it had been common, in that context, to all music up to this moment. With the eyes of hindsight we may attempt to descry here a glimpse of the academic, of the professor of the Max-Stern Conservatoire, the editor of Beethoven's Piano Sonatas, the conductor who is alleged to have meddled with the harmonies of Beethoven's symphonies. Is it not enough to remark that, while this passage could not have come from Wagner's own pen, this chord is the only feature which is out of place?

Bülow's critical edition of the Beethoven Sonatas, written concurrently with the productions of *Tristan* and *Meistersinger* in Munich, his activity as director of the new Music School there, and a growing schedule of concerts

both as pianist and conductor, give as complete a picture of Bülow the inter-
petative artist as we could wish for. They also tell us something of the man.
In a letter to Wagner in April 1869, Bülow wrote:

> I have been suffering so severely from a nervous attack for the
> past six days, *lieber Meister*, that I stayed in altogether to recover . . .
> I have employed this involuntary leisure in working at my edition
> of Beethoven and have finished Op. 106, at the cost of much exer-
> tion . . . Will you allow me to dedicate this work publicly to you
> (with a carefully considered preface)? It will not be an entirely
> unworthy contribution to your *"deutsche Vortragstil"*.
>   I saw Richter yesterday morning. When he called the day before,
> I was too exhausted to have him admitted . . . I put it seriously to
> him that he must warn Perfall[7] to obey your orders with regard to
> *Rheingold* promptly, precisely and good naturedly, and not to put up
> any opposition as in the case of *Meistersinger* . . .[8]

The penetrating—if now controversial—musicianship which animates the
nine hundred-odd pages of the Beethoven edition, side by side with the priceless technical secrets which they disclose, was (as Bülow's reference to
Op. 106 reveals) nearing the end and apotheosis of its task with the great last
sonatas—*le ultime cinque*, as he called them when, in later life, he incorporated
all five into the same programme in a series of historic recitals. The passage of
time has lent colour to the legend of Bülow's eccentricities—of which this was
labelled as but one instance—and of the extremes of *rubato* in which he would
indulge himself as an executive artist. Here is what Bülow himself writes,
concerning the use of *rubato*:

> . . . In the editor's opinion, even the freest cadenza must retain a
> rhythmically fluent pattern, and even the most eccentric *tempo rubato*
> must eschew unintelligent caprice if it is to be artistically justified.
> The privilege of coherent subjectivity is accorded by nature to but
> few, and its expression will always display that logic—albeit in-
> stinctively so—which lends intelligible form to an objective read-
> ing . . .[9]

The musical scholarship with which Bülow writes here—and the
authority which is implicit in his letter to Wagner, with all its overtones of

[7] Intendant of the Royal Opera House in Munich, strongly opposed to Wagner.
[8] *The letters of Hans von Bülow*, edited by Moulin Eckhart (1931), trans. Hannah Waller.
[9] Vol. IV, Op. 77.
   *Nach seine Ansicht muss auch die freieste Cadenz eine rhythmisch-plastische Gestalt
gewinnen können und aus dem excentrischsten 'tempo rubato', wenn es künstlerische
Berechtigung beansprucht, jede unverständliche Willküre verbannt sein. Das Privileg
einer interessanten Subjectivität ist nur Wenigen von der Natur verliehen; die
Äusserungen einer solchen werden stets von jener instinktiven Logik zeugen, die eine
objective Darstellung in verständlicher Form ermöglicht . . .*

political intrigue which had accompanied the first performance of *Meister-singer* and was so to accompany the production of *Rheingold* the following September—are in vivid contrast to the impetuous letters of his youth, but the artist's self-assurance remains unchanged. His desire to dedicate the work to Wagner, and to the latter's lifelong campaign for a *deutsche Vortragstil*— a standard of performance whose dignity would match the inspiration of its composers—this was undiminished. Yet if the task embodied in his edition of the Beethoven Sonatas was reaching its climax, so was his private life. His wife Cosima, daughter of his teacher and idol, Franz Liszt, had already borne Wagner two children and was carrying his third. It would be easy to attribute to Bülow's apparent unconcern a spirit of complaisance, a single-minded pre-occupation with the musical edifice which was being created—yet the letter which he wrote to Cosima in Lucerne on 17 June, eleven days after Siegfried Wagner had been born and the final and irreparable break had long since come about, is not consistent with such a view. We may see something of the King Mark in this letter[10], and it is ironical that it should have been the first production of *Tristan* which was to provide the stage for this human tragedy. It is sufficient to understand that, given three such brilliant characters, and a *mise-en-scène* which was to establish the supremacy of Wagner as an opera-composer, and Munich as the leading opera house of the world, the course which this tragedy had pursued was predestined and inevitable. One can only marvel at the utter fidelity which all three retained, in the face of their own emotional involvement and of enormous physical opposition from the Bavarian Court, towards the artistic goal which providence, in the form of the young King Ludwig, had placed within their grasp.

But for Bülow it was the end, in more ways than one, of an epoch which had begun for him with the towering artistic achievement of the first per-formance of *Tristan und Isolde* on 10 June, 1865. On 21 June, 1869—four days after he had signed Cosima's *quietus est*—he wrote to Wagner in Lucerne:

> The fifth performance (newly rehearsed) of *Tristan und Isolde*, *lieber Meister*, really came off yesterday . . . Herr und Frau Vogel achieved wonders from the musical side. The big dialogue in the second act was in fact more effective as regards tone and words than four years ago, when the blissful Ludwig damped his voice to please the noble Malwina[11]. The orchestra was quite attentive and discreet except for a few minor details. I for my part conducted far better and with more composure than before. This was due to my practice with the baton in between . . . Richter is conducting *Meistersinger* on the 27th., with Betz and Mallinger. He put it aside for the whole of

10 *The Letters of Hans von Bülow*, Moulin-Eckart.
11 Ludwig and Malwina Schnorr, who first created the roles of Tristan and Isolde.

last week to make way for the orchestra and piano rehearsals of
Tristan[12]. I should still have the strength to conduct it (*Meistersinger*) for the tenth time but, for one thing, I owe it to Richter and
his magnificent achievements to give him this pleasant satisfaction,
and, for another, there is more point in closing my career with
Tristan, for so I come full circle . . . As I shall be kept here next
month by the Music School and also do not feel well enough to come
and see you (as I once suggested); as, in addition, a meeting with me
would be painful and embarrassing for you while I, in my present
state of mind, should inevitably be dangerously upset by it; and as,
finally, Cosima has received a complete explanation in a lengthy
letter, it seems to me that a meeting between us two is superfluous.
It is better that I should bid you a last goodbye in writing when I
definitely leave Munich . . .[13]

A week later he wrote to Karl Klindworth, his friend and fellow-pupil under
Liszt, in Moscow:

> . . . *Rheingold* is still announced for 25 August. The rebuilding of the
> stage and orchestra-pit will soon be finished, scenic preparation also.
> Richter is in charge of the music. I hear from other people that
> Liszt is coming for the performance. It is quite impossible for me to
> stay and listen to it. My health is ruined, physically and morally.
> I can hardly pull myself together to carry on my official duties until
> the holidays. My career as conductor came to an end with the newly
> rehearsed *Tristan* on 22 June[14]: You will wonder why (I have
> resigned), but there will soon be plenty of people to solve the
> mystery for you. Spare me the necessity, I beg.
> How glad I should have been to arrange for you to succeed me
> here! Alas, I have now no say in the matter. I no longer have any
> communication with Switzerland . . . I am afraid I shall soon go to
> pieces, but am trying the last radical remedy, that of absolute
> personal resignation . . .[15]

It is difficult to see here "the man of keen temper, wayward as a child"
whom one writer, at least, discerns in the character of Bülow[16]. Certainly he
had a temper ready to match that of Wagner's, and in this was reflected the
abiding respect which each bore for the other as artist. Bülow was capable
of abusive language in inveighing against the mediocrities with which he met

[12] *Orchester mit Klavier-Proben*, Miss Waller's translation confuses the two separate
functions by translating this as "orchestral rehearsals with pianoforte". Orchestral rehearsals
are for orchestra alone, and piano rehearsals for singers alone.
[13] *The Letters of Hans von Bülow*: Moulin-Eckart.
[14] A second (and private) performance of the new production for Ludwig II.
[15] *The Letters of Hans von Bülow*: Moulin-Eckart.
[16] Preface, by Scott Goddard, to *The Letters of Hans von Bülow*. He also makes the
statement that Bülow gave the first performance of the Tchaikowsky Piano Concerto in 1880.
This had taken place under Fritz Lang, with Bülow as soloist, in Boston on 29 October, 1875.

in the course of his daily work, but of waywardness there is little trace in the meticulous care with which he approached and executed his work. And indeed it was probably the very predictability and security which he offered Cosima, echoing the princely punctilio of her own father, which drove her to exchange her life with Bülow for one of elemental unpredictability with Richard Wagner.

For Bülow, the journey from Weimar to Munich had been long and frustrating. His task at the Max-Stern Conservatoire in Berlin he regarded as a monstrous tedium, alleviated only by the rare pupil of outstanding talent, and occasional concerts as soloist or as conductor of the Berlin orchestra—precursor of the famous Berlin Philharmonic—in which, so he complained to Wagner in 1859, he had found a total of only twelve violins (six firsts and six seconds), and insufficient for the Prelude to Act I of *Lohengrin*. For opera, he had had to content himself with the vicarious pleasure of routine performances under Hülsen, and in his letters there is a growing sense of awareness —if also a growing one of frustration which reached its peak with the collapse of the project of staging *Tristan* at Karlsruhe, and with it his hopes of gaining employment as a permanent opera conductor. Thus it was that, when Wagner was at last in the position to call him to Munich at the age of thirty-four, he approached the ambiance of opera with the score of *Tristan* already familiar to him through and through—for he had been working on it, and preparing the piano-reduction, for the last five years—but with no first-hand experience of the operatic medium other than the paltry and stimulating months in Zurich and St. Gall fourteen years earlier.

The immensity of his achievement cannot be overestimated, for he laid the foundation of modern opera routine in discovering and inventing a routine which was capable of translating the pages of *Tristan* into a musical reality, and which was to give to the Munich Hofoper a position unique to German music-making. He inherited little from Franz Lachner, the previous incumbent in Munich and an equivocating routinier who had held his position for over thirty years by always accepting the least line of resistance. In Dresden, the town of his birth, there was Julius Rietz, who possessed much the same qualifications as Lachner, and had inherited his position from Reissiger, an incumbent of thirty-two years standing "who had destroyed everything which Weber, over a period of six years, had built up". There were of course Vienna and Prague, which could claim the musical sponsorship of so much Gluck and Mozart, but these too had suffered and finally capitulated beneath the assault of provincial standards. That *Lohengrin* and *Tannhäuser* had remained in the repertoire of the leading European houses at all had been largely due to the example of Weimar, and the Paris première of *Tannhäuser* (incorporating the

Bacchanale) had of course been a fiasco. Now came an opera whose score was as far removed from these in its idiom of musical speech as the Ninth Symphony had been from the Eighth, or—as Bülow himself expressed it—[17] the posthumous quartets from Op. 18. He was compelled to coach the singers himself, and to coach the coaches, who were unable to decipher the musical complexities of the score. He had to inspire the concept of an entirely new kind of vocal sound in his singers, and train them to produce this sound. He had to interpret for them, musically and dramatically, the logic and line of their parts, to unravel for them the intricacies and subtleties of their grammar and syntax, and to create for them their roles. And above all he had to train an indifferent orchestra, now augmented beyond its wildest imaginings, and numbering in its ranks many musicians of limited competence and musical understanding, first to play with articulation, then with accuracy, then with precision, and lastly with a dawning but ever-growing comprehension and awareness music whose technical and interpretative difficulties had seemed to Wagner himself insuperable. Finally, through an unprecedented series of *Hauptproben*[18], he had to weld the whole into the vast symphonic unity which is *Tristan und Isolde*, and bring it before the public on 10 June, 1865, without the aid of the score.

This last point is not in itself remarkable. Long before the first *Hauptprobe* Bülow must have had every note and every nuance of *Tristan* ineradicably engraved on his receptive—but by no means photographic—memory, and it would have been astonishing if he *had* needed a score for the performance. What is remarkable is that he should have been the first conductor to dispense with its use, not only in the performance, but in rehearsal as well— a fact far less readily remembered. That learning a score by heart did not come easily to him, we know from his own candid admission to his sister, when he was working with Wagner at Zürich—although it was a faculty which he acquired with increasing facility through practice and experience. That he took the trouble to do so is a testament to the amount of work which went into his study of the score—his editions of Beethoven and other piano music bear ample witness to this—and we may be sure that he did not cultivate the practice for reasons of vanity and showmanship, for it provoked in Munich as much adverse comment as the resort to a score by the conductor of a first-class orchestra would provoke in us today.

There must be, and there evidently are, charlatans in every profession who will seek refuge behind any device to cover up the miserable short-

[17] Letter to Wagner of 24 August, 1859.
[18] Undress rehearsals with full cast, orchestra, scenery, properties and lighting. Rudolf Hartmann, intendant in Munich until 1966, speaks of there having been eleven for the first performance of *Tristan*. Usually there is one.

comings of their own dilettantism, but they fall outside the province of this enquiry. So does the practice of dispensing with the score before one is properly qualified to do so—though it should be mentioned in passing that nothing so illuminates the gaps in one's awareness than the coming before an orchestra with an interpretation which is less than fully prepared. It is an experience akin to the actor who is thrust onstage in a role, the broad outline of which he may have mastered, but in the detailed interpretation of which he is less than word-perfect. Every nuance of expression and every secret shade of meaning wherein he has failed to make a decision become for him magnified to a dimension which will ensure that such inattentiveness will never again find its repetition in the diligent artist. For the conductor, such a situation is less transparently obvious to the public than it is for the actor, for a reputable orchestra will always carry him through these lacunae in his awareness— though at the expense of an immediate loss of contact and a lingering loss of respect, for it is impossible to deceive the orchestra where it may yet be possible to deceive the public. For the serious musician, the decision to work without the score is not taken lightly—any more than the analogous decision of the surgeon or the general or the barrister, no more ludicrous picture than which could be their unfamiliarity with the case history of a patient, or the plan of campaign, or the client's brief, at the moment where the patient is on the operating table, or definitive orders have to be given, or the client's case presented before court. Aside from the fact that a proper mastery of the content of the score must render its presence or absence on the music stand superfluous, the presence of the music-stand itself constitutes a physical and psychological obstacle. Its removal, on the other hand, presents an unambiguous and tacitly acceptable challenge to the orchestra, in exposing the conductor to their closest scrutiny—both in the physical and musical sense— and in its establishment of an immediate communion between the two, nothing could be more welcome to the conductor who is fully prepared. This is not to preclude the use of the score for the sake of expediency, on occasions where there has been no time to master it and one must rely to a more or less extent upon the ability to read and interpret at sight, but it is to condemn those competent routine performances whose standard would be raised a hundredfold if their authors were to take the trouble to master the score to the point where they no longer had need of it. Always providing that one knows how to conduct in the fullest sense of the word, the practice of conducting effectively without score is largely dependent upon that diligent mastery which one should expect every performance to enjoy in its preparation at the hands of a serious artist. To give a successful performance with the score in front of one demands, on the other hand, the possession of a very special gift which few conductors and no soloist within my experience can be seen to possess. I use the word "seen" advisedly; that some will maintain that great music—unlike little children—should be heard and not seen is a point on which I do not propose to enlarge at this juncture.

The psychological impact of Bülow's decision to give the rehearsals and performances of *Tristan* without score must have been tremendous, for it gave to the musicians in his charge that confidence and reassurance which were needed to surmount musical terrors only since equalled in the first performance, under Erich Kleiber in Berlin, of Alban Berg's *Wozzeck*. The first performances of *Meistersinger*, three years later, posed for Bülow an even greater challenge. For although its musical idiom was more accessible than that of *Tristan* had been, its texture was far more complex in the richness of its polyphony and the enormous intricacy—for that time—of its ensemble problems. Nor did Bülow enjoy the close association with Wagner which had been his for five or more years in the preparation of the score of *Tristan*, and which in *Meistersinger* had now been inherited, in his almost daily contact with Wagner at Triebschen, by Hans Richter—just as he was to inherit the traditions of Wagnerian conducting which Bülow had established. In a letter to Wagner at the end of 1868, Bülow wrote:

> ... The ninth performance of *Meistersinger* went very well in parts. Richter took first horn[19] after he had played the organ [in the opening scene] ... Fräulein Stehler was excellent—Sigl not in such good voice ... Kindermann dragged and went wrong a good deal (I had to beat time on my desk once or twice) ... Orchestra excellent ...

The excellent orchestra was to become Bülow's main preoccupation as a conductor, and just as he had set new standards of German operatic conducting which are—in those instances where they are still upheld—essentially those which we know today, so now he was to set an entirely new standard of orchestral playing in the symphony orchestra.

In 1860, Georg II of Saxe-Meiningen, with a predilection for instrumental music, had withdrawn his patronage of opera and turned his attention to the foundation of a symphony orchestra of thirty-five players in his principality. Five years later, while *Tristan* was being produced in Munich under the patronage of Ludwig II of Bavaria, he engaged Büchner—namesake and distant relative of the famous author of *Woyzeck*—who served as conductor of the Meiningen Orchestra until his death in 1879. On 7 November of the

---

[19] A position normally occupied by Richard Strauss's father, whom Bülow would not, however, allow in the orchestra-pit during his own performances. He was one of the first of the "conductor-baiters".

following year Bülow, now nearly fifty-one, succeeded him as permanent conductor at a salary of five thousand Reichsthalern. But the intervening years since he had fled Munich to try and build a new life for himself in Florence had been ones of savagely hard work, during which his international reputation as a pianist was established, and his spiritual, mental and physical wellbeing all but shattered. He had had to decline the offer of conductor of the Gesellschaft der Musikfreunde in Vienna in 1870, and Anton Rubinstein had been appointed in his stead. The following year—and at an age when Liszt had long since given up all public appearances as a pianist—he set out on the first of his historic recital-tours, and at the beginning of 1871 made the interesting comment in a letter to Carl Bechstein[20]: " . . . The current programme I am playing without music at all, and this, so far as I know, no one else has done—not even myself to date . . ."[21]

The famous tour of America, where he gave one hundred and thirty-nine concerts in the eight months from October 1875 to June 1876, placed him at the pinnacle of his profession as a solo pianist, but he was still far from financially secure, for he had not yet fulfilled his promise to Cosima to set up a trust-fund for their children, and it seems clear that she was not prepared to let him see them again, or even correspond with them, until this had been done. He conducted little—revisions of *Tristan* and *Meistersinger* in Munich in the summer of 1872, a few concerts in London in 1873 and 1874, and in Brighton in 1878, further disappointment over an operatic appointment in Karlsruhe, and the beginnings of an association with the Hanover opera. But the inevitable intransigence of the administration only resulted in a breakdown in negotiations and in Bülow's nervous health, and he was driven to attempt suicide—an attempt which was foiled by Carl Bechstein.

The artistic conditions which Bülow inherited in Meiningen were not favourable, and it must seem incredible to us that within five years—which included seventeen months of complete inactivity—he should have created, out of a nonentity of the forty-five players whom he had made his initial condition of acceptance, what was to become the most famous orchestra in Europe and numbering, by the turn of the century, nearly one hundred. Nor could he give his undivided attention to this, for much of his time was still devoted to gruelling recital-tours in the face of competition from Anton Rubinstein and Karl Tausig. And it was certainly the combination of the physical exhaustion of these tours, Cosima's unwillingness to let him attend the wedding of their daughter Blandine or the first performance of *Parsifal* at Bayreuth, the death of his friend Joachim Raff, together with internal difficulties within the

[20] Head of the famous firm of piano manufacturers, whose instrument Bülow preferred.
[21] This would seem to dispose of the legend that Liszt always—or indeed ever—played from memory.

orchestra, which led to his utter collapse and complete nervous breakdown of 1882—from which this remarkable man was still to recover and go forward to his greatest work.

Hitherto there had been only one symphony orchestra in Germany which could, by contemporary standards, be defined as a great orchestra—the famous Gewandhaus orchestra in Leipzig, whose origins went back to the first half of the eighteenth century when Bach had still been alive. Notwithstanding Wagner's comments, it had owed its stature and reputation in very large measure to the work of Felix Mendelssohn during the eight years from 1835 to 1843. And it is fair indication of how far contemporary standards were below those which we would consider valid today, and which Wagner considered essential to the performance of the classical literature, that he should have felt impelled to pass such judgement. But that Wagner had not exaggerated is borne out by Bülow's youthful account of a programme typical of the tradition of his day, and whose constitution transgressed every tenet of musical and artistic good taste. Apart from Leipzig there was only the Vienna Philharmonic, founded under Nicolai in 1842, and which with Richter's accession in 1875 had begun to offer the Gewandhaus orchestra serious competition. The eighteenth-century traditions of Mannheim, Stuttgart and Berlin had vanished, and that of the formidable Berlin Philharmonic was yet to emerge.

Three months after Bülow took over the Meiningen orchestra, Liszt wrote to the editor of the Hungarian Gazette in Pest:

> ... To Bülow it has been given to do battle better and with greater perseverance than I. His admirable Beethoven edition is dedicated to me[22] as the "fruit of my tuition". Here however it was for the master to learn from his pupil, and Bülow continues to teach by his astonishing performances as a virtuoso, as well as by his extraordinary learning as a musician, and now by his matchless direction of the Meiningen orchestra. Here you have musical progress in our time ...

The progress of the Meiningen orchestra must indeed have been unique, for by the summer of 1881 it had given a cycle of all nine Beethoven symphonies in one week in Munich, in performances to which even the hostile *Suddeutsche Zeitung* could not take exception. Nevertheless, the difficulties were still formidable, and in December 1881 Bülow wrote—Cosima's embargo having now been lifted—to his daughter Daniela:

> ... I can only hope to breathe again next week, when the seventh subscription concert and the sixth and last chamber music recital

[22] Wagner had, understandably enough, declined Bülow's initial offer of dedication.

(for this season) will be over ... I am hoping for the support of your grandfather's sympathy[23] when he hears that I have not yet sent in my resignation and may possibly not be forced to do so. The Duke appears to be more and more aware of the fact that I must now be a *freier Herr* in more ways than one if he wished to keep me partially and employ me occasionally. He is sensible enough to see that he can offer me no equivalent for the sacrifices I have made in health, time, comfort, money—yes, money!—and must therefore ease things for me in other ways. The engagement of a serviceable (assistant) conductor for next season would be of paramount importance to me. I have already found one who would do, in the person of young Mannstädt[24], who is probably known and appreciated at Bayreuth, where he coached Betz, Niemann and others ... Up to 3 January I shall have all I can do to polish my players, now that I have brought them out of the rough, for we have twenty concerts ahead of us in Berlin, Hamburg and Breslau. On 4, 5 and 6 January there is a cycle of Beethoven concerts at the Singakademie, on the 7th a Mendelssohn evening, and on the 8th and 9th two Brahms concerts, with the composer playing one of his concertos (No. 2 in B flat) with me as conductor, and conducting the other (No. 1 in D minor) which I am to play. This is a crushing blow for Joachim and his Crusca[25], my child—something which he never dreamed of, something from which he will *not* recover ...

And on 10 January, 1882, from Hamburg, where the orchestra was giving two concerts:

On 12 and 13 January we are in Kiel; 14 in Bremen; 15 Hamburg again; 16, 17, 18 Berlin; 19, 20, 21 Leipzig, Cöthen, Halberstadt. On the 22 back to Meiningen, after which I propose to start my pianist's tour on the 26 or 27 ... The Crown Prince was there (Berlin) five times, and last night the Kaiser came too. What a triumph over Hanover! Whether deserved or not, I can honestly say it was *essential* to me ... In between I have had a visit from the future director [of the Hamburg Opera] Stägemann ... He tells me that Hans Richter and César Franck are here and will come to the concert tonight ... Brahms has arrived here from Berlin, for no other reason than to come and hear us! So he has a heart, you see ...

It had been Bülow's original intention to take the Meiningen orchestra as far as London the year before, and a performance of the Beethoven Ninth,

---

[23] Daniela was nursing her grandfather, Liszt, in Rome.

[24] Mannstädt took over the orchestra during the 1882–83 season of Bülow's complete breakdown, and later conducted with him in Berlin.

[25] Joachim was by now director of the Royal Conservatory in Berlin. "Crusca" refers to the latter, drawn by Bülow from the original Accademia della Crusca which had been founded in Florence in 1583, but being also a pun on the Italian word for "chaff".

expressly in aid of the orchestra, had been scheduled for 22 May, 1881, in the Leipzig Gewandhaus. It is clear that the largesse of the Grand Duke of Meiningen did not immediately extend to the sponsorship of extra players and extra rehearsals which Bülow would have wished, and that during the first season he had had to pay for these out of his own pocket—an expense which he could ill afford. The kudos which the presence at the Berlin concerts of the Kaiser and the Crown Prince had provided was therefore of the utmost significance to the orchestra's future, as was that of such musicians as Brahms and Franck to Bülow's own reputation, and it is astonishing to see him, at the age of fifty-two still preoccupied by his failure to obtain an appointment in Hanover three years earlier, and to realise by what a narrow thread the future of his career still hung—in his own estimation, at all events. The programme of this tour of twenty concerts in eighteen days, across the breadth of north Germany, would be formidable by present-day standards, but in 1882 it was unprecedented, and is eloquent of the orchestral discipline which Bülow had instilled. His hopes of an appointment at the Hamburg Opera, which he had hoped to combine with his duties in Meiningen, were now dashed. The orchestra having acquired a reputation, its best players now responded to offers which they would not otherwise have received, and with an alacrity and fickleness which have a familiar ring. Bülow had of course been unable to secure them contracts which committed them beyond the current season:

> I am hoping to annul my Hamburg contract [he wrote to Daniela from Copenhagen in August 1882 while on a recital-tour] both on account of my lack of the greatest of all good things (since live one must) good health, and because of unforeseen obstacles in Meiningen; for instance, a number of my most reliable players have thrown me over for better jobs elsewhere. It is now my pleasing duty to find substitutes, paste and patch up as best I can. I spare you the details. You can imagine from this, if you did not already know, what a bed of thorns mine is ...

Many of the players in question, among them Fleischhauer, the concertmaster, and his brother, Cossman, the 'cellist, and Mühlfeld, the famous self-taught clarinetist, had in fact accepted engagements for the summer from Wagner in Bayreuth, where *Parsifal* was about to have its first performance, and this event must also have caused Bülow some mixed feelings. His ensuing nervous breakdown was relieved only by the gentle ministrations of his second wife, Marie Schanzer, an actress at the Meiningen municipal theatre, whom he had just married, and he was not to make another public appearance until 12 October, 1883. But notwithstanding this inactivity, and the need to create the orchestra anew, a festival was given in December 1883 in honour of Liszt, which the latter recounts in his famous article which accompanied the publication of a march in Bülow's honour:

> ... Under Bülow's conducting the Meiningen orchestra achieves miracles. Nowhere is there to be found such intelligence in diverse works—precision in performance with the most correct and subtle rhythmic and dynamic shading. The fact of opera having been abolished at Meiningen by the Duke some twenty years ago is most favourable to the concerts. In this way the orchestra has time to have a proper number of sectional and full rehearsals without too much fatigue, as the opera work has been done away with. Bülow is almost as lavish of rehearsals as Berlioz would have been, had he had the means ... The result is admirable and in certain respects matchless—not excepting the Paris Conservatoire and other celebrated concert institutions. The little Meiningen phalanx, thanks to its present general, is in advance of the largest battalions. It is said that Rubinstein and some others have expressed themselves disapprovingly about some of the unusual tempi and nuances of Bülow, but to my thinking their criticism is devoid of foundation ...
>
> Besides the Beethoven programme, the orchestra gave a special concert in the morning, with performances of the Overture to *King Lear* (Berlioz) and *Meistersinger*, my march *Vom Fels am Meer* and *Die Ideale*, and Brahms's Variations on a Theme by Haydn.[26] Always the same complete understanding both in the ensemble and the detail of these scores—the same vigour, energy, refinement, accuracy, relief, vitality and superior characterisation in their interpretation.
>
> The most difficult of Beethoven's Quartets, one which on account of its complexities never appears on any programme—the *Grosse Füge*, Op. 133—is played with perfect ensemble by the Meiningen orchestra. On a previous occasion I also heard Bach's celebrated Chaconne played in unison and with real authority by some ten violins at Meiningen ...

It is not impossible to discern the faintest whisper of senility in this unbroken paean, which has none of the searching discrimination which had characterised Liszt's earlier artistic judgement, and which now came from the pen of a seventy-two-year-old man who had acquired the widespread reputation of falling asleep during those performances which pleased him most. And one may readily seize upon those very points which he most praises as typifying the breaches of musical taste of which Bülow has stood accused by many of his critics. But it is important to see the figure of Bülow in its historical

---

[26] This at Liszt's own request, as he had not heard the work in its orchestral form, though he of course knew the two-piano version.

context, and to sift legend from fact, and the interpretation of that fact. Above all, Bülow was a teacher—not in the sense of a conservatoire professor whose occupation he openly despised, but in the sense which Mahler, Kleiber, Koussevitsky and all great musicians have been teachers—in the sense that his own mentor, Franz Liszt, had been pre-eminently a teacher.

Chapter 4

FELIX WEINGARTNER AND RICHARD STRAUSS

Liszt's coming to Weimar, the founding of an orchestra at Meiningen, and the staging of *Tristan* and *Meistersinger* and the first two operas of the *Ring* in Munich had been, alike, the enterprises of young men who yet conformed to the pattern of the old-style patron and autocrat. In the case of the Meiningen orchestra the financial outlay for a band of forty-five musicians when Bülow took over its direction cannot have been immense, and its meteoric rise to international fame can only have redounded to the credit of the young Grand Duke. Meiningen was in any case in Saxony, a rich industrial state which had thrived on the political poverty of Germany and could already claim the orchestra of the Leipzig Gewandhaus, now well over a hundred years old, and the Dresden Court Theatre which had inspired Frederick the Great to build his own opera house in Berlin in 1742. But for Bavaria there were no such precedents—save for the isolated premières of Mozart's *Idomeneo* in 1780 and Weber's *Abu Hassan* in 1811 at the Residenz Theater in Munich—and the money which the young king had, in the view of his ministers and his historians, squandered on these huge Wagnerian follies had been prodigious. Historians have been consistent in their mockery of the Wittelsbach family: Ludwig I, who had built the Nationaltheater in 1825, and had paid more attention to the actress, Lola Montez, than to the speeches of Metternich—and Ludwig II, the 'mad king' who had succeeded to the throne at the age of nineteen and had thereupon set about bringing Wagner and his operas to Munich, and building his famous castle in the Hohenschwangau. It is astonishing how barren are the accounts of historians of any awareness of the sociological role which music had played in European history. They accept as a matter of course the influence of the Church at the time of the Renaissance and the Reformation, but are deaf to the fact that it was through the medium of music that the Church communicated and sustained its dogma to the multitudes. They accept the political influences of Versailles and its ultimate generation of the forces of revolution, but cannot connect this with the political intrigues which took place under the guise of music-making—the

most obvious excuse for a large assembly of people and, due to the universality of its language, the most direct and the most immediate propagator of
the liberal ideal. The medium of the congress, which had become a powerful
element in the political life of Germany, had followed the pattern of the
annual Tonkünstler-Versammlungen founded by Liszt. And it is no exaggeration to say that, if Ludwig II, with his contempt for the Hohenzollern
parvenus, had not been preoccupied with the first performance of *Tristan
und Isolde* in June 1865, Bavaria might well have joined Saxony in throwing in
her lot with Austria against Prussia. By the beginning of July, Austria had
been decisively defeated by the Prussians at Sadowa, and within two months
Bismarck had completed his design for German unification.

The conventional picture which is drawn of Ludwig II fails to take into
account that madness did not drive him to suicide in the Starnbergersee until
he was forty, and that in his youth he was able to manipulate two successive
and powerful ministers—Pfordten and Holstein—to his own ends, which he
saw as the pursuit of intelligent pleasures and the service of posterity, and the
holding at bay of repeated and concerted attempts to depose him.

The pattern had by this time emerged of the powerful monarch as a
diligent and enlightened sponsor of the arts—whether that power was manifest intellectually, as in the case of Ludwig of Bavaria, or politically, as in the
case of Louis XIV and Napoleon Bonaparte in France, and Maria Theresa
and Franz Josef in Austria. Where that power had faltered, or had been
usurped by the politicians, so had effective sponsorship of the arts declined,
and the ill-starred Second Republic in France finds an exact mirror in the
decline in the fortunes of French music-making from those standards which
Wagner had so praised to a nadir of provincialism, with the demise of Napoleon III, from which it was never to recover.

This too had been the pattern in Prussia, and specifically in Berlin. By
the middle of the nineteenth century, those standards with which the Royal
Opera House had been invested by Frederick the Great had declined to those
of routine provincialism under the deadening influence of Friedrich Wilhelm
IV—a monarch possessed of pathological vanity, and all the eccentricity of
Ludwig of Bavaria with none of the latter's inspired and purposeful fantasy.
With the parvenu's obsequiousness he idolised the Habsburgs, and secretly
favoured union with Austria and the *Grossdeutsch-Solution*—this at a time
when the Austrian throne was at its feeblest, and Austria herself virtually
governed by Metternich. The accession, in 1858, of the future Kaiser Wilhelm I as regent should have brought with it some measure of relief, for his
wife was the daughter of the Duke of Weimar who had been Goethe's patron.
But a nervous conservatism continued to stifle every advance, Bismarck

(though not devoid of poetic susceptibilities, as his letters reveal) was pre-occupied with blood and iron, and the directorship of the Royal Opera persisted in the unimaginative and barely competent hands of Botho von Hülsen. No change in Prussia's musical fortunes was to take place until 1881, and then everything began to happen at once. In April 1881, the Meiningen orchestra played in Berlin under Bülow for the first time. In May, the forces of the Berlin Wagner-Verein, with an orchestra of a hundred players, assembled in the Victoria Theatre under Karl Klindworth, and in the presence of Richard Wagner, to give the first Berlin performance of the *Ring* cycle—to the embarrassment of Hülsen and the discomfiture of the Royal Opera. The following year—1882—an independent orchestra, drawing on the resources of the Wagner-Verein, weary of the pedestrian standards of the Royal Opera and its concert-giving Hofkapelle, and fired with enthusiasm by the example of the little band of Meiningers who had just revisited Berlin under Bülow, sprang into being under Klindworth, bearing the name of the Berlin Philharmonic Orchestra. In 1886 Bülow succeeded Klindworth at its head, and on his death in 1894 was in turn succeeded by his young disciple, Richard Strauss. Hülsen had meanwhile been replaced as intendant of the Royal Opera in 1886 by the more dynamic Bolko von Hochberg (though Strauss was later to describe him as "that great ass"), and in 1891 Felix Weingartner was appointed first conductor with Karl Muck.

Bülow, Klindworth and Weingartner had all three been outstanding pupils of Franz Liszt—and Weingartner remained a distinguished champion of Liszt's orchestral music until the end of his life. Strauss, whose father had played under Bülow during his forty years as first horn at the Munich opera, had been Bülow's assistant and successor at Meiningen, becoming first conductor under Eduard Lassen—Liszt's successor at Weimar—from 1889 to 1894, when he took over the Berlin Philharmonic. The following year he became general musical director in Munich, and in 1898 associate director with Karl Muck of the Berlin Opera. The transcendental authority of Liszt's musical personality, which had dominated more than half a century's music-making, had come full circle.

The influence which Weingartner was to have on the art of conducting—and especially in the performance of Beethoven's music—has another place in this book, but it is pertinent here to examine what he had to say about other conductors, and Bülow in particular, and to decide what were the interpretative principles and techniques which consciously informed music-making in Germany at the end of the last century. Weingartner's contribution as a conductor was too profound for us to attach overmuch importance to the persistent note of bitterness which his writing betrays—bitterness at the success

Leading German and Austrian Opera Houses and Symphony Orchestras from 1800 until World War II, with their respective "General Musical Directors".

	DRESDEN HOFTHEATRE 1642 Elector of Saxony (arch: Semper)	BERLIN SCHAUSPIELHAUS 1742 Frederick the Great (arch: Knobelsdorff)	LEIPZIG GEWANDHAUS 1781	MUNICH NATIONALTHEATRE 1821 Ludwig I of Bavaria (arch: Fischer)
1800		HIMMEL (1800–17)		
1810	MORLACCHI (1810–19) WEBER (1817–23)	(Burnt down 1817) SPONTINI (1819–41)	SCHULZ (1810–27)	
1820	MARSCHNER (1823–26) REISSIGER (1826–59)		MARSCHNER (1827–31)	AIBLINGER (1825–36)
1830			POHLENZ (1831–35) MENDELSSOHN (1835–43)	LACHNER (1836–64)
1840	WAGNER (1843–48)	MEYERBEER (1841–64) (Burnt down 1843) Nicolai (1847–49)	F. HILLER (1843–44) GADE (1844–48) RIETZ (1848–60)	
1850				
1860	RIETZ (1860–72)	HÜLSEN (1865–91)	REINECKE (1860–95)	BÜLOW (1864–69) Richter (1868–69) LEVI (1869–96)
1870	WÜLLNER (1872–82)			
1880	SCHUCH (1882–1914)		Mahler (1886–88)	Strauss (1886–89)
1890		WEINGARTNER (1891–98) STRAUSS (1898–1908)	NIKISCH (1895–1922)	STRAUSS (1896–1903)
1900		MUCK (1908–12)		(Prinzregenten-Theater: built 1901) MOTTL (1903–11)
1910	REINER (1914–21)	PAUR (1912–13) BLECH (1913–23)		WALTER (1912–22)
1920	BUSCH (1922–33)	KLEIBER (1923–35)	FURTWÄNGLER (1922–29) WALTER (1929–33)	HAUSEGGER (1922–23) KNAPPERTSBUSCH (1923–36)
1930	BOHM (1933–43)	KRAUSS (1935–36) Karajan (1938–42)	ABENDROTH (1933–44)	KRAUSS (1936–44)
1940	(Destroyed 1943)	(Destroyed 1944)	(Destroyed 1944)	(Destroyed 1944)

IMPORTANT PREMIÈRES

DRESDEN	BERLIN		MUNICH
Rienzi (1842) Fliegende Hollander (1843) Tannhäuser (1845) Feuersnot (1901) Salome (1905) Elektra (1907) Rosenkavalier (1911) Aegyptische Helena (1928) Arabella (1933) Schweigsame Frau (1935) Daphne (1936)	Freischütz (1821) Euryanthe (1825) Wozeck (1926)		Tristan (1865) Meistersinger (1868) Rheingold (1869) Walküre (1871) Mahler 4 (1901) Mahler 8 (1910) Lied von der Erde (1911) Friedenstag (1938)

"First Conductors"—i.e. First Assistant Conductors—appear (but not in capitals) where their names receive prominent mention in this book.

VIENNA PHILHARMONIC 1842	MEININGEN HOFKAPELLE 1845 Duke of Saxe-Meiningen	WEIMAR HOFTHEATRE 1847 Duke of Saxe-Weimar-Eisenach	VIENNA HOFOPER 1869 Kaiser Franz Joseph (arch: van der Null)	BERLIN PHILHARMONIC 1882
NICOLAI (1842–48) HELLMESBERGER (1845–48) ECKERT (1848–60)		LISZT (1848–59)		
		LASSEN (1859–1904)		
DESSOF (1861–75)	BÜCHNER (1865–80)			
			HERBECK (1870–75) JAUNER (1875–80)	
RICHTER (1878–98) Jahn (1882–98)	BÜLOW (1880–85) Strauss (1885–6) STEINBACH (1886–1902)	Strauss (1889–94)	RICHTER-JAHN (1880–96)	KLINDWORTH (1882–85) BÜLOW (1885–94)
MAHLER (1898–1901)			MAHLER (1896–1907)	STRAUSS (1895–96) NIKISCH (1896–1922)
J. HELLMESBERGER (1901–03) WEINGARTNER (1908–27)		RAABE (1904–33)	WEINGARTNER (1907–11)	
			GREGOR (1911–18) SCHALK (1918–29)	
			STRAUSS (1920–24)	
FURTWÄNGLER (1928–30)			KRAUSS (1929–35)	FURTWÄNGLER (1922–54)
KRAUSS (1930–33) FURTWÄNGLER-WALTER (1933–38		SIXT (1933–44)	WEINGARTNER (1935–36) WALTER (1936–38) KNAPPERTSBUSCH (1938–45)	KARAJAN (1954 to date)
			(Destroyed 1945)	
	Brahms 4 (1885)	Lohengrin (1850) Benvenuto Cellini (1852) Don Juan (1889)	Rossini: Zelmira (1822) Frau Ohne Schatten (1919	Mahler 2 (1895) Heldenleben (1898)

of others, and especially at that of Richard Strauss and Artur Nikisch, whose names are conspicuously absent from his writing, and bitterness at his own failure in the field of opera. Certainly his writing betrays a temperament which was fundamentally alien to the operatic idiom, and which refused to see music in its third dimension. Yet his appointment to the Berlin Opera at the age of twenty-eight, when its fortunes were at an all-time ebb, and his ability, in conjunction with Karl Muck, to raise them once again to standards of professional integrity, were in themselves no minor accomplishment.

Weingartner had gone to Meiningen at Liszt's recommendation in 1884, when he was twenty-one, to seek the post of assistant conductor in succession to Franz Mannstadt, who had left to join Wagner in Bayreuth. But to subjugate himself to Bülow's musical personality and carry out his every wish —imperative to any successful apprenticeship—Weingartner had not been prepared to do, claiming an independent spirit which would not suffer domination. Bülow had sensibly advised him to seek any position, however lowly, where he would be free to exercise that independence, and accordingly accepted Richard Strauss in his stead. It must have come as a bitter stroke to Weingartner when, thirteen years later, Strauss replaced him at the Berlin Opera, and for the next eleven years he found himself without an operatic post of any kind.

Weingartner's own essay on conducting, modelled on that of Wagner, was first published in 1895 when it championed Bülow and censured the Bayreuth administration for not having engaged his services after Wagner's death. It reappeared in 1905 in a totally revised form which constituted a vitriolic attack on his former colleague, giving rise to any number of erroneous ideas which subsequently acquired common currency. The burden of his charges against Bülow lay in his personal aversion to the use of *rubato* in orchestral playing—a practice which, with Strauss and Mahler as the two supreme operatic conductors in Germany and Austria of that time, we may judge to have become universally prevalent. Weingartner rightly condemns what he terms "over-characterisation"—the imparting to each and every turn of phrase of an emphasis of meaning quite out of context with the whole:

> It would of course be just as wrong to play a succession of quarter-notes (crotchets) with metronomic precision. But inflections of tempo—many of which Mendelssohn has marked himself— must be accomplished in such a way as to preserve the organic structure of the whole—its *melos*, the proper understanding of which, as Wagner rightly says, will also determine the right tempo[1]. At one

[1] But Wagner had said that only a proper understanding of the tempo would reveal the *melos!*

moment the sea laps quietly around the rocks of Fingal's cave, while at the next wind and water rise to beat upon its shore with the white foam of breaking waves. *But the picture of the seascape remains the same*, and there is nothing in Mendelssohn's overture to suggest an actual, elemental storm which could give to this picture a radically different perspective. The atmosphere of quiet and austere melancholy which lends to the Hebrides their individual charm is also preserved in the music.

The analogy is striking, stating Weingartner's own position vividly. But it does not for long hold true, for in its very evocation of the medium of painting it fails to take into account that the quality of Mendelssohn's miniature masterpiece lies as much in its choice of subject as in its fidelity to that subject. The Hebrides derive their character of pervading calm and brooding immutability from the very fact that they are continually exposed to the caprice of the elements, and Mendelssohn's is no picture-postcard of the islands viewed on a calm summer's day, with splashes of white foam and sea-gulls crying. Its quality lies in its ability to enter the timelessness of the painting which can transcend the limitations of its two dimensions and convey not an objective observation, but an experience with which every observer may identify himself. The picture does not change, but no two people will see the picture in quite the same light, and this is its very strength as a work of art rather than a travel-poster. It is Weingartner, who has clearly taken the trouble to observe the Hebrides Islands for himself, who is trying to impose his own literal impression on Mendelssohn's music, like the gentleman in Hugo's *Hunchback of Notre-Dame* who declared that the world must be flat because he was a much-travelled man, and had everywhere observed it to be flat.

Herein lies the crux of the problem of interpretation, for Weingartner is continually complaining of those *rubato*-conductors who must impose their own "conception" on the orchestra and the audience—as though the creative mind had any alternative. It is in the very nature of the great painting or the great piece of music which is universal to lend itself to widely differing interpretations, and though these may in themselves lack universality in that they are questionable, this does not detract from the merit of the original which is to provoke a reaction, to impregnate the mind of the interpretative artist and cause it to conceive. For this is the real meaning of the word "conception", and in the process of gestation a work will inevitably partake of the musical personalities both of its author and its interpreter. To ask the interpretative artist to remain "objective", to play no constructive or creative role in his performance, is to enter the madness of *Brave New World*, and to decry such terms as Furtwängler's Wagner, or Toscanini's Verdi, or Kleiber's Strauss, and to search always for the "definitive" performance or even to suppose that such a thing were desirable or even possible, is to be deaf to the fact that it is the genius of these composers that their works lend themselves to constant regeneration at the hands of successive interpretative artists. We should as well ask the painter to paint the "definitive" Crucifixion, or the composer to write the "definitive" Requiem, for every artist of integrity must search for the truth of a composition and discover its essence for himself, and to impose canons of objectivity is to deny temperament and nature herself.

In recounting Bülow's idiosyncrasies of interpretation, Weingartner became censorious to the point of pronouncing anathema, attributing no matter what infringement or variation of the printed text by no matter which conductor to the direct and malignant influence of Bülow. Three points of importance emerge from an examination of his argument. Firstly, that the great interpretative artist—whether from a spirit of caprice or from innermost conviction—may vary the broader indications of the printed text and yet by so doing reveal the greater insight into a work. It is perfectly possible to take the Prelude to Act I of Carmen very much slower than Bizet's marking of *Allegro giocoso* $\quartnote = 116$ and yet imbue it with a quality of transcendent good-humour, and to play Escamillo's *Toreador* aria *quasi adagio* and yet elevate the music into an embodiment of the whole Spanish mystique of bull-fighting. But if that is what Bizet wanted, why did he not mark the score accordingly? And it must be observed here that the composer, like any artist, frequently lights upon a universal truth the full implications of which he himself is un-aware, and if the interpretative artist can discover a facet of that truth which the composer had unwittingly allowed to remain hidden, he is fully justified in doing so. The only criterion is whether such an action justifies itself in per-formance, and while Weingartner regarded the above-mentioned practices as having been a gigantic leg-pull on the part of Bülow, he—Bülow—has had distinguished followers in Richard Strauss and Erich Kleiber. Likewise, the variations of a basic tempo which Weingartner deplored in Bülow's inter-pretations of Beethoven, though certainly exaggerated as he recounts them to us, have none the less found their way into many a significant performance of Beethoven's music in one guise or another.

Weingartner goes on to accuse Bülow of altering details in the printed text—the second bassoon part at bar 470 in the Scherzo of Beethoven's Ninth to B natural, and the first note of the great string cadenza of *Leonora* No. 3 from C to a "characterless D". (But the D is Beethoven's! It was Strauss who insisted that the first note should be C.) The altering of such details, when prompted by a conviction that there has been an error on the

part of the author or his publisher, is an inevitable incident in the life of any
composition which is automatically redeemed by subsequent generations if it
is not justified. But when prompted by such conviction, and not by an indolent
desire for quick effect, such action shows a necessary enquiry and awareness
that a passage is not straightforward and may require special treatment.
Bülow's ear was the first to spot that there was something untoward in the
second bassoon part of the Ninth at this point, and applied a solution—the
wrong solution, to be sure, but how often have we not been prepared to go to
the stake for our conviction that the composer (and Beethoven in particular)
must have committed an error of judgement, only to marvel at our own
ingenuousness when we discover the overwhelming simplicity and logic of the
passage in question? Even Toscanini, in our own time, proposed as a solution
to the passage in the first movement of Beethoven's Eighth Symphony, where
the main theme reappears in the basses and is never heard, the monstrous
vulgarity of doubling brass and kettledrums on each and every note of the
bass-line—a procedure which was rehearsed, but mercifully never performed:

Ex. 6

Beethoven's use of *fff* is rare—although it occurs twice in the third *Leonora* overture—and there is perhaps no effective solution to this passage within the terms of the Beethoven orchestra. Yet Weingartner confesses to having employed the same solution so far as kettledrums were concerned[2], and Bernard Shore ascribes the practice to the late Sir Henry Wood[3], which is somehow more characteristic, for Wood was nothing if not a solid craftsman. The enduring sentiment of these musicians seems to have been that, while the actual pitch of the notes in Beethoven's texts must of course be sacrosanct, it was perfectly legitimate to meddle with the instrumentation. But this, as we shall see, required infinitely greater caution than they would seem to have been prepared to accord.

The final point which emerges from Weingartner's essay is the extent to which fact and fable become intermingled where the artist's reputation has become legendary within his own lifetime, and any plausible anecdote together with the rankest hearsay acquire common currency. There are musicians who will invoke the name of Toscanini in defence of musical ideas which are poverty-stricken, and to which Toscanini's own reactions would have been unprintable. And there are conductors and critics who claim the authority of having heard him say such-and-such at a rehearsal which they could never have attended, for it is common knowledge that he never allowed outsiders into his rehearsals on any pretext whatsoever. Yet the deception continues—"as Toscanini used to say"—and another myth finds substance. I have tried to trace to its source the famous legend that Bülow wore black gloves to conduct the *Eroica*—an event which no lesser an authority than Bruno Walter recalls, in his autobiography, having witnessed—sixty years earlier—though he has no very clear recollection of the actual occasion. But there are those who are quite hysterically certain that they *saw* him do so, or at least that they had personally known someone who knew someone who had seen him do so, and I can find no firmer substance to the legend than that an ingenuous admirer had declared that Bülow had conducted the Funeral March from the *Eroica* Symphony *as though* he had been wearing black gloves. Equally, but more seriously, Bülow has been cited by many eminent scholars—upon what authority I do not know—as having tampered with Beethoven's text in the first movement of the *Eroica*, where the second horn makes its precipitate entry just before the recapitulation, by altering the A flat suspension in the second violins to G:

---

[2] Felix Weingartner: *Ratschläge für Aufführungen der Sinfonien Beethovens*, Breitkopf & Härtel, Leipzig, 1906.
[3] Bernard Shore: *The Orchestra Speaks*, Longmans, Green & Co., London, 1938.

Ex. 7

Weingartner in fact blames Wagner for having introduced this practice, a fabrication to which the following quotation by Robert Elkin must give the lie:

> Smart [Henry Smart of *The Sunday Times*] also gives us the interesting information that, at the famous horn entry in the first movement of the *Eroica*, Wagner restored the A flat in the second violins which Costa[4] had "emended" to G[5].

If Bülow in fact changed the A flat suspension to G to correspond with the notes of the second-horn part, this is at strange variance with his quite unequivocal remarks concerning a very analogous passage in the same key from the first movement coda of the Sonata, Op. 81a (*Les Adieux*):

Ex. 8

In his footnote to the sonata, Bülow says:

> An attack against the abusers and improvers of these four bars, which appear, it is true, to belong more to the music of nature than

---

[4] Michael (later Sir Michael) Costa, conductor of the orchestra of the London Philharmonic Society from 1845 to 1855.

[5] Robert Elkin: *Royal Philharmonic*. Rich & Co., London & New York, 1946.

D

of art, must come too late. The general understanding of music has made such an advance during the last ten years that we must now wonder, not so much at Beethoven's audacity, but at that of Oulibicheff and others ... [6]

Oulibicheff was the notorious amateur musicologist who, in his book *Beethoven, ses critiques et ses glossateurs*, published in Paris in 1857, had claimed that Beethoven did not understand the elements of musical grammar, and cited the above example together with the following passage from the beginning of the finale of the *Pastoral* Symphony:

Ex. 9

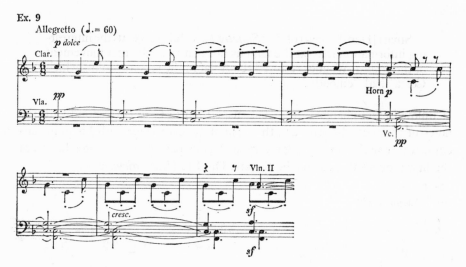

A study of the German text of Bülow's edition of the Beethoven piano works is ample evidence of his faithfulness to the printed text, except where he acknowledges an intentional departure, and we have no reason to suppose that he behaved otherwise as a conductor. But in introducing into the art of orchestral ensemble elements of *rubato* which in solo playing had long been taken for granted, he was doing something so new that it would have been very surprising if it had not excited adverse as well as enthusiastic comment. A convincing orchestral *rubato* is enormously difficult to accomplish, and there is today still only a handful of conductors who can obtain one without betraying an incipient vulgarity. Rather than questioning its use and abuse, we do better to enquire how it was that Bülow was able to inculcate the practice into the indifferent Meiningen string section and so to confound the international world of music a bare year later.

Liszt had written in December 1883 of the performance of the *Grosse*

[6] Vol. II of the critical edition by Hans von Bülow.

Fuge by the Meiningen orchestra's entire string section, and of the Bach D minor Chaconne (heard on a previous occasion, presumably in 1881) by a section of ten violins—probably the combined strength of the first and second violin sections of that orchestra. The musician who will take exception to such practices is also he who will have been embarrassed by Liszt's use of the word "virtuosity" in the context of Bach—as though Bach had been anything less than a virtuoso. The *Grosse Fuge* has been too often heard played by an entire string section for such a practice to excite overmuch comment nowadays, though even the best orchestral string players never know the work as well as they should, and invariably invoke the sanctity of the medium of the string quartet rather than settling down to master its gruelling difficulties. But the Chaconne is another matter. Even the Busoni transcription is still regarded with suspicion, while that by Brahms for the left-hand alone is seen more in the light of a study which was not intended for public consumption. How then should we view the prospect of ten violinists playing it strung out across the stage of the Meiningen theatre, and playing it without music—or conductor? Should we regard it as a circus-stunt by the Meiningen menagerie, a vulgar debasement of Bach's intentions?

Whatever those intentions may have been—and there are those who maintain that the solo sonatas were never intended for public performance in any case—there have been singularly few violinists of any generation who have been equal to making music out of the Chaconne which amounted to anything more than an inspired approximation. That Meiningen should have possessed ten violinists who, after two years' training under Bülow, were equal to its challenge is in itself remarkable. That he should then have led them through the towering technical difficulties which its performance was to impose, and have taught them to contain that performance in perfect ensemble, and with every nuance of phrasing and tempo which are here imperative—for even Weingartner would have conceded that the Chaconne cannot be played in strict tempi, like a ballroom dance—reveal an insight into ensemble discipline which was yet without precedent, and which can only compel our warmest admiration and endorsement. How such an experience must later have informed the string-playing of the third Brandenburg Concerto, or Berlioz's *Corsair* Overture, or the slow movement of Brahms's Fourth Symphony of which the Meiningen orchestra was to give the first performance in 1885, we can only begin to imagine.

The formation of the Berlin Philharmonic in 1882 can be seen as a facet of a growing spirit of democracy in a Germany still manifesting all the symptoms of moral schizophrenia, nurturing such opposing philosophies as those of Marx and Nietzsche, and breeding side by side a capitalist imperialism and an increasingly powerful proletariat. The humanitarian values which had inspired *Fidelio* and the Ninth Symphony, and which were deemed by many to have escaped Wagner, were lost in a world of growing avarice, the cult of socialism from a position of plenty, and the retreat of the sensitive behind the doctrines of nihilism. It had been the essential property of the German creative spirit to pursue the idea of "atonement", the reconciliation of man with, and within, his world (evidenced in the *Bildungsroman* of Goethe's *Wilhelm Meister*) and it was from the logical extension of this idea that the German interpretative artist derived his instinct of integrating and teaching —not as a pedagogue, but in the sense of re-creating and reconciling a text with the environmental expediency of its performance. Such teachers had been Wagner, Liszt and Bülow, in their relentless pursuit of a performance ideal, not as an abstract and unattainable concept, but as the realisable goal of each and every performance which, by the turn of the century, had established a tradition of orchestral playing throughout the continent of Europe and found new and dynamic expression in the New World.

Bülow's association with the newly formed Berlin Philharmonic, from 1886 until his death eight years later (and now coincidental with his duties at the Hamburg Opera) was fateful, for he could inculcate from the start his massive insight and concentration of experience of the young art of orchestral conducting, unhampered by the strictures of his Meiningen orchestra which had limited him at best to only forty-nine players, and free of the increasing caprice of his former patron, Georg II. It was the Berlin Philharmonic which Bülow's disciple, Richard Strauss, inherited for one season in 1894, on Bülow's death, before leaving to become musical director in his native Munich until 1898, when he combined his Munich duties with those of musical director—in conjunction with Muck—of the Royal Opera in Berlin. Artur Nikisch had meanwhile succeeded him as director of the Berlin Philharmonic in 1895, a post which he retained until his own death in 1922 when he was succeeded by Wilhelm Furtwängler.

Adherent and adversary, biographer and critic alike, have been predominantly concerned with an examination of Strauss the composer, and while they have shown a more or less cursory interest in his activities as conductor, it has never seriously been suggested that these were anything more than incidental to his activities as a "creative artist". It is not the purpose of this book to try to assess Strauss's importance as a composer, save to remark that the musical ideal to which he subscribed in his composition was that which he consistently applied in his music-making, and to assert that every page of his operas and orchestral writing furnishes abundant evidence of his mastery as a conductor. That Strauss did not retire from the stage of active and full-time music-making until he was sixty is testimony enough of the emphasis which he placed upon his work as an interpretative artist, always regarding composition as of secondary importance to his career as a conductor. Nor was he preoccupied with the performance of his own works. Of his fifteen operas he directed the first performances of only two—the early *Guntram* in Weimar in 1894, and the first version of *Ariadne auf Naxos* in Stuttgart in 1912. On the other hand, he gave the first complete performances of Mahler's First Symphony in Weimar in 1894, and of the Second Symphony in Berlin on 4 March of the following year[7], and was the constant executive champion of his contemporaries. It is only since the composer and the performer have parted company, the composer ceasing to perform and the performer ceasing to compose, and each arrogantly disdaining the activity of the other, that our music has become bankrupt.

Bülow had discovered the twenty-three-year-old Richard Strauss through the medium of his Wind Serenade, which he had accepted and re-hearsed for performance with the Meiningen orchestra in Munich. As Wagner's faith in the young Bülow's potential as a conductor had been aroused by the latter's youthful compositions, so now was that of Bülow in Strauss, and he thrust the young composer, who had never held a baton in his life, onto the concert-platform of the Deutsches Museum in his stead, re-maining in the artist's room during the performance, and engaging him afterwards—unseen and unheard, but with unerring instinct—as his assistant in Meiningen. The association was brief, for Bülow left for concerts in St. Petersburg (where he was to complain at being allowed only three rehearsals for each) a bare month after Strauss's arrival, and never returned to Meiningen. Yet it was to provide the basis for a lifelong devotion to Bülow's artistry, and in 1919, at the age of fifty-five, Strauss wrote:

> He who heard him play Beethoven or conduct Wagner, or attended his piano classes or listened to him at an orchestral rehearsal, will have found in him the model of all the shining virtues of the interpretative artist. His touching kindness to me, his influence on the development of my artistic abilities, was—apart from my friendship with Alexander Ritter who, to my father's dismay, made a Wagnerian out of me—the most decisive moment of my career ... On 1 October, 1885, I began my new apprenticeship, and a more interesting, more meaningful and more amusing one can-not be imagined. His memorable rehearsals—such as only Bülow could hold—took place daily from 9 until 12. The impression of those works which he rehearsed at that time—always from memory

[7] The eminent Mahler scholar, Prof. H. F. Redlich, maintains that both performances were conducted by Mahler himself, although he quotes no source. But *cf.* Strauss' corres-pondence.

—has ever since remained indelibly imprinted on my mind. The way in which he used to draw out the poetic content, particularly of the works of Beethoven and Wagner, was absolutely convincing. Here there was not a trace of wilfulness—everything sprang from a compelling necessity of the form and content of the works themselves. His compelling temperament, always governed by the strictest artistic discipline and fidelity to the spirit *and the letter* of the works—for the two are more synonymous than is generally believed—achieved by way of painstaking rehearsals a finesse of presentation which still remains for me today the summit of perfection in the performance of orchestral music ... His dictum— "First learn to read the score of a Beethoven symphony accurately, and you will already have the key to its interpretation"—might well be writ large over the doors of every conservatoire ... [8]

It was during this month of November 1885 that Brahms's Fourth Symphony (Beethoven XIII, as Bülow called it) received its first performance. "Bülow rehearsed with incredible care," wrote Strauss, "and his zeal and conscientiousness were often at strange variance with the open indifference which Brahms displayed over matters of dynamics and interpretation in his work ... " It was in fact a dispute over the interpretation of this symphony which led Bülow to tender his resignation, and Strauss remained in control of the orchestra until the end of the season when he was appointed second conductor in Munich, and his place in Meiningen taken— on Brahms's recommendation—by Fritz Steinbach. The rift with Bülow was temporary, and Brahms became a loyal attendant at Bülow's later concerts in Berlin. Steinbach in his turn became an outstanding exponent of Brahms's music, touring the Meiningen orchestra in programmes of his works whose conducting he shared with Brahms. On Steinbach's death in 1902, the Meiningen Orchestra was disbanded.

Strauss described his years in Munich—from 1886 to 1889—as ones of growing tedium and necessary routine. With the death of Ludwig II on 13 June, 1886, creative impetus had left the life of the opera, and there was increasing hostility from the intendant, Perfall—never a friend of Wagner or of Bülow, and openly hostile to Strauss's increasing success as a composer and self-evident gifts as a conductor. Hermann Levi, the general musical director, was pedestrian, and Fischer, the first conductor, incompetent, and it was with great reluctance that Strauss was accorded the responsibility of *Tristan* and *Die Meistersinger*—works which were to become among his greatest performances. In October 1887 Strauss wrote to Bülow in Berlin, asking him to

[8] Richard Strauss: *Betrachtungen und Erinnerungen*, Atlantis Verlag, Zürich and Freiburg, 1949.

accept the dedication of his orchestral fantasy *Aus Italien,* and mentioning a visit to Leipzig where he had conducted his F minor Symphony:

> The new concert hall excited me to wildest delight . . . I made a new and very attractive acquaintance in Herr Mahler, who seemed to me a highly intelligent musician and conductor—one of the few modern conductors who knows about *tempo rubato,* and expressed splendid ideas generally, particularly about Wagner's tempi . . . His arrangement of Weber's *Drei Pintos* appears to me a masterpiece— I was quite delighted with the first act, which Mahler played to me . . . [9]

Mahler's arrangement of Weber's unfinished opera did not however impress Bülow, who had immediately sent for the score on Strauss' recommendation, and now took his young colleague severely to task. *"Wo Weberei, wo Mahlerei, einerlei*—[10] the whole thing is infamous, antiquated rubbish . . . " and Strauss admitted that he had not, when he had written to Bülow earlier, seen the full score of the later acts, where the legendary orchestrator Mahler had taken the oboes up to F and G *in alt,* and the horns up to D *in alt*—*"and he is a conductor!"* lamented Strauss. A year later he wrote with nostalgia of a return visit to Meiningen, where "the orchestra is still in the best condition, and Steinbach an absolutely splendid musician", and spoke of his own life in the "Munich swamp" as becoming intolerable. Bülow had been using his influence in a quiet way to get Strauss appointed to the Karlruhe Opera as a replacement to Felix Mottl—a conductor whom he had known, and much admired, from his Munich days twenty years earlier. But Mottl was not yet ready to leave Karlsruhe—nor did he in fact do so until 1903, when he replaced Strauss as general musical director in Munich. With his friend Hans von Bronsart, intendant at Weimar and another former pupil of Liszt, Bülow had more success however, and in October 1889 Strauss wrote enthusiastically of his new position as first conductor under Liszt's successor, Eduard Lassen.

In the preface to his last opera, *Capriccio,* Strauss mentions the vain struggles which Mottl had experienced during his twenty-three years at Karlsruhe in trying to get the first-violin section increased from ten players to twelve—*"bis zu zehn Geigen ist halt 'Kammermusik'!"* as Mottl had said. A section of ten first violins—Meiningen had carried eight in Bülow's final year there—implies a string section of about thirty-five players, which remained the standard string complement for all but the leading symphony

---

[9] *Der Briefwechsel Hans von Bülow und Richard Strauss:* Boosey Hawkes G.m.b.h., Bonn, 1954.
[10] A play on words, literally meaning "whether *weaving* or *painting,* it makes no difference . . ."

orchestras until well into the present century. Strauss's habit of employing an ever larger wind section—which Bülow did his utmost to discourage, on the grounds of expediency—was balanced by an attitude toward wind playing in general which is constantly in evidence in the meticulous markings of his own scores. In his "Ten Golden Rules for the Conductor" he was to say:

> Never look at the brass—it only encourages them ... on the other hand, never let the horns and the woodwind out of your sight: if you can hear them at all, they are too loud ... if you think that the brass are not loud enough, reduce their dynamics by two degrees ...

In later years he was to say to the Vienna Philharmonic, *à propos* a famous passage in *Don Juan*:

> I was a shy [!] young man, and the brass used to frighten me. Besides, there were never enough strings—not strings like these, at all events. If you will not deem it an impertinence, I will ask the gentlemen of the trombone section, and the horns [*die verehrte Herrn Posaunisten, bzw. Hornisten*] to play their entries here with a princely, that is to say *zivilizierte, fortissimo*:

Ex. 10

Don Juan received its first performance, under Strauss, with the Weimar orchestra on 11 November, 1889, and we know with what dismay its diminutive string section greeted the following famous passages—the opening of the first of which Strauss later taught the Vienna Philharmonic to play *spiccato*, which has since become the tradition with that orchestra:

Ex. 11

(i)

Ex. II. *(continued)*

(ii)

(iii)

Just as this famous work revealed a new virtuoso potential in the symphony orchestra which was not to find its fulfilment until the great days of the Berlin and Vienna Philharmonic, and their companion orchestras in Amsterdam and the United States, so did it reveal the potential of the virtuoso conductor. It is significant that the twenty-four-year-old Strauss declined the opportunities of conducting its Dresden and Berlin premières, which took place respectively on 10 January, 1890, under Adolf Hagen, and on 30 January under Bülow. On 15 January, Strauss had written to Bülow to give him a résumé of the tempi of *Don Juan,* whose detail reveals both the uncommon decision of the young composer and the painstaking care which he attributed to the older conductor, albeit that their strict observance must necessarily result in the reduction by more than two minutes of the printed timing:

> In reponse to your *specific* wishes, the following are the nearest possible metronome markings for *Don Juan*:
>
> First tempo: 𝅗𝅥 = 84
> Letter C : 𝅗𝅥 = 88
> Letter D : 𝅗𝅥 = 76
>
> From the B major melody onwards, starting rather more quietly, the whole passage up to 7 bars before G (𝅗𝅥 = 60) very *rubato*, and increasing in expression more than in tempo.
>
> 3 bars before G: 𝅗𝅥 = 76
> H: 𝅗𝅥 = 84
> K: starting 𝅗𝅥 = 92
> L: 𝅗𝅥 = 76 (at the modulations)
>
> From the twenty-second bar after M, modify the tempo considerably, and from the seventh to the twelfth bar after N, go back to 𝅗𝅥 = 69.
>
> *A tempo*, 18 bars before O: 𝅗𝅥 = 84 (but very heavy)
> *Tempo giocoso* after P: 𝅗𝅥 = 92
> 4 bars after U: ○ = 63, but very soon quieter, until
> V: 𝅗𝅥 = 72
> Cc: starting 𝅗𝅥 = 100
> 8 bars before the fermata: starting ○ = 84
> after the fermata: starting 𝅗𝅥 = 72
>
> I hope, *sehr verehrte Meister*, that these metronome markings—in my opinion wholly unneeded by you—are specific enough. Where they do not fit in with your own conception, I implore you urgently to disregard them.

In the summer of 1892, Strauss fell victim to serious illness, and was sent on a long Mediterranean holiday. On 4 June, 1893, in one of his last letters to Bülow, he wrote from the house of Bülow's daughter, Blandine, in Sicily:

> Amidst the mummies of ancient Egyptian princesses there percolated to me here and there news of the progressive mummification of the Philharmonic concerts [Bülow had been absent on his last extended recital-tour, and his place in Berlin taken by Joseph Joachim], then suddenly the good news that you were conducting again, and I saw the spirits of Beethoven and Haydn rise rejuvenated from the rocks and tombs which had been designated for them . . .

Less than two years later, Strauss took over the concerts of the Berlin Philharmonic, and one of his first actions was to include in the season's programmes the gigantic second symphony of his colleague and contemporary Gustav Mahler—the *Resurrection* Symphony, calling upon the resources of an orchestra of a hundred and twenty, solo voices and mixed chorus. It is eloquent of the authority which Strauss by now commanded that he was able to persuade Wolff, the impresario who managed the Philharmonic, to mount such a performance, which Mahler had been unable to accomplish in Vienna and had declared himself unable to conduct. But Strauss's reputation in the opera house, and particularly his performances of *Tristan, Zauberflöte* and *Entführung* (the concert-ending of whose overture he had revised from the wholly inappropriate Beethoven scoring which it had been given by Johann André), were already international, and the overtures to engage his services at the Royal Opera which had begun immediately after his arrival in Berlin were now echoed in Munich where, with the retirement of Hermann Levi, he was now offered the post of musical director. For all his abiding contempt for the city of his birth, this was too strong an inducement for him to refuse, and from this time onward, the thirty-two-year-old Strauss had no peers on the German operatic conductor's podium.

The reference which Bülow had made, in a letter to Wagner in 1869, to having spent the afternoon "practising his baton-technique" (and of the consequent improvement in that evening's performance of *Tristan*) is the first instance of the use of that term which I know, and the first recorded suggestion by a musician that baton-technique might amount to something more than the clear beating of time—principles which Berlioz had laid down for the first time in the appendix to his treatise on instrumentation. The baton had originally appeared as a substitute for the violin bow, and was for a time quite simply this—a large piece of wood the size of a military baton constructed for the sole purpose of beating time, and as a visual aid to the orchestra. But the wrists and fingers of the violin-conductors who now gained access to an independent rostrum were attuned to the more sensitive handling of the bow, and so the baton which Berlioz prescribed had come into being. There are differing schools of thought as to how the baton should be held—whether between the thumb and first two fingers, allowing greater flexibility and precision in the control of the point, or loosely held in the palm of the hand, allowing more expressive gesture from a flexible wrist—but there are significantly few conductors who have mastered, and employ, both techniques. That most conductors in fact conduct with the elbow—and this includes many would-be conductors in the form of orchestral musicians who have played under some of the finest conductors in the world—does not alter the fact that this looks hideous and sounds appalling, and is only to be surpassed in the grossness of its resultant sound by the ape-like antics of the choral conductor who conducts from the shoulder. The purpose of the baton is to provide a visual focal-point for the assembled orchestra, and the more concentrated are its movements, the more concentrated will that focus and the resultant orchestral sound be. That Strauss belonged to the former school can be clearly seen from the drawing by Eduard Grützner—Lenbach's portrait of Bülow, with the arm raised in eloquent gesture, tells us the same thing—and everything which we know about Strauss the conductor informs us that his movements and gestures were precise and economical. The left hand was to be placed in the waistcoat pocket, he said, or at most reserved for a slight gesture or some small detail—which could however be equally well accomplished by swift glance of the eyes:

"How unimportant it is to beat out every quarter- and eighth-note I have discovered during some fifty years of experience", he wrote in 1934. "The essential thing is the rhythmically exact up-beat which contains every element of the ensuing tempo, together with a precise down-beat . . ." (The absence of fuss with which Strauss negotiated such notorious openings as those of *Don Juan*, the Fifth Symphony by Beethoven, and the overture to *Zauberflöte*, have become legendary.)

The second part of the bar is inessential, and I often give it in the style of an *Alla breve* . . . Eighty years ago, in the finale of Schubert's Great C major Symphony at a Rhineland music-festival, Franz Liszt conducted only the periods—that is to say that he gave a down-beat only to every fourth bar. The poor orchestra, quite unused to such inspired refinements, had of course no idea how to control its chains of triplets, and straightway decided that Liszt was no conductor! In their painstaking study of rhythmic details it is just the 'subaltern-conductors' who miss the sensitive and urgent conception of the entire phrase, the compelling *melos* of the singing line, which in its broad outlines must be grasped as a complete idea by the listener. Any variation of the tempo which is demanded by the character of a phrase must be accomplished imperceptibly, so that one is never aware of a disturbance of the fundamental tempo . . .

Strauss goes on to endorse what must seem to us some astonishing practices by Wagner and Bülow—notably the *poco a poco accellerando* up to *Presto* in the string cadenza of the third *Leonora* overture, only reaching the ultimate *Presto* three bars before the *fff*—and this would seem at strange variance with his above-mentioned words, which appear on the contrary to endorse Weingartner's earlier strictures of Bülow. But the operative word is "imperceptibly"—the *allmähliche Steigerung* which pervaded Bülow's edition of Beethoven's piano works, and which pervades the scores of Mahler and Strauss. The points are so fine, so easily misconstrued by even the most sensitive orchestral player, so easily unheard by the unheeding ear, that we must wonder all the more at Weingartner's outburst. For, however much he may have disapproved of the practice of *rubato*, he cannot with his own superlative musicianship have been deaf to a quality of finesse which was entirely in keeping with his own highest ideals of performance.

The question of metronome markings cannot however be ignored. Maelzel's metronome acquired its apotheosis at the hands of Beethoven, and although it is patently obvious that many of his metronome-markings are hopelessly inexact, and it is known that Beethoven's metronome was itself inaccurate—and even today the accurate metronome is the exception rather than the rule—yet the myth is compelled to persist that, because *Beethoven* wrote them, they are sacrosanct. They are of course immensely valuable, for no matter how inaccurate his metronome, they tell us for example that the *Allegro vivace* of the first movement and the *Allegro ma non troppo* of the finale of his Fourth Symphony are to be taken at exactly the same speed— something which is neither self-evident from the Italian tempo-markings nor from the majority of performances which one hears of this work. But Strauss's own misjudgements of the metronome markings in *Don Juan*, his report of Brahms's unconcern over choice of exact tempi in his Fourth Symphony, and the complete absence of metronome-markings from so many works written after the metronome had come into general use—all these factors must make us doubt whether the metronome has any absolute value. One point is abundantly clear. For while it is, in all conscience, difficult enough to pick up an exact tempo from the metronome—as any orchestral-player who has played under a conductor who only beats time like a metronome will readily confirm—to set a metronome to a preconceived tempo which exists either in the composer's mind, or to match it in the act of performance, is well-nigh impossible. When we consider that Beethoven could no longer physically hear his own music, and could only *see* the metronome which he was using, we should concede that the chance of any serious co-incidence of accuracy with his intentions must have been very small indeed— and too small to warrant serious attention with a composer who was so un-compromisingly exact about his other indications. Why then should he have bothered with the medium of the metronome at all? Was it perhaps with something of the childish pleasure of a new-found toy which we may perceive in Berlioz's description of the electric time-beater which enabled the opera-conductor to give backstage signals to his sub-conductor of the backstage chorus? It seems more reasonable to suppose that Beethoven resorted to metronome markings for precisely the same reason that every composer before him had found no need of such a device—because he could no longer establish a tradition of tempi for his own works himself, by the act of performance which for Bach and Handel had made even Italian markings largely superfluous. It must be emphasised again that the tempo marking—whether expressed in metronomic or in more general terms—serves an identical purpose with the stage-direction in drama and which, in the classics, is characterized by its sparseness and infrequency. If it has any value at all, it is to define the composer's concept of an ideal tempo. But there can be no such thing as the "definitive" tempo, which must vary from conductor to conductor for the very reason that he is not himself a metronome. "We have no metronome markings for our classical literature", wrote Strauss. "Only our music-critics have authentic information concerning them, direct from Olympus."

Chapter 5

RICHTER, NIKISCH AND MAHLER

The formation of the Berlin Philharmonic Orchestra in 1882 heralded the breakaway from an operatic domination which—always excluding Leipzig—extended to every major city in Europe, and which had reached its climax in July of the same year with the triumphant first seven performances of *Parsifal* at Bayreuth. Yet the portents were already unmistakable. Despite a deepening awareness and sense of artistic regeneration—and perhaps because of them—operatic standards had everywhere dwindled save for the very instance of Munich, where the influences of Wagner and Ludwig II had been most directly felt. Since Beethoven's *Fidelio*, the frivolous approach to Mozart had become unauthentic, and an uncritical profession and undiscriminating audience—as yet unready to assume the mantle of maturity which the performance of the classics imposed—sought refuge behind the medial and undemanding virtues of Meyerbeer's *Les Huguenots* and Gounod's *Faust*. Nor had a redeeming veneer of elegance, in the better traditions of Spontini, Spohr and Mendelssohn, survived to furnish a vestige of professional gloss. Writing to his daughter Daniela in 1879, Bülow had declared Dresden moribund—what chance was there of staging the *Ring* in a city which could no longer command an audience for *Götz von Berlichingen*? He could not foresee that with the promotion of Fritz Schuch to general musical director in Dresden, in the same month that the Berlin Philharmonic was to make its first appearance, a gradual return to those standards which had promoted *Fliegende Holländer* and *Tannhäuser* under Wagner's baton would be able to meet the challenge of Strauss' *Don Juan* in January 1890. Between 1901 and his retirement in 1914, Schuch had given the historic first performances of *Feuersnot*, *Salome*, *Elektra* and *Rosenkavalier*, and on its four-hundredth anniversary in 1942, Strauss described the Dresden Opera Orchestra as the greatest in the world.[1]

The reference to the *Ring* in Bülow's letter of 1879 was certainly prompted

---

[1] Needless to say, in 1542, no permanent orchestra had existed as such—and certainly not in those proportions which Orlandus Lassus was later to experience in Munich.

by the production which had been given earlier that year by Angelo Neumann —a young intendant of more initiative than artistic conscience—in the totally inadequate house of the Leipzig opera, a production which Liszt had championed and Wagner ignored. But it was nonetheless the citizens of the town of Wagner's and Bülow's birth who held the formula for future developments in the shape of their Gewandhaus Orchestra. It needed but the example of the visiting Meiningen band in 1881 to translate the insipid vulgarity of conventional music-making which Bülow had described in his youth, into the three-dimensional experience of the great symphony orchestra. The inauguration of the Berlin Philharmonic in 1882 was doubly portentous, for Leipzig and Berlin were to share a common destiny lasting nearly half a century.

In fulfilling Wagner's dream of a national opera house which could stage the *Ring*, the small Franconian town of Bayreuth had once again emulated the pattern of local initiative through which every artistic development has found substance. Whether, nearly a century later, we can be certain that the Bayreuth image fulfils every promise which Wagner held out for it is another matter—but this does not diminish the civic achievement of the Festspielhaus nor lessen the stature which Wagner commanded among his fellow musicians at the time. For it should be remembered that when the foundation stone at Bayreuth was laid on 22 May, 1872, much of Wagner's music was still largely unknown to the musical profession and the general public, and much of that which was known was cordially disliked and treated with the gravest suspicion. But Wagner the musician—the conductor—held an unqualified fascination for the musical world. The historic performance of Beethoven's Ninth at the foundation ceremony had been able to draw upon the finest musicians in Europe—among the first-violins alone were no less than ten famous concertmasters, led by August Wilhelmj, and such was the response to Wagner's appeal that he had been able to handpick the wind sections. He only insisted that the kettledrums should be played by his friend and disciple, Hans Richter—"since no professional timpanist yet understands the part".

Richter's association with Wagner had begun in Munich where, from 1866 to 1868, he had shared the position of co-principal horn with Strauss's father. Just as Bülow had worked in close collaboration with Wagner in the preparation of the score of *Tristan*, so now Richter became his assistant in the preparation of the score of *Meistersinger* at Triebschen in 1886 and 1887. In 1868, Richter became third conductor under Bülow and Hermann Levi, and with the mounting domestic tension over Cosima von Bülow, Wagner began to place increasing faith in Richter's judgement—though he was quick to admonish the young man for having gone over Bülow's head over the matter of a performance of *Figaro*. When Bülow finally fled from Munich in 1869, it was only natural that Wagner should have turned to Richter as his conductor for the forthcoming première of *Rheingold*. Wagner had wished to preserve the first performance of all the operas which constitute the *Ring* for an ideal ambience, but the young King Ludwig—to whom Wagner owed his pension —had been insistent. At all events the preparation of *Rheingold* under the twenty-six-year-old Richter was a shambles from which responsibility he had done his utmost to release himself, declaring that the soloists and orchestra were in no sense ready for performance. A typical opera house scandal ensued, involving the usual political machinations at which intendants are so adept—and Perfall could be counted upon to have surpassed himself—and three weeks before the première of 22 September, 1869, Richter was suspended from service. Exactly six months later, entirely on his own initiative, he had staged the first Belgian performance of *Lohengrin* at the Théâtre de la Monnaie in Brussels. It is from this point that a subtle change can be seen in Wagner's attitude, from a former indulgence in a favourite and gifted pupil, to a growing regard and respect for an artist of stature. His impatience that Richter had not time to deal with the piano reduction of *Walküre* (which he accordingly instructed Richter to send to Klindworth in Moscow—"insured for 100 francs") gave way to active attempts at helping him in his career, and a trace of dismay that the *Lohengrin* performance should have won for Richter other champions. Wagner's letter to the intendant of the Budapest opera was in vain, for the addressee was dead and his temporary successor, Zichy, powerless to offer Richter an appointment. With the arrival of Felix Orczy as intendant, Liszt interceded on Richter's behalf, and in September 1871 he became second conductor in Budapest.

Wagner had written to Richter in July, commenting that confirmation of the Budapest appointment coincided with the death, two days earlier, of the thirty-year-old Karl Tausig, a brilliant pupil of Liszt who had planned the formation of the 100-piece Wagner-Verein orchestra in Berlin which was to give the *Ring* there under Karl Klindworth ten years later. "My first thought was that you should take his place if the undertaking should materialise", wrote Wagner, and four months later—"God knows who else one can find to do the job". Five weeks later still—"Dr. Theodor Kafka writes to me that the Wagner-Verein in Vienna is flourishing...". But Richter, with the arduous routine of regular performances confronting him, was not to be drawn. On 6 February, 1872, Wagner wrote again:

> I think that I shall be ready to leave Triebschen by the end of April. About the second week in May I shall be giving the Viennese

their promised concert. Try and get leave to be with me from the middle of May. On 22 May the foundation stone of the Bayreuth theatre will be laid, and for this I want to give a really model performance of the Ninth. I am already promised a specially chosen chorus from the Berlin and Leipzig choral societies, and I want as well an 'élite-orchestra' of 100 players. I have been in touch with the concertmasters in Vienna, Berlin, Dresden, Karlruhe etc., and asked them to collect together their best musicians, who will need five days' leave—two for the journey to Bayreuth and back, and three for rehearsals and performance. They will receive no fee, but travelling expenses and board and loging in Bayreuth will be provided. Now I must wait and see who will accept. If they do, then I shall need you for my *"Generalkonzertmeister"* . . .

And on 23 February:

I am delighted with your musicians, and should be more so if you could find fourteen instead of four. Twelve from Vienna have accepted. We shall see . . .

And again on 27 April:

I am still counting on the remaining musicians from you: two first fiddles, two second fiddles, two violas (good ones), a 'cellist, a double-bass, a first clarinet and a first trumpet. Hellmesberger[2] is finding the horns for me. But now, you who are always chattering about the contrabassoon—find me one! Beethoven is in need! I shan't ask anyone else . . .[3]

Preparations continued for the opening of the Bayreuth Festspielhaus, first in 1874, postponed until 1875 and then again until 1876 because the architect Brandt could not be ready. Rehearsals of the *Ring* occupied Wagner and Richter at Bayreuth from the beginning of May until the end of August 1874, which as early as 1 April of that year Wagner had ready planned as a work schedule to be repeated in 1875 and 1876—"and of these 12 months, not one moment is to be lost". In October 1874, Richter was promoted to musical director of the Budapest Opera, but it was an appointment which came too

---

[2] Principal of the Vienna Music Academy and former conductor of the Vienna Philharmonic, 1845–48.

[3] Wagner's reliance upon Richter for a contrabassoon, and principal clarinet and trumpet, has an interesting geographical significance, for as far back as the middle of the eighteenth century, when the clarinet and bassoon had first begun to find general acceptance in the symphony orchestra, their best exponents had come from south-eastern Europe—Czechoslovakia, Hungary, and what is now Yugoslavia, and the same remains true to the present day. The clarinet and trumpet also display an incredible degree of virtuosity in the hands of gipsy musicians of south-eastern Europe, rivalling that of her gipsy fiddlers, and the *mariacci* trumpeters of Mexico. This is especially evident in Dvorak's writing for the trumpet—notably in his Slavonic Dances, Op. 72.

late, for he had already been approached to accept the position of second conductor at the Vienna Opera, and conductor of the Vienna Philharmonic. On 1 April, 1875, he took up his duties in Vienna. Wagner was evidently annoyed that Richter's acceptance of this post would prevent his joining him in Bayreuth for the summer, since the Vienna opera season began in August, and the Vienna press tried to make capital out of a seeming rift in the Wagner-Richter relationship:

> Even Hans Richter's enthusiasm appears to have been dampened, and his doubts aroused, by the monstrous proportions of the vocal and orchestral writing of the *Ring* rehearsals now taking place in Bayreuth . . .

Wagner had indeed engaged the services of Felix Mottl, the twenty-year-old conductor of the newly-formed Wagner-Verein in Vienna, to assist him at the Bayreuth rehearsals in Richter's place, together with Anton Seidl—also twenty years old—who since 1872 had been living at Bayreuth and making the complete fair copy of the *Ring*. But there was never any question in Wagner's mind but that Richter should conduct the opening performances at Bayreuth in 1876, and it was under Richter that the ill-starred premières took place. They yielded a deficit of some £10,000—a crippling sum for Wagner at that time—and the *Ring* was not performed again at Bayreuth for the next twenty years, nor did Richter conduct there again for another ten, though he remained a devoted disciple of Wagner, accompanying him to London for the concerts at the Royal Albert Hall in 1877—the beginning of a lasting association with England—and the first to hurry to Venice at the news of Wagner's death on 13 February, 1883. But for the rest, he was prepared to immerse himself in his duties in Vienna, rising to the position of associate musical director with Wilhelm Jahn in 1880, at the age of thirty-seven.

The spirit of musical regeneration which, at the hands of Wagner, Liszt and Bülow, had played so vital a share in the movement towards social and political integration in nineteenth-century Germany found little to mirror it in the feudal empire of the Habsburgs. The extraordinary epoch which had nurtured the genius of Gluck and Haydn, and so atrociously neglected its responsibilities towards Mozart, Beethoven and Schubert, had come to an end under the nebulous influences of the Emperor Francis and his successor, the feeble-minded Ferdinand—frightened men, haunted by the spectre of the murdered Marie-Antoinette, and the rising forces of revolution throughout Europe. So contentious a voice as Beethoven's might by all means be allowed to remain silent, and the Ninth Symphony did not receive its first professional performance in Vienna until 1843—sixteen years after its composer's death, and four years after Wagner had heard it under Habaeneck in Paris. Just as Bismarck's political domination of Germany was to smother any significant cultural advance in a national sense, so the influence of Metternich until his fall in 1848 had—in the absence of a powerful and enlightened monarchy—stifled the continuation of the extraordinary musical heritage of Empress Maria Theresa. With the revolution of 1848, Ferdinand abdicated in favour of his eighteen-year-old nephew, Franz Josef, and there began the slow return to a semblance of that cultural enlightenment which, through its union with Savoie, had graced the earlier years of the Habsburg dynasty.

But, as if by way of punishment for her perennial irresponsibility towards those artists to whom she most owed her cultural reputation, Austria now possessed no composers—certainly none who could speak with the unequivocating voice of Richard Wagner, and envisage a musical grand design to match Austria's political designs in becoming the centre of a German-speaking empire of seventy-million people. In 1865, her sole composer of lasting magnitude was the forty-one-year-old Anton Bruckner, who was regarded as a village simpleton, while the presence of the Hamburger Brahms in this city of his adoption constituted an acute embarrassment for the Viennese. The one redeeming feature lay in Emperor Franz Josef's willingness, after being soundly defeated by Prussia at the battle of Sadowa, to disburse funds for the building of a proper opera house, so bringing Vienna into line with the remaining capitals of Europe. And on 25 May, 1869, the Vienna Hofoper opened its doors on the Ringstrasse for the first time, with Heinrich Esser, former conductor of the Mannheim Hofoper, as its musical director. The Vienna Philharmonic, whose function was and still is identical with that of other concert-giving opera orchestras in Europe, had been founded in 1842, and gave its first concert as a separate entity of sixty-four players in the Redoutensaal of the Vienna Court on 28 March under the thirty-two-year-old Carl Nicolai, better known as the composer of *The Merry Wives of Windsor*. Since the services of the orchestra were required at the existing opera of the Hofburg during the week, concerts were given on Sunday mornings—a tradition which has persisted to the present day—and in 1860 an annual subscription series of eight concerts for the general public was initiated. While Vienna was the last European city to indulge in a full-sized opera-house which was open to the general public, she may fairly claim to have been the first major city to have possessed a permanent symphony orchestra.[4]

The musical climate of Vienna immediately prior to Richter's appointment to the Hofoper was described by the young Artur Nikisch as a student at

[4] Leipzig was not, of course, a major city in the political sense.

the Vienna Music Academy and an unofficial deputy violinist in the opera orchestra, or Vienna Philharmonic, as it is better known. For violin he had as his professor Joseph Hellmesberger—Nicolai's successor in 1845, and one of the last violin-conductors—and for composition Felix Dessoff, conductor of the Vienna Philharmonic and a native of Leipzig.

> It was the year 1872 [wrote Nikisch]. Spring had come with all its glory, and with a magic which affects the senses in no other city in quite the same way as in Vienna. Through the good offices of Hellmesberger I was already allowed to deputise, in the case of absence or illness, in the ranks of the second violins at the opera and the Philharmonic concerts, and was very fortunate in getting to know the masterworks in a more comfortable way than hitherto, when I had had to queue from three o'clock in the afternoon to get a reasonable seat in the fourth gallery . . . Suddenly the news spread like wildfire through the city—Wagner was coming to Vienna to conduct a big symphony concert.

The concert, which took place on Sunday 12 May, 1872, consisted of the *Eroica* Symphony, the Overture and Bacchanale from the Paris version of *Tannhäuser*, and Wotan's Farewell and the Magic Fire Music from *Walküre*. After the concert, Wagner announced the forthcoming performance, in ten days' time, of Beethoven's Ninth at Bayreuth, and through Hellmesberger the young Nikisch found himself among the twenty musicians from Vienna who were now participating.

> I can say [he wrote], that Wagner's *Eroica* in Vienna and then the Ninth at Bayreuth were an absolutely decisive influence, not only on my later grasp of Beethoven, but on my whole understanding of orchestral interpretation. To speak only of the obvious things: Wagner was certainly not what one might describe as a "routine conductor"—his very gestures were music in themselves. I have said before that the conductor's baton-technique—if he is not just an uninspired time-beater—is a language whose mastery enables the listener to penetrate the feelings of the artist, and helps his understanding of the work being played. This was Wagner through and through . . .

Richter was to sustain his position as musical director of the Vienna Hofoper until 1896—a period of twenty-one years of uninterrupted association with the opera house and Philharmonic which remains a record in a city where a lazy and corrupt administration, with too much time on its hands, had traditionally resorted to the diversions of politics and musical intrigue. Hanslick, reviewing Richter's first Vienna concert in January 1875—shortly before his appointment to the opera—was indulgent and full of praise, but Richter's name does not again appear in his published reviews. Bülow had spoken—with an understandable trace of asperity—of Richter's "beery complacency", and we may well imagine that, as a younger man, he had possessed a jovial and easy-going temperament which appealed to the Viennese and allowed him to escape any compromising limelight. The Wagner operas which were new to Vienna were introduced in due course—*Walküre* in 1877 and the remainder of the *Ring* in 1878—but Richter was responsible for introducing no first performances in Vienna save for Bruckner's Fourth Symphony on 20 February, 1881, Brahms's Third Symphony on 2 December, 1883, and Bruckner's Eighth on 18 December, 1892. This was well in keeping with Viennese conservatism, whose experience of operatic premières was confined, for the space of 105 years between the final version of *Fidelio* in 1812 and the production of *Die Frau ohne Schatten* in 1919, to the solitary instance of Rossini's *Zelmira* in 1822. If it were not for the unqualified veneration with which those English players who are still alive and who played under Richter speak of him, it would be easy to conclude that his chief virtue in Vienna had lain in his ability to remain anonymous. For reference books are unanimous in their appraisal of Mahler—Richter's successor in Vienna—as having "done much to enhance the prestige of the opera", which must suggest that Vienna's prestige, vis-à-vis the German houses of Berlin, Munich, Dresden, Hamburg and Karlsruhe, was lacking. It has been said of Richter and Strauss that, while Richter saw the performance of *Meistersinger* through the eyes of Hans Sachs, Richard Strauss saw it through those of Walther von Stolzing. And again, of Richter and Nikisch, that Richter "was the devil before one's eyes" while Nikisch "was the devil at one's shoulder, hounding incessantly". If this is to suggest that Richter's approach was direct, uncompromising, and perhaps a little unimaginative—which may account for the stolid and over-ponderous tradition of Wagnerian performance in this country—then it must also underline the poetic and dynamic elements which Strauss, Mahler and Nikisch introduced into their music-making.

The final years of the nineteenth century were fateful. Nikisch succeeded Reinecke as permanent director of the Leipzig Gewandhaus Orchestra in 1895, and Strauss as permanent director of the Berlin Philharmonic two years later. In the same year Gustav Mahler succeeded Richter as general musical director of the Vienna Hofoper, while Richter took over the Hallé Concerts in Manchester, and in 1898 Richard Strauss became musical director of the Berlin Hofoper. The great heritage had been established. It had now to be proven and defended.

As in the case of Richard Strauss, the biographer and critic of Gustav

Mahler has been chiefly concerned with an examination of his work as a composer, and the adherent of the one has tended to find himself called upon to be the adversary of the other. More astonishing than the obvious differences between the two men—whether as composers or conductors—is the extent to which their viewpoint and approach to interpretative problems was similar and, in many instances, identical. Only with Mahler, nothing came easily. His professional career was fraught with continual battles with successive administrations, and his early symphonies he gave into the hands of other conductors to present, neither possessing the influence to mount such performances himself, nor feeling confident of directing their first performances. Indeed, as late as *Das Lied von der Erde*, he confessed to Bruno Walter that he had no notion of how to conduct the *Abschied* movement. Walter concluded that his illustrious master was quietly pulling his leg, and it is only when we realise how barely this work has even yet entered our repertoire, in the sense that conductors know how to bring it off successfully on each and every occasion, that we see that Mahler was speaking in all seriousness. With Strauss, on the other hand—the "opportunist", as Mahler called him, who seemed to be riding the royal road to success and from whose path all difficulties seemed miraculously to vanish—we have difficulty in reconciling his taut and economical style of conducting with the ebullience and extravagance of his writing, while the decadence which so many of his critics are ready to descry in his later composition (if not all of it) is at strange variance with the creative vitality which imbued all his music-making until his final retirement from the conductor's rostrum. Closer attention to his scores reveals an economy and vitality in Strauss's writing which are still but seldom accurately observed, and the writing itself displays an innate sense of the conductor's art, as has already been said. With Mahler this economy, within the vast instrumental textures which he employs, is even more in evidence, and it is the vitality which must sometimes seem to have been superimposed. But the mind of the conductor is equally apparent, and more explicitly so than in the case of Strauss. Barely a page of his orchestral-writing passes without some footnote drawing one or another detail to the attention of the conductor, from which we may deduce that, despite the influence of Bülow, neither the correct readings of *crescendo* and *diminuendo*, nor the gradual and imperceptible change of tempo—to quote obvious examples from Mahler's scores—had acquired common usage. If, as Professor Redlich maintains, Mahler conducted the performances of his first two symphonies in Weimar and Berlin, then these footnotes cannot have been written for the benefit of Strauss, who would in any case have understood their implications. It will be recalled that the conversation between Strauss and Mahler at their first meeting in Leipzig had centred around "tempo-modification", with especial reference to Wagner's interpretations.

Like Strauss, Mahler's baton-technique became progressively simpler and more subtle. Walter recalls that, during his early years in Vienna, Mahler had indulged in extremes of gesture—even though he always conducted opera sitting down—but that his bearing gradually became calmer, and his seemingly innocent beat allowed his musicians the utmost freedom of expression while always maintaining an unfailing precision. "I remember a performance of Strauss's *Sinfonia Domestica*", wrote Walter, "where the contrast between the tumult of the orchestra and the immobility of him who was causing it became quite uncanny." Like Strauss, and like Bülow and Wagner, Mahler's performances were pursued with an inevitability which made each and every one of them an unique experience. There was for him in Vienna no such thing as the "routine performance", and each was prepared as though it were to be the first and the last in the whole world. These qualities imbued his whole work in the opera house, where an inner compulsion as to what *must be* dictated every aspect of his productions—music, acting, staging and lighting— and brooked no interference or opposition. His particular genius as an operatic conductor lay in his particular ability to identify himself with each and every one of his characters on stage, engaging a comparable sense of commitment from his orchestra who now felt themselves an integral part not only of the music, but of the action of the opera as well. His introduction of the third *Leonora* overture into the body of *Fidelio*, just before the final scene, was no brainwave which he had come upon by chance and decided, like Winnie-the-Pooh, was "a good idea". It arose out of the conviction that Beethoven had written *Leonora* No. 3, whether consciously or not, as a final peroration, a complete summing-up of the whole drama of *Fidelio*, which found as natural a place in the dramatic entity of the opera as the symphonic epilogue was to find in Berg's *Wozzeck*. By contrast, Mahler found the opposite solution for the opening of Act II of *Figaro*. It is a notorious first entry for the Countess, who must wait during a long orchestral introduction, growing (though she be the most experienced opera singer in the world) progressively more nervous, while successive producers have racked their brains to find her something to do to occupy both her own attention and that of the audience. Mahler sought a solution in the music itself, which he allowed to acquire such intensity and independence of expression that the Countess' treacherous entry became almost incidental—a commentary on the musical text which, like *Leonora* No. 3, embodied the complete sentiment of the whole opera.

Mahler's experience in the opera had been hard won, embracing appointments in seven different theatres during the first eleven years of his career up to the age of thirty-one. Save for Prague and Leipzig, none of these had afforded the resources or the standards for which he could have wished, and it was only with his appointment as first conductor in Hamburg in 1891— where he found a champion and an example in Bülow—that he was first exposed to anything approaching metropolitan standards and traditions for which he had instinctively been fighting. If ever there was a conductor who was self-made, and who brought to his art an intuitive vision and sense of purpose, it was Gustav Mahler, and with his collaboration with the scenic-designer, Alfred Roller, in the productions of *Tristan, Walküre, Fidelio, Don Giovanni, Figaro* and *Zauberflöte* in Vienna, these qualities found their pinnacle of artistic achievement, and placed the Vienna Opera for the first time at the forefront of European music-making.

It was a manifestation of single-minded genius which Vienna could not indefinitely endure. Mahler, as musical director, had acquired absolute powers and had used them without scruple, engaging and dismissing artists at will, and employing tyranny and extravagance with the same want of foresight which had terminated a ten-year contract with the Budapest Opera after only two seasons. Yet such powers, and such intractability in their employment, are essential to the musical director who must, if he is to succeed in the absolute service of his muse, play the part of the autocrat, and must be allowed and encouraged to do so. One possible end dictates the only possible means, and the misfortune lay not in Mahler's uncompromising personality, but in his geographical location. Inevitably, on the expiration of his ten-year contract with Vienna in 1907, the forces of intrigue cultivated in her political hot-bed compelled Mahler's resignation under circumstances which con-stituted yet another abiding disgrace to the social conscience of Austria's capital. At the age of forty-seven, world-famous but still financially harassed, Mahler accepted the invitation to conduct at the Metropolitan Opera in New York, making his debut there with the same historic production of *Tristan* which had established his Vienna reputation—the same opera which had established the reputations of Bülow, Strauss and Nikisch before him.

As Mahler's career was to end in the United States, when he collapsed during a concert near the end of a second long season with the New York Philharmonic and was brought back to Europe to die, so Artur Nikisch's career could be said to have started, in a decisive way, in America. Nikisch had left Vienna in 1878, at the age of twenty-one, to become chorus-master— at the recommendation of the Leipzig-born Dessof, of the Leipzig Opera under its intendant, Angelo Neumann, who, in April of that year, had staged the first complete performance of the *Ring* outside Bayreuth. Four years later Nikisch was promoted to first conductor, and in 1888 elicited the following

testimonial from Tchaikowsky, who was visiting Leipzig on a conducting-
tour of Europe:

> The Leipzig Opera can be proud of its inspired young conductor
> Artur Nikisch, who is a specialist in the Wagner music-dramas of the
> latest period. I heard *Rheingold* and *Meistersinger* there—the
> orchestra, which is the same as that at the Gewandhaus, is absolutely
> first-class. They play well under Reinecke, but one can only see to
> what heights of perfection they can rise when one hears a per-
> formance of the difficult and complex scores of Wagner under so
> miraculous a young master as Mr. Nikisch. His conducting has none
> of the showmanship—inimitable in its own way—of Mr. Hans von
> Bülow . . . it is calm, sparing of superfluous gesture, yet exhibiting
> extraordinary authority and a complete and compelling self-
> confidence. He does not conduct, but rather imparts a kind of
> hidden magic—he does so little to attract attention to himself that
> one scarcely notices him, and yet one has the feeling that the whole
> orchestra is completely subject to his will, like an instrument in the
> hands of a great master. This conductor is small of stature, a pallid
> young man of about thirty [actually thirty-three] with magnificent
> eyes full of poetry, but must in fact possess some magic power which
> compels the orchestra, now to coo like a dove, now to freeze in
> breathtaking mysticism. And all this is achieved in such a way that
> the audience does not notice the little conductor, who commands
> the orchestra like obedient slaves, at all . . .

Tchaikowsky had long-standing associations with the United States, and
especially with Boston where Bülow had given the first performance of the
B flat minor Concerto under Fritz Lang in 1875. The following year—1889—
Nikisch left Leipzig to become resident conductor of the Boston Symphony
Orchestra which had been inaugurated as a permanent body of eighty-three
players under the English conductor, Sir George Henschel, in 1881. It has
of course been suggested by his German biographers that Nikisch was
attracted by the fee, which at $10,000 was nearly four times as much as he
had been receiving in Leipzig—and twice as much as Bülow had received in
Meiningen. The European is so justly proud of the musical traditions which
had been established in central Europe during the eighteenth and nineteenth
centuries that he is apt to forget that those traditions are today largely ex-
hausted, while a new tradition, based upon the more enduring elements of the
old, had sprung up in the New World and was already flourishing well
before the end of the last century. The Metropolitan Opera House had been
built in 1883, and the New York Philharmonic founded in 1842—the same
year in which the Vienna Philharmonic had given its first private concert
under Carl Nicolai.

The provincial standards of the Leipzig Opera, which Mahler had abandoned in favour of Budapest after only two seasons as second conductor to Nikisch—1886–88—had been a valuable but arduous apprenticeship for the older conductor, and they could not have held him there indefinitely, especially since access to the Gewandhaus Orchestra, which had been firmly held in the hands of the unimaginative Reinecke since 1860, was becoming progressively more difficult. The decision to go to America was for Nikisch a departure from the operatic field which was to prove decisive, for although he returned to the opera house at the conclusion of his four-year engagement in Boston—to succeed Mahler in Budapest at the latter's recommendation—the American experience had established for him the reputation as a concert conductor of an entirely new kind. Nikisch was in London, giving concerts with Richter's orchestra—later to become the London Symphony Orchestra—when, in June 1895, Reinecke announced his retirement after thirty-five years in office, and the directors of the Gewandhaus immediately cabled Nikisch with the offer of the position of permanent conductor. For Nikisch this was both the fulfilment of his dearest wish, and a merciful release from the tedium of Budapest which both his fellow-Hungarian, Hans Richter, and Gustav Mahler had found intolerable. Two years later, after a series of guest appearances in Berlin, he succeeded Bülow and Strauss as permanent conductor of the Berlin Philharmonic, and was to hold both positions—together with the annual series of subscription concerts by the Berlin Philharmonic, founded by Bülow in Hamburg—until his death in 1922.

The early years of the Berlin Philharmonic had been difficult ones. The orchestra did not, in 1882, enjoy a municipal subsidy like that of the Leipzig Gewandhaus, nor a wealthy private patron like Higginson, who was to shoulder the burden of the Boston Symphony, founded in 1881, single-handed for thirty-seven years. The idiom of the symphony orchestra was new, and Leipzig had been the only city in Germany to maintain one long enough for the symphony concert to acquire a tradition independent of the opera house. The Berlin orchestra was compelled to be entirely self-supporting, and although it enjoyed the success of novelty in its first four years under Karl Klindworth, and sold-out houses under the figurehead of Hans von Bülow, its position at his death, and after only twelve years in existence, was precarious. Richard Strauss, as a disciple of Bülow, possessed all the qualities of musicianship and initiative required of a suitable successor, but he was never at home on the concert platform with all the ancillary responsibilities which the position of permanent conductor of a symphony orchestra must entail, and which for him had none of the magic of the opera house. In the critical season which followed Strauss's appointment to the opera house in

Munich in the summer of 1896, a succession of guest conductors were engaged by the Berlin Philharmonic—Hans Richter, Felix Mottl, Gustav
Mahler, Hermann Levi and Felix Weingartner. But none was free to accept
a permanent engagement in Berlin, or else they did not possess the personality which was so crucial to the success of this new enterprise. The guest
engagement of Artur Nikisch by the orchestra's manager in the person of
Hermann Wolff came almost as an afterthought, for his position at the head
of the Gewandhaus orchestra carried no especial kudos at that time—Leipzig
was just a worthy little provincial town whose excellent orchestra had seen
better days under Mendelssohn, and its opera house nothing to compare with
the Royal Opera Houses of Munich, Berlin, Vienna and Karlsruhe. Wolff's
decision to try out Nikisch as a potential successor to Bülow came from the
distant recollection of Liszt's enthusiasm for one of his performances at a
festival of the Tonkünstler-Verein in Magdeburg in 1884. It was a historic
decision, for not only did the permanent appointment when it came, in 1897,
carry with it the dual responsibility of eighteen subscription concerts in
Hamburg, but Nikisch insisted on retaining his post in Leipzig as well,
besides being allowed leave for outside engagements.

The debt of gratitude which Nikisch avowed to Bülow went back to the
year 1882, when the Meiningen orchestra had visited Leipzig, and it found
expression when Nikisch commemorated—as did Strauss, in his article of that
time—the twenty-fifth anniversary of Bülow's death with a performance of
the *Eroica* Symphony in Berlin in 1919:

> The modern conductor [wrote Nikisch] must create anew, and
> therein lies the independent and creative nature of his art. That is
> why his individuality must play so significant a role today. The con-
> temporary composer understands this perfectly well. Once when I
> was rehearsing a Brahms symphony in Leipzig in the composer's
> presence, he could hardly get over his surprise and became quite
> nervous, repeating over and over again: "Is it possible? Did I really
> write that?" But afterwards the Master came to me, his face beaming
> with pleasure, and said: "You have changed everything. But you are
> right—it *must* be like that." It is only since Hans von Bülow that
> there have been conductors who understood their task in this way.
> Berlioz understood—but he only conducted his own works. Once I
> have made a piece of music part of me, I can only build it up again
> from the beginning—but I must follow my own conviction, other-
> wise it will not be a reconstruction of integrity.

These sentiments suggest a strong spiritual affinity between Nikisch and
Bülow—not to mention Strauss and Mahler—though it would be hard to
imagine two musical personalities more unalike, if we are to believe the

accounts of their contemporaries, and Tchaikowsky in particular. Ferdinand Pfohl, the Czech composer and critic, who settled in Hamburg in 1892 as music editor of the *Hamburger Nachrichten*, made the following comparison thirty years later:

> There are few names which one can mention in the same breath as Artur Nikisch. Hans von Bülow, Hans Richter—the Wagner disciples. Perhaps Felix Mottl as well—but then, only perhaps. For in Felix Mottl there was still something of the old German school— especially in his technique—albeit imbued with a warm-blooded Austrian nature, a sense of style and a passionate musical intensity. His identification with the music was nowhere more compelling than in the final section of the *Parsifal* Prelude—the transformation from the tremolo in the timpani and double-basses [bar 78] through to the infinite anguish of Amfortas's cry for redemption—who could ever forget this?
>
> Hans Richter was another proposition altogether. As a conductor he was not really a personality of striking character. Neither roman- tic nor subjective, neither demon nor showman, he represented neither a movement nor a school. He possessed spirit and feeling, but no sinew. His profile as a conductor was etched with typical German thoroughness, and reveals a calm and cordial greatness. He was no ascetic, like Parsifal, no recluse lost in mystical rapture, but a man of the earth—and that is why he was no conductor of *Parsifal*. Yet there was a trace of Sachs' good humour, something of the utter honesty and simplicity of the German artistic conscience, and that is why he was an ideal conductor of *Meistersinger*. And in the natural strength of his musical gift and his understanding and per- ception of humanity, he was also the ideal exponent of the Beet- hoven symphony . . .
>
> But Hans von Bülow! The master of an art of expression which had only been made possible through the rich expressive values of Wagner's music, and the resolution of the technical problems which they imposed—the man who, for all his idiosyncrasy and impredict- ability established a pattern and an example and a criterion for all who followed him wherever his genius had the opportunity to blaze its trail! The musical analyst whose dialectic penetration brought to light—through the process of "de-composition" as he used to call it—all the hidden shades of meaning in line and architecture, and clarified all the subtle relationships within the parts. Above all the teacher, who gave a double performance of Beethoven's Ninth with the Berlin Philharmonic [and also at Meiningen!] in the selfsame concert. Nikisch would never have been capable of that . . . Bülow was the classicist, the master of line—Nikisch the romantic, the master of colour. Contour and colour were for him one and the same thing. Bülow's interpretations had the sharp clarity and the clear, cool light of a winter landscape. The same music in Nikisch's hands

had the youthfulness and freshness of spring. It is above all those incomparably great strokes of intuitive tone-painting, when his musical instinct seemed to surge up from some demon depth, and a sudden blinding inspiration to transfigure his interpretation, which must distinguish him once and for all from Hans von Bülow, for whom instinct and improvisation were anathema, and whose artistry lay in his penetrating intelligence and his brilliant and authoritarian intellect. Nikisch's gestures made the music visible, gave it substance, made it change before our very eyes. When he raised hand and arm high into the air, as if to draw tone and expression from the very heart of the orchestra, his movements would carry with them a sense of exaltation and revelation. It was exactly the movement of someone throwing open a curtain, the gesture of the priest in lifting the veil from the sanctuary. For the artistic personality of Nikisch there was no precedent, no historical preparation. It burst upon the world as something entirely new . . .

It is reasonable to ask at this juncture whether an account such as this—vivid though it is in conjuring up a picture of the artists in question—can resurrect anything more than the musical personalities of a bygone generation of great conductors. What of their methods of work, their use of the baton, their general interpretative habits? What—above all in the case of Artur Nikisch—of the tone-quality which they produced from the orchestra, their sense of colour? How would they define it in technical terms? In so far as they were also composers, the markings of their own scores present an attitude of mind toward specific problems of tempo, balance, dynamics and orchestral colour. Just as Strauss maintained that the meticulous observance of his dynamic markings would ensure proper balance within the orchestra and between orchestra and stage, so may we assume that balance for him was a matter of prime importance in the performance of other composers' music. Colour was secondary, for it was also implicit in his writing and needed no further emphasis. Because it was innate in his own nature and temperament and required no special treatment, he also found it implicit in the writing of Mozart, Beethoven, Wagner and Mahler. Mahler's works, on the other hand, are meticulous in the markings of gradations of tempo and abound with indications evocative of shades of tone-colour which are not themselves implicit in his writing. Questions of balance, however, together with in-structions for this or that part to be brought into prominence, or for this or that section of the orchestra to be given preference to another section, are confined for the most part to footnotes for the conductor—as in the very open-ing octaves of his First Symphony. Such points do not appear in the or-chestral parts because Mahler regarded them as being subject to the visual control of the conductor without resort to long-winded explanations or elaborate rehearsal. An attentive glance at the last desk of double-basses just before the down-beat of his first symphony was enough to ensure that they treat their entry with care. Good balance came naturally to Mahler, and where it was not implicit in the instrumentation—as in the symphonies of Schumann—he was impelled to revise it. It was the perfect control of a flexible tempo which was Mahler's preoccupation as a conductor, and which required for him fastidious rehearsal.

Interpretative style and baton-technique—more closely associated than most musicians would give credence—are more elusive, however, since accounts are so often conflicting. The writer on Strauss speaks of the economy of his baton-technique—for which there is ample supporting evidence—and which had, he declares, nothing of the extravagance of gesture and over-interpretation of Artur Nikisch. The writer on Nikisch, on the other hand, speaks of *his* economy of gesture—for which we have Tchaikowsky's endorsement—and which had nothing of the explosive impetuosity of Richard Strauss. Bülow is described at one moment as an analytical pedagogue with a scrupulous regard for the smallest textual detail, and at the next as a flamboyant eccentric, prone to speech-making, and with an utter disregard for fidelity to the composer's intentions. Bruno Walter remarks a radical transformation in Mahler's conducting style from compulsive violence up to the age of forty-one to almost motionless repose less than six years later, whereas our experience of living conductors is that their techniques do not undergo any significant change at all once they have acquired an initial mastery—though there is always a tendency to greater economy as they grow older. Whom then shall we believe? Certainly the contemporary critics tell us nothing, and even so renowned a critic as Eduard Hanslick—whose opinions we are bound to acknowledge because he enjoyed the intimate friendship and respect of so towering a musical intelligence as that of Brahms—has little to say which has any meaning for us today. His evaluations of contemporary composers are not very much at variance with the judgement of posterity—for there is a grudging respect for Wagner beneath the violence of his fulminations against that composer—but his opinions are no longer viable because they reveal the expression of a *partie prise* and carry no authority over the distance of eighty and ninety years. Only when he tells us that the Meiningen Orchestra played in Vienna *standing up* does he reveal something of factual significance which is rich in musical overtones, and from which we can draw further musical conclusions about this remarkable orchestra. (It was of course customary for the German orchestra to perform standing until the last years of the nineteenth century—a caricature of the Leipzig Gewandhaus performing *Leonora* No. 3

under Reinecke tells us this—but it is interesting to discover that this practice was considered foreign in Vienna in 1884.)

But what are the facts? Why has it been so difficult for the musical historian and the musician himself to record the evidence of his own ears? In part, because the art of conducting was less generally understood sixty and seventy years ago than it is even today. But the fact of the matter is that not only our memories, but also our ears and our eyes, constantly deceive us. If we could hear again the performance of twenty or thirty years ago which is still so memorable for us, we should be surprised—not because our assessment of that performance was so misjudged, but because we ourselves have changed. The recording heard on the acoustic gramophone which captivated us in our childhood will not have the same effect on ears which are conditioned to the refinements of high-fidelity and stereophonic sound. Indeed, the impression which we had at that time, when our ears were conditioned to other standards of sound reproduction, may in fact be much more valuable than the seemingly incontestable evidence of the recording itself. For the enduring quality of a great musical experience lies in the very fact that it is unique, instantaneous and unrepeatable, defying any process of recording save that made indelibly on the mind of the listener in the instant of its occurrence. Nor can we always trust the evidence of our eyes, for we shall always come back to the score which we have known in the minutest detail and discover some new secret staring us in the face. And there will always be the Mahlerian scholar to draw our attention to the massive use of percussion in *Das Lied von der Erde* (which has the shortest timpani part in the whole symphonic literature) or its exotic use in the first movement (where its activity is confined to the sparing use of the glockenspiel)—proving conclusively that the eyes of the scholar in question have deceived him. We can trust nothing save our own ability to derive fresh insight into the language of music-making from the few clues which are available to us, and with that insight to experience the sense of fresh revelation which must accompany every great performance.

Chapter 6

STOCK AND STOKOWSKI

The idea of a North American culture is still for many people a contradiction in terms. Apart from the popular superstition—particularly rife in Central Europe—that the American belongs to a materialist society for whom the higher things in life can as yet have no meaning, there is the more serious contention that a country with so short a civilized history could hardly be expected to have attained that depth of cultural perception which, in Europe, had been the fruit of five (if not indeed of twenty-five) centuries of artistic growth. The contention is not wholly false. The artist who fled Europe in search of a new world sought freedom from the intolerable burden of his European cultural tradition quite as much as from material persecution, and in doing so bound himself spiritually and morally to abandoning that heritage as being "unreal" in terms of his adoptive society.

But if the creative artist grew new roots in the soil of his adoption, the re-creative artist continued to draw upon his European heritage. This is no paradox. The vital force in music-making today is the symphony orchestra, and that instrument was still in its infancy—albeit growing with astonishing vigour—when art-music was experiencing its first awakenings in the United States. The inclusion by a growing society of an instrumental idiom which has only within living memory risen to its zenith was therefore completely valid. The New York Philharmonic is, as has already been mentioned, the third oldest orchestra in the world, and most if not all America's leading orchestras had been established by the turn of the century—a time when the full symphony orchestra as we know it today (if only by hearsay in our own thrifty country) came to be established in its own right.

These were the vintage years of the great conductors, and America was swift to engage their services: Nikisch, Strauss, Mahler, Mottl, Muck, Weingartner—all were associated with the early years of her leading or-chestras. Soon however there were appointed permanent conductors whose terms of office, by comparison with Europe, were exceptionally long—men who, though European-born, were to fashion instruments which were essentially American, and whose seriousness, dedication, integrity, discipline and artistic stamina ranked them with the vaunted orchestras of Berlin, Vienna and Amsterdam. Europe had experienced a period of moral, material and artistic bankruptcy, and with the advent of the First World War came an inevitable wave of nationalism. Richter renounced his connections with the Hallé Orchestra, Wagner and even Beethoven were pronounced anathema at Queen's Hall and l'Opéra, and Toscanini returned from America to his native Italy with loud protestations of patriotism. The opera houses of Germany and Austria underwent tenuous and increasingly uneasy interregna, which descended to a nadir with the cessation of hostilities and the ensuing political and cultural anarchy. Having won the war for us, America experienced an incipient spirit of isolationism, a policy of retrenchment. The European was welcome in her midst, but only if he was prepared to identify himself with American culture, and to invest in it rather than living off its capital. Before her belated entry into the war she had given freely of her riches to all comers, but now she felt that she had burned her fingers in the process, and was unwilling to repeat the experience. Her conscience could not easily overlook the impetuous action of a Toscanini in deserting the Metropolitan Opera, for whatever reason. Mahler had been something different, for he was a refugee from the Vienna Court Opera and was duly accorded the asylum of the Metropolitan Opera and the New York Philharmonic until New York doctors diagnosed his fatal disease of the heart, and he returned to Vienna, a dying man. She could welcome an Artur Bodanzky, from Mannheim, for in the year 1915 America was still a neutral country, and he responded to that hospitality with twenty-four years of faithful service to the Metropolitan Opera. But she could not countenance a Karl Muck in 1918 when, with nationalist zeal, he was denounced and arrested as an "enemy alien".

The Metropolitan Opera had been built in 1883 and leased to its manager, Henry Abbey, a man of no great operatic experience and who finished his first season with a deficit which has been variously placed at $300,000 and $600,000. The lessors allowed the opera house to be used for a benefit which realised only $100,000, and their guarantee, posted at $60,000, was used up. The following season saw a board of nineteen directors closely watching the situation, and allowing Leopold Damrosch, as conductor-manager, little leeway. Nor did his death in mid-season augur well for the new enterprise. His son, Walter Damrosch, finished out the season, and in September 1885 Anton Seidl was appointed conductor-in-chief, and served for twelve years, which incidentally involved the famous episode "Parsifal".

Edmond Stanton was manager for the first six of these, and Henry Abbey returned in the capacity of manager for the next six, accompanied by

Maurice Grau and Edward Schoeffel as colleagues. Maurice Grau remained as manager during the 1898–99 season (when Franz Schalk was conductor-in-chief), the 1899–1900 season (when Ernst Schuch was conductor-in-chief), and for the next three seasons, which witnessed a return to the routine standards of Walter Damrosch. Yet it should be said for Walter Damrosch—though he was never again to venture inside the stage-door of the Metropolitan as an opera conductor—that he was a man not without courage, and a supreme salesman. It is not generally recognised that such composers as Stravinsky, Sibelius, Delius, Elgar, Ravel and Honegger—not to mention Wagner—had in Damrosch their first American champion. But to the native American composer, Charles Ives, Damrosch's behaviour was one of insufferable condescension.

Heinrich Conreid as manager, and Alfred Hertz as conductor-in-chief, now took over the Metropolitan for the next five years, in the last of which Gustav Mahler made his American début with *Tristan*. Press notices from this time testify to the sense of tremendous occasion which attended his first appearance, while their enthusiasm for his later performances of *Fidelio* and *Don Giovanni* knew no bounds. The following year—1908—saw a change of management to that of Giulio Gatti-Casazza, who was destined to remain with the Metropolitan until his retirement, twenty-seven years later. As manager of La Scala, Milan until 1908, he brought to his task a wealth of experience, and he brought something else as well—the figure of Arturo Toscanini, at the age of forty-one making his first of a number of American débuts. Press notices of the time were delirious in their praise of Toscanini's *Aïda*, slightly more reserved for his *Götterdämmerung*, and provided no clue, six years later, to his abrupt resignation in mid-season. Rumour was rife that he had returned to Italy for reasons of patriotism, but he could be observed for months afterwards, publicly drinking coffee in Times Square while Francesco Spetrino was conducting in his place. Toscanini was never to return to the Metropolitan, and whatever justice there may have been on his side, New York and America as a whole felt, with equal justice, slighted. Next season Giulio Gatti-Casazza played for safety, and Artur Bodanzky was engaged—a reliable and predictable German.

The New York Philharmonic, meanwhile, had witnessed the truly amazing transfiguration which a great conductor can effect, and in the two seasons in which Gustav Mahler had been their director he had made them for the first time cognizant of European standards. The pressure of work, involving forty-six concerts in the season of 1909–10, and sixty-five—of which he completed only forty-eight—in the season of 1910–11, friction with the orchestra as well as the committee of the Philharmonic Society early in

1911, and the long and strenuous out-of-town journeys, did their share in undermining his indifferent health which had already given more than usual trouble during the final preparations for the first performance of his Eighth Symphony in Munich, which duly received its world-première there on 12 September, 1910, under its composer's baton. Mahler's final performance was to be in America, on 21 February, 1911, and it was clear that he was mortally ill. The New York Philharmonic now returned to its pedestrian sloth for nine long years until, in 1920, it was awakened by the garrulous voice of Willem Mengelberg. But it was not to achieve an identity which was recognisably American for more than twenty-five years with the advent, as successor to Artur Rodzinski, of Dimitri Mitropoulos. In the interim it was destined to remain a conglomerate, cosmopolitan as New York herself is cosmopolitan, reflecting in its successive musical directors—Mengelberg, Toscanini, Barbirolli and Rodzinski—the similitude of internationalism, without partaking of its essence. With Mitropoulos and Bernstein, the progression to a recognisable entity was to be—in part—fulfilled.

Founded by the Boston banker, Henry Lee Higginson, in 1881—one year before the Berlin Philharmonic—the Boston Symphony Orchestra is America's second oldest orchestra, and the world's sixth, ceding place to the Meiningen Orchestra under Bülow by a short head. Higginson, who had been a student of music in Vienna before he became a colonel in the American Civil War, had heard the famous Vienna Philharmonic and was determined to create such an orchestra in his native country, and from his own pocket he furnished a guarantee of $1 million to the Bostonians. Such a guarantee allowed an annual budget of $100,000 (the annual budget of the New York Philharmonic was $7,000 at this time) and was the first instance in America of a private subsidy of such regal proportions. For thirty-seven years Higginson had borne the weight of this burden single-handed, involving the meeting of all and every deficit until, in 1918, he felt unable to continue, and entrusted its responsibility to a board of nine trustees on the occasion of its incorporation on 7 May, 1918. He had seen an unbroken succession of conductors in London's Sir George Henschel, Germany's Wilhelm Gericke, Hungary's Artur Nikisch, Austria's Emil Paur, a return engagement of Gericke, and now Karl Muck, who had come to Boston initially for one season in 1906 and, twelve years later, had been arrested in a frenzy of nationalist hysteria, the experience of which America was mercifully accorded but a brief eighteen months.

Much had been hoped for under Muck, for although he undoubtedly possessed some objectionable qualities—arrogance of manner, a vicious tongue, and the merciless severity of a Junker officer—he had been a master of every phase of the conductor's art, and an interpreter of supreme attainments. It had been expected that under him the Boston Symphony would achieve international fame, for it is doubtful that there was at that time any other orchestra in the world, of the same level—unless in Philadelphia. The orchestra was offered to Rachmaninoff, who had experienced a conspicuous success with it in 1909, in the dual role of pianist and conductor, but he declined. Successors were found in Henri Rabaud and Pierre Monteux, but they were not capable of maintaining the orchestra's glory—Rabaud because he had neither the necessary capacity nor gift, and Monteux, who was a remarkable conductor, though certainly not a Muck—because the failure of the orchestra to establish a union had resulted in wholesale resignations, and Monteux was compelled to work with an orchestra which had become a skeleton of itself. Frantically, the board of the Boston Symphony searched for a conductor who had the experience, authority, skill, prestige and temperament with which to reconstitute the orchestra, and to restore to it that orchestral prestige and honour which had once been Boston's. Such a conductor was to be Serge Koussevitsky.

Ten years after the foundation of the Boston orchestra, on 7 October, 1891, the Chicago Symphony Orchestra had given its inaugural concert under Theodore Thomas, with Rafael Joseffy as soloist in the Tchaikowsky B flat minor Concerto, and that Thomas was determined to transcend the level of popular taste in Chicago may be seen from the programmes of his subsequent concerts held in the now historic Auditorium—Bach, Gluck, Schumann, Beethoven, Wagner, Schubert, Tchaikowsky—a rigorous diet for an audience which had hitherto been fed on trifles and whipped cream.

> If it is desirable to educate the "masses" to a liking for any certain style of music [wrote a Chicago critic who voiced the sentiments of many of the orchestra's patrons], sound policy dictates that some effective means be adopted for bringing the "masses" aforesaid within the reach of the educative influences, and that the uniform and exclusive offering of what they will not tolerate is hardly to be reckoned among effective means. Mr. Thomas and his advisers seem to think otherwise, and if the Orchestral Association members are willing for their own gratification to pay the cost of what has been given them, nobody else has the right to object . . .

The mid-West in the 1890s was composed of largely pioneering stock of German and Scandinavian heritage, which had little of the culture or sophistication of the East Coast, and it was therefore not unnatural that public and critics alike should give vent to the expression of such sentiments. But the backers of the Chicago Symphony met the deficits of $53,000 for the first season and $50,000 for the second without complaint, for they had faith in their conductor and complete confidence in his ultimate victory—nor was it misplaced, for the antagonism of the Chicago audiences to Thomas and his programmes was finally overcome. The Auditorium grew more and more crowded with each successive season, and deficits decreased sharply. Then, in 1904, came tangible evidence of the esteem in which the citizens of Chicago held their orchestra: a public appeal was launched for the building of a new auditorium for the orchestra, at a cost of $750,000:

> The money began to come in, not only from millionaires and such men of means as had hitherto paid the orchestra's deficit; it came from the public at large, including that great part of the public that is never supposed to know or care a stricken thing about classical music. The rich were asked to give, but it was the common run of humanity to whom we turned and that now spoke out. Working men, merchants, clerks, bookkeepers, schoolteachers, shop girls, scrub women—it is the most amazing thing I know, but these were the people who responded.[1]

Theodore Thomas died the following year, on 4 January, 1905, and it fell to his assistant, Frederick Stock, to assume control of the orchestra for the time being. Born in 1872, Stock had come to the Chicago Symphony as a viola-player from Europe at the age of twenty-three, with an already impressive musical background. He had graduated from the Cologne Conservatoire at the age of fifteen, and had been given the post of a violist in the Municipal Orchestra where, for eight years, he had played under the batons of many famous musicians—Bülow, Brahms, Strauss and Tchaikowsky. Thomas discovered him in Cologne, and urged him to come to America, and it was with no little amazement—both to Stock and to his colleagues—when Thomas selected him as his assistant, for Stock had been an unassuming musician with no very obvious talent for conducting. It is a tribute to Thomas's intuitive powers that he recognised in Stock a potential successor, for while the directors of the orchestra scanned the European horizon with searching eyes, and many Europeans expressed their readiness to come to Chicago, it remained in the event to Frederick Stock to continue, and to build upon, the orchestra's traditions for well-nigh forty years.

A conductor who rises from the orchestra is in an unenviable position, and there has been only one other conductor of distinction who has successfully accomplished the leap which is inevitably involved in crossing, after anything but a very few years, from one side of the orchestra to the other—Charles Munch, an outstanding concertmaster of the Leipzig Gewandhaus

[1] Charles Russell: *The American Symphony Orchestra and Theodore Thomas*, Doubleday, New York, 1927.

Orchestra until his forty-first year. But Munch had been able—and indeed compelled—to return to Paris (for he refused to become a German citizen again, having acquired French citizenship when his native Alsace was returned to France at the end of the First World War), and had been able to abandon his activities as a concertmaster and successfully assume those of a conductor before making his spectacular eighteen-year climb into the saddle of the Boston Symphony Orchestra as Koussevitsky's successor. But for Frederick Stock there had been no such opportunity, and the moment called for supreme tact and innate wisdom for, although he was now amply equipped to conduct most of the works in the repertoire from memory, and could master a new score in the course of a two-hour train ride, he was now in a position where he had to exert his authority over former colleagues, and where his success demanded that he take command and be obeyed. To have given himself airs would have been to instantly antagonise his players, and an antagonistic orchestra can sabotage even the most carefully prepared performance by a great and experienced conductor. Stock maintained a warm and friendly relationship with his orchestra, accepting—and gratefully so— the advice and the opinions of his fellow musicians, but at the same time letting it be understood that his authority was not to be questioned. At another time, and under quite different circumstances, he was to profit from his innate sense of tact, and it was just after America's belated entry into the First World War, when war hysteria was rife, that Stock sensed a situation and rose to it, asking to be excused from his duties as conductor until his American citizenship should become official. But from 1919 until his death in 1944, he conducted the Chicago Symphony uninterruptedly for twenty-five years.

Philadelphia had still been a musical suburb when, in 1900, Fritz Scheel—a friend of Brahms, Bülow, Rubinstein and Tchaikowsky—had conducted four excellent concerts there, and his success had inspired the foundation of an orchestra on some permanent basis. The Philadelphia Orchestra Association was founded the following year and incorporated in 1903, Scheel remaining at its head until his death on 13 March, 1907. He had been a musician of discrimination and taste, refusing to pamper his audiences by offering them salon pieces as so many other conductors were in the habit of doing at that time throughout America—and Great Britain. Indeed, it had taken fully sixty years to educate Leipzig, Dresden and Vienna away from such habits—witness the young Bülow's letter to his mother in 1848. Scheel's programmes had been musically sound, and sometimes even adventurous: in 1903 he had conducted a Beethoven cycle, and in 1904 invited Richard Strauss to conduct three programmes devoted to his own works, with his wife as soloist. Felix Weingartner had appeared as guest conductor for one concert in 1905, and Scheel had been a receptive host to other living composers, giving the American premières of works by Dvořák, Sibelius and Rimsky-Korsakov. He had stubbornly refused to relinquish those standards which he had set for himself and his orchestra, and this had resulted in small audiences and large deficits. With his death in 1907, Campanini, from the Metropolitan, Otto Neitzel, and Scheel's assistant, August Rodemann, completed the season, and were succeeded for the next five years by Karl Pohlig—a competent but colourless musician who had his admirers in Philadelphia but who, during the tours outside that city which the orchestra was frequently called upon to make, was greeted with something less than enthusiasm.

In Boston and New York, the Philadelphia Orchestra had been regarded with something akin to condescension, as being a small-town orchestra from a musically insignificant city. Now, in 1912, it was taken over by Leopold Stokowski, fresh from triumphs in Cincinnati where, since 1909, he had won a tremendous following and had transformed its orchestra—founded in 1895 by Van der Stucken, with Anton Seidl and Henry Schradieck as guest-conductors—from standards of pedestrian routine to those of a near-virtuoso ensemble. Within four years Stokowski had placed Philadelphia on the American musical map with the American première of Mahler's Eighth Symphony in 1916, performed nine times in Philadelphia and twice in New York, and proving an unprecedented triumph for the orchestra and the prelude to its international reputation.

Leopold Anton Stanislas Stokowski had been born in London on 18 April, 1882, the son of a Polish father—who had anglicised his name to Stokes—and an Irish mother. He had come to America in 1905 as organist of St. Bartholomew's Church in New York from St. James's Church, Piccadilly, where he had been organist since graduating from the Royal College of Music two years earlier, and, as a musician, had clung legitimately to his original family name. The Cincinnati orchestra had been disbanded after the 1907 season, in defiance of the American Federation of Musicians[2], and when it was reconstituted in 1909, a new conductor had been found in Leopold Stokowski who had spent the previous summer in Europe studying conducting, and had been accorded some summer concerts in London by Sir Henry Wood. Stokowski's career in Cincinnati is of interest not because he at once showed himself to be a great conductor—which was not the case, and would in any event have been impossible—but because of his autocratic methods and programmes which, by European or any other standards, were incredibly progressive and were to remain consistently so throughout his life: not for

[2] Cincinnati was the first American city to come under the jurisdiction of the A. F. M., and has the dubious honour of having been designated "Local 1" of this American equivalent of the Musicians' Union.

nothing had he been a disciple and admirer of Henry Wood. Like Bülow in his later life, Stokowski in his youth was something of a speech-maker, inculcating discipline into his Cincinnati audiences and admonishing them for unruly behaviour, and his mane of golden hair and magnificent profile lent authority and glamour to his personality. When, in 1912, with the Philadelphia contract already in his pocket, he announced his resignation from the Cincinnati Orchestra—giving as his reasons for so doing his inability to secure the full co-operation of orchestra and management—near panic ensued: the directors of the orchestra came to him with promises of every kind if he would but reconsider his decision, while a spokesman from the orchestra declared on behalf of his colleagues that if he would be prepared to stay, he would assuredly have no further grounds for complaint. But Stokowski remained adamant, saying simply that he had lost the enthusiasm for his task essential to the work of creating an orchestra of consequence.

No other living artist is quite such a contradiction in terms as is Stokowski, combining as he still does extravagant good looks and the flair of the master showman with a rigid asceticism and simplicity of manner both on and off the concert-platform. No other living artist has been so misrepresented, nor has been to such an extent the victim of his own successes, for there is in Stokowski's make-up an element of the naive and the obtuse which are at strange variance with the shrewdness of his perception and the bitterness of his sarcasm. Occasionally a shaft of ironic humour will pierce his cold and uncompromising exterior, as when—at a rehearsal of the Shostakovitch Fifth with the London Symphony Orchestra some eight years ago—he took a second-violinist to task for not marking a bowing in his part, adding, with a perfect sense of timing: "We cannot remember everything we do in this life . . . thank God!" But such moments are rare, and to the uninitiated Stokowski remains an enigma and something of a charlatan. Those London critics who recently voiced their disapproval of his reading of the Beethoven Ninth (a performance which it had been his long-cherished ambition to offer our capital) seemed to have forgotten—or perhaps they never knew—that Stokowski was giving immaculate performances of this work before ever they were born, and that numberless critics before them had come to similar conclusions, and as many had profoundly disagreed with them. There is, too, a supreme logic behind his layout of the orchestra, which was the fruit of many years of experimentation in Philadelphia, and is patently more logical than the division of first and second violins to the left and right of the conductor. (A number of illustrious persons have recently deplored the passing of this practice—which is supremely *illogical*—maintaining that without it, the element of antiphony between first and second violins is lost. I have searched my scores of Haydn, Mozart and

Beethoven in vain to discover more than the most fleeting examples of this alleged "antiphony", which in any case is surely the antithesis of "symphony". By extension, one surely achieves a greater element of antiphony between strings and winds by separating *them*—the principle which governs Stokowski's practice.) Although its present incumbent has by now fulfilled the longer term of office, the Philadelphia Orchestra remains to this day synonymous with the name of Leopold Stokowski for her musicians. The traditions to which her members aspire—the traditions of Kincaid, Tabuteau, Maclaine and Glanz— have all had their origin in the search for perfection which was Stokowski's. The sound of her magnificent string-section under his direction was unique and unmistakable, bearing no vestige of similarity to the chromium-plated gloss with which his successor has imbued it, but rather the thin and characteristic veneer of French polish, with a fine and subtle finish. Stokowski is too austere a man, always intractable in his habits both in his public and private life, to have indulged the opulent tone with which his name is nowadays identified, though it has tended to become richer and mellower with his advancing years. And the vanity of his old-world charm is too refined and too sensitive to have engaged in those antics for which he is often attacked today. To listen to those recordings of Beethoven and Brahms which the Philadelphia Orchestra made under Stokowski's direction in the early 'thirties is to hear some very remarkable music-making indeed—remarkable for its restrained warmth, its youthful sophistry, and the elegance of its control. Comparisons are odious, but there can be no comparison to the brittle harshness of the accompaniments to those recordings of the Rachmaninoff concertos which were made after his resignation with those—of the Paganini Rhapsody and the ubiquitous Second Concerto—which Stokowski made before he resigned, and which belong to an entirely different dimension.

Then, too, Stokowski was—and has remained—an eminently inquisitive man, ever curious to unearth new talent and unknown and undiscovered repertoire. His first performance of Mahler's Eighth Symphony was but the prelude, now echoed a thousandfold, to the American and world premières of countless new works, great and small, distinguished and undistinguished, which but for his initiative would either have had to wait, or would never have seen the light of day at all. Regularly every week throughout his term of office with the Philadelphia Orchestra, Stokowski's Wednesday morning rehearsals were devoted to the reading of new material, much of which would subsequently find its way into his programmes, and this accomplished a dual purpose. Not only did it allow its composers a hearing, but it also kept the orchestra on its toes, and gave them a practice in sight-reading which was to establish a tradition of its own among American orchestras, who now have no rivals in this sphere. British orchestras are proud of their sight-reading ability, and I think without justice, for they have always had to sight-read out of necessity rather than from choice, and do so well only with a literature with whose idiom they are already familiar—and a very parochial idiom it tends nowadays to be, for the days of Henry Wood have seen no continuing tradition in this country. In America, only Koussevitsky and Stock shared with Stokowski that compulsive appetite for new music and that passionate concern which identifies the cultural pioneer. Had this concern for the new been simply for its own sake—had it been made to be their exclusive occupation, rather than drawing strength from the conventional repertoire—then it would have swiftly relegated these artists to the ranks of a Hermann Scherchen or a Pierre Boulez, and the London critics' reactions to Stokowski's performance of the Beethoven Ninth might have been understandable. Both Scherchen and Boulez are—or were—conversant with this masterpiece, which they chose to dissect like a time and motion study, neglecting however to reassemble its component parts. Boulez's 1966 performance with the Philharmonia Orchestra was a conspicuously virgin reading, and this writer could find nothing to recommend it whatsoever—least of all his literal observation of metronome markings which are not only dubious but patently absurd, and which drew from the critics the unqualified praise which is normally reserved for a serious performance. Mr. Boulez is an excellent interpreter of contemporary repertoire, but he should not meddle—or be encouraged to meddle—with the classics until he has found the time and the humility, as has Stokowski, to devote patient and penetrating study to them and to make them, metronome markings and all, his own.

In 1918, when Stokowski had held office for six years, the Philadelphia Orchestra was threatened by a major crisis. It had been his practice, and has remained so, to be adamant over questions of repertoire, with the result that his audiences had been frightened away by the strange and often austere programmes which included works by such then ultramodernists as Schoenberg, Stravinsky and Bartók, and this had been reflected in the management's annual returns. Stokowski had counted on their unwavering support for his principle, which was the education of the Philadelphia public into the ready acceptance of such novelties as being an integral part of their normal diet of Brahms, Beethoven and Strauss, and while the board of directors had been sympathetic to this principle, the hard fact of the alarmingly mounting deficit had to be faced. An anonymous donor—subsequently identified as Edward Box—agreed to underwrite the deficit for the next five years, on condition that a permanent endowment of $500,000 were raised on the orchestra's behalf, and the crisis was averted. This, like most acts of philanthropy, showed a shrewd and acute business sense quite apart from its expression of an implicit faith in Stokowski's abilities, for in appealing to her sense of pride and prestige, it provided a challenge to the city of Philadelphia which she could not reasonably have failed to meet. Nor did she do so, and the next sixteen years saw a prospering of her orchestra's fortunes under the leadership of Leopold Stokowski raising it from the position of a leading provincial orchestra to that, in turn, of national and then of international consequence. Willem Mengelberg conducted two concerts in the 1920–21 season, and subsequent guest-conductors included Ernest Bloch, Alfredo Casella, George Chadwick, Vincent d'Indy, Georges Enesco, Ossip Gabrilowitsch, Eugene Goossens, Darius Milhaud, Pierre Monteux, Horatio Parker, Sergei Rachmaninoff, Frederick Stock and Igor Stravinsky. In 1930, Arturo Toscanini conducted the Philadelphia Orchestra for two weeks while Stokowski did similar service for him in New York. But the vastly greater burden of concerts —including many of the Youth Concerts—had been carried by Stokowski himself, and in 1934, at the age of fifty-two, he tendered his resignation.

There has been much speculation as to what prompted Stokowski to do this, and it is not improbable that a disparity of interests with his manager and contemporary, Arthur Judson, was the root cause. Judson had been appointed manager of the Philadelphia Orchestra in 1915—three years after Stokowski's appointment as conductor—and combined the post with the continuing management of his own concert-agency, Concert Management Arthur Judson, first in Philadelphia and then with an additional office in New York. In 1922 he acquired the management of the New York Philharmonic in addition to that of Philadelphia, in 1926 founded the Judson Radio Program Corporation to meet the demand for artists and programmes for the new medium of broadcasting, in 1928 absorbed the Wolfsohn Musical Bureau which had been founded in 1884 and was the oldest concert-agency in America, and in 1930 merged all these agencies under the corporate title of Columbia Artists, of which he appointed himself president. In the course of creating this empire, Judson had all the while retained his managerial position in Philadelphia (together with that of the New York Philharmonic), and it is significant that, when in 1934 Stokowski proffered his resignation, and the alarmed directors immediately came to him with the offer of the post of "musical director"—carrying with it dictatorial powers—it was Judson who resigned, on a date which has been variously defined as that of June 1934 and June 1935. Stokowski continued in his capacity of musical director for the next four years, undertaking transcontinental tours with the Philadelphia Orchestra in the spring of 1936 and 1937, with Saul Caston and Charles O'Connell as assistant conductors. Eugene Ormandy, whose appointment as associate conductor had been announced in 1936, finally superseded Stokowski in 1938.

There was at the time considerable conjecture as to why Stokowski should have finally retired from his position at the head of a world-famous ensemble with whom his name had become synonymous and inseparable, and conjecture—dissipated into the superfluous anecdote of blind supporter and blind detractor—continues to this day. At this distance of time Stokowski himself has certainly forgotten the reason why, and equally certain is the fact that so restive a soul as his could not indefinitely continue to inhabit a world which he had conquered so completely. After a brief excursion into the realm of the Hollywood film—for which the musical puritan has never been able to excuse him—he turned in 1940 to the youth of his country and founded the "All American Youth Orchestra", a selection of eighty-two of nearly fifteen thousand applicants whose average age was eighteen, and with whom he made the triumphant tour of Central and South America where, in Santiago, his path crossed with that of Erich Kleiber. He has continued to repeat this phenomenon—in 1944 with the New York City Symphony, which was later to play under Leonard Bernstein, in 1954 with the Houston Symphony, and in 1964 again with the American Youth Orchestra, this time in New York and with of course an entirely new personnel, the orchestra of 1940 being now in its early forties. At eighty-seven, youth remains Stokowski's abiding preoccupation, and there is an Aeschylean irony in his ready and near implicit acceptance by the musical youth of America, and his neglect and near disdain by the musical *conneur*. But this preoccupation has not been to the exclusion of all else, and in 1960, for example, he commuted between New York and Philadelphia for twelve performances of *Turandot* at the Metropolitan Opera and six performances of *Gurrelieder* with the Philadelphia Orchestra within the space of three weeks, using crutches occasioned by a fall which had resulted from his playing football with his two young sons by his third wife, Gloria Vanderbilt.

But the most enduring testament to Stokowski's art must be the first performance—later recorded—which he gave on 26 April, 1965, shortly after his eighty-third birthday, of the remarkable Fourth Symphony by Charles Ives. This extraordinary work was Ives' last major composition, written in 1916, when he was forty-one, and anticipates, as do most of his last writings, the techniques, compositional devices, and frequently the actual thematic material of Berg, Schoenberg, Varèse and their disciples by ten years and more.

Ives was born in Danbury, Connecticut, on 20 October, 1874, graduated from the music department of Yale University in 1898, and died in his eightieth year, in New York City, on 19 May, 1954. He was a "week-end" composer, who rose to the head of a successful insurance business in New York, and his most productive work was achieved between 1907 and 1916. His earlier output, which includes the first three symphonies, shows little originality save a gift for melody—which he was evidently unwilling to trust— and a command of counterpoint which was second to none, including that of Brahms. What induced him to make so radical a departure from conventional writing, from his *Soliloquy* of 1907, and *The Unanswered Question* and first violin sonata of 1908 onwards, must remain one of music's enigmas, and for the next eight years he produced music which at that time looked—on paper, and certainly to the musicologists—as though its author had passed the fringe of lunacy. Ives stopped composing altogether after 1916—save for a few songs, and some experiments with quarter-tone music—and here again it was the insidious influences of the musicologists which were to blame. That such a violinist as Milcke, concertmaster to Anton Seidl in New York, should have found his first violin sonata technically and aesthetically un-playable, gave Ives due pause—but not undue pause. That such a musician as Gustav Mahler, with whom Ives shared many musical attributes, should have been eager to mount a performance of the Third Symphony with the New York Philharmonic, only to be dissuaded before he had even seen the score because the "experts" thought the work "derivative" Ives found, not intoler-able, but infinitely discouraging. The Third Symphony is of course derivative —as are his first two Symphonies—and that is one of the essentials of its strength. So are his unconventional harmonic progressions—when they occur—which the musicologists took to be sheer ignorance of "the rules", and were incapable of evaluating the wealth of conventional harmony and counter-point. To Ives's formal weaknesses—which, in 1904, the year of the Third Symphony, were those not of the unconventional but of the *too*-conventional —the musicologists were evidently deaf.

The Fourth Symphony comes as the climax to five years of incredible creative activity which start with the completion of the final draft of the Third Symphony[3] and the beginning of the three *Tone Roads* for chamber orchestra in 1911, and encompass the *Holidays* Symphony (*Washington's Birthday, Decoration Day, Fourth of July* and *Thanksgiving*), completed in 1913, and the *Concord* Sonata, completed in 1915. A *Universe* Symphony was left uncompleted in 1916. The Fourth Symphony itself is a four-movement work which shares many points in common with the *Holidays* Symphony, and in particular a prophetic predisposition to the musical language of Alban

---

[3] Mahler took a copy of the score of the Third Symphony back with him to Europe in 1911, but died before he had the chance of performing it.

Berg. The initial bass-entry in the *Fourth of July* is in many respects identical with the bass-entry at the beginning of the symphonic epilogue (bars 319–21) of *Wozzeck*—not so much in terms of literal notation or harmonic structure as of their spiritual affinity:

Ex. 12

(i)

Ives: *Fourth of July*: [1901-1911]

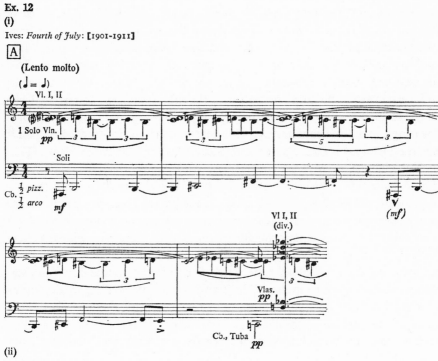

(ii)

Berg: Symphonic Epilogue from *Wozzeck*: [1914-1921]

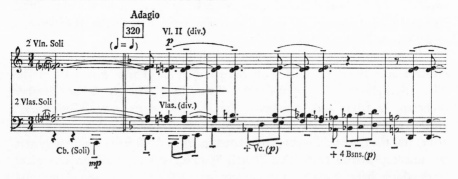

And the opening bars of the *Prelude* of the Fourth Symphony are very prophetic of those by Berg in Marie's monologue from the beginning of Act III of *Wozzeck*:

Ex. 13
(i)
Ives: Prelude from the Fourth Symphony: [1910-1916]

(ii)
Berg: Monologue from the beginning of Act III of *Wozzeck*

Wilfrid Mellers, an eminent British musicologist, in an otherwise laudatory
(if sadly incomplete and often inaccurate) assessment of Charles Ives's work,
produces this astonishing series of mis-statements:

> In some passages of his Fourth Symphony—the most "advanced"
> of all his works—Ives attempts to explore this free polyphony in the
> texture of a symphony orchestra. The first movement is turbulent
> and atonal—the strife of the personal life. The second . . . is diatonic,
> hymm-like, straightforward in rhythm—the simple, communal life.
> The third . . . is tipsily syncopated in its attempt to notate the im-
> provisatory rhythms of the bar-parlour. The fourth . . . seeks a
> "transcendental" synthesis in combining all these elements
> simultaneously, attaining a linear and rhythmic complexity so
> great that it would seem to require three or four conductors . . .[4]

Mellers has of course transposed the second and third movements in his
imagination. The final movement was incomplete until Stokowski located the
missing pages among Ives' papers shortly after his death, and the first performance, under Eugene Goossens in 1927, was—according to Goossens—of
the first three movements only. As such, it was musically necessary to interchange the second and third movements, and this is the origin of Dr. Mellers's
misapprehension, though he has obviously never taken the trouble to look at
the score. (It is arguable, too, whether this is in fact the most "advanced" of
Ives' works: the musical texture of the third *Tone Road* and of some of the
movements from the *Holidays* seems to me to be infinitely more complex.
It certainly sounds so, on paper.) The beginning of the first movement of the
Fourth Symphony is admittedly turbulent, but it is a turbulence which sub-
sides at bar 5, and a prevailing calm endures until the end of a movement
which is, substantially, a short choral-setting of the hymn *Watchman, tell us
of the night*. It represents neither the "strife of the personal (or any other)
life", nor is it atonal in any known sense of that much abused and utterly
misleading term. The second movement (which Mellers mistakenly calls the
third) is not "tipsily syncopated in its attempt to notate the improvisatory
rhythms of the bar-parlour", having nothing whatever to do with the bar-
parlour at all. In Ives's own words, it is "a comedy, in which an exciting, easy
and worldly progress through life is contrasted with the trials of the Pilgrims
in their journey through the swamps and rough country. The occasional slow
episodes—Pilgrims' hymns—are constantly crowded out and overwhelmed
by the former. The dream, or fantasy, ends with the interruption of reality—
the Fourth of July in Concord—brass bands, drum corps, etc." The final
movement does in fact require three conductors—like Stockhausen's *Gruppen*

[4] Wilfrid Mellers: *Music in a New Found Land*, Barrie & Rockliff, 1964, and Chilton,
1965.

—and for much the same reason. The percussion opening—identical with the opening of Varèse's *Ionization*, written in 1931—is scored for five timpani, snare drum, military drum, bass drum, cymbals, triangle, tom-toms, light and heavy gongs, high and low bells, and exists as an entity in itself, maintaining a rigid and immutable rhythm of its own against an orchestra which is called upon to indulge in frequent *rubati, accelerandi*, and *ritardandi*. The wordless chorus which is introduced in the closing pages of the symphony has likewise another rhythmic dimension altogether. Yet the movement's overall effect in terms of resultant sound is far from complex, and reveals supreme logic and supreme greatness.

The first complete performance of Ives's Fourth Symphony was therefore something of an historic occasion, and it is fitting that it should have been Leopold Stokowski who had been able to locate the missing pages of the last movement—with the active collaboration of John Kirkpatrick—simply because he had the musician's imagination to know where to look for them. Much the same thing can be said for Robbins Landon, who unearthed countless Haydn manuscripts which had defied the corporate efforts of other Haydn scholars, and much the same of Heinrich Schliemann or Michael Ventris in their respective discoveries of ancient Troy and the key to Linear B. There is nothing so alarming as a musicianship—or a scholarship—which is devoid of the imaginative processes. But the Carnegie Hall première was not only historic, it was musically significant as well, for Stokowski presented his audience with an immaculate and magnificent reading of what is, by any standards, a very great and very difficult work. Though no greater than those of *avant-garde* writing in recent years, its rhythmic complexities are on occasion enormous—nor are those occasions always so obvious as they would appear to be on paper. The opening of the second movement has—simultaneously—six eighth-notes to the bar in the flutes, brass, percussion and solo piano, five to the bar in the clarinets and second orchestral-piano, seven beats spread over two bars in the bassoons, and two to the bar in the first orchestral piano—while the double-basses have no bar-lines at all. Bar 144 contains no less than twenty different—and simultaneous—rhythmic combinations. Yet these are two perfectly innocuous-sounding passages, where the problems lie hidden far below the surface of actual performance. Both are undulating washes of sound, and we can only marvel that Ives's ear should have had the imagination—and the technique—to give substance to such sounds, and qualities of sound. For there can be no question but that every note fulfils a predetermined function—even when that function is purposely and purposefully indeterminate. There are other sounds which fall too easily on the ear— harmonic and melodic progressions which are sickly in the banality of their associations. Yet these are always lightly under or overscored with soft but jagged dissonances and curious, wayward, fleeting tone-clusters and broken rhythms. There is a violin phrase half way through the second movement (fig. 23) which emerges like a glistening strand of fire between passages of growing tumult, rising like a star over a gulf of chaotic darkness:

Ex. 14

No conductor in the world could fake the sound which Stokowski achieved here, nor the sheer intensity which he brought to the huge string *crescendo tremolando* a few pages later (Fig. 35):

Ex. 15

[*Square note = quarter-tone sharp]

Gunther Schuller's performance at a Promenade Concert on 13 September, 1966, was a pale mockery of the music, the offering of a lip-servant who has yet to be convinced of the stature of this music—as have the members of the BBC Symphony Orchestra. The final climaxes of the second movement, where Ives introduces a Fourth of July which is an intoxicating and ebullient reality, are far removed from the grim reality of the American national holiday which he presents in the third movement of the *Holidays* Symphony—a bitter, psychedelic dream-fantasy which was interpreted by Leonard Bernstein and

the New York Philharmonic, in spite of themselves, as Ives's secret commentary on the real implications of the War of American Independence and war in
general. On the two final pages of this *Fourth of July*, Ives lets loose a fantastic
display of five bars of overwhelming noise which has no equal in the symphonic literature, and it is perhaps significant that a passage very like this has
found its way into the ending of a recent record by one of Britain's leading
"pop" groups, whose especial target for scathing irony has been the sham, the
complacent, the credulous, and the insincere.

In the finale of the Fourth Symphony it became clear that the American
Symphony Orchestra—at least under Leopold Stokowski—is a very distinguished orchestra indeed. It is not a very experienced orchestra, for most
of its members are recent graduates of Juilliard and Curtis who join the
orchestra to gain one or two seasons' experience before moving on to a
permanent post in an established orchestra. The music itself is of immense
distinction, one huge arch of sound from which emerges a slow-paced, basic-
ally two-part exposition in some writing of monumental power:

Ex. 16

Ex. 16 (*continued*)

The absolute control which Stokowski exercises, in particular over his brass, and with the utmost economy, is uncanny, and infinitely more telling than Bernstein's efforts on Ives's behalf with the New York Philharmonic, where the playing is largely routine and lacking in conviction. The Carnegie Hall première of the Fourth Symphony served to give universal sanction to the work of Charles Ives—no longer as the spurious, but as the legitimate "Father of American Music"—and overnight his name became a household word, not only in America, but in this country as well. The Fourth Symphony in its turn furnished the ultimate sanction to the conducting art of Leopold Stokowski himself who, besides an immeasurable service to contemporary music, has served the romantic world of Brahms, the classical world of Beethoven, and the pre-classical world of Bach as far back as the music of Gabrieli, with a long life of constant rededication.

Chapter 7

KOUSSEVITSKY

Leopold Stokowski and Serge Koussevitsky had both been the candid admirers of Artur Nikisch, and it is the quality of Nikisch which unites two otherwise so disparate conductors. Stokowski knew Nikisch's art from the days of his own youth in London, and from Nikisch's tour of the United States with the London Symphony Orchestra in May 1912, which had been the final phase of Stokowski's apprenticeship with the Cincinnati Orchestra. Koussevitsky, eight years Stokowski's senior, had a veneration for Nikisch which went back to his years in Berlin and earlier still to the latter's visits to Russia, where he had heard his posthumous first performance of Tchaikowsky's Sixth Symphony in Moscow in 1895. But whereas Stokowski had emigrated to America at the age of twenty-three, and had forthwith taken out citizenship papers, Koussevitsky was already fifty when he went to the United States for the first time, and only became an American citizen in 1941, at the age of sixty-seven—"I'm sorry I didn't do this earlier", he is reported to have said, with endearing candour, to the immigration officials. Koussevitsky was in fact slow to identify himself with the American ways of life, and courted deserved criticism for using his earlier years with the Boston Symphony Orchestra simply as a good accommodation address during his enforced absences from Paris, which had become his home in the summer of 1920, and was to remain so in effect for nineteen years.

Koussevitsky came to conducting comparatively late, and only when—through his second marriage to the heiress Natalya Konstantinovna—had come the wedding-gift from his father-in-law of a symphony orchestra, which had enabled him to resign his position as principal double-bass with the orchestra of the Bolshoi Theatre. His description of contemporary theatre conditions, printed in the Moscow daily paper, *Russkoye Slovo*, of 28 September, 1905, was critical:

> I have devoted eleven years of my life to service with the orchestra of the Bolshoi Theatre. Access to this so-called temple of art is difficult—the need for many years of preparation, the exacting requirements of the competitive auditions and the scarcity of

vacancies—all these factors pose a series of obstacles to the aspiring young musician. But finally he has conquered them. He has become an artist of the Imperial Theatres. He has achieved the realisation of his hopes and entered the ranks of the chosen . . . In a few years the man is broken, his hopes are extinguished, and the exhausting day to day travail has undermined his strength . . . Daily rehearsals and performances, working on the improvement of one's technique at home, the need to take outside work to supplement the meagre salary—these are the "opportunities" of the chosen one. Add to this the arrogant treatment of some conductors, and of the authorities in general, and the condition of orchestral players becomes a picture which must compel your attention. Your temple has become one of Hades . . . The stultifying spirit of police bureaucracy has penetrated to where it should have no place whatsoever, and has transformed the artist into an artisan and the work of the spirit into the enforced labour of the slave.

Paying sixty to seventy roubles [about £10] a month, demanding every moment of the working day, permitting no leisure, have you the right to expect inspiration, expression, attentiveness? Nowhere in the West do musicians earn so little, and nowhere do they work as hard and without a ray of hope. In the West such orchestras are seen to be schools and seats of learning for the talented, but for us they appear the graveyards of musical talent. Destroying the strength of the young, the theatre destroys itself . . .

Does not the management know of all the defects which I could point out to them, or does it not *want* to know? I am leaving the Theatre—leaving in spite of the fact that my situation there was much better than that of others . . .

Koussevitsky, having effective control of a fortune which ran to many millions, could well afford to leave, but this does not detract from the courage of his statement to the press. Indeed, it would have been musical suicide so to have expressed himself as an existing employee of the Theatre, but now the article—which was reprinted in full in the Russian *Musical Gazette*—gained the added weight of a man of independent means. But this did not prevent his being compelled to flee the country with his wife to avoid arrest by an outraged Tsar (later reported in the *New York Evening Post* of 2 March, 1944), and in the spring of 1906 the Koussevitskys installed themselves in the exclusive Tiergarten district of Berlin. By November 1906, Koussevitsky had emerged as a virtuoso of the double-bass, giving two recitals in Berlin and two in Leipzig—where he also performed the astonishing feat of playing the Saint-Saëns 'Cello Concerto on the double-bass with an *ad hoc* orchestra. In the spring of 1907 he gave two concerts in London, and two more in Paris— the second of these in collaboration with Henri Casadesus, uncle of the distinguished pianist and a viola d'amore player who had founded the Société des Instruments Anciens six years earlier. On 30 and 31 January, 1908, he scored a major triumph in Leipzig, playing under Artur Nikisch at a pair of concerts given by the Gewandhaus Orchestra. There had been considerable embarrassment when Nikisch had earlier withdrawn an invitation for Koussevitsky to play there, on the ground that the Gewandhaus directors did not consider the double-bass to be a musical instrument. But they had witnessed his virtuosity for themselves when Koussevitsky had played there on his own in December of the previous year, and recognised their mistake. Koussevitsky was now, however, preoccupied with more important matters, for on 23 January, 1908, he had made his debut as a conductor—for which he had been preparing for two years—with the Berlin Philharmonic Orchestra and in the Berlin Beethoven Saal, in a programme which consisted of Tchaikowsky's overture to *Romeo and Juliet*, the Rachmaninoff C minor Concerto—with the composer as soloist—the entr'acte from Taneiev's *Orestes*, and Glière's Symphony in C minor. He was now thirty-three, and whatever in later life he may have claimed, he had never been a pupil of Artur Nikisch. Not only do we have Arthur Lourié's testimony for that, but there is also the conclusive evidence that Nikisch was not giving classes in conducting in Berlin during the period of Koussevitsky's residence there. But it is true that he studied the techniques of conducting exclusively from the living examples of famous conductors—Nikisch, Mahler, Strauss, Weingartner, Mottl and Schuch—which yielded him vastly greater profit than the academic ambience of the classroom, whether inhabited by Nikisch or some lesser mortal. No conductor of any distinction has owed his beginnings to the orthodox training of a conservatoire of music, and his subsequent success has always been in spite of rather than because of its insidious influences, which have perverted more real talent than they have laid bare. Whether or not he has grown up in the environment of the opera house, the conductor of consequence has always been "thrown in at the deep end", and has had to learn the bare essentials of his art almost overnight. To that extent Koussevitsky's art was suspect, for he could afford to buy his way into the profession with the services of a great orchestra and unlimited rehearsal time, preceded by weekly rehearsals with a student orchestra in his own home over a period of nearly two years in which he painstakingly learned a large portion of the classical repertoire. If he could not conduct after this he would never be able to—but Koussevitsky *could* conduct after this, though the excellence of his baton technique was never to become one of the distinguishing features of his musical personality.

If this was really Koussevitsky's first essay in conducting [wrote August Spanuth, editor of *Die Signale*, after his Berlin debut], it

must certainly be said that much is to be expected of him . . . After
this sample we can understand how the double-bass, with its limited
literature, did not satisfy his nature . . .

A little over a month later Koussevitsky gave another concert in the same
auditorium and with the same orchestra, conducting—as if to give the Berlin
public a more familiar criterion by which to assess the qualities of the new
conductor—music which now included the *Egmont* overture and Seventh
Symphony by Beethoven.

Now successfully launched on a second career, Koussevitsky embarked on
a third, in collaboration with his wife Natalya—that of music-publishing—
and on 16 March, 1909, *Les Editions Russes de Musique* were officially initiated
with a working capital of half a million roubles. Meanwhile, Koussevitsky had
been pursuing his first career with undiminished zeal, appearing as double-
bass soloist with the Orchestre Colonne in February 1908, in May a further
recital—with the assistance of Henri Casadesus—in London, while in the
spring of 1909 he gave solo recitals in Berlin, Budapest, Dresden, Breslau and
again in London. During this time he was using at least three instruments,
two by old makers—Maggini and Andrea Guarneri—and a third, dated 1889,
by the Saxon firm of Glaessel and Herbig. The charge that Koussevitsky
employed an undersized bass, whose dimensions were more those of the
'cello, was frequently levelled—now and even later—and critics seemed to be
in disagreement on a point which can however be resolved without resort to
the observation that the size of the double-bass is in any case far from
standardised. For its tone-quality and sonority are not appreciably altered by
having the projecting corners at the top of the instrument removed, since
neither the overall length of the belly, nor its width at the bottom, are affected.
But there is a big effective increase in the performer's reach, and he can
negotiate passages in the extreme positions which would otherwise have been
virtually impossible with the small hands which Koussevitsky possessed. The
other charge that he employed *scordatura* and used 'cello strings is of no
significant interest, for so long as he played the music in its original key, his
choice of tuning was very much his own affair, while much the same thing had
been said, over and over again, about choice of strings when 'cellists began
to adopt the now universally accepted practice of using metal strings instead
of gut.

Koussevitsky's London recital in May 1908 was followed by the immediate offer of two concerts as guest conductor of the London Symphony
Orchestra, repeated in the following year with the addition of a Beethoven
concert with the Orchestre Colonne. Then, in the late summer of 1909,
Koussevitsky made a triumphant return to Russia, after an absence of four

years, to conduct a series of eight concerts in Moscow and four in St. Petersburg. Koussevitsky's advance press was hostile, and on 16 September, 1909—
before the new season had even started—the Moscow paper *Russkoye Slovo*
had some acid remarks to make about his predilection for self-advertisement,
declaring in lordly style: "Such methods of self-advertising may not be considered unusual abroad, but here they make a very poor impression indeed . . ."

Koussevitsky's Russian debut took place in St. Petersburg on 27 October,
1909, in a programme consisting of Beethoven's *Egmont* Overture, Bach's
Third Brandenburg Concerto, Weber's *Oberon* Overture, and the Chopin E
minor Concerto with Leopold Godowsky as soloist, and which was repeated
the following week in Moscow. Although the music critic of *Russkoye Slovo*
could not restrain himself from the element of "quite good for a beginner" in
an otherwise laudatory review, it was apparent to the audience from the very
first moment that Koussevitsky's was a talent to be reckoned with—a conclusion which subsequent history was to confirm so abundantly. In the same
critic's review of Koussevitsky's second programme, devoted exclusively to
Russian music, he was however compelled to recognise the "signal talents" of
the new conductor, commenting at length upon the dearth of native talent in
this as compared with other fields, remarking Koussevitsky's virtuoso temperament, the firmness of his beat (which is debatable), and declaring his
ability to say "almost with certainty" that Koussevitsky would become "an
outstanding conductor". Scarcely had Koussevitsky's initial season come to
its end, than he announced his plans for the forthcoming 1910–11 season,
with an array of soloists which was to include Kreisler, Busoni, Scriabin,
Godowsky, and Koussevitsky himself.

Russian musical life, concentrated in her two principal cities of Moscow
and St. Petersburg, was by now the most brilliant—if also the most diffuse—
in the world, although the world still continued to regard Austrian and
German music as being the apotheosis of all that was excellent. It was not
unusual for there to be forty and fifty concerts in the season of each city,
while their respective opera houses were playing to capacity audiences six
nights of the week. Once again, it had been Franz Liszt who had been to a
large extent responsible for this renaissance of musical interest, a tradition
which had been carried further by Bülow and Klindworth and was now led
by Russian musicians—Anton Rubinstein, Alexander Siloti and Vassili
Safonov, with Mengelberg, Strauss and Nikisch as frequent visitors. Safonov,
who had been born on 5 February, 1852, and only made his debut as a conductor at the age of forty-five—having been a distinguished concert pianist
until that time—was in fact the first Russian conductor of consequence,
appearing with the New York Philharmonic in 1904, and as their permanent

conductor from 1906 to 1909, when he was succeeded by Mahler. In 1911, after some guest appearances with the London Philharmonic Society, he became permanent conductor of the concerts of the Imperial Russian Music Society in St. Petersburg, and Koussevitsky found himself with a serious rival, twenty-two years his senior, for the first time—for his contemporary, Sergei Rachmaninoff, had been the permanent conductor of the Bolshoi Theatre in Moscow for only two seasons, 1905–07, and his activities in this field, although impressive, now became increasingly spasmodic.

On 11 March, 1910, Koussevitsky gave another concert with the Berlin Philharmonic—his third—which was attended by Artur Nikisch, who is quoted as having said to Koussevitsky:

> I am astonished. You have been conducting only for such a short time and you can do all this? You are a born conductor. Everything is there—you have the technique, you have the imagination, you have temperament and you bring out everything with such plasticity. It was wonderful, and I really know of no one who could have conducted these works better[1].

There followed, in May, the first of three tours—or, more properly, voyages—down the 2,300 mile length of the Volga river to the Caspian Sea and back with an orchestra of sixty-five players, accompanied by the wives and children of many of them and a number of guest-artists, including Alexander Scriabin as soloist in his own piano concerto. For the tour, which occupied more than two months, Koussevitsky had chartered the steamer *Perivyi*, one of the huge pleasure-boats which used to ply the Volga river in the days before the First World War, and concerts were given in the serviceable theatres of the provincial towns along its banks. It was an inspired masterstroke, bringing the symphonic literature within the reach of many who had never known it at all, and others for whom it was a distant memory of a youth enjoyed in one or another of the larger Russian cities. And it displayed for the first time the astonishing pioneering instinct of its author, as well as providing him with much valuable publicity—for the enterprise did not go unreported in the national press. Nor did Koussevitsky play down to his largely untutored audiences, offering them solid and—so it would have appeared—heavy musical fare, but the evidence of the dividends which accrued was overwhelming. Koussevitsky was asked back again and yet again, and the tours—each time engaging an increased number of musicians—continued biennially until 1914, after which the advent of the First World War made their continuance impossible.

[1] Arthur Lourié: *Koussevitzky and his Epoch*, Alfred A. Knopf, New York, 1931.

Meanwhile, Vassili Safonov had returned to St. Petersburg, and Koussevitsky resolved to found his own orchestra in Moscow, which made its debut there in October 1911 with the performance within a single week of all nine symphonies, the Fourth Piano Concerto and the Violin Concerto by Beethoven. The season continued with fortnightly concerts in Moscow—each repeated the following weeek in St. Petersburg—and the musicians were engaged on an annual and exclusive basis. Profits of the enterprise—if any—were to go to the orchestra, while the possibility of deficit was guaranteed by Koussevitsky. At the end of the first season, which had had only two guest-conductors—Artur Bodanzky with Mahler's Fourth Symphony, a novelty for Russia, and Ernst Wendel with a Liszt memorial programme—twenty musicians were given notice, and duly replaced. The 1912–13 season opened once again with a festival of four concerts within a single week, this time devoted to the music of Tchaikowsky which—strange though it may now seem—had become rather neglected in Russia, as indeed elsewhere. The remainder of the season followed the pattern of its predecessors—there were again two guest conductors, Bodanzky being re-engaged to conduct Mahler's Seventh Symphony—and was followed by a provincial tour with four-day cycles of all nine Beethoven symphonies in Odessa, Kiev, Kharkov and Rostov. The 1913–14 season was Koussevitsky's most brilliant in Russia. Artur Nikisch and Claude Debussy were the guest conductors—the latter in a programme of his own works—and Ferruccio Busoni was soloist in his Concerto for Piano, Chorus and Orchestra. At the opening pair of concerts, Koussevitsky conducted an impassioned reading of the Verdi *Requiem*, and at its close the first concert performance of Stravinsky's *Le Sacre du Printemps*—preceding the Paris concert-première under Pierre Monteux by five weeks—and when his championship of new music was once again attacked. The Russian *Musical Gazette* praised Koussevitsky and his orchestra for doing their best in "trying to overcome that negation of rhythm which is the substance of Stravinsky's music".

The outbreak of war in August 1914 was naturally to have serious repercussions on the organised musical life of Russia, and within a few months all but two of the concert-giving enterprises in Moscow had disappeared. One exception was Koussevitsky's orchestra, and the other the orchestra of the Imperial Russian Music Society, which had been deterred from disbanding largely by Koussevitsky's example. Almost immediately there broke out in the Russian national press the familiar controversy over "alien music," the more conservative of Russian music enjoyed a frenzy of nationalist zeal, and French, Polish, English and Scandinavian composers became *personae non gratae*. St. Petersburg was re-christened Petrograd, and Koussevitsky made a virtue of necessity by engaging young Russian artists in place of foreign celebrities who were no longer available. A concert given by Koussevitsky in memory of Liadov, who had died on 28 August, 1914, inevitably invited comparison by the critics with another concert of that composer's works given shortly afterwards under the baton of Rachmaninoff, and this is not without significance when one considers the distinction to which Koussevitsky had by now attained. Infrequent though Rachmaninoff's appearances on the rostrum had by now become, his serious comparison with a personality of the stature of Koussevitsky must account for the offer, five years previously and again four years later, of the conductorship of the Boston Symphony Orchestra to Sergei Rachmaninoff.

The summer of 1915 witnessed an important advance in the fortunes of Koussevitsky's publishing house, when it bought out, for 300,000 roubles, the firm of Guttheil of Moscow which had itself succeeded the old St. Petersburg house of Stellkowski many years before, acquiring in the process a priceless collection of old Russian manuscripts. The house of Guttheil had been run on a strictly commercial basis, confining itself largely to reprinting prestige material from old plates, and only publishing the music of Rachmaninoff because it could be seen to be commercially viable—chiefly as a result of the ubiquitous C sharp minor *Prelude*. The new season began with a cycle of four concerts in memory of Scriabin, who had died on 25 April, 1915, at the age of forty-three, and at which all the major orchestral works by Scriabin were played, including the Piano Concerto, with Rachmaninoff as soloist. The body of the 1915–16 season contained a programme devoted to the music of Glazounov, with the fifteen-year-old Jascha Heifetz as soloist in the Violin Concerto, and another devoted to the music of Rachmaninoff, including the Third Piano Concerto with the composer as soloist, and the *Bells* Symphony—set to a translation of the text of the same name by Edgar Allan Poe. Further programmes included Scriabin's *Prometheus*, Berlioz's *Damnation of Faust*, and Tchaikowsky's *Manfred*, but thereafter the progress of the war made any organised music-making increasingly impossible. Yet Koussevitsky somehow managed to prevail over the wartime difficulties, and was able to present a Beethoven programme in Moscow in October 1916 with a pick-up orchestra, which prompted the press to acknowledge his essential value as a really significant conductor.

With the fall of the Tsar in February 1917, the new government, led by Kerensky, reorganised the Imperial Orchestra in St. Petersburg to meet the new conditions, changing its name to the State Symphony Orchestra, and in recognition of Koussevitsky's services to Russian music and his reputation for democratic tendencies, he was appointed musical director on 15 May. Then came the October Revolution, and the Kerensky government was in turn succeeded by the Bolsheviki. Koussevitsky's attitude towards his official position, and towards the Bolshevikaya government, was expressed in a letter to the press shortly afterwards, which is prophetic of Furtwängler's attitude to the Nazi regime some sixteen years later:

> In circles closely connected with the State Orchestra and interested in its existence, certain persons have spread the report that I, who am in command of the orchestra, am in full accord with the government of the People's Commissars. Furthermore, the fact that in the present circumstances I continue to give concerts is held by these persons to be proof of my readiness to come to terms with the "existing state of things"—that is, to recognise them as being lawful and moral.
>
> All this is entirely false. As I definitely stated in the course of the first few days after the recent revolution, there can be no question of an "accord" between myself and the new government: like all sensible people, I shall submit only to the government which shall be appointed by constituent assembly. Until then, I shall remain in charge of the State Orchestra, on the distinct understanding that no new "powers that be" shall interfere in any way with its affairs.
>
> In regard to the concerts, I shall continue to give them—not, of course, to show my approval of the harshest, most despotic and most violent regime which has ever reigned over us—but for the sake of those chosen, sensitive representatives of our suffering society to whom music is the equivalent of their daily bread and who seek in it a respite, albeit a brief one, from the hideous element of baseness and brutality which has us in its grasp.[2]

The fact that this letter did not lead to his immediate arrest is eloquent of the popularity and respect which Koussevitsky enjoyed—eloquent too of a fear among the youthful Boshevikaya of Koussevitsky's power as a man of immense wealth. For even after Mme. Koussevitsky's fortune had been nationalised, the Koussevitskys continued to live in style, and there was clearly a limit to the amount of privation to which they could be subjected without incurring a popular outcry. Koussevitsky continued to give concerts, and in April 1919 made his operatic debut at the Bolshoi Theatre with Tchaikowsky's *Pique Dame*. But this period, with its overt political orientation, is of little musical interest. When, in late May of 1920, after an abortive earlier attempt to flee the country, the Koussevitskys were finally given leave by the authorities to go abroad for a year, it must have been obvious to everyone that they would never return.

From Moscow their way led to Berlin—to investigate the condition of

[2] Arthur Lourié: *Sergei Koussevitsky and his Epoch.*

F

their publishing house which had been transferred to that city soon after its foundation, and which was not in such a bad way as they had been led to believe—and thence to Paris, which was to become their home for the next four years, and from where they could finally take stock of the situation. In December 1920, Koussevitsky was invited to make two appearances at the Accademia Santa Caecilia in Rome—one, under Molinari, on the double-bass—and shortly after the New Year he gave a short series of Sunday concerts with a nondescript orchestra at the Royal Albert Hall in London. In April and May 1921, he gave three concerts at the Salle Gaveau in Paris, and in June returned to London for a further series, now with the established London Symphony Orchestra—including, on 10 June, the controversial first performance of Stravinsky's *Symphonies pour les Instruments à Vent*, which was reported at length by the late Ernest Newman and which, fifteen years later, Stravinsky himself was to comment on in his autobiography. Then, in November 1921, were inaugurated at the Paris Opéra the Concerts Symphoniques Koussevitsky, which came to consist of four concerts given twice yearly, in the spring and autumn, and enjoyed a tremendous vogue, for Koussevitsky had quickly become the *grand seigneur* of Parisian musical life. He gave intermittent concerts with the Berlin Philharmonic, and more regular concerts with the London Symphony Orchestra, and ventured further into the field of opera with performances, in Paris and Barcelona, of *Boris Godounoff*, *Khovantshchina*, *Prince Igor* and *Pique Dame*. Then, in the summer of 1923, came the announcement of his appointment as conductor of the Boston Symphony Orchestra, to take effect from the autumn of 1924. Koussevitsky was to have, at long last, and beyond the income which was still pouring in from his wife's fortune, that salary which can alone constitute a competence of good living and artistic independence.

Writing in the *Baltimore Sun* of 6 April, 1924, Henrietta Strauss gave voice—in the course of a review devoted to a concert by Koussevitsky's predecessor, Pierre Monteux—to remarks whose scurrility leaves little to the imagination, and an extremely bad taste in the mouth:

> He [Monteux] has done more than rescue the Boston Symphony Orchestra from a threatened disintegration—he has made it once more supreme. His successor—Koussevitsky—will doubtless reap the glory, for Koussevitsky is one of the *prima donna* species. But in the memory of the few it will be Pierre Monteux who deserved our gratitude for saving our greatest orchestra.

Whatever may have been the merits of the late Pierre Monteux—and as a conductor he possibly possessed greater musicianship than did Koussevitsky —he could not by any stretch of the imagination have been called a musical personality in the sense that that term is usually intended to convey. His extreme vanity and exaggerated sense of *amour propre* were never of an order to sustain the burden of the great tradition of musical personalities who —though their nature be extrovert or introvert—must always be *seen* to be musical personalities, and larger than life. In the language of our American friends, Monteux was, in short, something of a "cold fish". So was Wein-gartner. Their vocations could both of them have been that of teaching in its broader sense, were it not for the fact that this too was to be Koussevitsky's vocation—as it had been that of Nikisch and Bülow and Liszt before him. A member of the Boston Symphony Orchestra told me, after a concert given by Pierre Monteux at Tanglewood in 1956:

> Koussevitsky was about the best-hated conductor we ever had to play under, and there were times when I would have gladly forfeited my career for the pleasure of spitting in his face. But there was something about him which stopped you—something which made you realise in time that you were proud to belong to such an orchestra as this, although, and even because, it entailed having to play under him.

The professional orchestral musician dislikes almost nothing more than to submit to the leadership of one whose professionalism is not complete, and he resents it as a personal indignity although, as a professional, he knows that he is bound to obey orders. If, in addition, he has any artistic conscience or human sympathy, he can assist the incompetent conductor by effectively con-cealing from the audience that conductor's more glaring errors, though this will only be at the expense of his personal respect. Koussevitsky, having initially won the respect of the orchestra at their New York debut on 27 November, 1924—a respect which the Bostonian audience was too shabbily genteel to have seriously entertained of a newcomer—he promptly forfeited it when, at the end of the season, he went to the trustees with the demand for wholesale dismissals. But almost from the first Koussevitsky had realised that the Boston orchestra was not the peerless ensemble which he had been led to believe when, in the summer of 1923, he had agreed to become its conductor. It was not so bad, it is true, as he and his supporters made it out to be, but neither was it as good as the apologists for Monteux had claimed. His action inevitably backfired, and he found himself facing the very charge of in-competence which he had levelled against nearly twenty of the orchestra's musicians, for even the most indulgent and far-sighted orchestral player will question the competence of a conductor whose detailed purpose he does not understand. In some respects, of course, Koussevitsky *was* incompetent, call-ing extra rehearsals to assist him with unfamiliar scores which he should have been able to bring before the orchestra already mastered, and picking the most senseless quarrels with musicians whom he did not like. It was to be another two years before Koussevitsky could—or would—provide them with the evidence that his own musicianship was not at fault, and by this time the complement of the Boston Symphony Orchestra had become stable.

On 4 October, 1927, Koussevitsky gave his first public recital in America on the double-bass—an event which was repeated the following season in New York, when it occasioned the following comment from Samuel Chotzinoff, critic of the New York *World*:

> Had Mr. Koussevitsky played the double-bass for us before he assumed his duties with the Boston Symphony Orchestra, we would have been made aware at once of his peculiar fitness for the regeneration of the late Mr. Higginson's pride and joy . . . We have known conductors who were excellent musicians, but never having mastered an orchestral instrument themselves, they were content with performances that on the technical side left much to be desired.

This shows faulty reasoning on the part of the New York critic, and a lack of comprehension of that standard of professionalism to which Koussevitsky the conductor subscribed. Any display of instrumental prowess on the part of a conductor is of course always interesting, but it should never be allowed to assume the guise of special pleading. The position of the conductor must be absolute—or as absolute as he can reasonably make it—and to have to resort to the medium of the orchestral instrument as a means of identifying himself with the orchestra of which he has charge must inevitably undermine his authority in the long run. Koussevitsky knew instinctively that he had first to make his point as a conductor, and in conductor's terms, and only then could he afford to provide his musicians and his public with the gratuitous evidence of mastery in a field which had long since become secondary. "If he can play the bass like that", his musicians would now say, "he must assuredly have qualities as a conductor which we have been missing". And every distinguished conductor assuredly has qualities which even the most distinguished orchestra will inevitably miss, for the orchestral player—who might seem to be in the best position to assess a conductor's merits—is notoriously obtuse by very reason of the fact that such an assessment can never be objective. The only person qualified to pass final judgement on a conductor is another conductor of equal or greater calibre, and in that such a judgement can never be spontaneous, and requires a detailed examination of every aspect of the conductor's art, it can never be effectively realised.

Koussevitsky's Paris concerts continued twice-yearly until 1929, and he and his wife continued to visit Europe every summer, until the outbreak of the Second World War made any continuance impossible. With the growing spirit of isolationism in the United States, Koussevitsky invited much criticism on this account, although his service to contemporary music—and to contemporary American music in particular—was pursued with continuing and undiminishing zeal at his Boston concerts and on the orchestra's tours to New York and the mid-West. Between 1924 and 1941, when Koussevitsky became an American citizen, he gave the world first performances of ninety-nine works, of which no fewer than seventy-five were American or American-orientated—two in 1924, two in 1925, four in 1926, seven in 1927, nine in 1928, two in 1929 (the first year of the depression), six in 1930, six in 1931, six in 1932, three in 1933, four in 1934, four in 1935, three in 1936, one only in 1937, five in 1938, five in 1939, two in 1940, and four in 1941. Nor was this to the neglect of the conventional repertoire, which was extremely catholic in the breadth of its taste—though there were naturally those works for which Koussevitsky's temperament was better suited, and those which were his especial favourites (which is not by any means necessarily the same thing.) His predilection for Russian repertoire was offset by an equal respect for the music of Bach and Haydn, and when, in March 1941, Richard Burgin—concertmaster and, by this time, assistant-conductor—was chosen to lead the Boston Symphony Orchestra in Koussevitsky's transcription for winds of Bach's C major Prelude and Fugue, Koussevisky found himself favourably compared with Stokowski, the subtlety of whose Bach transcriptions had become legendary[3]. In 1927, Koussevitsky added to his labours the additional burden of an elaborate Beethoven Festival, which drew from Ernest Newman the comment: "I never want nor expect to hear more exquisite orchestral playing than I have heard during the last few days in Boston".

Having undergone a crisis the previous year, when Koussevitsky had announced that he would not seek a renewal of the original three-year term of his contract when it expired at the end of the 1926–27 season, Koussevitsky had now conquered the unforeseen difficulties which a season of more than a hundred concerts imposed, and began to settle into his work at Symphony Hall with increasing enthusiasm. The twenty-six years of his ultimate tenure of office in Boston is remarkable—as that of his colleague Leopold Stokowski was legendary—not by reason of the turbulence of his personality or his self-assured caprice (though such factors did of course provide incidental stimulus), but for that sense of pride which has already been referred to and which

[3] The transcription of Bach's famous Toccata and Fugue in D minor—a controversial showpiece whose authorship is generally attributed to Stokowski—was in reality an occasional piece written by a member of the Philadelphia Orchestra who persuaded Stokowski to give it the blessing of his own name. Stokowski's own transcriptions, while using large forces, are characteristic for their economy and restraint, and fidelity to the native spirit of Bach.

Koussevitsky generated and maintained among his players and the community at large. This ability to restore the belief of his musicians in the jaded classic, to instil and sustain it through the rehearsals and performances of initially antipathetic contemporary works, is the essential and seemingly uneventful aspect of truly great conducting—an aspect shared by Frederick Stock in Chicago for more than forty years, and more recently by Georg Szell in Cleveland. It is the unique end-product of the interpretative art, and how wrong-headed even the most distinguished authority can be over this point may be adduced from the following extracts—one from the mouth of no less a musical personality than Igor Stravinsky:

> It was romantic music that unduly inflated the personality of the Kapellmeister even to the point of conferring upon him—along with the prestige that he today enjoys on his podium, which in itself concentrates attention upon him—the discretionary power which he exerts over music committed to his care. Perched on his sybilline tripod, he imposes his own tempi, his own particular nuances on the compositions he conducts, and he even reaches the point of talking with naïve impudence of his specialities, of *his* Fifth, of *his* Seventh, the way a chef boasts of a dish of his own concoction.

Perhaps Stravinsky would prefer that flavour which results from the ministrations of the cook-general. Again, in the other extract:

> Koussevitsky's thesis (for his Honorary Doctorate at Harvard University) . . . is basically a "rationalisation" of his desire to present music in accordance with his personal impulses. It is briefly suggested as follows: The great music of the past was written in a different social *milieu* from ours, for listeners having different intellectual, moral and aesthetic concepts. If the contemporary listener is to be affected by this music of the past in the same way as the listeners of the past for whom it was written, it must be reinterpreted for him in terms of the present. If Beethoven's music, for example, is interpreted today in the same way as it was interpreted in Beethoven's day, it misses its mark on present-day listeners.
>
> This argument is plausible but deceptive. An analogy with the other arts seems to me proper. Does anyone seriously suggest that, to make Spenser more understandable to twentieth-century readers, his text should be revised? Or that a painting of Michelangelo be touched up for twentieth-century onlookers? Or that the ruins of the Acropolis be remodelled so that they may "live" for people postdating them by more than twenty centuries? The last suggestion is patently absurd, and for that very reason suggests the key to the fallacy of the Koussevitskian argument . . .[4]

[4] Moses Smith: *Koussevitsky*: Allen, Towne and Heath, 1947.

It is however Mr. Smith's own argument which is fallacious. No one is seriously suggesting that Spenser's text be revised, but rather that the twentieth-century reader will read his poetry with an emphasis which has been informed—as that of Spenser's contemporaries could not have been—by the vastly wider experience of twentieth-century life. No one is seriously suggesting that Michelangelo be "touched-up"—though his unrestored paintings invite an unfavourable comparison with those of his sculptures (the *David*, for example) which have been preserved more or less intact, while restoration does generally speaking evoke the reaction that the onlooker is seeing the picture quite literally "for the first time". And the last observation is itself patently absurd, for if Koussevitsky had been suggesting that the ruins of the Acropolis be remodelled, he would have been saying the exact opposite of what he did in fact say. It is we who change, as Mr. Smith quite rightly concludes, but the architecture also changes (as does the Michelangelo painting), being subject to a constant process of decay from the very moment of its realisation—although it will acquire other qualities in that self-same process. This is not so with music, which is a dynamic and not a static element—and here the fallacies of both Mr. Stravinsky's and Mr. Smith's arguments become self-apparent. It is the burden of Stravinsky's complaint that everything which the composer demands is (or should be) in the score—though Mr. Smith does not find himself in agreement with this contention. Both however agree that the educated man should be able to project himself into the past and appreciate its culture, and this—outside the moribund influences of the museum—is exactly what he cannot do. The historically accurate—but too literal—castle of Hollywood's creation transgresses and offends his sense of history, for it no longer presents for him any sense of magic or wonder. Neither, so many people will argue, does the music of Stravinsky when it is conducted by Stravinsky—though the fervent admirer will always be able to invent that magic and wonder for himself, which is precisely what Stravinsky is requiring his listeners *not* to do, if I have understood him correctly or at all.

Koussevitsky's decision, in 1941, to follow the example of the twenty-three-year old Stokowski in 1905, and become an American citizen, was but the outward manifestation of a growing inner resolve to identify himself with the myriad facet which is American culture, and with the American way of life as a whole. Ten years earlier, during the brilliant fiftieth anniversary season of the Boston Symphony Orchestra, he had had the occasion to remark that, in his view, the orchestra was now vastly superior to anything which France possessed, or had ever possessed since the days of Wagner's youth—and this despite the fact that the Boston orchestra was by now predominantly

French or Franco-Russian in its origin, which must have given Koussevitsky substantial food for reflection. By 1941 the Boston Symphony Orchestra had unquestionably become the greatest orchestra in the world, with the Philadelphia Orchestra—on those occasions when Leopold Stokowski still conducted them—as a close rival. Certainly nothing to compete with them existed at that time in Europe, for she was benighted by the evil genius of Hitler which had perverted the native talents of Germany and Austria, and overwhelmed those of Amsterdam. But it is a moot question whether, even under those conditions of normalcy which had obtained until eight years previously, Europe could have boasted two such institutions as the orchestras of Boston and Philadelphia had, by the middle 'thirties, become.

Chapter 8

MENGELBERG AND TOSCANINI

Everything which can be said about America as a whole can be said about New York. The paradox of a unified diversity—mitigated by the vast distances which separate and divide, within one and the same country, New England from Los Angeles and New Orleans from Lake Superior—finds in the island of Manhattan a concentration of expression in her beauty and her brashness, her candour and her cruelty, which makes her at one and the same time the most representative and the least typical city of the United States. America is a nation of contradictions, and the most flagrant contradiction of all is New York City—not, as the American provincial naïvely believes, a city to be visited, but very definitely a city to live in, to identify oneself with, to explore endlessly and patiently, for New York is above all jealous and ultra-sensitive, and yields but rarely and then unwillingly to the inquisitive stranger the true riches which lie buried beneath her granite subsoil. New York is a synthesis of all that is best and worst in the American way of life: but more than this, she has inherited from the metropolitan cities of Europe which engendered her—from Berlin, Paris, Rome, London and Amsterdam—identical qualities which are reflected in her constant conflict between acceptance of the Old World and a suspicion of its ways, and a faith in the New which is tempered by an incipient sense of inadequacy. Of every three people whom one meets on her streets, so the saying goes, one will be a musician. (Of the other two, one will be a millionaire—or his widow—and the other the PR man for all three.) For music in New York is synonymous with big business and public relations—a thriving, expert, cynical industry which brooks no dilettantism and suffers no fool gladly, or at all.

The history of the first hundred years of her Philharmonic Society is one of an almost uninterrupted succession of European conductors, with here and there the name of a native American who was in more than one sense a musical pioneer—Ureli Corelli Hill, her founder and first conductor, George Loder, William Alpers, Theodore Thomas, Leopold and Walter Damrosch. From 1892—the fiftieth anniversary of the foundation of the New York

Philharmonic Society on 7 December, 1842—the balance of visiting European conductors became marked, and from 1903, when Walter Damrosch conducted the Philharmonic for one season, no native American was to be their permanent conductor until the accession of Leonard Bernstein in 1958. In 1892, Anton Seidl became their first conductor of any permanency, holding office for six years and combining his activities with those of musical director of the Metropolitan Opera, which had been opened nine years earlier. He was succeeded on his death in 1898 by Emil Paur, who conducted the Philharmonic for the next four years—combining this with activity at the Metropolitan only during the 1899–1900 season, however, for the orchestra was by this time beginning to acquire an articulate identity, and made ever-increasing calls on her conductor's attention. After Walter Damrosch's brief interregnum in the 1902–03 season, there followed in the course of the next three years the engagement of a succession of guest conductors in the attempt to discover a new permanent musical director, and the roster of names includes those of Edouard Colonne, Max Fiedler, Victor Herbert, Karl Panzer, Vassili Safonov, Richard Strauss and Henry Wood. Safonov was engaged in 1906, but three years later returned to Russia where Koussevitsky had recently appeared as a serious rival. Gustav Mahler, who had been hounded from the Vienna Opera after ten years of unremitting service, was at that time engaged by the Metropolitan Opera, and was accordingly offered the appointment to the Philharmonic in 1909.

Mahler's merits as a conductor—though as a composer he wrote nothing in the operatic medium—were those of the opera-house, and it had been at the start of his first productive term of office at the Hamburg Stadttheater in 1891 that he had won the accolade of Hans von Bülow—then director of the Berlin Philharmonic. Mahler, in short, was as yet unfamiliar with the workings of a great symphony orchestra—witness his abandonment of the Vienna Philharmonic to Felix Weingartner six years previously—and this the New York Philharmonic was now tending to become. Mahler found his duties irksome and the pressure of work, in an already weakened condition, arduous to the point of physical collapse. During the first season, which included the first performance with the New York Philharmonic of Rachmaninoff's Third Piano Concerto—a work written specifically for America—he had had to conduct no less than sixty-five concerts, and a similar number was scheduled for the following season, although Mahler was destined never to complete it. (Rachmaninoff has remarked the meticulous attention which Mahler accorded his concerto—a work with whose idiom Mahler cannot have had any very great sympathy—and which was, he declared, a revelation largely instrumental to his own success, in December 1909, in the role of conductor-pianist with the Boston Symphony Orchestra. It was not without gentle irony, however, that he described Mahler's discussion with the concertmaster of the New York Philharmonic of a bowing which he himself had already discussed with the concertmaster of the Moscow Philharmonic. Mahler was for changing it, but the New York concertmaster expressed his reluctance to do so, and in the event it was left as it stood.)[1]

It was at Mahler's recommendation that Josef Stransky, who had been first conductor at the Prague Landestheater from 1898 to 1903, and at the Hamburg Stadttheater from 1903 to 1911, succeeded him when he collapsed in February 1911, and mortal illness was diagnosed. Stransky, though of a somewhat pedestrian disposition, appears to have made an initially favourable impression, and Joseph Pulitzer's bequest to the New York Philharmonic the following year enabled him to further Mahler's reforms, which included the establishment of daily rehearsals throughout the twenty-six week season, as it then was. He retained the post of conductor of the Philharmonic throughout the increasingly difficult war years, and their immediate aftermath, when few European artists were available, but although Stransky continued to conduct until 1923, it had become clear to the directors of the orchestra two years earlier that a personality was needed who could more effectively carry on the traditions of Mahler. Accordingly his pupil and disciple, Willem Mengelberg, was appointed musical director of the Philharmonic in 1921.

Born in Utrecht in 1871, Mengelberg had become conductor of the Lucerne orchestra at the age of twenty-one, and followed this with his appointment as musical director in 1895, at the age of twenty-four, of the Amsterdam Concertgebouw Orchestra which had been conducted since the opening of the Concertgebouw seven years earlier by Willem Kes, who was later to go to Moscow. Mengelberg quickly brought the orchestra to a high level of virtuosity, and gave the first world performance of Richard Strauss's *Ein Heldenleben*—which had been completed on 27 December, 1898, and is dedicated to Mengelberg—in the early months of 1899[2]. (Strauss, it will be recalled, had been appointed general musical director of the Berlin Opera on 1 November, 1898.) Although a passionate disciple of Mahler's music—he was to give a Mahler Festival during his first New York season—Mengelberg was to make something of a *cause célèbre* of *Heldenleben*, and would lavish on it a care and attention which exceeded (if that were possible) that devoted to the more familiar works of the repertoire as it then was. (Even today *Heldenleben*, in common with *Don Quixote*, *Also sprach Zarathustra* and *Macbeth*, is surprisingly unfamiliar to even first-class orchestras unless their members have had to play it at all recently. But this may be said of the greater part of the standard repertoire.) I make no apology for quoting Bernard Shore here at considerable length, for the passage[3]—referring to Mengelberg's first encounter with the BBC Symphony Orchestra, which had been founded in 1930—not only provides the musician with an object lesson which can immediately be related to Mengelberg's work with other orchestras, but also the general reader with a substantial picture of the insight which every great conductor should be able to bring to every work with which he has to deal:

> Tuning with him [Mengelberg] is a ceremony which may take anything from five minutes to (in extreme cases) two hours. The first violins are directed to take the A only from the first oboe, followed by the seconds, violas, 'celli and basses. The rest of the orchestra then tunes, starting with the flutes and ending with the tuba. Not until the whole orchestra has the A are the strings allowed to tune their other strings. The oboe officiates like a High Priest, and has to stand and turn to the department concerned, for the benefit of those further away, while Mengelberg, sitting like a Buddha on the rostrum, criticises the slightest deviation in pitch. On the first occasion tuning took twenty-five minutes, and gave rise to his first dissertation:
>
> "It has taken twenty-five minutes to tune—it should take two minutes! You may be first-class orchestra, but if you play not in tune?—It is difficult for musicians—Fifty years ago it did not matter so much perhaps: but now it is necessary to have full house, and if you play not in tune, well—the house, it will be empty! The first oboe, first clarinet must help their colleagues, like a mother her children: and you, Mr. Oboe, must make the face, if someone play bad A!—You must watch, like the cat the mouse—There—that little double-bass, you hear him behind there?"
>
> Tuning eventually comes down to a matter of five or six minutes. If he is starting the programme with *A Midsummer Night's Dream*, he will have all the woodwind chords played to him at the last moment, before going on the platform.
>
> Usually he likes five rehearsals for a symphony concert—two for the winds, two for the strings, and the final rehearsal together. He does not find it necessary to have more than one general rehearsal, for he says that if sufficient detailed work is put in by the two halves of the orchestra, he has no difficulty in joining them up. Mostly he rehearses from memory. The whole of his first rehearsal with the BBC Orchestra was devoted to the opening portion of *Ein Helden-leben*, as far as the entry of the solo violin.
>
> Thoroughly characteristic of his methods was the way in which he tackled the great opening phrase. Each note of the arpeggio had to be detached, in spite of the composer's direction, because, he said, the audience should hear every note, "and if they are all slurred by

[3] Bernard Shore: *The Orchestra Speaks*, Longman, Green & Co., London, 1938.

the strings, there will be no definition, and the passage will sound like a chord of E flat", whereas he wants to make the effect of a brilliantly clear arpeggio. The first two notes after the tied minim [half-note] are invariably lost in performance, consequently he puts a rest or comma in place of the tie. For the same reason he places another in the second bar, after the dotted minim C, to ensure an incisive attack on the last beat of the bar, and the strings are directed to hit the E flat with the point of the bow. However, the next phrase is played *legatissimo* to the last beat of bar 4, in front of which a breath-mark allows for another attack leading to the two heavily accented minims.

Four bars after fig. 1, he again cuts out the ties and inserts rests. This may, on paper, seem very drastic, but the effect in playing is brilliant, and the sharp contrast between *sostenuto* and *staccato* stands out with the greatest effect. Not only is this opening passage typical of his genius for producing superb playing, but it also shows his attitude to the composition he is interpreting. Nothing will induce him to obey blindly the composer's directions if his own experience tells him that they could be made more effective by a slight alteration. In his own words: "Beethoven, like many other composers, sometimes makes *changements* in his scores, even after publication, and then he was also deaf. So why not the conductor also, who often knows much better than the composer? I was the best pupil of Schindler[4], who was the best pupil of Beethoven, so I know what Beethoven meant. So, in this work of Strauss: I have been great friend of Richard Strauss since I was a boy, and I know just what he wants, and we will make some *changements* also!"

He rehearses the opening as far as fig. 2 at great length, first of all taking the violas, 'celli and horns, until there is complete unanimity in ensemble, phrasing, intonation and style, and all trace of untidiness at these inserted breath-gaps is removed. He arrives at the episode of the Critics (first bars before fig. 14) after two hours' work, and makes the flute play his subject *staccatissimo* and as spitefully as he can, and the counter-subject in the oboe drawled and wooden, with each entry of the other woodwinds almost overblown in the anxiety to be heard. The celebrated fifths of the two tubas are considerably broadened with a big *crescendo* and *diminuendo* to the held note. So much are they elongated that the rest of the orchestra has to adjust its playing to them as in Example 17, over the page.

He spent a long time at each rehearsal over this tuba motif. "This motif represents one of Strauss's most hated critics, M. Quentin, and it must sound like MON-SIEUR-QUEN-TIN: Play it to me! —No, it is not together! But you don't give me the *crescendo* to the second beat and then *diminuendo*! Now, for the last time . . .!"

[4] Not strictly speaking true, since Schindler had died in 1865, six years before Mengelberg was born. However, Mengelberg *did* study with Wüllner, who had himself been an illustrious pupil of Schindler's, so we may allow this poetic licence since Mengelberg clearly understood the Beethoven tradition.

Ex. 17

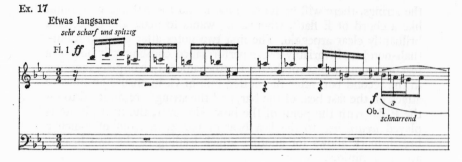

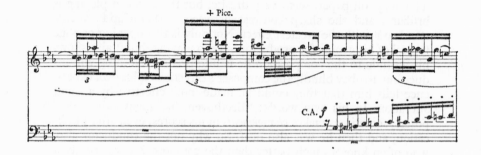

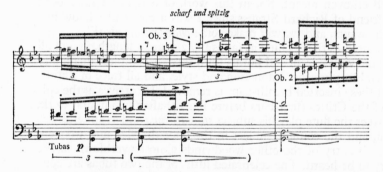

He rehearses all the first part of this section until all the contra-puntal parts are clear in every detail, and the utmost character portrayed in the different themes. At the end of this episode for wind he finds the accompaniment too heavy at the *pianissimo* syncopated chords in bassoons and horns, and later in the strings as well, so it gives him another opportunity to discourse on the playing of accompaniments in general:

"You must play with just the right amount of tone, neither too much, not too little: if you play an accompaniment too soft, it is just as wrong as playing it too loud. Listen to the soloist! Then, if you *are* the soloist, you must be heard, even if the mark is *pianissimo*.

Not forgotten that if you are accompanying, play less than what you have, and when you are the soloist, play a little more.   It must be a hundred-per-cent, and not just seventy-five-per-cent!"

At the *Festes Zeitmass* two bars before fig. 22 he plays the four-bar passage six or seven times until the rhythm is sufficiently accurate and *staccato*, with frequent interjections of *"Ter-*der!!" [Mengelberg's favourite expression for blurred or cumbersome playing]:

Ex. 18

The unfortunate solo violin does not get the opportunity to set out on his difficult solo until well into the middle of the second rehearsal—a very trying experience—for each time the conductor arrives at his entry he stops him in mid-air, on his first C sharp, and returns to a figure some way back. Much the same thing happened in Brahms' B flat Piano Concerto. He would let the pianist play one chord in his second big solo, and then stop him and start again, working at considerable length over the first *tutti* and stopping the pianist each time in his stride.

The ensuing passage in *Heldenleben* contains many difficulties for the orchestra, as well as the exacting solo for the violin. The first one crops up in the 'celli, basses and horns at the end of the fifth bar of fig 23, and continues much in evidence throughout the whole of the accompaniment to the violin. This is the elusive semiquaver which always precedes the principal subject of this section. *"Ter-*der! I don't hear that sixteenth-note—what do you call it?—SEMI-QUAVER! Put the bow on the string and separate the note from the next bar. Give me the first 'celli—so. Now the double-basses—again!

Ex. 19

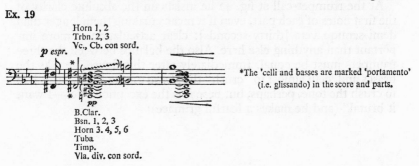

*The 'celli and basses are marked 'portamento' (i.e. glissando) in the score and parts.

It is difficult! Better! Now the first and second horn. You will have
to play louder, second horn! Now 'celli, basses, and first and second
horn. Ah ha! I begin to hear it at last! It is no longer *Ter*-der, and
nearly eighty-per-cent. 'Celli and bassi, use *more glissando!*"

About ten bars further on he practises the *pizzicato* chords in the
second violins for ensemble and intonation, both times the passage
occurs, demanding a clear but quiet plucking of the strings at right-
angles for a dry sound, and not along the string for a more sustained
sound. At the end of the solo violin passage, at fig. 32, he has further
trouble with the "semiquaver" and does not continue until the
'celli, basses, oboes, clarinets and bassoons articulate the note distinctly, before the great G flat chord.

The next section might almost be labelled the "left hand of the
violin", so frequently does he demand the utmost warmth and life in
the *vibrato*, as much as in great breadth of bowing. He continues to
take all those playing the same phrases in unison or octaves separately,
and often one department at a time, aiming at a rich and glowing
sound where perfect intonation and ensemble increase the volume.
Not until he obtains the right volume given him by these two
elements—"one hundred-per-cent, and not just seventy-five-per-
cent"—does he turn to the balancing of the parts:

Ex. 20

Four bars after fig. 38 he makes the utmost of the first and
second violin passage in octaves, by getting both departments to
take exactly the same amount of bow in exactly the same style and
position, stopping instantly if any player is taking obviously too
much or playing in the wrong part of the bow. "It is not good, that
long bow in the orchestra. It looks well, yes, in the front—but the
notes are not there! A soloist may do it, perhaps, but it is not good
in the orchestra."

At the trumpet-call at fig. 42 he insists on the absolute clarity of
the first notes of each part, even if it means making them longer than
demi-semiquavers [thirty-seconds]: clear articulation is more important than anything else here. Also the balance between the three
trumpets must be equal. Immediately after this figure, he asks the
basses and 'celli almost to "crush" the *sforza* on the B flat. "It is bad
to crush the tone, perhaps, but here it is the exception! Yes—I want
it brutal" (and he makes a fearful grimace):

Ex. 21

He does not spend much time on the battle-scene, and only insists
that those tunes which stand out from the general din be clearly and
accurately handled. The insistent rhythm which appears on the
strings and side-drum at the *Festes Zeitmass* after fig. 49 is hammered
out as hard as possible, with short jabbing strokes of the bow, near
the heel, and percussion and strings have to clear up some ragged
ensemble, the side-drum being a long distance away. At the climax
two bars after fig. 75 he again insists on the perfect articulation of
the ♫ figure.

The tuba again fails to satisfy him before fig. 85, but the violas and
second clarinet fortunately get over their shaky bridge at fig. 85 without mishap:

Ex. 22

A typical stroke of Mengelberg's comes out in the 'celli, a few bars further on, their last sextolet being drawn out in a *molto allargando e diminuendo*, making an exquisite sound with the bows just brushing the string before falling at length on the G major chord:

Ex. 23

He touches on the various quotations from Strauss's earlier works in the next episode, particularly demanding a special effort from the horns in their *Don Juan* motif. After fig. 94, in the semiquaver passages, he makes a terrific effect from the strings by forbidding too much bow, and as near the heel as possible, so that he gets articulation and *staccato*, even at high speed. Should any player forget himself and let his bow trickle to the point, he shouts: "Why do you play *there*? It is no good—I have told you! You are not playing as soloist—you are in the orchestra." The offending player is then eyed for a few moments. "Now we must do it again!"

Ex. 24

For the last time, he makes sure of getting every semiquaver clearly played after the tied notes, between figs. 95 and 96, and at the end of the episode he takes the great descending quintuplet in two beats, making groups of two and three.

In the concluding scene, a Mengelberg of extreme gentleness appears, capable of exquisite tenderness, and the lovely interjectory phrases on the first and second violins—during the cor anglais solo —are made to sound as if there were all humanity in them. The left hand of the violins is singled out for his medium of expression, the bows held well in control to avoid over-emphasis. The violin solo to the end is made to tell on every note, both in expression and delicacy, with the rest of the orchestra hushed to an extreme *pianissimo* which is yet alive—the colour of a moving part just coming to the surface now and again:

Ex. 25

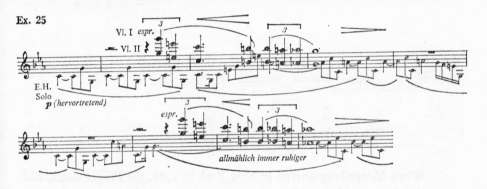

Another facet of Mengelberg's extraordinary command of the orchestral situation—which he shared with other eminent colleagues—was his ability to hear things from the point of view of the last row of the audience. This faculty lay behind many of the apparently arbitrary decisions which he made over composers' music—of which Strauss was but one instance—and which stemmed from his conviction that the performance from the orchestra's point of view must take such things into consideration. One must be over-articulate, he used to say, for what sounded brilliant enough from his conductor's rostrum would sound less than brilliant to the audience. The slurred passages from Tchaikowsky's *Romeo and Juliet*, for example, did not bear for Mengelberg that degree of articulation which they had for Tchaikowsky the composer, and which for the audience became a blurred murmur of sound. Therefore he changed the slurs to *spiccato*, thus:

Ex. 26

When Mengelberg arrived in New York in 1921, the Philharmonic had just absorbed the National Symphony Orchestra, and eighteen months later it merged with the New York City Symphony. Mengelberg had, however, no wish to sever his connections with the Concertgebouw, which he had already brought to a standard which vied with that of the Berlin Philharmonic, and he accordingly shared his concerts during his eight remaining years in New York with a series of co-conductors, and spent two annual periods of three months each in his native Amsterdam. American players who played under him during this time agree that Mengelberg was inclined to talk too much, but they bore him that mute respect which, from the orchestral player, is the equivalent of high praise, and certainly nothing of that open hostility of their English colleagues, at a Philharmonic Society concert in 1938, who considered that, because they had played the *Prelude and Liebestod* under Sir

Thomas Beecham—not to mention Wilhelm Furtwängler—there was nothing which Mengelberg could teach them. Artur Bodanzky and Josef Stransky shared the season with Mengelberg in 1923, Willem van Hoogstraten—with Igor Stravinsky as a guest conductor—in 1924, and Wilhelm Furtwängler during the next two seasons, which also saw, in 1926, the arrival on the Philharmonic scene as guest conductor of Arturo Toscanini, who was destined to conduct the orchestra for the next ten years, becoming its musical director in 1928, when the Philharmonic merged with the New York Symphony and became the New York Philharmonic-Symphony. Bernardino Molinari was an associate conductor for the next three seasons, and during Mengelberg's final New York season—for Toscanini was by no means yet *persona grata*—a number of guest conductors was engaged, including Arthur Honegger, Clemens Krauss, Fritz Reiner and Ossip Gabrilowitsch. For the next three years Toscanini shared his duties with Erich Kleiber, general musical director of the Berlin State Opera, and Leopold Stokowski was a two-week guest while Toscanini rendered similar service with the Philadelphia Orchestra. In 1931, Bruno Walter, then musical director of the Leipzig Gewandhaus, appeared as a guest and was re-engaged as an associate for the next three seasons. Issay Dobrowen became an associate in 1932, with Sir Thomas Beecham, Vladimir Golschmann and Ottorino Respighi as guests, Hans Lange an associate for three seasons in 1933, Otto Klemperer an associate for two seasons in 1934, with Artur Rodzinski and Werner Janssen as guests, and Beecham an associate in 1935, whereupon Toscanini announced his resignation—though whether this was a direct result of Beecham's appointment, over which he had of course no control, history does not relate with any substance of reliability. Toscanini was succeeded by John Barbirolli —then aged thirty-seven—as principal conductor in 1936, and as musical director the following year, and doubtless furnished a happy Anglo-Italian compromise.

The name of Toscanini evokes manifold sentiments in the music-lover, and there has been an unconscionable amount of literature—good and bad, light-hearted and serious, fact and fiction—written of the man who was to become a legend within his own lifetime. Arturo Toscanini was born in Parma on 25 March, 1867, and received his diploma in 'cello and composition from the Parma Conservatorio at the age of eighteen. Musical conditions in Italy at that time—1885—were such that he found himself the following year the first of a section of two 'cellos in a travelling opera company in Rio de Janeiro. Their conductor was Leopoldo Miguez, a Brazilian, and his substitute an Italian by the name of Carlo Superti. The exact circumstances of their quarrel are not clear, for there are at least three conflicting accounts, but the upshot of the quarrel which undoubtedly took place was that both conductors resigned, and Toscanini—who, because of the shortness of his vision, could be relied upon to know at least his own part from memory—found himself conducting a performance of *Aïda* in their place, and in fact conducted the next sixteen performances. The resultant artistic standard, with a 'cello section now reduced to a single player, cannot of course have been very high.

In the autumn of 1886, on his return from Brazil, Toscanini was engaged as a coach at the Teatro Carignano in Turin, and made his debut as a conductor there in Catalini's *Edmea*—memorable music set to an execrable libretto, with which Toscanini, however, contrived to do something more than justice. But in spite of Catalini's testimonials, couched in glowing terms, the debut remained isolated, and when he found that his engagement at the Teatro Carignano was not to be renewed, Toscanini reverted once more to the 'cello. So began his years as an itinerant musician, which were to last until 1895 when he received his first permanent appointment to the Teatro Regio in Turin. In December 1886 he played in the orchestra of the Teatro Vittorio Emanuele for two concerts under Bolzoni, besides giving a 'cello recital at Asti, and on 5 February, 1887, was fourth 'cellist in the première of *Otello* at La Scala, Milan, where Verdi singled him out in public for not having played loudly enough in the 'cello quartet. Toscanini protested that he had observed Verdi's marking of *pp*, to which Verdi replied that the marking had to take account of the acoustics of La Scala, and that a true *pp* was absolutely lost in that building.

There followed modest engagements as conductor in Casale Monferrato, with Meyerbeer's *L'Africaine* and Verdi's *I Lombardi*, and in the spring season of 1888 the Teatro Dal Verme in Milan engaged him for *La Forza del Destino*, Ponchielli's *I Promessi Sposi* and Cagnoni's *Francesca da Rimini*, which was a failure. The remainder of the year found Toscanini conducting *Aïda* in Macerata and *Les Huguenots* in Novara, to which he added *Aïda* and *La Forza del Destino* in the early spring of 1889. From Novara he returned to the Teatro Vittorio Emanuele in Turin to conduct *Carmen* and *Mignon*, and there followed a period of complete unemployment (apart from a very short season at Brescia, where he conducted Puccini's *Le Villi*) until October 1890, when he was offered a six-month engagement in Barcelona. Thence Toscanini went to Senigallia, on the Adriatic, to conduct *Cavalleria Rusticana*.

It was not until 1892 that there came a decisive change in Toscanini's fortunes, when the Teatro Dal Verme in Milan engaged him to conduct the première, on 17 May, of Leoncavallo's *I Pagliacci*, which was an unqualified success. Later in the same year he took over from Mancinelli on the third

night of the world-première of Franchetti's *Cristofo Colombo* in Genoa—
Mancinelli and Franchetti having quarrelled in true Italian style (without,
however, an immediate reconciliation on this occasion), and Toscanini having
been summoned overnight from Milan, and having learned the score in the
train. Meanwhile Toscanini revived Catalini's *Lorelei* in 1892, and the following year gave the first Pisa performance of Puccini's *Manon Lescaut*, which
had received its première under Mancinelli in Turin on 1 February, 1893. In
1894 he was once again in Genoa, conducting *Tannhäuser* and *Falstaff*.

Turin, which had been Toscanini's base since 1892, represented at that
time the centre of a new movement which had come to condemn the attitudes
both of audiences and management in opera in particular for their indifference
to the unbelievable liberties which were taken by singers, and the unwarrant-
able tyranny which the leading publishing houses exercised inside the opera
house over the choice of operas. This was a movement to which Toscanini
could subscribe fully, and the revolution which was to take place throughout
Italy during the course of the next twenty-five years may be attributed largely
to Toscanini's influences. Nor were there any permanent orchestras in the
Italian theatre at that time, and still less in the Italian concert hall, which
was virtually non-existent—*vide* Hans von Bülow's letters from Florence,
and the situation had not changed one whit in twenty years. When, in 1895,
Toscanini secured his first permanent appointment, at the age of twenty-
eight and for an initial term of three years, at the Teatro Regio in Turin, it
furnished him with the opportunity of initiating those principles which had
by now become very near to his heart—fidelity to the composer's text, and
the creation of permanent orchestras in the theatres which would provide
the performances of that composer's music (not to mention his fight against
the practice of not dimming the lights in the theatre during the performance
of opera, on which Stendhal had commented in his notes on Italian theatrical
customs).

Toscanini gave the Italian première of *Gotterdämmerung*—in Italian—on
22 December, 1895, and followed this with Verdi's *Falstaff* five days later.
Tristan followed in 1896, and *Walküre* in 1897, and scattered between were
the normal repertory operas of Boito's *Mefistofele*, Bellini's *Norma*, and the
new operas—Canti's *Savitri*, Puccini's *La Bohème* (which received its world
première in Turin on 1 February, 1896), Lozzi's *Emma Lioni*, Giordano's
Andrea Chénier (premièred at La Scala on 23 March of the previous year
under Martucci, and repeated at the New York Academy of Music in November 1896), Buzzi Peccia's *Forza d'Amore*, Mancinelli's *Ero e Leandro*, and di
Levo's *La Carmago*, representing a selection from no less than eighty new
operas which were performed at one theatre or another in Italy during the

year 1896. Toscanini had given four symphony concerts at La Scala in 1896, and these had prepared the way for his performance, at the World Exhibition of 1898 in Turin, of no less than forty-three concerts with the Turin Municipal Orchestra which Toscanini had founded the previous year. But they also prepared the way for his return to La Scala, on 26 December, 1898, in another capacity.

When the original ducal theatre in Milan had been destroyed by fire in 1776, Empress Maria Theresa had commissioned the construction of a new theatre on the site of Santa Maria alla Scala, which was opened officially on 3 August, 1778 with the performance of Salieri's *Europa Riconosciuta*, and was at that time the finest theatre in the world. Private individuals from among the well-to-do had bought the land on which the Teatro alla Scala was to be built and had financed its construction, in return for which they became the owners in perpetuity of its four main tiers of boxes. When it succeeded the Austrian royal house, the municipality of Milan inherited the least profitable part which had until that time enjoyed royal largesse—the fifth tier, stalls and galleries—and now derived the precarious revenue, which was needed to make good the deficit, from the practice of gambling in the bars and foyers of the opera house. When Milan came once more under Austrian rule in 1815, Emperor Franz II imposed a ban on gambling and the theatre was compelled to close for the next two years until he was persuaded to grant an annual subsidy of 200,000 lire—a considerable sum for those days—and which continued up until the end of Austria's rule in 1859. The Italian Royal House had none of the instincts to patronage of their Austrian cousins however, and the municipality of Milan was now looked to to finance the opera house, and little by little parted reluctantly with increasing sums which, by July 1898, had reached the figure of 240,000 lire. Meanwhile a Socialist majority had recently been elected to the municipal council, and was not slow to point out the burden and the injustice of spending 240,000 lire on an opera house to which the general public had no access. When it was rumoured that La Scala would have to close its doors, a public subscription was opened and a committee elected with the object of forming a limited company, and of inducing the box-holders to increase their subscriptions—at that time purely nominal, since they were one and all jealous of their ancient birth-right—and the municipality to grant at least a small subsidy. The president of the committee was Guido Visconti di Modrone, and had as his right-hand men Boito, the librettist of many of Verdi's operas and composer of *Mefistofele*, and Giulio Gatti-Casazza who, as intendant, was responsible for finding a new conductor.

Toscanini was their choice, and he was careful to ensure that the clauses

of his contract should provide guarantees of his independence and authority—
an authority which was to be put to the test at the very outset, when he insisted that the opening production of *Norma* should be abandoned. During the
first four seasons, which represented the initial term of his contract, Toscanini
presented *Die Meistersinger* and *Falstaff*, *Siegfried*, *Lohengrin* and *Otello*,
Tristan, *Walküre* and the *Verdi Requiem*, and the third act of *Parsifal*, reviving
at the same time *Elisir d'Amore*, *William Tell*, *Linda*, *Trovatore*, *Luisa Miller*,
and *Ballo in Maschera*. On 11 March, 1903, during a performance of *Ballo in
Maschera*, Toscanini suddenly stepped off the rostrum and left the theatre.
He left Genoa the following day for Buenos Aires, and it transpired that he
had been upset by the audience's bad manners, and their crude insistence on
an encore from Zenatello, the Riccardo of *Ballo in Maschera*. But it appeared
that he had in any case been booked to leave Genoa on 12 March, and had
been engaged—as he had been the previous year, and was to be the following
year—for a winter season in Buenos Aires. The 1904 season in Buenos Aires
witnessed a repetition of his conduct at La Scala the previous year, and he
was not re-engaged. In Italy, having provoked a scandal of major proportions
in 1903, Toscanini was—needless to say—*persona non grata*, and had to wait
until the 1906 season for Depanis, intendant of the Teatro Regio in Milan, to
arrange for him to conduct some opera there during the annual carnival, which
was followed by a concert-tour when Toscanini conducted Debussy's *Nuages*
and *L'après-midi d'un faune* for the first time. Meanwhile Cleofonte Campanini had succeeded him at La Scala in 1903, without conspicuous success,
and a mass walk-out on the part of the orchestra during a rehearsal of *Fra
Diavolo* led to his resignation in May 1906. In the same month Toscanini
enjoyed the sweet victory of a return to Buenos Aires, and in the autumn to
La Scala. He forthwith made the banning of all encores official, but when he
insisted that Umberto di Modrone, who had inherited his father's position as
president of the theatre, should be barred from rehearsals, his days at La
Scala were numbered. In 1908 Gatti-Casazza left La Scala for the Metropolitan, and took Toscanini with him.

Toscanini's seven seasons with the Metropolitan Opera have been re-
counted in an earlier chapter, but mention should be made of a concert
which he gave with the chorus and orchestra of the Metropolitan on 13 April,
and again on 18 April, 1913, with Frieda Hempel, Louise Homer, Karl Jörn
and Putnam Griswold as soloists. The programme, whose lack of discrimination may be offensive to the fastidious, consisted of Wagner's *Faust* Overture,
Strauss' *Till Eulenspiegel*, and the Beethoven Ninth Symphony.

From 1915 until 1920, Toscanini did not earn one penny, and was
thrown back on the resources which he had saved from his annual $42,000

contract with the Metropolitan. Nor did he conduct very much, although he had placed himself at the disposal of the Italian government. But with the formation of the "Ente Autonomo del Teatro alla Scala" under Emilio Caldara, the socialist mayor of Milan, Toscanini set to work forming a new orchestra—the "Toscanini-Scala Orchestra" as it came to be known in America—taking them on a concentrated training tour from Italy to the United States and Canada and back to Italy again, and giving 134 concerts in just over six months. On 26 December, 1921—twenty-three years to the very day after his first appointment to La Scala—the theatre was reopened with all attendant ceremony, Toscanini conducting *Falstaff*: and twenty-five years later, on 11 May, 1946, he was to conduct another programme of Italian music in a rebuilt La Scala.

Toscanini had lived constantly on the fringe of politics, but these had been the petty politics of the theatre or the everyday grouses of the people, and in his early flirtation with Fascism of these years he was voicing a protest with which most radically-minded Italians were in accord. But by 1926 he sensed that he was being carried out of his depth. There had been an alarming increase in the number of blackshirts in the Piazza della Scala, and the ever-growing chanting of *Giovinezza*. Toscanini accepted a guest engagement with the New York Philharmonic with alacrity, and became co-conductor with Mengelberg the following year. But when, in 1928, the Philharmonic merged with the New York Symphony, and Toscanini was appointed musical director with authority to select and reject players from the two orchestras, his position became prone to increasing hostility from musicians and management alike. Accordingly, he arranged the European tour of the New York Philharmonic-Symphony in the spring of 1930, which was to bring him to Bayreuth that summer—an invitation which backfired for all concerned when it was repeated the following year and, true to pattern, he walked out of a memorial performance for Siegfried Wagner. For Furtwängler had been appointed musical director at Bayreuth, and Furtwängler was one conductor whom Toscanini could not abide: Mahler had been another, Koussevitsky was another, Beecham yet another—"i dilettanti" as he described them. No more could he tolerate any other conductor save the gentle Bruno Walter, to whom no one could take exception, and Mengelberg, for whom he had a grudging respect, and Stokowski, in whom he perhaps felt a kindred spirit, and Kleiber, the one conductor who commanded his unqualified admiration. Toscanini became musical director of the Salzburg Festival in 1935, having given a concert there two years previously, and on 29 April, 1936, gave his farewell concert with the New York Philharmonic. On 26 December, 1936, he gave his first concert with Hubermann's orchestra in Tel-Aviv, and

exactly one year later the Christmas night concert which marked the start
of his last and longest association—that of seventeen years with the NBC
Symphony Orchestra.

The Toscanini legend has by now acquired adherents without number,
and it is not without poetic justice that he should have died, on 17 January,
1957, in the city which had been effectively his home for over thirty years, for
he belongs—in so far as anyone may ever claim to belong—to New York.
Filippo Sacchi has written this of him: "His creative attitude to his work in
the theatre is illustrated by his remarks to a violinist during a rehearsal of the
overture to *Traviata*. One phrase was not to his liking, and eventually he
burst out: "But can't you read what it says? It's quite plainly written down."
"It says *Lamentoso*", answered the player. "Well, weep then, *weep*, in the
name of God!"[5]. So much for sentiment. That Toscanini could be ill-
tempered is an understatement. He could be violent, and physically so, to the
point where one must seriously question who it was that struck the first blow
in the Bologna incident of 1931 of which he was to make so much capital. He
could be childish to the point of throwing every sort of tantrum, crying tears
of impotent rage, and finally sulking when he did not get his own way. He
could be hysterical to the point of throwing his stand onto the floor, grinding
his watch into the floorboards, wilfully breaking his baton, and hurling in-
vective at his players, which would subside dramatically so that they imagined
the danger had passed, only to recommence with a renewed volley of abuse
in the vilest of language, followed invariably by his petulant exit. His cries of:

"Piano—PIANO—*PIAAAAAAAAAAAAAAAAANO!*"
or: "Canta—CANTA—*CAAAAAAAAAAAAAAAANTA!*"

would provide a grating crescendo which tore at the nerve ends until his
players felt physically ill, and could with justice retort—as one of them did:

"Grida—GRIDA—*GRIIIIIIIIIIIIDA!*"

His exits from the very heart of actual performances were as legion as they
were invariably dramatic, and were as irrevocable as they betrayed a lack of
professional stamina. And they would never have been tolerated for one
moment from a conductor of less stature than Toscanini consistently and
successfully made himself out to be.

So much could be forgiven Toscanini, for it is in the final analysis the
music which counts. And so much has been forgiven him, in the name of
music, by fellow-artists and music-lovers more tolerant than he the world over,
who chose to overlook his monstrous egocentricities for the sake of the music

[5] Filippo Sacchi: *The Magic Baton*, G. P. Putnam's Sons, New York, 1957.

which he gave them. But where is that music now? Certainly there is precious little evidence of it in those recordings which he has left to us, representing as they do some of the least attractive aspects of a commercialism usually confined to Madison Avenue. A talented conductor—yes. A great conductor—perhaps. But the greatest conductor which the world has ever known—assuredly not.

Chapter 9

KLEIBER AND FURTWÄNGLER

With Mahler's departure for the United States in 1908, Felix Weingartner had been summoned from Munich to take his place at the Vienna Court Opera—an unenviable task for a conductor for whom, with his over-literal sense of musical perspective, the medium of opera had already proved to be alien on more than one occasion. Nor was he destined to succeed there— though the intrigues, treacheries, and petty criminalities of the *Opernhaus am Ring* have, to this day, never enjoined the services of outstanding conductors for more than a very few seasons: Mahler's ten-year term is a record, and his only substantial successors—Richard Strauss, Bruno Walter, Hans Knappertsbusch, and Herbert von Karajan—have none of them stayed the course for even half this period of time before they were compelled to resign in the face of the scheming incompetence of an administration which comprehended only the routine and the second-rate. At all events, Weingartner left in 1912 for the more congenial surroundings of the Hamburg Stadttheater, and was succeeded at the Vienna Opera by Hans Gregor—a routine appointment which endured until the end of the First World War. But Weingartner's fortunes did not prosper in Hamburg either, and two years later he found himself in the post of musical director in the town of Darmstadt—and encountered in the person of Erich Kleiber a youthful third Kapellmeister who was very definitely on his way up. Weingartner maintained his position in Darmstadt for seven years, thereafter abandoning it—save for one brief season at the Vienna State Opera (as it had now become) in 1935, which terminated in his resignation, and occasional appearances at the Volksoper, Vienna's second opera house—for the more sanguine and impersonal atmosphere of the concert hall, for which he had a more natural affinity.

Erich Kleiber had shared (as Weingartner had not) an admiration for the art of Nikisch with Wilhelm Furtwängler—five years Kleiber's senior, and Nikisch's successor at the head of the Berlin Philharmonic and Leipzig Gewandhaus orchestras—and throughout his life declared that, with each advancing step in his career, his veneration for Nikisch grew stronger.

It was one of the greatest pieces of good fortune that ever befell
me [wrote Kleiber], that Artur Nikisch should have come to Darmstadt when I was third conductor there. One of his orchestral rehearsals for *Tristan* was an object lesson which I shall never forget.
A few of us had gathered in the darkened auditorium to hear it. The
Isolde was not present, and Nikisch rehearsed the *Liebestod* with
orchestra alone. Our orchestra seemed suddenly transformed. We
could none of us understand how Nikisch, with a single rehearsal,
could draw from them such beauty of sound and such ecstatic depth
of feeling. The score rang out as it rings out in the silence of one's
work-room after repeated sessions of intensive study. The mighty
crescendos were absolutely uncanny: where other conductors flail
away with both arms, Nikisch just slowly raised his left hand until
the orchestra roared around him like the sea. It was an effect of art
such as only he and Richard Strauss—as I was later to realise—
could produce with the last pages of *Tristan*[1].

Kleiber left Darmstadt in 1919 to become principal conductor at the
Staatstheater in Wuppertal, in Düsseldorf in 1921, and in Mannheim in 1922
—succeeding at an interval of two years Furtwängler, who had taken over the
Leipzig and Berlin orchestras with the death, on 23 January, 1922, of Artur
Nikisch. Furtwängler's first concert with the Gewandhaus Orchestra—"In
Memoriam Artur Nikisch"—was on 6 February, 1922, and with the Berlin
Philharmonic in the following October. His successor in Mannheim, mean-
while, had quickly made his mark, and on 26 August, 1923—following a
guest appearance with *Fidelio* made on a single rehearsal—his appointment
as general musical director of the Berlin State Opera was publicly announced.
Kleiber was thirty-three, and had succeeded Leo Blech—who had held the
post since Strauss's resignation in 1910, and had now left to take charge of the
Charlottenburg theatre—in the face of rival competition from Bruno Walter
and Otto Klemperer. Kleiber's appointment, moreover, was to be for an
initial period of five years, and provoked a storm of protest. Fritz Stiedry,
first conductor under Blech, immediately resigned, and the press singled out
the intendant, Max von Schillings, for heavy fire. On 17 September he wrote
to Kleiber:

The quarrel is assuming grotesque proportions. We must realise
that a part of the press will be very much up in arms against you.
Already they are creating a most horrible atmosphere in readiness
for your arrival ... And now: in early October we must have
Falstaff and a Strauss cycle and the *Ring*. We are not free to do as we
like in respect of these, because the soloists have already been engaged ... I shall soon put on a new production of *Lohengrin*. The

[1] John Russell: *Erich Kleiber*, André Deutsch, London, 1957.

Paris *Tannhäuser* will make way for the original Dresden version, *Don Giovanni* has recently had a new production, which you can take over. *Aïda* and *Carmen* I should like, and we must discuss *Freischütz*. As for the Strauss cycle (all his operas, excepting *Feuersnot*), and the new works, and the contracts with the publishers—all this we can discuss when you come ...

Kleiber was always a prodigious worker, and the eight major productions —including *Fidelio*—which he undertook during his first five weeks in Berlin brought him into contact with singers who were to form one of the last great permanent ensembles in the world—Herbert Janssen, Zinaida Jurjewskaya, Barbara Kemp, Frida Leider, Marherr-Wagner, Friedrich Schorr, Maria Müller, Leo Schützendorf, Heinrich Schlusmus and Fritz Soot. Kleiber's conducting technique at that time had little of the sovereign economy which was to characterize it in later years, and many of his critics were distracted by what they described as his *Bülow-Allüren*—Bülowesque gestures. "But those who kept their beards in the score noticed that even the trumpet-calls in *Leonora* had been restudied, and that the many unexpected nuances in his readings were there because the composer had intended them, and not for their own sake alone."[2] The extent of Kleiber's repertoire was all-embracing (save for a blind-spot for the music of Brahms, and no great enthusiasm for that of Bach) and found an especial emphasis in his programmes for the concert hall which championed not only the contemporary composer—his programmes during his one year at Düsseldorf had contained Schoenberg's *Kammersinfonie* No. 1 and *Pierrot Lunaire, Das Lied von der Erde*, an evening devoted to the music of local composers, and a Hindemith concert directed by Hindemith himself—but also delved back into the past, and more than once had the critics reaching for their musical dictionaries, besides introducing novelties by such familiar composers as Mozart, Schubert, Beethoven and Weber. For these concerts there were never less than five rehearsals— including the public general rehearsal—nor did Kleiber neglect the standard repertoire, imbuing it with a new life which inspired in his musicians and his audience alike the sensation of hearing even the most familiar work as if for the very first time, whereas unknown or little-known repertoire acquired at his hands an essence of familiarity. But it was to be in his operatic direction— as it had already been for ten years and more—that the specific qualities of Kleiber's genius lay, and which in turn informed and enriched his frequent appearances (or as frequent, at all events, as his duties as musical director of a metropolitan opera-house would allow) on the concert platform.

Kleiber had the unerring instinct of attracting and consolidating

[2] Ibid.

talent, and he was never at this time—as was Furtwängler—jealous of colleagues. Walter, Klemperer, Toscanini, Strauss and Furtwängler himself were accorded unimpeded access to his rostrum, and in 1926 Leo Blech—who was nearly twenty years Kleiber's senior, and who had conducted at the Staatsoper uninterruptedly from 1906 to 1923—was persuaded by Kleiber to return from the Charlottenburg. Leo Blech recalls their first meeting in Darmstadt, where he had been invited by the Grand Duke of Hesse to give *Un Ballo in Maschera*:

> After one of the performances a very young man approached me and introduced himself as Erich Kleiber. He had such a vivid and engaging personality that I gave myself the pleasure of inviting him to dinner. He asked me if I could spare the time to hear him conduct Oscar Straus's *Waltz Dream*, and so I went along. I saw at once that he was a born conductor—and that is how it is, to my way of thinking: one day you get up in front of an orchestra, and either you know how to conduct—or nobody will ever be able to teach you ... [3]

Kleiber attracted younger colleagues as well—Dimitri Mitropoulos, who was a répétiteur under him from 1923 to 1925, when he returned to his native Greece to take command of the Athens orchestra, and Georg Szell, who was his first conductor from 1924 to 1929, when he went to Prague. Both were to become leading conductors in America, and both testified to the debt which they owed to Kleiber—their senior by five and six years respectively.

Kleiber's performance on 3 March, 1924, of *Jenufa*, which Janáček had begun thirty years earlier, and had completed in March 1903, and whose Berlin première was in the original Czech—a language which Kleiber had mastered in his youth in Prague—was an unqualified success, confirming his sponsor's beliefs in his prodigious gifts, and paving the way to the world-première, in December of the following year, of the opera with which Kleiber's name has become synonymous—Alban Berg's *Wozzeck*, a work which was to be the biggest single factor in confirming that belief with the public at large. That *Wozzeck* survived its ten initial performances and remained in the repertoire during the ensuing seasons is conclusive evidence, not only of the stature of the music, but of that of Kleiber himself, for he devoted the same meticulous care to every work which he touched, and their number was legion.

Erich Kleiber had been born on 5 August, 1890, and his childhood was spent alternately in Vienna, Prague, and again in Vienna where, in 1906, he first heard and saw Mahler conduct, and became thenceforward an incessant,

[3] John Russell: *Erich Kleiber*, André Deutsch, London, 1957.

though humble, patron of the Court Opera. Mahler had by this time achieved an ensemble of the greatest distinction, having under him Franz Schalk as first conductor and Bruno Walter as second, and taking in his stride—in addition to the standard repertoire—such now little known works as Bizet's *Djamileh*, Lortzing's *Zar und Zimmermann*, Charpentier's *Louise*, Rezniček's *Donna Diana*, Weber's *Euryanthe* and Leoncavallo's *La Bohème* (which had been written earlier than that of Puccini). In 1908 Kleiber returned to Prague to divide his time between the university and the conservatoire, where he had been conditionally admitted on the evidence of his compositions. But he found the life of the conservatoire—like that of the university—irksome, and became an increasingly frequent unofficial visitor to the rehearsals of the Deutsches Theater. There, early in 1911, he was discovered by the intendant, Angelo Neumann, during a rehearsal of *Götterdämmerung*, and was engaged, on the strength of his bona fides, as an unpaid volunteer. He had had no formal training on the piano at all, and had in fact only started to study that instrument in an unorthodox fashion in 1906, at the instance of his friend and exact contemporary, Hans Gál. But by the autumn of 1911 he had acquired sufficient mastery of the keyboard to coach a number of minor roles, and on 4 January, 1912, made his first public appearance as the accompanist of Alfred Piccaver.[4] Meanwhile Kleiber, on 1 October, 1911, had made his debut as conductor in the stage-music of a Nestroy comedy, at the instance of Paul Eger, the newly-appointed intendant of the Darmstadt Court Theatre, who was visiting Prague. This was followed, on 21 November, with the *Euryanthe* Overture, as a prelude to Kleist's *Prinz von Homberg*, which prompted a woman journalist to comment: "Kleiber made himself conspicuous by his excessive agility. A baby Mahler, he may learn in time that there is more to his great model than growling and spitting." Kleiber's debut proper came on 10 March, 1912, with Hervé's *Mam'zelle Nitouche*, and on the strength of this, Eger offered him a three-year contract as third conductor at Darmstadt.

Darmstadt is a provincial town, somewhat smaller than Coventry, and ruled over at that time by the interested, intelligent and benevolent eye of Crown Prince Ludwig of Hesse, then in his early fifties. Yet it could command the occasional services—as we have seen—of Nikisch and Blech, and the permanent services, from 1914 to 1921, of Felix Weingartner. Its theatre had a tradition which extended back into the seventeenth century, and was well up to the times—and in advance of them, as the town's identification with the centre of *avant-garde* music in recent years must suggest. Kleiber's first assignment in Darmstadt was Offenbach's *La Belle Hélène*, and operetta was

---

[4] Alfred Piccaver, English operatic tenor, b. 5 February, 1887. Made his debut at the Landestheater, Prague, on 25 September, 1907.

to be the substance of his musical fare until April 1916, when he took over the general rehearsal of *Rosenkavalier* at twelve hours' notice—Ottenheimer, the first conductor, having fallen ill. Ottenheimer was well enough to conduct the first two performances, but accorded the third and fourth to Kleiber by way of recompense. Yet he never regretted his apprenticeship with operetta, which provides the discipline of technique and style so necessary to grand opera as does no other. Writing in 1917, Kleiber said: "I used to have to feel my way in music, but now I am quite sure of myself. The only thing which remains wholly and wonderfully mysterious to me is the elusive magic-of-the-moment in performance—the moment of inspiration when you *know*, as assuredly as if you had composed it yourself, how it *must* sound . . . " On 1 May, 1919, when his appointment to Wuppertal—or Barmen-Elberfeld, as it was then known—was confirmed, Nikisch wrote to Kleiber:

> My heartiest congratulations for Elberfeld! Now you have reached your goal—to be first in command. Volkener is an ideal intendant, and you will certainly get on well with him. I view the whole situation with one happy and one tearful eye—for what shall *I* do in Darmstadt without Kleiber now? But as I could not expect you to stay there just because of me, I shall make do—for better or for worse—as best I can . . .

The Germany of 1919 was one of moral and economic chaos, and a society which no longer acknowledged the principle of hereditary rule found itself groping for an adequate substitute. The Austro-Hungarian Empire, embracing eleven different nationalities, and the last great empire of Europe, had collapsed with her German ally, and the practice of court subsidy, which had established Vienna (in her own eyes, at all events) as the world centre of music-making for nigh on two hundred years, came to an abrupt end. It is to the lasting credit of an otherwise discredited Weimar Republic that it forthwith assumed, as a moral onus, the responsibility for subsidising German arts, introducing legislation which was to secure the future of her theatres and opera houses, and to provide state pensions for their artists and employees. The case for the new Austrian Republic was parallel.

In December 1918 Wilhelm Furtwängler, then resident conductor of the Mannheim orchestra, had made his debut with the Vienna Symphony Orchestra in a concert which included Brahms's Third Symphony, and from this moment Vienna had sought his services whenever possible. The following year, at the age of thirty-five, he was made a director of the Gesellschaft der Musikfreunde—an honorary post which he occupied until the appointment of Herbert von Karajan in 1949. In 1920, his contract in Mannheim having expired, he was unanimously appointed conductor of the Berlin Staatskapelle

—the Berlin opera orchestra which had given concerts under Richard Strauss until his resignation and—with his appointment as musical director of the Vienna State Opera in 1920—return to the operatic field. Two years later, at the behest of the Leipzig trustees, Fürtwängler succeeded Nikisch as conductor of the Gewandhaus Orchestra, and later inherited from him the Berlin Philharmonic—a post which he was effectively to retain until his death in 1954, when he was succeeded by Karajan.

Furtwängler had always been an imposing figure, with—as his biographer, Dr. Geissmar, has written—"a little of the Parsifal about him"[5]. Certainly, there was about him a naïve innocence, a preoccupation with philosophical concepts, which rendered him awkward and obtuse in the face of the unfamiliar and the everyday, and to a very large extent oblivious of a changing Germany—which was to change radically in the early 'thirties. He had always been a fluent pianist, and had had none of the early struggles with that instrument with which Kleiber had had to contend in his youth—although, unlike Kleiber, his baton-technique was in no sense immaculate, and was in fact a constant source of embarrassment to him (and to the musicians who played under him, if they were unfamiliar with its convolutions). Consequently Furtwängler had never been compelled to undergo the strenuous apprenticeship of operetta which Kleiber had had to, and had in fact fallen asleep, by reason of overwork, during one of his rare performances of operetta in Zürich in 1905. Although he was no stranger to the opera house, he never in fact held a continuous post of consequence there, and, like Weingartner, was clearly more at home in the concert hall. Here, too, Furtwängler's repertoire was more limited than that of Kleiber, but in those works which they shared in common they were of equal—though disparate—stature, and without question the greatest conductors of their generation.

In 1927 Furtwängler added to the Berlin and Leipzig orchestras a third prize in that of the Vienna Philharmonic, which he had conducted for the first time in 1922, and the following year was offered the Vienna State Opera, but declined. He had, he felt, too little experience of the operatic medium at this level, and above and beyond his standard repertoire—which could never have embraced an operatic première of the order of *Wozzeck*—and very probably had little desire to contaminate himself with that particular brand of politics which must result from prolonged association with any opera house—and particularly that of Vienna. The offer was immediately extended to Kleiber, Walter and Klemperer, without result, and Schneiderhan, the intendant and director of Austrian State Theatres, remained conspicuously

[5] Berta Geissmar: *The Baton and the Jackboot*: Hamish Hamilton, London, 1944: issued in the United States as *Two Worlds of Music*: Creative Age Press, New York, 1946.

silent. Franz Schalk had become the opera's musical director in 1918, and from 1920 to 1924 had worked in conjunction with Richard Strauss who had then resigned, on reaching the age of sixty, and gone into a composer's retreat at his home in Garmisch. Schalk was determined to resign himself at the conclusion of the 1927–28 season, when he would be sixty-five, and in the event it was Clemens Krauss who succeeded him, at the age of thirty-five. (And it was Clemens Krauss who—at Hitler's express wish, according to Dr. Geissmar's informant[6] was to succeed Kleiber when the latter resigned from the Berlin Staatsoper on 4 December, 1934, after a concert performance of the symphonic excerpts from Berg's *Lulu*.) Meanwhile, Furtwängler had relinquished permanent directorship of the Leipzig Gewandhaus Orchestra in 1928, and was succeeded in 1930 by Bruno Walter, and in 1933 by Hermann Abendroth.

The history of a great symphony orchestra must to a very considerable extent be the history of its tours and its guest conductors. The day-to-day routine in the life of an orchestra is—or should be—comparatively uneventful, and the life of a resident conductor in a major city is one of extreme loneliness and constant battle to maintain the status quo—"a battle which" (to quote Charles Munch, who had served as concertmaster of the Gewandhaus Orchestra under Furtwängler since 1922) "you must always win". He can afford to have no friends among his orchestra or the management, and sentiment must never be allowed to intrude over the principle of a musical discipline which he must always be prepared to enforce. On the other hand, he must present the image of a public figure constantly, indulge an instinct for showmanship in its best sense, and imbue with a sense of occasion every performance and every rehearsal. But the orchestra on tour, or the conductor appearing in the capacity of a guest, will provide their own sense of occasion, and are accorded a courtesy which is their rightful due. And they provide the local public in both instances with a yardstick by which to measure their capabilities, and which must put them on their mettle, and in both cases it is only the resident conductor who has anything to lose.

Furtwängler's terms of office with the Berlin and Vienna orchestras were only exceeded—in Europe—by Mengelberg's forty-three years with the Amsterdam Concertgebouw, and in America, by Frederick Stock's thirty-eight years with the Chicago Symphony. Kleiber had conducted the Vienna Philharmonic in Vienna in December 1927, as he had conducted them on tour earlier in the year and two years previously, but Furtwängler can have had no

---

[6] "Clemens Krauss, who had been hanging about in Berlin, was immediately engaged as director of the [State] Opera in place of Furtwängler. This, we were informed, was at Hitler's special request." It is, of course, Dr. Geissmar's wishful thinking that Furtwängler ever *had* been "director of the Staatsoper".

control over these engagements. Common hospitality, it is true, compelled
him to engage Kleiber as guest conductor of the Berlin Philharmonic, with
whom he made his debut in 1924 and thereafter more or less annually, in
return for which Furtwängler was accorded an equivalent number of Sunday
night concerts with the Berlin Staatskapelle. But I can find no further record
of Furtwängler's sanction of guest conductors of calibre—other than of
Bruno Walter and Sir Thomas Beecham—with those orchestras over which he
exercised jurisdiction, and certainly nothing of the hospitality which was
accorded both him and his European colleagues by Mengelberg in Amsterdam, and Stokowski, Mengelberg and Koussevitsky in America. It is convenient to impute jealousy to Furtwängler's motives, and there has been many
a German Kapellmeister who has taken refuge behind the excuse that Furtwängler had stood in their way at some crucial juncture of their lives. Certainly he had a predisposition to jealousy which amounted at times almost to
paranoia—but whether this was a jealousy of those conductors whose concerts
he so studiously avoided, or a jealousy of his own orchestras in the hands of
those conductors, is a point which might repay closer investigation.

In 1930, the Bayreuth Festival had witnessed the death, on 4 August, of
Siegfried Wagner, and at its close Karl Muck, the last disciple of Richard
Wagner, tendered his resignation. Toscanini, who had conducted *Tristan* and
the Paris version of *Tannhäuser* at this, his first Bayreuth season, had promised to conduct the following summer, and Furtwängler was invited to
replace Muck as the Festival's musical director, with the responsibility of
assembling the Festival orchestra, and to take over *Tristan*. The quaint and
self-conscious mystique of Bayreuth seems now, at nearly forty years' remove,
a monstrous anachronism and a grave disservice to Wagner's memory, but in
1931 it was seen as a noble tradition which followed faithfully in the footsteps
of the Bayreuth *Meister*. (Nor can one entirely commend the current reversal
of that tradition which allows M. Boulez to cut ninety minutes off the perfor-
mance-time of *Parsifal*. Richard Strauss, who after all knew something about
singing—as did Wagner himself—and had conducted *Parsifal* in the summer
of 1933, had insisted that there was a "just" tempo which would suffer very
little modification if the singers were to be accorded sufficient time to enun-
ciate correctly and well, without having to gabble their words[7]. There are of
course no metronome markings in the score of *Parsifal*.) The 1931 Bayreuth
Festival was not without its crises—an annual event which the presence of so
many prima donnas of both sexes amply ensured. Furtwängler made a
spectacular and somewhat tardy arrival, explaining that his private plane had
crashed on the way there, Lauritz Melchior (the Tristan of Furtwängler's

---

[7] Richard Strauss: *Betrachtungen und Erinnerungen*.

first Bayreuth performance) wanted to leave immediately and declared that he would never return—nor did he in fact ever do so—and Toscanini made his famous exit from the rostrum during the memorial concert for Siegfried Wagner and betook himself to Marienbad to sulk, and thence home to Italy. Furtwängler himself resigned before the beginning of the next season, publishing his reasons for so doing in the *Vossische Zeitung* of June 1932. But he was to return in 1936.

The annual tour of the Leipzig Gewandhaus Orchestra—a tradition which had been established by Nikisch—was maintained under Furtwängler, and took the orchestra in 1922 as far as Switzerland. It was followed by the tour, in 1924, of the Berlin Philharmonic, which thereafter became an annual event, the orchestra visiting England for the first time in 1927 for two concerts in London and one in Manchester, followed the next year by the first post-war visit to Paris. In 1931 the Vienna Philharmonic visited England for the first time, and was followed by the Berlin Philharmonic on a tour of Germany, Holland, Belgium and England at the end of the same year. In January 1934— by which time the Third Reich had come into being—the tour was repeated, and in the spring was extended to include Paris and Rome. The Nazi propaganda machine had begun to function, and was functioning well. Meanwhile, Furtwängler had been following a spectacular career as a guest conductor outside the German-speaking countries, making his Italian debut in Florence in 1922, which had inspired the famous cry from a member of the orchestra— Furtwängler never having possessed the clearest of beats—of "coraggio, Maestro!", his London debut with the orchestra of the Royal Philharmonic Society in 1924, and his American debut with the New York Philharmonic early in 1925. As an obtuse student of orchestral psychology, however, Furtwängler was re-engaged the following season for one concert only (by the Royal Philharmonic Society), and for the next two seasons for two weeks and one week respectively by the New York Philharmonic Society. The Italian has always made a particular cult of the prima donna, and Furtwängler continued to be welcome in Italy—and especially so after Toscanini's departure for America in 1926.

The advent of the Nazi regime in January 1933 found Kleiber and Furtwängler rivals of equal standing in Berlin, and it was inevitable that politics, for so long buried beneath a courtesy *de convenance*, should now come into the open. There can be little doubt that Kleiber regarded Furtwängler as his only serious rival for the post of director of the Berlin State Opera, and this underlay his rejection of the offer of the Metropolitan Opera on more than one occasion—lest, in his absence, he should find that Furtwängler had unseated him in Berlin. Though a brilliant student of orchestral psychology, Kleiber was something more than obtuse in the realm of *Realpolitik*, whereas Furt-wängler, although a poor student of orchestral psychology, had a shrewd political sense and could not resist dabbling in polemics. In April 1933, following the burning of the Reichstag on 27 February, he was induced to write an open letter to Dr. Goebbels, making an impassioned plea for artistic neutrality and an end to racial discrimination:

> The contemporary world of music, already weakened by the world depression and the radio [he said], can stand up to no more experiments . . . When this fight is directed against the real artist, it is against the interests of culture as a whole . . . It must, therefore, be plainly stated that men like Walter, Klemperer and Reinhardt must be enabled to have their say in Germany in the future . . .

Goebbels's reply, published in conjunction with Furtwängler's letter in a national press which he—Goebbels—by now controlled, was a master-piece of equivocation, and revealed the vanity of Furtwängler in supposing that he could ever defeat the politicians on their own ground. During April, the Berlin Philharmonic visited Mannheim to perform in a joint concert with the Mannheim orchestra, and the attempt was made to replace the Berlin concertmaster, Szymon Goldberg, with Mannheim's own concertmaster who was not—as Goldberg was—a Jew. Furtwängler declared that if the disposition of players was not to be left to him, he would cancel the concert. In the fol-lowing month fell the centenary of the birth of Johannes Brahms, who had been born in Hamburg, and the German Brahmsgesellschaft agreed to col-laborate with the Gesellschaft der Musikfreunde and hold a centenary concert in Vienna, where Brahms had spent the greater part of his life. Hubermann and Casals were engaged for the Double Concerto, and Schnabel for the Second Piano Concerto, provoking an immediate outcry from Nazi Berlin, with the result that foreign musicians, Jew and Gentile alike, began to boycott Germany. It became apparent that Furtwängler could not sit on the fence for very much longer, and would soon have to learn to distinguish and choose between his artistic conscience and the political sympathies with which he was becoming increasingly identified. His controversial article—*Der Fall Hinde-mith*—published in the *Deutsche Allgemeine Zeitung* of 25 November, 1934, in which he defended Hindemith and his music for reasons which are no longer historically cogent, led to his resignation both from the *Reichsmusik-kammer*, of which he had been vice-president, and the Berlin Philharmonic on 5 December, the day following Kleiber's own resignation from the Staatsoper. The Berlin Philharmonic's impending visit to England was accordingly can-celled, though Hitler refused to accept Furtwängler's resignation, and invited him to reconsider. In March 1935 Goebbels was reported on the German radio as having received Furtwängler, who had declared that he had never intended to introduce political considerations into the Hindemith Case, and regretted past misunderstanding. He was prepared to continue to conduct the Berlin Philharmonic—though not as their musical director—and would conduct at the Nuremberg Party Rally the following autumn. On 25 April he was photographed shaking hands with Hitler at a public concert in aid of the Winter Relief Fund, and in the summer his reinstatement as musical director for the forthcoming Bayreuth Festival in 1936—which Hitler would attend—was announced. In the light of these reports—whether true or no, and subsequent history shows them to have been substantially true—it is hardly surprising that when Furtwängler's appointment as permanent conductor of the New York Philharmonic in succession to Toscanini was announced on 29 February, 1936, it should have invited a holocaust of indignation, for the personnel of the New York Philharmonic was predominantly Jewish, and contained many members and their families who had been refugees from Nazi persecution. On 15 March, Furtwängler cancelled his New York engagement in the following cable:

> Political controversy disagreeable to me. Am not politician but exponent of German music which belongs to all humanity regardless of politics. I propose postpone my season in the interest of Philharmonic Society until the time public realises that politics and music are apart—FURTWÄNGLER.

Nothing could be calculated to have had more disastrous consequences on the American psychology, and Furtwängler was destined never to conduct in America again. In the summer of 1936 he fulfilled his engagement at the Bayreuth Festival, and remained its musical director until the outbreak of war in the summer of 1939. In 1938, following the Austrian *Anschluss* with Germany, he became musical director of the Salzburg Festival in succession to Toscanini, who had held the post since 1934.

Even at this distance of time, and with the wisdom of hindsight, it is difficult to assess the case of Furtwängler with complete impartiality. That he embraced a common cause with the Nazi regime, whose attitude—in those matters of art which touched them—was as superficially enlightened as their policy in broader terms was hideous, seems possible. That he helped prominent Jewish musicians to flee Germany when it became impossible to retain their services any longer, seems probable. But what is certain is that Furtwängler only registered annoyance at the material fact that those musicians who had become *untragbar* under the Nazi régime should no longer be available to him, in much the same way as he registered annoyance at the presence of an audience at the general rehearsal of the Ninth Symphony with the Vienna Philharmonic at the Royal Albert Hall in London in 1948. Furtwängler was in no sense a realist, and felt that because he was impelled to take up a particular position in a given situation, all reasonable people would be constrained to follow his example, and when they failed to do so he underwent the successive emotions of impatience and perplexity. That he should have meddled in politics, without understanding that the politics of Nazi Germany had nothing whatever to do with his own concept of political philosophy, and could only contaminate him in the eyes of the outside world, should not blind us to the fact that he was a very great conductor indeed—for that, at this distance of time and with the wisdom of hindsight, is the only issue which need concern us today.

With Kleiber's last two performances at the Berlin State Opera—of *Tannhäuser*, on 1 and 3 January, 1935—he now regarded himself as a free agent. Goering, as *Minister-Präsident* of German Theatres, had attempted to induce him to reconsider his resignation, and to return on his own terms, and at a salary payable in Swiss francs to any account in the world. (According to Max Lorenz, who was privy to their conversation, Kleiber had finally accepted, "on condition that he could give a Mendelssohn programme at his first concert".) The summer of 1935 saw him as a guest conductor—at the invitation of Toscanini—of the Salzburg Festival, and later in the year in Brussels, Amsterdam, Paris and London, where he made his debut in a Mozart programme at the Queen's Hall on 15 October. Paul Eger was now intendant of the Deutsches Theater in Prague, with Georg Szell as his general musical director, and Kleiber found an especially warm welcome there, conducting *Fidelio*, *Rosenkavalier* and Smetana's *The Kiss* and giving a series of concerts with the Czech Philharmonic. With the death of Alban Berg, on Christmas Eve 1935, Kleiber had not only lost a close and revered friend, but also his only reliable link with the Vienna opera house. Clemens Krauss, who had given the Austrian première of *Wozzeck* in 1929, had succeeded Kleiber at the Berlin State Opera, and his place at the Vienna State Opera was taken by Felix Weingartner. But Weingartner's unquestioned merits had never been those of an opera conductor, and he resigned at the close of the 1935–36 season. Speculation as to his successor was rife, and Kleiber was an obvious candidate. But his invitation to the Salzburg Festival was not renewed in 1936—nor was he even accorded that "audition" with the Vienna Philharmonic whose indignity he was to suffer in 1951. The 1936–37 season opened with Bruno Walter as "artistic director" of the Wiener Staatsoper, and Kleiber's visit in September to the Austrian Chancellor, Schuschnigg, can only be interpreted in the light of a formal protest from a fellow-Austrian. Austria was, in short, closed to Kleiber, and became increasingly so as the *Anschluss* drew nearer. Not unnaturally he felt that his middle years were slipping away from him, but there were compensations: his debuts at La Scala and Covent Garden, his popularity in Brussels and Prague, and his German opera season in Buenos Aires, which he had visited for the first time in 1926, and where he came nearest to the kind of cumulative work which he enjoyed most. Carlos Pessina, concertmaster of the Teatro Colón, has said of Kleiber:

> What gave Maestro Kleiber's rehearsals their especial flavour and character was his mixture of idiosyncratic injunctions, piercing inquisitory gaze, exact, exacting and ironical comment, kindness towards our individual dilemmas, and inflexible rigour where musical discipline and artistic obligation were concerned. With his original wit and brilliantly-timed jokes and comparisons, he fired the interest of even the most sluggish and ungifted members of the orchestra. He had a feeling for style that was really miraculous and showed itself as much in the Johann Strauss Waltzes and Dvořák Slavonic Dances in those early days as it did, years later, in the *Ring* and *Frau ohne Schatten* ... He never tired the orchestra with unnecessary remarks, nor rehearsed a bar longer than was absolutely needed. On the day of the performance the rehearsal would last less than half an hour, and it was rare for so much as a note to be played. Instead he would produce from his pocket a long roll of paper on which, he said, the composer had asked him to take note of the errors which had been committed the previous evening at the general rehearsal. Sometimes—before a Wagner opera, for example —the roll would be several feet long and covered from end to end with annotations in red and blue pencil ... As a psychologist, as well as a consummate pedagogue, he never appealed in vain to the will-power and *amour propre* of the orchestra, and he knew instinctively when they were about to flag and would be better for a break. If one of us made a mistake in performance he would never show that he had noticed. Often, in fact, he would deliberately turn his back. It was never safe, however, to conclude that one would not be called to order, later, in his room. I dare to assert that no musician who ever worked under him can remember him with anything other than the profoundest affection and respect.[8]

Orchestral training as Kleiber understood it was something quite new to the Argentine when he arrived there on his first visit in 1926—though it had clearly satisfied Toscanini on his last visit to Buenos Aires twenty years earlier. Rare visits by the great European and North American orchestras had of course given a vivid impression of what the end-product of such training could amount to, but of the work which was involved in acquiring those

[8] John Russell: *Erich Kleiber.*

standards the Argentinian musician had but little idea. During the first two months Kleiber had held exactly one hundred full rehearsals with the orchestra, and from the third of his fifteen concerts there was never an empty seat in his audience. His programmes for that first season introduced, among other things, the Argentinian premières of Mahler's Fourth and Beethoven's Sixth Symphonies, Brahms's *German Requiem*—in Spanish—and, the following season, Beethoven's centenary year, the *Missa Solemnis*. It was however his Covent Garden debut in May 1938 which represented the most important extension of Kleiber's activities after his resignation from the Berlin State Opera. His performances of *Fliegende Holländer* and *Rosenkavalier*—the latter with Lotte Lehmann as the Marschallin (save for the first performance, when she broke down at the end of Act I and her place was taken by Hilde Konetzni)—were an inspiration not only to the general public, the orchestra, and the cast, but one which extended to the stage-management as well. *Rosenkavalier* was only surpassed by his own performance, twelve years later, in the same house.

> *Der Rosenkavalier* is loved, of course, for its great lyrical scenes [writes John Russell in his biography of Kleiber], but it is primarily a narrative opera, in which the conductor's first task is that of setting an over-all tempo, and his second that of getting the words across without robbing the orchestra of the animal resource with which Strauss had endowed it . . . By never dwelling on moments of deep emotion he alienated those who like to lie in *Rosenkavalier* as others lie in a pine-bath. By keeping the orchestra down to a genuine *piano* and *pianissimo* he gave people more to listen to than they had expected to hear. And by bringing out the inner parts—producing, for instance, so great a clarity in the prelude to Act III that several members of the orchestra told him that they had never heard so many of the notes before—he altogether transcended the impact, inauthentic and gross, on which people had come to rely. Certain passages—Ochs's great narration in Act I, for instance, where he likens himself to "Jupiter, happy in a thousand guises"—had, it is true, a Handelian fullness: but they also had a Handelian fleetness of mind, and that is not what people expect of *Der Rosenkavalier*.
>
> For a glimpse of Kleiber's purely professional qualities we cannot do better than turn to the passage in Act I (fig. 124 *et seq.*) where Ochs talks to himself, to Octavian [Mariandl] and the Marschallin all at once. Ludwig Weber, who recorded the role with Kleiber, told me that, for sheer accomplishment, he had never seen anything to match the way in which Kleiber, both here and in the levée scene, kept the action transparently clear and the huge orchestra as nimble as that in *Ariadne auf Naxos*. But it is by the great lyrical moments that *Rosenkavalier* is remembered. The humour may go never so well, but if the heart is not touched, the evening's traffic will

seem long indeed. Kleiber did not subscribe to the *larmoyant* view. "Comedy", Strauss and Hoffmansthal had called it, and comedy it remains in Kleiber's recording. But this does not mean that his interpretation is without deep feeling—on the contrary, it is sentimentality which is lacking. His was not a performance which needed to force the pace, and when the music calls for a single decisive stroke (as in Act III when the word *vorbei* is passed from voice to voice like an envelope which none dares open) then the art of the *conteur* pays off a hundredfold and the stroke, for all its gentleness, is mortal. Kleiber's conduct of the opera is throughout a lesson in the uses of reserve—provided, of course, that the reserve comes from a superabundance of feeling: it is only the strong who can afford never to crave the audience's attention, or to put, too obviously a shoulder to the wheel.

But this is to overlook other and more important essences of *Rosenkavalier* which were peculiar to Kleiber's artistry, and so abundantly in evidence in his performances of the work. The very opening was wholly characteristic, the initial *slancio* of the horns being engaged summarily and without the usual formalities of acknowledgement of applause—which was stifled at birth, and the audience brought to the edge of their seats—while the exuberant conviction of the answering string section of the Covent Garden orchestra bore Kleiber's unmistakable stamp. The blatantly suggestive horn *glissandi* at bars 31–32 and their immediate release at fig. 5 were in impeccable taste—as they are in the score itself—because they allow of no possible ambiguity, unlike the trombone *glissandi* in *Lady Macbeth of Mtzensk*. The Marschallin's melody at fig. 11 was not accorded the extended treatment which, a few minutes later, it received after her words to Octavian—"Du bist mein Bub, du bist mein Schatz! Ich hab' dich lieb . . . "—for this is still the overture. Nor was this quotation at fig. 27 dwelt on with the same full-throated eloquence which it received at the end of Act I (fig. 321), for this is only the beginning of the act. The poetry of the Marshallin's words (four bars after fig. 25) are accompanied by the first sustained woodwind *pianissimo* of the opera, and provided a superlative vehicle for Lehmann's voice—as it did for that of Maria Reining in Kleiber's later recording—and promise of untold riches to come. For Kleiber was the supreme master of *pianissimo*, and nowhere was this more in evidence than in Sophie's exquisite phrase at fig. 30 of Act II:

Ex. 27

Wie himm—— lis-che nicht— ir - dis-che, wie Ro-sen von hoch ~ heil-i-gen Pa - — ra-dies

a phrase which, at fig. 35, is repeated a minor third higher, and provided the illusion of a sustained *forte*, simply because Kleiber took the trouble to observe Strauss's markings of *fpp*—the *pp* being retained for three full bars of broad 4/4 before swelling quickly back to *forte* again:

Ex. 28

Ex. 28 (*continued*)

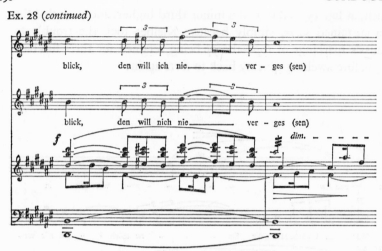

This control is identified with that sense of timing which was the hallmark of Kleiber's art, for where the climaxes finally arrive, he would accord them their supreme value—as at fig. 291 where, the strings having already reached *fortissimo*, the trombones enter *piano*, with a two-bar *crescendo* to *forte* at fig. 292, rising immediately to *fortissimo* only five bars later—four bars before fig. 293:

Ex. 29

Ex. 29 (continued)

This control was always purposeful, as Strauss intended that it should be, and where, earlier in Act III, at fig. 278, the first violins are required to answer Sophie's bewilderment with a sense of compassion which must be dramatically felt before the Marschallin gives it expression in the last half of the selfsame bar, Kleiber showed consummate mastery:

Ex. 30

It is the *portamento* of the first violins which gives this phrase its character, and the mysteries of the "audible shift" are generally thought to be the closely guarded secret of the practitioners of string playing themselves. Kleiber had been a violinist of modest dimensions in his youth, and had discovered many of these secrets for himself, but he had never been a virtuoso violinist of the calibre of Charles Munch, for example, who in the *Symphonie Fantastique* had confined the use of audible *portamento* in all three performances which I was to hear him give of the work to the solitary instance of a first violin phrase from the coda of the first movement. The virtue of *portamento* lies in direct relation to the infrequency of its use, and when that use becomes exaggerated, as it does under Eugene Ormandy, its virtues are abused and the whole purpose of the effect defeated. That is why orchestral string players are reluctant to employ it, feeling that if the conductor is a string player himself he will know how to ask for it if he wants it, and that if he is not he will not know where its use will be appropriate. But the distinguished conductor, whether he is a string player or not, will *always* know when its use is appropriate and when it is not, and if he does not know how to ask for it will take the trouble to find out. Among non string playing conductors who have continually astonished experienced string players with the acuteness of their perception into this subject are Georg Szell and Dimitri Mitropoulos, and it is extremely significant that both had worked under Kleiber at the Berlin State Opera. Mitropoulos's use of *portamenti* in the *due violini soli* passage from the slow movement of Mahler's First Symphony was especially apt, and utterly haunting in its effect.

Kleiber's own use of *portamento* was not lavish, and it was always discreet, but it served to bring an inner warmth to the texture of the music which immediately distinguished it from the readings of other conductors of equal distinction. The clearly audible *portamento* in the first violins at bar 43 (*Tempo I*) of the slow movement of the Beethoven Ninth was an obvious example, imbuing the appogiatura F with a significance which had escaped all conductors before him. But there were other and infinitely more subtle uses of the effect in Kleiber's reading of this movement in particular—from the C to the G of the first violins in the first beat of bar 105, for example, or the same notes in the last beat of bar 138. And he would examine the text exhaustively for any implied reference to other string effects, employing a *sul IV* in the first violins at bar 149—which cannot sensibly be played on any other string, but giving the performance the conscious conviction of G string tone at this point. He would endow the great passage immediately following letter B with a sequence of the heaviest of long and sustained accents—not only on the evidence of the text itself, but by drawing his analogy from the Schubert

Quintet, Op. 163. In the first movement, the insistent octave D's in the second violins beginning at bar 240 were rescued from their normal gross and perfunctory role and transfigured into a mighty fulfilment, dominating the entire passage, of the hushed string triplets which open the movement.

There were many other remarkable features about Kleiber's performance of the Beethoven Ninth, not least of which was his logical analysis of the problematic passage at bar 330 of the Scherzo. Weingartner used to direct the horns to play in unison with the woodwinds, and *fortissimo*, at this point, maintaining that the balance of the passage had been misjudged by Beethoven, and that the strength of the combined octaves in horns and trumpets which the text prescribes must be too loud for the all-important woodwind phrase at this point. Furtwängler and Munch were among other conductors who agreed with him, and indulged themselves in consequence in an orgy of horn tone which, far from giving support to the woodwinds, swamped them altogether. And very impressive the passage became, though it distorted Beethoven's original conception of it. Kleiber went to the root of the problem, agreeing that the balance was faulty, but maintaining that it was not the brass octaves which were too loud, but the woodwind which were too soft. And he accordingly instructed the horns—not four, but two—to play with the woodwind, and not *fortissimo*, but *piano*, thus according the woodwinds a token of support, and restoring the balance as Beethoven had conceived it.

On 24 June, 1939, Kleiber left Europe for five concerts in Montevideo—which embraced all nine symphonies by Beethoven—and arrived in Buenos Aires on 14 August, on a journey which was destined to separate him from his family for the next eleven months, and from Europe for the next nine years. War in Europe broke out in September 1939, and he found himself an initially unwilling exile in South America. Those artists who were not already in America were no longer available to him, and at the end of the Teatro Colón season in November, Kleiber was thrown back on his own resources. It was wholly characteristic of his inner reserves of strength that he found himself adopting, more or less unwittingly at first, the role of a pioneer, and in his letters to his family in 1940, Europe gradually passed out of his line of vision and was replaced by a preoccupation whose dimensions were purely local. During the next six years he discovered, rehearsed endlessly, patiently and tirelessly, and gave concerts with the local orchestras of Peru, Chile (where he gave the first Chilean performance of *Le Sacre du Printemps*), Uruguay (where he gave Berg's *Lyric Suite*, the three excerpts from *Wozzeck*, Bartók's Concerto for Orchestra, and Strauss's *Don Quixote*), Montevideo, Mexico, Guatemala and finally Cuba—returning the while for the annual season of German opera at the Colón in Buenos Aires, which was by now equal to such works as the *Ring, Parsifal, Elektra, Salome* and *Der Rosenkavalier*. Cuba was the last of his discoveries, and he gave the first of his concerts there on 25 March, 1943, with the Orquesta Filharmónica of Havana—an orchestra partially recruited from the local police and fire brigade bands. Yet this did not prevent Kleiber from introducing the first Cuban performances of *Mathis der Maler, Heldenleben,* de Falla's *Homenajes,* and Rameau's *Castor et Pollux*—the last named of course receiving as detailed attention as he gave to the Hindemith and Strauss. Yehudi Menuhin, who came to play the Beethoven Violin Concerto with him, found in Kleiber's "a quality of patience that is going out of life"—the capacity to work and wait which had been the secret of the great nineteenth-century executants, *vide* Liszt's letters to Franzisca von Bulow. Eighteen orchestral rehearsals preceded the three rehearsals with Menuhin, and even these three represented a rare luxury for an itinerant soloist who normally has to content himself with a single run-through.

With the end of the war it was now at long last possible to recruit international casts, and the 1947 *Ring* included List, Janssen, Svanholm and Varnay, and in the winter of 1947–48 Kleiber visited North America to conduct the NBC Symphony—one of the very few European conductors to be accorded this privilege. (Kleiber had previously conducted the New York Philharmonic, on two months' leave of absence from the Berlin Staatsoper, on the three consecutive occasions of the 1930–33 seasons. But he was not enamoured of the United States, although his wife, Ruth Kleiber, was American.) In February 1948, Kleiber returned to Europe for two concerts with the London Philharmonic Orchestra, and this invitation was repeated the following year when his two programmes consisted of the Haydn *Surprise* Symphony and the *Pathétique,* and the Mozart G minor Symphony and the *Eroica*. The following spring he concluded a contract for a series of guest appearances at the Royal Opera House, Covent Garden, and arrived there to take up his duties in November 1950. All opera at Covent Garden was, in principle, given in English at that time, and there was—to quote Mr. Russell:[9]

> about every Covent Garden production in English something in-
> expungably *triste*. Foreign visitors claim to admire the practice, in
> principle, and no doubt it has for them a certain exotic appeal. In
> smaller theatres, too, where the convinced patriot expects less, more
> is given ... Covent Garden is, by any standard, a great theatre, but
> it not an encouraging one. Anything that falls flat there falls flatter
> than almost anywhere else in the world. The audience too: a dull
> audience at Covent Garden is the very image of desperation. When
> to all these factors is added a continual drip of disparagement, singers

[9] John Russell: *Erich Kleiber.*

and orchestra cannot fail to become discouraged, even if they know that a great many of the unfavourable comments originate with people who have rarely been inside the theatre. Covent Garden was not, in short, a happy theatre at the time of Kleiber's arrival.

It was in fact a classic Kleiber situation, in which he arrived, wrought his private miracles with orchestra and singers (and with an especial word of praise to the young music staff), won the public to the last man—and almost to the last critic—paid two more visits and was offered the musical directorship, and finally left, after irreconcilable differences with the administration. It was given out after the Coronation season of 1953 that the differences had been financial, but this was patently not the root cause of the disagreement. Sir Steuart Wilson is reported to have published abroad the fact that "he did not think Kleiber had any personality", and for his part, Kleiber did not sense at Covent Garden what he had sensed at the Berlin Staatsoper and the Teatro Colón—an instinct to put art first, at whatever the cost. Mr. Russell goes on: "Kleiber was by nature an absolutist, and in a world like that of the English stage, where compromise is universal and a creeping gentility saps all that should be direct and unfearing, he could never have survived."

Nevertheless, Kleiber's three seasons at Covent Garden yielded performances, unsurpassable in their orchestral perfection, of *Der Rosenkavalier*, *Pique Dame*, *Rigoletto*, *Carmen*, *Elektra*, *Tristan* (in German, with Rudolf Hartmann as producer), *Figaro*, *Die Zauberflote* and *Wozzeck*. And it was perhaps this last which left on London the faintest, but most indelible impression, for the ultimate quality which the masterpiece of *Wozzeck* displays is one of extreme compassion, and this was Kleiber's own abiding quality, and one which distinguishes him from all other contemporary rivals. For London in 1952, *Wozzeck* could not have held that significance which it had held for the Berlin audience of 1926, nor could it have had that significance which it holds for a younger generation today, where Wozzeck's vision of an all-engulfing fire has more than a sense of immediacy. For the première of *Rosenkavalier* on 6 December, 1950, the critic Eric Blom had written, in a moment of rare enthusiasm: "On the evidence of one's ears alone one could have sworn that he [Kleiber] had brought some fine and assiduously drilled orchestra with him, from goodness knows where". For the première of *Wozzeck*, *The Times* could only declare: "Nasty and depressive it all is", in the course of a review which failed monumentally to grasp the point.

Furtwängler, meanwhile, had returned to London for the first time since 1938, when he had made a last, and in the event, unwelcome visit with the Berlin Philharmonic. Now his visit was with the Vienna Philharmonic, in a great performance of the Beethoven Ninth at the Royal Albert Hall, which resulted in guest engagements with the London Philharmonic and a recording contract with the newly-formed Philharmonia—an orchestra which at that time, and with the pressure of competition from so many other London orchestras, was over-inclined to stand on its dignity. Furtwängler was not popular, and there was an undisguised antipathy to him at first, which took the form of pointed and audible comments about his recent political affiliations, and an undercurrent of complaint about the inadequacy of his baton-technique. But within the space of a year the political affiliations had been forgotten, the purpose of his wayward technique understood and digested, and another English orchestra had begun to learn its lesson. In June 1951, Furtwängler visited East Berlin—not to conduct, on this occasion, but to hear Kleiber conduct *Der Rosenkavalier* at the Admiralspalast. He was accorded an ovation from the citizens of Berlin which was only exceeded by the appearance of Kleiber himself who, so great was the tumult which greeted him, was unable to start the performance for several minutes—a singular occurrence for one whose openings were habitually abrupt to the point of disdaining any applause at all. This was the only occasion, to my knowledge, of Kleiber and Furtwängler meeting (or nearly so) in the context of interpretative artist and listener, and for all its shrewd irony, there must have been an overwhelming mutual respect, and mutual sadness, that their several great gifts should ultimately have gone, in their several ways, by default.

Chapter 10

STRAVINSKY, WEINGARTNER AND OTHERS

It is necessary to distinguish two moments, or rather two states of music: potential music and actual music. Having been fixed upon paper or retained in the memory, music exists already prior to its actual performance, differing in this respect from all the other arts, just as it differs from them, as we have seen, in the categories that determine its perception.

The musical entity thus presents the remarkable singularity of embodying two aspects, of existing successively and distinctly in two forms separated from each other by a hiatus of silence. This peculiar nature of music determines its very life as well as its repercussions in the social world, since it presupposes two kinds of musicians: the creator and the performer[1].

Stravinsky goes on at once to include the theatre within this frame of reference, but with qualifications which tend to baffle the average intelligence. And his whole thesis, which is contained within the above two paragraphs, is inclined to break down when one points out that more than the architect is involved in building a building for which he has merely furnished the blueprint, and that the sculptor is likewise dependent on apprentice labour if he be a Benvenuto Cellini. In fact the only arts which fall within Stravinsky's claim of being essentially different from music are those of literature and painting, where the reader or the viewer becomes in any case his own interpreter. Just as architecture must to a greater or lesser extent reveal the personality not only of its architect, but also of the builder who actively supervises its building, so the performance of music must contain an element of the personality of its interpreter as well as that of its composer. The fundamental flaw in Stravinsky's argument becomes only too clear when one is compelled to point out that it is never his more familiar pieces which are of interest to the listener as much as Stravinsky's own interpretations of them, which are never outstanding as to matters of ensemble, but are none the less intensely personal and hold for us a continual fascination—even if it is only the fascination of listening to him bowdlerising his own text.

An analogy with the processes of history will be obvious, and the historian

[1] Igor Stravinsky: *Poetics in Music*, Harvard University Press, 1947.

who is completely faithful to the undeniable fact of history in its every aspect is a significant hypothesis. For the 'facts' are invariably ambiguous, and their ambiguity becomes the more marked at precisely those moments of history where available research is richest, and most "open to interpretation". To insist that the conscientious historian confine his activities to the recording of those facts of history which are not seriously in dispute must be supererogatory, and overlook the equally undisputed fact of that inspired conjecture which can alone bring his treatise to life. For historical fact will remain dead and inanimate unless and until the historian of integrity can resuscitate it with an interpretation which reveals demonstrably the conviction of his personality, and however unimpeachable the source, that interpretation will always reflect a quality which is ephemeral in direct relation as it fails to penetrate below the surface of accepted fact.

Tucked away in the pockets of recent musical history are four conductors, each of whose characters is distinctive but—for this writer, at least—whose personalities remain elusive: Felix Weingartner, Bruno Walter, Clemens Krauss and Otto Klemperer—of whom the last-named is, at the time of writing, still very much alive, and has long since become a British Institution. Only thirty years separate their respective dates of birth, and they find common ground in the service which they have rendered to a specific composer or composers—Beethoven in the case of Weingartner, Beethoven and Mahler in the case of Klemperer, Mozart and Mahler in the case of Walter, and Mozart and Strauss in the case of Clemens Krauss.

Felix Weingartner was born in Zara, on the Dalmatian coast, on 2 June, 1863, and read philosophy at the University of Leipzig until he was twenty, when he attended the summer master-class of Franz Liszt, and went thence to his first operatic appointment at Königsberg. In 1885 he became an assistant conductor in Danzig, two years later at the Hamburg Stadttheater, and two years later still at Mannheim. His subsequent history has been chronicled elsewhere, but it is undoubtedly his eleven years as a concert hall conductor of the Berlin Hofkapelle (from 1891 to 1902) and nineteen years with the Vienna Philharmonic (from 1908 to 1927) for which he is chiefly remembered, and wherein he was enabled to bring his performances of Beethoven to a pinnacle of perfection. His treatise on the performance of the Beethoven symphonies, published in 1906[2], swiftly became a standard textbook—in fact the only textbook—on the subject, and it is eloquent of its scholarship that, sixty years later, all British orchestras[3] of any distinction

---

[2] Felix Weingartner: *Ratschläge für Aufführungen der Sinfonien Beethovens*, Breitkopf & Härtel, Leipzig, 1906. Author's translation.
[3] With the exception of the Philharmonia, which has in recent years learned to play Beethoven *à la* Klemperer.

continue to play Beethoven in the manner which he advocated (Weingartner having been a frequent visitor to this country, making his debut here in 1898, and giving his last concert, with the London Philharmonic, in 1940) although Continental orchestras have long since discovered other and more penetrating possibilities. Like every treatise, the caution over its blind and verbatim adoption which Weingartner consistently pleaded has been largely ignored, with the result that practices, which in the light of later research have revealed themselves as being acutely personal to him, have acquired common currency—in Britain, at all events—while his critics have been ever ready to attack him on the very ground on which Weingartner was least sure of himself, and openly admitted it. On that ground where Weingartner took a confident, and as he thought, unimpugnable stand—over the vexed question of bassoons and/or horns in the reprise of the second subject in the first movement of the Fifth Symphony, for example—his critics are significantly silent.

I have tried in the first instance to enliven the execution by carefully editing the text [wrote Weingartner], and have endeavoured to clarify the obscurer passages without resort to alteration of the instrumentation. By careful editing I have brought the more important parts into prominence and relegated the less important ones to the background—not with the purpose of introducing arbitrary shades of expression, but simply to preserve unbroken the *melos* of the symphony, the clear understanding of which is the only safeguard against obscurity in execution. In many cases where I had originally thought an alteration in the instrumentation to be indispensable, I found to my joy that a carefully executed "edition" not only met my own requirements to the full, but also corresponded much more to Beethoven's intention than the contemplated alteration would have done.

Passages do occur, however, where editing alone does not suffice, and in such cases I have been obliged to have recourse to interference with the instrumentation. This book, in which every one of these cases is examined and justified in detail, should be sufficient evidence of the careful consideration with which I proceeded in this matter.

Such alterations are of two different kinds. In some cases I have made the second voice in the winds, where it has arrived at a rest, play in unison with the first with the object of strengthening it. In several symphonies I have not only employed double woodwind against a sufficiently numerous string section—this other conductors have done before me—but have also indicated with the utmost care where this doubling is to come in and where it was to stop in every passage and every divided part . . . Other alterations are necessary in those passages in which both horns or both trumpets should

play in octaves, and Beethoven was obliged—through want of a
"natural" note—to allow the second voice to make a dispropor-
tionate leap. Wagner, as he tells us himself, "generally" recommended
his second wind players to take the lower part and to play thus:

Ex. 31

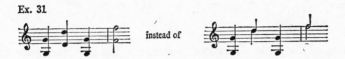

But this "generally" goes too far, for it is just these intervals
which are often so characteristic. And just as a great master can
often turn to advantage the very imperfection of the means at his
disposal, so here this striking use of natural notes often corresponds
exactly to the peculiarities of Beethoven's style, and any attempt
to improve upon it would only have the opposite effect. I have
therefore examined each of these cases on their own merits, and
have only ventured an alteration—i.e. a transposition to the lower
octave—where Beethoven's action is palpably due to the limited
compass of the instruments of his time.

Much less numerous than these modest modifications are those
passages in which I have made actual additions and have inserted
harmony notes where rests are prescribed for the brass, or have
changed slightly the course of the melody in these parts. I have
only done this where there can be absolutely no doubt that Beethoven would have written the same passage in exactly the same way,
had not the above-mentioned imperfection of these instruments
compelled him to do violence to his own conception, and he would
certainly thank us for these alterations were he still in the land of the
living.

Weingartner thereupon proceeds to examine the Beethoven symphonies
in meticulous detail—without, however, always justifying in their entirety the
changes which he advocates. That Beethoven must have been secretly aware
that a radical improvement in the inadequate brass instruments at his disposal had, by the end of his life, become long overdue is clear from the
number of stopped notes which proliferate in his works from the *Eroica* onwards. Nor can one entirely agree with Weingartner when he states, *à propos*
the following passage, which contains no less than seven stopped notes in the
third horn part:

Evidently Beethoven had a skilful player at his command. There
was less danger in this passage, however, of any harm being done
by the notes in question, since the 'celli and first bassoon
were playing [in unison] at the same time. *This passage proves,*

*however, that Beethoven did not abstain from stopped notes on principle,
but on purely technical grounds.*

Ex. 32

What, then, of the pitilessly exposed passage in the first horn part, earlier in
the same movement, whose responsibility it is to engender the impulse for the
ensuing string fugato and its monumental aftermath?

Ex. 33

I would, on the contrary, infer from Beethoven's text that it was precisely on
the matter of principle, and not "on purely technical grounds", that Beethoven abstained from using stopped notes, except where their employment
in the context of a whole phrase was characteristic, whereupon he would
examine the means at his disposal to discover whether or not the passage concerned were possible on the instrument (usually the horn) which was available
to him—and usually it was, for the instances of Beethoven's conceiving a
passage which should prove wholly uncharacteristic in its every aspect are
extremely rare.

In the famous passage from the first movement of the Fifth Symphony,
Weingartner states categorically that horns should replace Beethoven's
bassoons.

> The transference of the second subject from the horns in the expo-
> sition of this movement to the bassoons here, is merely a way out of
> a difficulty. Beethoven could not entrust the phrase to the E flat
> horns, as he could not use stopped notes for this powerful and
> luminous passage. There was no time for a change of crook (to C)
> and evidently he was unwilling to add a second pair of horns simply
> for the sake of these few bars. So there was no way out of the diffi-
> culty than to make use of bassoons. The effect which they produce,
> however, when compared with the idea which we obtain from this
> passage as it appears in the exposition, is lamentable—in fact it is
> simply comic . . . There is only one radical change which can be
> made and this is preferable to all these half-measures: that is, *to
> replace the bassoons by the horns, and that is certainly what Beethoven
> would have done had he had all our instruments at his disposal.*

Ex. 34

But would Beethoven have done this? Let us examine the context in detail. We may accept Weingartner's view that the use of E flat horns, involving as they would the employment of two prominent stopped notes, would have been out of the question for Beethoven. If Beethoven had really required the phrase to be played on the horns, a change of crook would therefore have been imperative. Weingartner asserts that there was no time to accomplish this (and this is the usual excuse which is given)—but is this in fact true? The last notes which the horns have to play without any manner of dispute occur in the pause bar of bar 252. At the important cadence at bars 267–8 the horns are significantly silent, and a change of crook (to C crooks) could have been accomplished here with ease—bearing in mind the length of the oboe cadenza at bar 268—before their next entry at bar 274, had Beethoven required it. Between bar 274 and the all-important entry at bar 303, all the intervening notes which the horns are required to play are available as open notes on C crooks, with the exception of three which are readily available as stopped notes. They include, it is true, the sustained (written) octave C at the *ff* at bar 296, but—bearing in mind his intolerance of compromise, and his aversion to the sound of stopped notes—Beethoven would have assuredly re-orchestrated this passage had he really wished the ensuing phrase at bar 303 to be played on the horns. Between bars 321 and bar 342, moreover, there is ample time for a reversion to E flat crooks. (The changing of crooks was accomplished, by virtue of long habit, extremely quickly in Beethoven's day, and the oft-cited example in the first movement of the *Eroica*—where Beethoven allows 41 bars for the first horn to change his crook from E flat to F, and no less than 89 to effect the change back—must not be misinterpreted. Crook-changing was as unusual in Beethoven's music as it was frequent in the music of lesser composers of his day, and the example of the *Eroica*—which is the first instance of the practice within the body of a Beethoven movement—must necessarily have excited curiosity and expectancy from his audience, for although crook-changing can be accomplished silently, it cannot be accomplished invisibly. Beethoven, as a profound psychologist where his own music was concerned, preferred to allow time for that curiosity to subside, so that the first horn entry on F should come with all its freshness. Nor could Beethoven's sensitive ear adjust to the sound of only two horns in the *tuttis* which precede and follow this entry without the substantial preparation of the ears of his audience.)

Beethoven wrote the bassoon entry at bar 303 of the Fifth Symphony because he wanted bassoons, and not horns, whose sound would have been uncharacteristic in the context of the whole movement—whether played as stopped notes on E flat crooks, or as open notes on C crooks—and alien to a mind which could think in symphonic terms more penetrating than those of Weingartner. But his expectation of the volume and quality of tone which the bassoons might be expected to produce was undoubtedly exaggerated—Beethoven was by this time already deaf—and the bassoon passages in the overture *Die Weihe des Hauses* furnish another example of a tonal image which had by then become further distorted. The only remedy consists in doubling the bassoons—which will in any case be already doubled in any performance of distinction—and to add horns (not one, but two, so as to preserve the symphonic texture) in *piano*, which will give the necessary tonal support to the bassoons for which Beethoven's inner ear was in all probability seeking. Erich Kleiber, who was a master of compromise once the composer's intentions had been established beyond dispute, used to play the phrase in question in this manner once he had penetrated through to the fundamental argument —that Beethoven did not want horns *in principle* to play at all. Having arrived on the pedal G, Kleiber directed the horns to carry their pedal-note over to the end of bar 322, in analogy with the corresponding passage in the exposition. (Clemens Krauss thought that Beethoven might have omitted this note because it gave the uncomfortable feeling of a 6/4 chord—the real bass being here in the timpani, as compared with the 'cellos and basses in the exposition which give a more conscious bass. But what of the timpani notes eight bars earlier? Bar 322 occurs at a page-turn in the original manuscript, so that Beethoven could have omitted the extra bar in the horn parts by accident. That he does not use a tie in the last bar of the preceding page is not, to my mind, conclusive—though some have thought it so. But although Beethoven had the opportunity of proof-reading the individual parts, he did not proof-read the first edition of the score, which had been assembled from those parts.)

Over the matter and manner of execution of the opening bars, and Beethoven's alteration of his own original text in every place where the passage recurs, Weingartner is unquestionably right, *in principle*. The opening is an organic part of the whole progress of the movement, and must be played up to speed and with the strictest observance of the quarter-note rests, that their length be not exceeded. Furtwängler has quarrelled with Weingartner's thesis here, claiming that Beethoven inserted the additional bar before the second pause only because he wanted it to be longer, on every

occasion where it recurs, than the first pause: and he rejects Weingartner's
assertion that its function is organic. But there is ample evidence in support
of Weingartner's view—and evidence to spare—if we examine Beethoven's
text in greater detail. (It goes without saying that, in either reading, the second
pause will in any case be longer than the first—always assuming that the
pause may be read as a constant factor in both instances, which also goes
without saying.) Weingartner groups the bars in pairs, with the strong
accent on the first (silent) beat, as though to anticipate the use of trombones
at the entry of the finale:

Ex. 35

which clearly has a more incisive logic than this:

Ex. 36

and finds its ultimate justification in the final statement of the phrase, near the
end of the first movement. This, however, leads to a confusion of up-beats
when we arrive at the second subject—so demonstrably derived as it is from
the first. With the entry of the *piano* at the sixth bar, the system of strong and
weak beats has become reversed—justifiably so, since the emphasis is now on
the lower note of the interval. With the arrival of the second subject at bar
59 we may either continue in the same system of weak to strong beats, or have
to contend with the proposition of a three-bar phrase in the preceding three
bars (56–58). Weingartner deduces the logic of the passage as follows:

Ex. 37

but then, at its recurrence just before the recapitulation, reverts to this reading:

Ex. 38

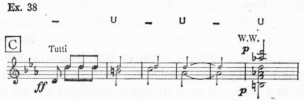

The abrupt nature of the *ff* entry at bar 228 can only be accomplished with the most dynamic and unambiguous of down-beats, and the reading of the analogous phrase at bar 59 must therefore be identical. This not only gives us a three-bar phrase at the cadence bars 56–58, but a phrasing of the counter-melody at bars 63–66 *et seq.*, which Weingartner finds—arbitrarily enough, because he has not examined the whole context—"completely wrong". If, however, we take the second subject motif from the point where it makes its entry on a dynamic down-beat in the closing stage of the development section, everything falls into place—two periods of eight bars each, followed by the gradual fragmentation of the motif, thus:

Ex. 39

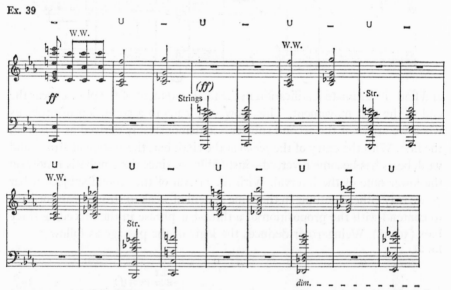

the accents falling in a manner diametrically opposed to normal practice—a manner, moreover, advocated by Weingartner himself, notwithstanding his rooted objections to the four-square execution of the original phrase (bars 59–66 *et seq.*): and this found its apotheosis in Kleiber's performances of the work.

Nor is this all. The second subject motif makes its appearance in the coda, as the natural culmination of the much discussed and bitterly disputed passage from bar 374 to bar 397 inclusive. Once again, if only we read the passage as a uniform progression of two, four and eight bars, consistently strong to weak, everything falls into place:

Ex. 40

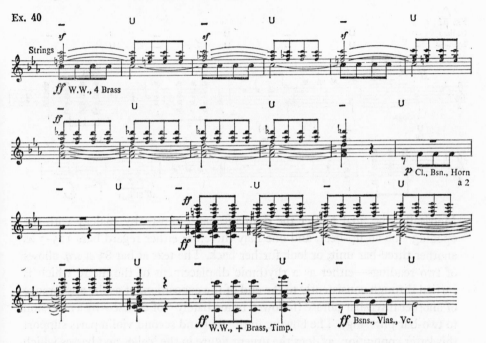

There remain the difficulties of the three-bar phrase (bars 56–58), and the preceding seven-bar phrase (bars 39–45 inclusive)—which, however, cancel themselves out if one applies Weingartner's principle of paired bars consistently, the twelve bars from bar 44 to bar 55 constituting a rhythmic displacement, or harmonic syncopation. Or one may read the passage, as Krauss suggested, as a seven-bar sequence arriving naturally at its climax with the *f* on the eighth bar—the upper octave. But yet another problem arises with the entry of the clarinets and horns at bar 83. These are marked *p cresc.*, while the direction of *cresc.* for the strings and bassoons comes only at the next bar (where the first oboe also makes its entry *p cresc.*), and the suggestion has been made that Beethoven has here made a mistake, and that one or the other of the dynamic markings should be transposed. If one reads the passage as it comes, however, as a displacement or syncopation of the metrical sequences of two bars, we arrive naturally at bar 124 in readiness for the return to the opening at the double-bar—though this does not imply that Beethoven's phrasing should be ignored, since Beethoven was fully aware of the implications of cross-phrasing. With the repeat of the exposition, however, the logic of Beethoven's seeming carelessness in his dynamic markings at bars 83–84 becomes at once apparent, for the bars which immediately follow the double-bar are intentionally ambiguous, looking as it were both forward and back:

Ex. 41

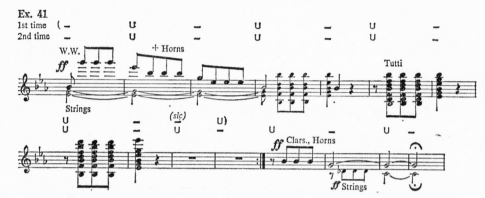

Metrically, the final *p* after the dramatic pause must—by analogy with the opening—be an up-beat, and one may therefore either regard bars 125–7 as another three-bar unit, or look further back. The text at bar 83 *et seq.* allows of two readings—either as a rhythmic displacement of the metre which is carried through consistently to the end of the exposition, or as the appearance of another three-bar phrase (followed immediately—of course—by a reversion to two-bar phrasing). The bowing in the first and second violin parts support this latter contention, as does the urgent figure in the 'cellos and basses which makes its presence felt at this moment with its insistent rising semitones. If, therefore, one reads the passage at its first statement as a syncopation across pairs of bars, the logic of the *crescendo* at bar 83 becomes apparent. If, however, one reads the passage at its second statement—the re-exposition—as a three-bar phrase, the logic of the *crescendo* at bar 84 becomes apparent. In fact, Beethoven has not been careless at all, and the duality of his dynamic markings in bars 83–84 only serves to underline two separate but distinct functions—a return to the opening in the first case, by way of a metrical displacement which naturally heightens the intensity of the passage immediately following, and a continuation into the development in the second place, where the adoption of an isolated three-bar metre at bars 83–85 finds its ultimate resolution at bars 125–7 *et seq.* Once again, Erich Kleiber made this subtle distinction demonstrably apparent in his readings of the Fifth Symphony, by imbuing the passage in question—at its first appearance—with that quality of tentative urgency which every true syncopation must provide of its own accord, and with that self-assurance—at its second appearance—which is confident of finding its resolution at the double-bar.

Only one further problem remains unresolved in this extraordinary movement—bars 469–482, whose constitution would seem to contradict the basis of Weingartner's whole thesis, for if we take the C minor resolution at bar 469 as being a strong beat, we arrive by the process of paired bars at bar 478 with an up-beat, followed immediately by a down-beat at the first of the two pauses:

Ex. 42

But a glance at bars 407–14 should be sufficient for the discerning analyst, for they constitute a sequence of nine bars—a changing-note sequence over the interval of one octave—whose function is absolutely organic: to displace the rhythm which appears nine bars later, at bar 423, and to imbue the entire passage from bar 423 to bar 477 with the quality of a gigantic syncopation such as only Brahms was to know how to equal. This is not to say that the trochaic metre at bars 423–4 *et seq.*, must be reversed—quite the contrary. The establishment of a pattern of syncopation carries with it, at the hands of a great artist, the ever-increasing expectation of ultimate resolution, which comes—in no uncertain manner—with bars 478–82. Here again, Kleiber's reading was unequivocal, and remains unsurpassed.

There is, notwithstanding its manifold and glaring lack of penetration and scholarship, very much to recommend in Weingartner's treatise. His injunction for the first flute to take the high B flat at bar 473 in the first movement of the *Eroica,* and more particularly for the first violins to take the high A in the analogous passage at bar 501 *et seq.*, in the first movement of the Ninth Symphony, is highly questionable. The high B flat on Beethoven's flutes was of uncertain and piercing quality (and even today, it requires expert control), while it is well known that Beethoven seldom took his violins above the high A—and when he did so, as in the overture to *Egmont,* where they are taken up to C—he is cautious to approach the note in question by step, and not from "out of the blue". While Weingartner's recommendations do ineradicable damage to Beethoven's concept of a characteristically tortured

H

leap at the climax of a phrase, they have the merit of a refusal to accept blindly
the printed text—and the demerit of then being blind to the merit of the
printed text. His injunctions over the use of doubled woodwinds are thoroughly sound in general—just as, in principle, is his recommendation for six
horns in the *Eroica* Symphony. If one is to allow the principle of doubled
winds, then three horns are clearly insufficient, but I think it wiser to confine
their use in the *Eroica* to only five—a standard practice in American orchestras, and one which Kleiber introduced to this country at one of his concerts
with the London Philharmonic in 1949. A further problem arises in this work,
for which Weingartner's solution is really only a half-measure. It concerns the
famous phrase, in the third horn and clarinets, in the fugato of the Funeral
March:

Ex. 43

Here an unequivocal decision must be taken—either to leave Beethoven's text
as it stands, or carry through the intentions implicit in the voice-leading of the
clarinets (and violas) to their logical conclusion. Kleiber and Munch, among
others, are conductors who have adopted this latter course, and I am convinced that they are right. If there is to be any doubling at all, then it is
necessary to double the passage in its entirety, and nothing less than three
clarinets and three horns will suffice for the complete expression of the
phrase's inherent majesty. A high C is called for in the trio of the Scherzo, so
it is no use arguing that Beethoven refrained from a voice-leading which
would give, at this point, E—F sharp—G sharp—A on the E flat horn on the
grounds that the passage is dangerously exposed—the trio of the Scherzo is
far more dangerously exposed, for all three horns are *soli*. But the use of the
E-flat horn to complete the phrase would, however, have demanded the use of
stopped notes in Beethoven's time—notes whose production was readily
available to his players, but whose quality Beethoven found repugnant. Why,
then, does he not complete the phrase on the first horn, which is in C in this
movement, and which would give the melodic progression of G—A—B
(natural)—C, the identical written notes which the first horn is required to
play in the trio of the Scherzo? The first four bars are unequivocally in E flat

major, and lay naturally on the E flat horn of Beethoven's time, which is why
he seizes on the instrument to express his symphonic idea at this juncture, for
it is of all horn phrases one of the most idiomatic. But it is not sufficient to
suggest that his fastidious symphonic instinct would have been outraged by
the transference of the phrase to another instrument at the fifth bar, where the
music moves to the dominant of C minor—although this may have been so.
Far more important—and absolutely conclusive, in my view—is the fact that
Beethoven considered, on balance, the octave C which enters at bar 142 to be
the decisive factor. Both notes of this octave are equally important, in the
symphonic context, and neither was available on the E flat horn, so that if
Beethoven had completed the preceding phrase on the first horn, he would
have had to sacrifice one or other of the horn notes in the lower octaves,
and this he was clearly unprepared to do. Here, the logic of the use of five
horns becomes manifest—though its logic is equally manifest on frequent
other and more obvious occasions—for three horns may now be used to complete the phrase in unison with the clarinets, while the other two may take
over the sustained octave C at bar 142. Three-fold woodwind is now sufficient to each and every occasion, for no more than three horns will now be
playing the same identical part, and these were the forces employed by
Kleiber at the above-mentioned London Philharmonic concert.

But the most obnoxious of Weingartner's recommendations does not
consist in his frequent emendations of Beethoven's text, and which—
whether or not one can agree with them—have a logic which has clearly been
well considered, although he will ignore the presence of conflicting evidence
if it suits his purposes to do so. Much more egregious—for all his claims to
self-justification—is his wholly arbitrary editing of dynamic markings into the
text of the symphonies, and it is precisely this which has acquired for Weingartner something approaching a cult in this country. The attempt at self-
justification carries with it the complementary tendency toward scepticism on
the part of the discerning critic, while Weingartner's evident conviction on
matters which must, by definition, be wholly personal is—such is human
nature—but seldom questioned, and the most abominable dynamic bowdler-
isations acquire widespread currency. Significantly, these do not include those
passages where Weingartner freely admits that his is a personal solution, and
made without recourse to the plea that he is only altering the dynamics or
introducing entirely new ones for the sake of clarity. The coda of the finale of
the Seventh Symphony is a case in point, and had, in Weingartner's reading
of it, a beauty whose eloquence I am fully prepared to acknowledge, although
it is one to which I cannot personally subscribe—because I have not traced its
logic and made it my own. But if the "dynamic *rubato*", as Liszt calls it in his

Faust Symphony, is admissible to Weingartner on quite personal grounds, why then not the metrical *rubato* so distinctly personal to Bülow and his disciples, which Weingartner so consistently and roundly condemns?

Reference to the Seventh Symphony reveals a hiatus in Weingartner's scholarship, with reference to the final bars of its *Allegretto*. The autograph, according to Dr. Köhler of the Berlin Staatsbibliothek, vanished during the war, but this apparently gave *arco* only at the final bar of the strings:

as compared with the first edition, which gives *arco* in the preceding bar of the second violins only:

and the current editions, which all give:

This shows a progressive bowdlerisation of the *Urtext*, if we take the first version as being authentic, and the Viennese printers of the first edition derived the logic of the alleged autograph as follows: Beethoven's prescription of *arco* for the octave A double-stop in the second violins, coming as it does immediately after the two eighth-notes F sharp and G sharp, seemed improbable, and they therefore drew the analogy from the *staccatissimo* F sharp and G sharp in the first violins of making the F sharp and G sharp in the seconds *arco* as well. But this also seemed rather improbable, musically speaking, so they extended the second violin *arco* to embrace the whole phrase. Beethoven himself did not have the opportunity of reading the first edition proofs of either the score or parts, and the first edition consequently went to press in this form. Nor, with the ensuing success of the symphony as a whole, and this movement in particular, did Beethoven have the opportunity of correcting the passage, for he was by this time completely deaf, and it seems, on balance, unlikely that he would have spotted the strings playing *arco* at this point in those performances where he was present. The current editions have extended the logic of the second violin part in the first edition by allowing *arco* to embrace the whole of the first violin phrase as well, restoring the > marking—and which the first edition conveniently omits altogether—in the first violins which they interpreted as a *decrescendo*, and extending the *decrescendo* to *pp* in the winds backwards to start immediately after the *f*—in conformity with the first violins.

But what other interpretation may be placed on the *Urtext*, if not one of these two? If we ignore the *arco* marking for the moment, everything falls into place. The string *pizzicato* can continue to the end of the movement, the *staccatissimo* markings implying a *crescendo* to *forte* in the second violin part— for it is impossible to play *staccatissimo pizzicato* without introducing an element of *crescendo*—and the > marking in the first violins now becoming, not a *decrescendo*, but a long accent. The beginning of the *decrescendo* in the winds, in both the autograph and the first edition, is now found to be perfectly in place. But what of Beethoven's apparently unambiguous marking of *arco*, which it seems impossible to reconcile with such a practice? Could it not be an instruction to the string section to take their bows in readiness for the ensuing Scherzo—which should follow without a break, for there is no *fermata* over the final bar or bar-line?

Erich Kleiber, who had the benefit of access to the autograph during his years in Berlin before the war, has drawn attention to the fact that the *arco* was placed over the *second* half of the penpenultimate bar, and that the placing of the *decrescendo* in the winds corresponds with its placing at the outset of the movement—a *forte* sustained for three-quarters of the bar before making a bar-and-a-quarter *decrescendo* to *pp*. Furthermore, the all-important *arco* marking appeared to have been added as an afterthought, for the handwriting is much heavier than the context, as though Beethoven had suddenly realised the implications of finishing a movement *pizzicato* and having the string-section suddenly scrabbling for their bows—which they would probably have laid aside at bar 254—at the page-turn into the Scherzo. (There is of course a page turn at this point in the string parts to the first edition.) At all events, Kleiber made it his consistent practice to play the final bars of the *Allegretto* pizzicato to the end of the movement, and this affected fundamentally his reading of the entire ending, and indeed of the movement as a whole, for the final 6/4 chord in the winds must acquire an entirely different character behind a dry *pizzicato* instead of a warm *arco*—and this is the chord with which the movement opens. And I find it rather ironic, in retrospect, that it should have been the conviction of my own insistence which occasioned me a solitary moment of respect in an otherwise rather disagreeable rehearsal with the Royal Philharmonic in 1958.

It has not been the object of this chapter to denigrate Weingartner, whose artistry in the concert hall was unimpugnable, but rather to emphasise his own dictum in urging the utmost caution before regarding any marking in Beethoven's works—or the works of any other composer, for the matter of that—as being conclusive evidence of anything at all. Weingartner's purpose —avowed or unwitting—was to stimulate an atmosphere for intelligent enquiry, and it is his ultimate vindication that he has succeeded conspic-uously. With his death in 1941 came the close of an epoch which has been variously described as the mortal sickness of the era of live music-making of stature, and the advent of a new era which was to culminate in the perfection of the long-playing gramophone record.

Chapter 11

BRUNO WALTER AND CLEMENS KRAUSS

The conductor himself produces no music, but does so by means of others, whom he must lead by gestures, words, and the power of his personality, and the result depends on his ability to handle people. In this respect, too, innate talent is of decisive importance—a talent for asserting one's own personality—and it needs to be developed by constant endeavour and by making the most of daily experiences. He who has been born without authority and is lacking in the essential dynamics originating in the sphere of the will cannot gain a firm footing as a conductor, even if he possesses musical talent, ability or knowledge. He may reach a point at which he will be able to express himself with masterly skill on the piano or the violin, but he will never be successful in welding an orchestra or an operatic company into an instrument of his own. The result of his conducting will be more impersonal, insignificant, and ineffective than that of a musician of lesser ability who has the natural gift of authority.

These words, from Bruno Walter's autobiography[1], were written in 1945, when he was sixty-nine, and concern his first crisis of introspection, which had occurred fifty years earlier as a boy of nineteen. Walter was born in Berlin on 15 September, 1876, with the family name of Schlesinger, and the eighty years of his life were to constitute a kaleidoscope of achievement, success, disappointment and—sometimes—failure which found but ill-concealed resentment. There is an evasiveness about the way in which he writes, a continual searching for extra-musical causes and extra-musical personalities behind his manifold disappointments, a certain moral dishonesty in his mention only by inference those who bore him open hostility, which conflict oddly with the picture which we have of him and which he would have wished to paint of himself.

Success came early to Bruno Walter, who became a coach at the Cologne Stadttheater in 1893, at the Hamburg Stadttheater in 1894—where he came into contact with Mahler for the first time, and was allowed to conduct some

[1] Bruno Walter: *Theme & Variations:* trans. by James Galston, Alfred A. Knopf, New York; Hamish Hamilton, London, 1947.

performances—and two years later, at the age of twenty, third conductor of the Breslau Stadttheater, where he was commissioned to stage and conduct Donizetti's *Lucrezia Borgia* and a revival of *Zäuberflöte*. There followed a six-month engagement as first conductor in Pressburg the following year, and his appointment as first conductor in Riga—where Wagner had conducted—in 1898, at the age of twenty-two. That year Mahler wrote to him from Vienna, where he was by now installed as general musical director, offering Walter the post of junior conductor at the Vienna Opera when his two-year contract in Riga terminated in 1900. But Walter declined, feeling that he would not be ready to expose himself to Mahler's powerful influence by that time, and accepted instead a five-year contract as junior conductor at the Berlin Opera in succession to Franz Schalk, who joined Mahler in Vienna. This brought Walter into contact with Richard Strauss and Karl Muck and one Karl Halir, concertmaster of the Royal Opera orchestra, who is the only personage whom Walter has the courage to mention by name, in his autobiography, in the context of their open hostility. The following year—1901—Walter was released from his Berlin contract, and went to Mahler in Vienna where he now found himself working under Franz Schalk, who was in any case thirteen years his senior and a near contemporary of Mahler himself. In Vienna, the twenty-five-year-old Walter quickly made enemies with the press in the form of the *Neues Wiener Tageblatt* with his performance—the first as an independent conductor—of *Tannhäuser*, and the sense of outrage to which that newspaper gave vehement expression was quickly taken up by its colleagues. A post at the Cologne Opera became available, and Mahler advised Walter to take it, declaring that "he had lost the game in Vienna", and adding that he who lost in Vienna could never hope to be victorious again there.

Thus far the tragedy of a success which had come too early and too easily was all too clearly manifest. Walter had possessed all the talent, the flair, and the musical equipment of the first-class artist, but he did not possess the all-important talent and flair of personality, magnetism and orchestral psychology which is synonymous with creative industry. There came the second crisis of introspection in his life, accompanied by the resolve first to be victorious in Vienna—accompanied too by a nervous ailment which attacked his conducting-arm, and for the treatment of which he went to Sigmund Freud. Walter's painful shyness, and preoccupation over his extreme youth (now no longer as extreme as he liked to think) were by gradual stages overcome—though never entirely so, as his autobiography testifies—and his eleven years in Vienna bear witness to the slow and painful acquisition of artistic maturity. On 1 January, 1913, at the age of thirty-seven, Walter was appointed general musical director of the Bavarian Court Theatre in Munich, and could be said to have well and truly "arrived".

Felix Mottl had collapsed at a performance of *Tristan* at the end of June 1911, and died a few days later, on 2 July, at the age of fifty-four, having been general musical director in Munich since 1903. Walter, who had harboured pretensions to the general musical directorship in Vienna, had been unable to conceal his disappointment when, having been passed over by Weingartner in 1907, he was passed over again in 1911 by Hans Gregor—who was not even a conductor, but a *régisseur*—and found himself continuing to work as the subordinate of Franz Schalk. He therefore applied for his release from the five-year contract which had just been renewed, but Gregor was unwilling to let him go, for he recognised in Walter a talent which was not to be lost to Munich, and there followed lengthy negotiations which ultimately involved Prince Montenuovo, major-domo to Emperor Franz Josef, and director of the Royal Theatres. In his autobiography, Walter claims that Montenuovo declared that Mahler had recommended him—Walter—as his successor, and that Montenuovo made his release conditional on a "secret understanding" that Walter should return to the Vienna Opera when his six-year contract in Munich expired. His resignation was finally accepted at the end of 1912, and Walter was free to take up his Bavarian post. But Franz Schalk succeeded Gregor in Vienna on the latter's death in 1918—a post which he held until his retirement in 1929, when he was in turn succeeded by Clemens Krauss. Walter was only to return to Vienna in 1936—after Weingartner had replaced Krauss, who had in turn replaced Kleiber in Berlin—and then it was only in the capacity of musical adviser to the general musical director, Erwin Kerber. Walter's ultimate victory in Vienna was not to come until 1955, at the age of seventy-nine, with his performance of the Beethoven Ninth Symphony at the Staatsoper—as it had become after the First World War—and which had just opened its doors after the Second. Vienna, ever true to character, was according Walter a *coup de grâce*.

Munich had been the scene of Walter's first performance of Mahler's *Das Lied von der Erde* on 20 November, 1911—six months after Mahler's death—and he followed this with the première, in Vienna, of Mahler's Ninth Symphony on 12 June, 1912. Mahler had heard neither work, and was even reluctant to play them to Walter on the piano, being sceptical both of their effect in public and even of his own ability to conduct them—so Walter relates with significant surprise. Mahler had for him been the *Meister* in its fullest sense, but in the final year of Mahler's life Walter had not yet learned that degree of humility and self-criticism which had continually informed and nourished Mahler's work as a conductor—and was so to inform Walter's own work in the extraordinary performances which he gave of Mahler's Ninth Symphony and *Das Lied von der Erde* with the Vienna Philharmonic in 1937—performances which are preserved in the Mahler Society recordings. But it was not only Mahler whom Walter was continually to rediscover during his ten-year incumbency in Munich, but also Mozart—that never-failing source of inspiration for every great musician without exception.

Meanwhile war had been declared in Europe on 31 July, 1914, and its repercussions were felt within the walls of the Bavarian Court Opera. Walter had to accept severe reductions in his opera house staff, Strauss was prepared to accept reductions from eight to four clarinets in his opera *Elektra* both in Munich and elsewhere, and amateur deputies became increasingly evident in the rank and file of the orchestra. In his autobiography, Walter wrote:

> A sense of sincerity requires me to define my attitude to the First World War. Although I was convinced of the outrageous conduct of Baron Berchthold, the Austrian Secretary of State for Foreign Affairs, and of the grave mistakes made by the German Kaiser and other personages in the governments of the Central Powers, and although I had been horrified by Germany's violation of Belgium's neutrality and by Bethmann-Hollweg's reference to a "scrap of paper", my heart was still partial to Germany and Austria. I wished to see preserved undamaged the cultural life in which I had my roots. So closely was I in contact with noble spiritual currents and moral tendencies in both countries, so wholly was I cut off from contacts with the outside world, and so constantly was I under the influence of spoken and printed pro-German propaganda that I wished with all my heart a termination of the war that would assure their world position to the Germany and Austria I loved—not to the Germany of the Kaiser and the Junkers, but to that of Goethe, Hölderlin, Beethoven and Bach, and to the Austria of Mozart, Schubert and Grillparzer . . . Yet I considered the outcome of the war a misfortune and looked forward to Europe's future with presentiments of fear.

Italian, French, Russian and—needless to say—British music had disappeared from Germany's programmes at the outset of the war, and remained on the Central Powers' index for the duration. Walter's principal 'cellist, a Belgian by the name of Disclez, became the target for a local press campaign for his removal as an enemy alien, but Walter succeeded in keeping him at his first desk throughout the war—eloquent testimony, to quote Walter, "That all counter-currents notwithstanding, it was then still possible to appeal to reason and tolerance".

Walter's prime talent was that of moderation, and it was this quality which was to sustain his activities at the opera house during the immediate post-war period when anarchy was rife throughout central Europe. Musical conditions, which had faltered increasingly during the war years, were among those swiftest to return to a semblance of normality, and when in the spring of 1920 Karl Muck appeared in Munich, after the regrettable episode in Boston of two years earlier, Walter was able to offer him part of the summer Wagner festival at the Prinzregenten Theater. Muck, in return, was later to be able to offer Walter some guest engagements with the Hamburg Philharmonic, the directorship of which he took over from 1922 until 1933. Walter, meanwhile, had accepted a series of guest engagements with the Berlin Philharmonic through the Wolff Agency in Berlin, who controlled the interests of every major artist in Germany, but in Munich he encountered growing undercurrents of opposition which led finally to his resignation from the opera house in the summer of 1922, on the grounds of "spiritual fatigue". But in reality, America was calling him with the offer, from Walter Damrosch, of a four-week engagement with the New York Symphony early in 1923, and similar offers from Detroit and Minneapolis. His engagement with the last-named orchestra was in fact in the nature of a four-week trial, the previous permanent conductor since the orchestra's foundation in 1903—Emil Oberhoffer—having retired the previous year, and a series of guest conductors having been engaged for the 1922–23 season. Minneapolis was, in the event, unimpressed by Walter's gifts, and the appointment of permanent conductor for the next eight years went to Henry Verbrugghen, who was succeeded in 1931 by Eugene Ormandy, and six years later by Dimitri Mitropoulos. So began Walter's years as an itinerant musician—not so pronounced as had been those of Toscanini, for Walter enjoyed long periods of respite, first at the Charlottenburg Opera in Berlin from 1925 to 1929, then at the Leipzig Gewandhaus from 1929 to 1933, followed three years later by his appointment as artistic adviser to the Vienna State Opera until the advent of the *Anschluss*.

Little can be said in retrospect of Walter's years at the Charlottenburg Opera, save for his increasing emphasis on a quality of excellence whose essence resided in its moderation. But there can be little doubt that Walter grew increasingly jealous of his colleague, Erich Kleiber—his junior by fourteen years and whose success as general musical director of the more important Berlin State Opera had been spectacular, and was likely to remain so. When, on his fiftieth birthday (15 September, 1926), Walter read of Heinz Tietjen's appointment as intendant of the State Opera in succession to Max von Schillings, after only one year's collaboration with him at the Charlottenburg, he telephoned him at once to demand an explanation. Tietjen prevaricated, maintained a foot in both camps for the next two years, and when confronted by an ultimatum from Walter, decided in favour of Kleiber and the State Opera, whereupon Walter resigned from the Charlottenburg. Kleiber had the good grace to offer him a guest engagement at the State Opera in a performance of Weber's *Oberon*, but references to Kleiber in his writing remain significantly sparse—there is only one, and that is extremely casual.

Walter's Covent Garden debut had been in 1909, at the age of thirty-three, when he gave a performance of Ethel Smyth's *The Wreckers*, and this association had been renewed in 1924 and continued uninterruptedly until 1931, reaching its climax with his Mozart cycle in 1928, which was repeated the following year in Paris, at the instance of Georges Caurier, in the Théâtre des Champs-Elysées. His resignation from the Charlottenburg in 1929 had been prompted by many considerations—the offer of a permanent position at the Leipzig Gewandhaus, in succession to Furtwängler, his continuing associations with the Berlin Philharmonic, the Amsterdam Concertgebouw and Covent Garden, and once again the lure of the Vienna State Opera, whose general musical directorship would fall vacant with Schalk's retirement. Furtwängler had already declined the post, which left the field open to all comers, but Walter—like Kleiber—was destined to be disappointed, although —unlike Kleiber—he refused to accept the situation philosophically, and insisted on discerning in the situation every manner of political intrigue. These there undoubtedly were, this being Vienna and concerning the future of her opera house, and Clemens Krauss, a firm favourite with the Viennese, was appointed Schalk's successor at the age of thirty-six. Walter took up his residence in Leipzig, where he was to remain for the next four seasons, until 1933.

Walter had become an Austrian citizen in 1911, so that he had little to fear in the strictly physical sense when the National Socialist Party came to power at the beginning of 1933—little, that is to say, in the sense which his German colleagues of Jewish blood had to fear, and Walter expressed a naïve surprise that Hans Hinckel should have ordered a boycott of his impending Gewandhaus concert, and a naïve indignation that Richard Strauss should have volunteered to substitute for him. Germany was forthwith closed to Walter, and he was compelled to leave Berlin that very night. He had not foreseen the situation, and neither had any rational German—Jew or Gentile— but he should not have been surprised, for the portents had been sufficiently ominous. As for Richard Strauss, a German Gentile of nearly seventy who had been brought up in the bourgeois atmosphere of a Munich of the days of Kaiser Wilhelm I and Ludwig II of Bavaria, and had been nurtured since childhood on a brand of anti-semitism which was as mildly conventional as it was universal, and which certainly contemplated nothing of the hideous

extremism of the Nazi era—how much less was he able to foresee a situation
to which Walter himself, a man in his middle fifties, had been manifestly
blind. Strauss, with his eternal spirit of opportunism, probably felt quite
sincerely that he was helping a colleague out of an unfortunate situation at a
moment of political aberration which would swiftly return to normal. Walter
had meanwhile lost his connections with Covent Garden since Sir Thomas
Beecham had assumed its entire control in 1931, and his last appearance with
the Royal Philharmonic Society had been in 1926. There remained to him his
guest appearances with the Amsterdam Concertgebouw, at the Salzburg
Festival, and with the Vienna Philharmonic during the winter season. To
these he had now added, since the 1931–32 season, guest appearances with the
New York Philharmonic which were to persist until the announcement, in
1935, of his pending appointment as musical adviser to the Vienna State
Opera, to take effect from the following year—a year which also saw his
appointment as co-musical director with Toscanini of the Salzburg Festival.
But with Germany's ultimatum to Schuschnigg, the Austrian Chancellor, on
11 March, 1938, Walter's Austrian citizenship could no longer afford him a
protection long since denied his German colleagues in race, and he now
became a citizen of France. There followed tours of the Balkans, France,
Holland and Scandinavia—involving a circuitous route so as to avoid
Germany—thence back to London for a concert with the BBC Symphony
Orchestra and the Royal Philharmonic Society in January 1939, and finally
to New York at the invitation of Toscanini, for engagements with the NBC
Orchestra which had been founded just over one year earlier. In August 1939
Walter visited Switzerland for the Lucerne Festival at Villa Triebschen—
where Wagner had prepared the score of the *Ring*—and was greeted with the
tragic news of his younger daughter's death. He sailed for New York from
Genoa on 31 October, 1939, accompanied by his wife and surviving daughter,
and within a few months France—the country of his most recent adoption—
had fallen.

In America, Walter now divided his time between the Los Angeles
Symphony—having succeeded Otto Klemperer there—and the NBC
Symphony in New York, returning to the New York Philharmonic in 1941 for
guest engagements which continued, in conjunction with his nominal
activities at the Metropolitan Opera, for the next four years. But Walter had
never been a fighter, and was not to become one now, and there was never any
serious question of his becoming permanent musical director of the Philharmonic. Is it a commentary on Walter himself, or upon the professional
attitude of the New York Philharmonic as a whole, which prompted one of
its violinists—himself a conductor of moderate talent—to remark to me in

Cleveland in 1956: "It took us five years to have Bruno Walter realise there was nothing he could teach us."

★   ★   ★   ★   ★

Clemens Krauss, who was born in Vienna on 31 March, 1893, shared with Walter the same fluency of musical talent combined with a specific flair for the music of Mozart. But there all similarity ceased: Walter had been the Jewish-born son of Berlin *petit-bourgeoisie*, Krauss—so legend has it—the natural-born son of the Archbishop of Vienna, and as such possessed of that innate sense of aristocratic *laissez-faire* which typifies the upper strata of society in the Austrian capital. At the age of eight Krauss became a chorister at the Vienna Hofburg (home of the Wiener Sängerknaben), and at thirteen, when he entered the Academy, could—in his own words—already "give a creditable account of myself in both *Königin der Nacht* arias". He was a model student at the Music Academy, passing his *Reifeprüfung* in 1912, at the age of nineteen, and after a short period spent as chorus-master at the municipal theatre in Brünn, receiving his first operatic post in the autumn of 1913 in Riga, where Walter had himself held office fifteen years earlier. With Germany's declaration of war in July 1914, the Latvian post was terminated, and Krauss spent the war years successively as first conductor in Nuremberg, Stettin and—at the end of the war—Graz. In 1922, he found himself appointed to the Vienna State Opera as second conductor under Franz Schalk, with Richard Strauss as general musical director. The post of general musical director had been vacant since Weingartner's resignation in 1911 and until Strauss's engagement in 1920, and from Krauss's appointment in 1922 dates the beginning of the life-long collaboration between Strauss and Krauss which was to culminate in the latter's libretto to Strauss's last opera, *Capriccio*. When Strauss retired from the Vienna Opera in 1924 at the age of sixty, Schalk became general musical director, and Krauss became intendant of the Frankfurt Opera and took over—at Strauss's recommendation—the Frankfurt Museum Concerts from Willem Mengelberg who had relinquished them because of his growing commitments in New York. Krauss continued to commute with Vienna, however, for concerts with the Philharmonic and his activities with the *Kapellmeisterschule* at the Music Academy, which he had instituted in 1922.

Richard Strauss had maintained his relationship with the Vienna Opera after his retirement to Garmisch, and when in 1929 Franz Schalk announced his own retirement on reaching the age of sixty-five, Strauss had proposed two candidates to Schneiderhan, the intendant—Furtwängler and Krauss.

Furtwängler had declined because of his prior commitments with the Berlin, Leipzig and Vienna orchestras, and Clemens Krauss was duly appointed general musical director—to the aforementioned dismay of a number of other candidates for the position. Krauss forthwith introduced a number of—for Vienna —new works into the repertoire, including an outstanding performance of *Wozzeck* and all the Strauss operas to date, besides reviving all the Mozart repertoire, and a performance of *Tristan* which was distinguished by the youthfulness of its conception. (It was also the shortest *Tristan* on record: Toscanini's, significantly, was the longest.) On 1 July, 1933, Krauss appeared in Dresden as a guest in the world première of *Arabella* with his wife, Viorica Ursuleac, in the title role—a performance which was repeated in Vienna the following October and at Covent Garden early in 1934. Early in 1935 he succeeded Kleiber—who had resigned the previous December—as general musical director of the Berlin State Opera, and his duties in Vienna were taken over until the conclusion of the 1936 season by Felix Weingartner. In the autumn of 1936 Krauss joined the Bavarian State Opera in succession to Hans Knappertsbusch—who had himself succeeded Walter in 1922— dividing his time between Berlin and Munich until 1938 when he was appointed to the dual role of general musical director and intendant in the latter city, and his activities in Berlin had to be curtailed. Strauss's opera, *Friedenstag*, which was dedicated to Krauss and his wife, received its première in Munich under Clemens Krauss on 24 July, 1938, with Ursuleac in the role of Maria. He retained his dual post of general musical director and intendant of the Bavarian State Opera until 1944, when the opera house was destroyed by a direct hit in the course of an air raid.

Krauss returned to Vienna, where Knappertsbusch had now been installed since Walter's enforced flight and Kerber's resignation in 1938. Early in 1945, the Staatsoper became a victim of American bombing, and the company transferred its headquarters to the Theater an der Wien—the scene of the première of *Fidelio* on 20 November, 1805—and which was to be their home for the next eleven years. Knappertsbusch returned to Munich in 1950, and Krauss was appointed chief conductor—although Hilbert, the intendant, was not prepared to dispense the title of General Musical Director until the Staatsoper had been rebuilt. The history of the closing years of Krauss's life is one of a continual rearguard action, for he had himself become embroiled long since in the favourite Viennese pastime of petty politics, and his avowed policy became one of keeping out intruders at all costs—or, if he could not keep them out altogether, of ensuring that they appeared at something less than their best. With the end of the war, Vienna had become an international den of intrigue. The city was still under the control of the four powers, and a game which the Viennese loved to play was to go and watch the Russian garrison taking over command from the American—or vice-versa—or to go and see George London in the role of Boris Godounoff (which he sang in Russian) *selbstverständlich* before an audience which included American and Russian officers and diplomats. Furtwängler was still the conductor of the Vienna Philharmonic—in addition to that of Berlin—and gave a guest performance of *Götterdämmerung* at the Theater an der Wien in 1953: Karl Böhm was a refugee from a Dresden which now lay in East Germany, and a frequent guest conductor at the Staatsoper's temporary head-quarters: and even John Pritchard constituted a brief threat to Krauss' position when he first appeared there in 1952—at the recommendation of Fritz Busch—and was re-engaged for six performances the following season. In March 1951 Erich Kleiber had been accorded a guest performance of *Rosenkavalier*, together with a performance of the *Eroica* with the Vienna Philharmonic, and had fallen title to the claim of the opera's new musical director—a claim which had been widely voiced since 1945, and which Krauss did his utmost to prevent and, in the event, succeeded. It is ironic that his last days were to be spent in that very city which, almost twelve years earlier, had witnessed yet another of Kleiber's miracles of orchestral transfiguration, for Krauss died in Mexico City, in the course of a guest engagement with the Mexican National Orchestra, on 16 May, 1954. The rebuilt Vienna State Opera re-opened eighteen months later, with Karl Böhm conducting *Fidelio*—in the Mahler version which interpolates *Leonora* No. 3 before the Finale—Karajan conducting *Meistersinger*, and Knappertsbusch conducting Krauss's beloved *Rosenkavalier*.

Much has been said of Krauss's palpable Nazi sympathies. That he should have been available to take over Kleiber's duties in Berlin at the beginning of 1935, when the Nazi cause had shown its true colours beyond the remotest shadow of a doubt, is of course significant. Krauss pursued the Nazi ideology for ten years after its proclamation of power, and when at last he perceived the heinous error of its ways, it was too late: he had become tainted, and for the remaining eleven years of his life could—here too—only fight a rearguard action. But he never sought to deny his one-time membership of the Nazi Party, and a certain shamefacedness betrayed, in retrospect, a sense of corporate guilt which was shared by few of his compatriots of lesser distinction who, the war over and the atrocities unambiguously revealed, one and all pro-tested that "there was nothing they could have done". Nor did Krauss once refer to the countless victims of Nazi persecution whom he had helped to escape from Germany and Austria, at a time when his Nazi idealism must have been at its very height. But that he assuredly did so I have from many of the victims in question, among them Elsa Mayer-Lismann. The whole question of corporate blameworthiness during the Nazi era is one which has been dealt with *in extenso*, but the following extract from Arnold Schoenberg's *Style and Idea*, entitled *A Dangerous Game*, deserves to be quoted in full:

There are a great many categories of collaborators in Germany and the conquered countries. One must distinguish between the many who have been forced to collaborate and those who have done so voluntarily. There are others, besides, who simply "missed the bus", who would have preferred to emigrate rather than bow to dictates, if it had not become too late for them to do so. And there are those whose stupid egotism led them to believe that evil could only happen to others while they themselves would be spared. Some did only what they were ordered to do, others functioned as agitators, prosecuting those who did not conform to the prescribed style, and based their conduct on the theoretical party line.

With the thought in mind that the captain in *Carmen* is not intended to represent a coward but simply a man who yields to the argument of the guns which confront him, it may be said that only those should be authorized to blame the forced collaborator who have themselves proved fearless before the menace of the concentration camp and of torture. People like that of course also exist.

Curiously, few realise that politics, a nice topic to talk about, is a rather dangerous game into which one should enter only if he is aware that his life and that of his opponent are at stake and if he is willing to pay for his conviction—even that price.

Artists generally deal with this problem as thoughtlessly as if it were merely a controversy on artistic matters; just as if they were discussing merely "art for art's sake" as contrasted with "objectivity in art". Even in such arguments a participant's life may be at stake. I wonder whether Richard Wagner knew that he would be living in exile as an outlaw for so many years when, because of artistic corruption, he participated in setting the Dresden Hoftheater on fire.

On the other hand, very few of those who emigrated can ask to be honoured for their political or artistic straightforwardness. Most of them had no other chance of being spared, either because of their race or that of their matrimonial partner. Many had been politically implicated and others came under the ban of *Kultur-Bolschewismus*. There are probably not many who emigrated voluntarily; and even among such "real" émigrés there are some who tried hard to come to an agreement with the powers only to give up in the end.

Yet despite the fact that little personal merit attaches to the inability of many to swim with the official current (*Gleichschaltung*), there is this to be said for them: they all had to abandon their homes, their positions, their countries, their friends, their business, their fortune. They all had to go abroad, to try to start life anew, and generally at a much lower level of living, of influence, of esteem; many even had to change their occupations and to suffer humiliation.

There may be no merit in that; still, if those who had to do it could do it—why should not others also have preferred to preserve their honesty, their integrity, their character, by taking upon themselves of their own free will the suffering of the émigré, like those who had no other way?

That would have been of some merit!

I am inclined to say:

Those who here acted like politicians are politicians and should be treated in the same manner in which politicians are treated.

Those who did not so act should escape punishment.

But considering the low mental and moral standards of artists in general, I would say:

Treat them like immature children.

Call them children and let them escape.[2]

When the National Socialist Party came to power in 1933, Dr. Goebbels was proclaimed Minister of Propaganda and Public Enlightenment, and on 22 September, 1933, instituted the Reichskulturkammer (Chamber of Culture), consisting of the seven independent departments of theatre, music, cinema, radio, journalism, writing, and art, and it was to the second of these —the Reichsmusikkammer (Chamber of Music)—that Richard Strauss was elected President on 15 November, 1933, in his seventieth year, with Wilhelm Furtwängler, then aged forty-seven, as one of the two Vice-Presidents. The Chamber of Music contained the further sub-divisions having charge respectively of the cultural, economic and legal aspects, and it was the responsibility of the cultural division to outline the policy of the department as a whole, and to be the final arbiter in all matters relating to music and the science of music, and to act in liaison with public archives, libraries, academies and conservatoires of music, student orchestras, concerts for schools, and to supervise professional examinations and the disbursement of scholarships. The economic division had charge of all matters concerning financial administration, the collection and payment of royalties, procurement of work for unemployed musicians, administration of nursing homes and recreation camps for disabled artists, printing of important works by composers having no means of their own, subsidising municipal orchestras, and awarding scholarships. Membership of the Chamber of Music—which was mandatory for all musicians—fell into the nine categories of composers, solo operatic and concert artists, radio artists, operetta and music-hall artists, orchestral

---

[2] Published as part of a symposium "On Artists and Collaboration" in *Modern Music*, XXII, 2, November–December, 1944. Reprinted in: Arnold Schoenberg: *Style and Idea*. Williams & Norgate Ltd., London, 1951.

players and chorus members, amateur and professional choirs, music publishers, concert agents and instrument manufacturers and dealers. The organisation was in fact thorough—on paper—and as such calculated to appeal to the German temperament. But it had two drawbacks—the fact that membership was obligatory for all "aryan" musicians, and that all artists of Jewish birth came under the separate control of one of the sub-divisions of the Ministry of Propaganda in the person of Dr. Hans Hinckel. Nor were the meetings of the president and council of the Reichsmusikkammer conspicuously frequent: there were two meetings in 1934, two in 1935, one in 1936, and none in 1937, and the activities of Strauss and Furtwängler were therefore largely nominal. Four days after his first performance of the five pieces from Berg's *Lulu*, on 4 December, 1934, Kleiber resigned his membership of the Chamber, and Furtwängler's resignation as its vice-president followed the next day. Early in 1935 Strauss himself resigned, and was succeeded by Peter Raabe, a distinguished musician of sixty-two who had shared duties at the head of the Kaim orchestra in Munich with Felix Weingartner in the 1903-04 season, and had taken over from Lassen, Liszt's successor in Weimar, in 1907. His most recent post had been in Aachen, where he had been superseded by Herbert von Karajan. Krauss had acquired membership of the Reichsmusikkammer in 1934, when he first had occasion to conduct in Germany following Goebbels's proclamation, and succeeded Furtwängler as its vice-president in 1935, joining the Nazi Party in 1938 when Germany absorbed Austria and the Reichsmusikkammer extended its activities to that country.

Chapter 12

OTTO KLEMPERER AND THE BRITISH INSTITUTION

The history of the British orchestra in the nineteenth century is largely that of the orchestra of the Philharmonic Society, which had been founded in 1813 and gave its inaugural concert on 8 March. Near the end of his life, Liszt was to write to Walter Bache in London:

> You are miserably taken in by foreigners in England—which is entirely your own fault. But the way in which mediocre foreign talent —and especially singers—has been pushed over and over again, at the expense of the native, is simply scandalous . . .

Many years earlier, during the 1829–30 season, the twenty-year-old Felix Mendelssohn had written from London to the German baritone, Eduard Devrient, in Berlin:

> I am very happy here, and enjoy myself very much—especially when I can shut my eyes and ears to music and musicians—which is fortunately not difficult. Were I to tell them my opinion of their music-making they would think me rude, and were I to speak to them of music in general they would think me quite mad. So I do not trouble them with my ideas, but wander about looking at the splendid life of this city and her streets . . . buying a bunch of lilies-of-the-valley from some bawling old woman in the crowd, and finding in it more music than in all the concerts which I survived yesterday, shall endure tomorrow, and put up with again on Friday. Of the English style of singing I shall say nothing, but will give you a sample in December—you will fall off your chair laughing . . .

And again, in 1855, during Wagner's second visit to London, he wrote to Liszt:

> I am living here like a soul damned in hell—I never thought that I should be obliged to sink so low again. I cannot describe how contemptible I feel at holding on, under circumstances so repugnant to me, and I realise now that it was a downright sin and a crime to

accept this London engagement, which even under the most
favourable conditions could only have led me from my real path . . .

At the end of Wagner's London season, Henry Smart of the *Sunday
Times*, who had shown a conspicuous and scrupulous fair-mindedness at the
season's outset, wrote that Wagner was:

> without doubt, the worst conductor to whom the Philharmonic baton
> has yet been entrusted . . . The same wavering, fidgety and uncertain
> beat which had bewildered the band at the first concert remained to
> puzzle them at the last, and sufficed to prove that, in the mechanical
> indication of time, he had the first of the conductor's duties yet to
> acquire.[1]

This last testimony is not quite borne out by the consensus of opinion
of Hans von Bülow, Alexander Ritter and Liszt himself, and later endorsed
by Hans Richter, Artur Nikisch, Gustav Mahler and Richard Strauss. It was
clearly—on this occasion, at all events—the audience and the critics themselves who were to be found wanting, together with an orchestra whose
members had accorded Wagner scant courtesy and a flagrant disregard for all
his wishes. But the combined testimonies of Liszt, Mendelssohn and Wagner
point to a national condition in this country symptomatic of a disease more
serious and widespread than any which could be defined under the manifold
aspects of inattentiveness, for in musical matters, and indeed in all matters
concerning the arts—with the exception of literature—we are, as a nation,
notoriously obtuse. We will allow the foreigner into our midst, or permit the
musical establishment to invite him, without due regard for his qualifications,
and when this causes an outcry from our native artists—whether with justice
or no—will then espouse the cause of the native artist and declare all foreign
musicians suspect. On the other hand we will betray an intuitive instinct
which declares to us that, for all their undeniable qualifications as artists,
there is among our own musicians an inbred lacking of professional stamina,
and embrace the cause of those very musicians from abroad whose most
brazen qualification is just such a want of professional stamina.

The sleeping sickness which afflicts our arts in Britain today—as in the
last century—is inherent in the very strength of our literary tradition. Our
theatre, avid for realism, yet seemingly deaf to the real drama of language,
gives us the social documentary and the conversation piece, now removed
from the drawing-room to a kitchen which is no longer even below stairs.
For all that our art critics—unaware of the work, let us say, of Ruprecht
Geiger or Gerhardt Fietz—bandy about the abstractionist label, our painting

[1] Robert Elkin: *Royal Philharmonic Society* (Chap. V), Rider & Co., London and New
York, 1947.

and sculpture remain firmly representational, and with strong literary overtones. And in music, for an older generation at least, nothing is quite as
popular as Gilbert and Sullivan or Handel's *Messiah*.

Literature used once to be simply that branch of the arts which found
its medium of expression in the written word. But its overriding predominance
in this country has led to its colonization of the sovereign territory of the other
arts as independent media, and to the gradual confusion of the role of the
artist with that of the intellectual. No one would deny the artist the potential
of a logic and intelligence quite as penetrating as that of the intellectual, and
indeed one hopes that the maundering myth which portrays the artist as
being a creature of instinct, moving by the light of nature, has long since been
dispelled. The artist's terms of reference are utterly different from those of the
intellectual, however, and in music at least, the qualifications of the general
practitioner—let alone of the specialist—demand a clinical experience, in
constant and direct contact with the substance of his profession, quite as long
and as arduous as that of medicine. Far from allowing room or time for
liberal contemplation or congenial debate, they must exact a rigid immunity
from such disseminating influences.

There are no musical institutions—unless they be in Russia—which can
emulate the singleness of purpose of the medical school. The musical
specialist, whose point of real contact as a teacher should only be with the
prodigiously gifted, is not accorded the prerogatives of his colleagues in the
sphere of specialised medicine, and must concern himself with the largely
mediocre talent which floods our schools of music. These have been led, in
the main, by men whose tradition has been one of church music—a tradition
which, up to the time of Bach, had been a vital influence on music-making,
and one which still lingers in this country, as a further witness to literary
influences, to the present day. As long as the Church continued to wield a
creative influence on music, these men—who by their very vocation had
grown out of and substantially contributed to the amateur tradition—held a
rightful place in society. Be it the fault of the Church, or be it that of a
twentieth-century society with other preoccupations, music is now overwhelmingly secular in its appeal, and its attention focussed on our concert
halls and opera houses, and the persistence of these men as the principals
and professors of our schools of music constitutes an anachronism. In a more
leisured society, too, the serious amateur of music had the time and the
opportunity to acquire an acceptable degree of accomplishment, and his
participation in a level of music-making whose technical demands were less
exacting than those of today was not disagreeable. But with the disappearance
of that society, and the tremendous increase in the resources of the instru-

mentalist which came with his final emancipation from vocal music—an emancipation which was already felt two hundred years ago in central Europe —the continued effective participation of the dilettante became impossible and his influence (particularly in the sphere of conducting) pernicious.

But while the British love of institutionalism is happy to accord the welfare of her schools of music to indigenous talents—and would, indeed, provoke an outcry if the appointment of foreign talent were ever to be seriously entertained—she is exceedingly reluctant to entrust to native hands, where there is a suitable foreign candidate, those institutions of the opera house and the concert hall which are more in the eye of the musical public at large, and the initiative of the BBC in appointing Colin Davis in 1967 as their musical director is the more to be welcomed. Combined with this institutional sense is the widespread illusion, shared by our Anglo-Saxon brethren on the other side of the Atlantic, that the musical prerequisite of any artist is the possession of some tangible characteristic of personality with which to provide the public a convenient peg on which to hang its label. In all fairness it should be said that the whole world shares in this illusion, which is only misguided when—and to the extent that—it precludes the artist from the opportunity of allowing his personality to develop in its own time and in an ambience which is purely musical. The unique institution of the opera house affords such an opportunity—on the continent of Europe, at least—and the personality of the young conductor can develop within its walls unimpeded by extra-musical considerations.

Otto Klemperer is one of countless conductors who enjoyed the advantages of the opera house in his younger years, and has acquired in his old age, largely by virtue of that experience, a reputation in this country which is as legendary as it is unassailable. In his office as musical director of the Philharmonia—now, since the abdication of Walter Legge, the New Philharmonia—he cannot truthfully be said to conduct any longer: rather does he *preside* over the musical deliberations of that orchestra. It is in fact only during the last fifteen or so years of his association with the Philharmonia—an association originally instigated by Walter Legge—that Klemperer's reputation has prospered to that of a conductor of international pretensions, and that is why he is generally recognised for the conductor which he so very really is in this country alone. Before 1950, few British musicians had ever heard of him, and to the musical world at large he still remains comparatively unknown.

Klemperer was born in Breslau on 14 May, 1885, and spent his childhood in Hamburg. He was a student at the Hochschule für Musik in Frankfurt, and completed his musical studies under James Kwast and Hans Pfitzner at the Stern Conservatoire in Berlin—where Bülow had taught until 1865. In 1907, on the evidence of a testimonial from Gustav Mahler—who had never seen him conduct, but was evidently impressed by the sheer size of the youth—he was appointed third conductor of the Deutsches Landestheater in Prague, and two years later, at the age of twenty-five, second conductor of the Hamburg Stadttheater. In 1914, Hans Pfitzner invited him to Strasbourg—which was then German territory—to become first conductor of the opera house of which he was musical director, and to teach at the conservatoire, of which he was also the head, and had as one of his pupils the twenty-year-old Charles Munch. Klemperer became general musical director in Strasbourg in 1916, but left the following year to become first conductor in Cologne where he gained a certain reputation as a conductor of contemporary music in a city whose musical tastes have been traditionally *avant-garde*. In 1923 he was considered as a candidate for the Berlin State Opera, but his choice was never seriously entertained, and in 1924, at the age of thirty-nine, he left Cologne to become general musical director in Wiesbaden. Three years later he was appointed general musical director of the Kroll Theatre in Berlin at the recommendation of Erich Kleiber, who had inaugurated the new theatre as an adjunct to the Staatsoper on 1 January, 1924, with a performance of *Meistersinger*. The Kroll Theatre had, at the time of Klemperer's arrival, a repertoire of forty-four operas, most of which had come from the pens of contemporary composers, and he furthered the policy of the theatre, introducing a notable first performance of Hindemith's *Cardillac*, besides giving concerts at the Staatsoper with Hindemith and Schnabel as soloists. In 1929, at the age of forty-two, he founded the Berlin Philharmonic Choir, but reactionary elements had meanwhile campaigned, since his appointment to the Kroll Theatre, against tendencies which they saw as becoming increasingly "progressive". In 1931 their campaign proved successful, and the theatre was closed, to reopen in 1933 as the temporary home of the Reichstag. Klemperer had meanwhile become second conductor under Erich Kleiber and Leo Blech at the Staatsoper.

In 1933, with the advent of the Nazi régime, his contract with the Staatsoper was terminated overnight and at the stroke of a pen. Klemperer appealed to Richard Strauss, who declared—not without wry humour—that this was a fine time to ask him to intercede on behalf of a Jew: no more was it, as immediate history was so abundantly to endorse. Klemperer joined the émigré battalions to America, and received the appointment in September 1933 as conductor of the Los Angeles Philharmonic in succession to Artur Rodzinski, who had gone to Cleveland. During the next two seasons—1934-34 and 1935-36—he appeared as guest conductor of the New York Philharmonic, and in 1937 was engaged for six weeks to reconstitute the

Pittsburgh Symphony, which had enjoyed a chequered career since its in-auguration in 1895, and had once again fallen upon hard times. Then, in 1939, shortly before the outbreak of war in Europe, he fell victim to a tumour of the brain, and his Los Angeles contract went by default, to be taken up in due course by Bruno Walter, and in 1943 by Alfred Wallenstein.

The history of Klemperer's illness, incorporating a subsequent stroke which paralysed the whole of one side of his body, is one of indomitable courage and almost superhuman physical strength. Not only could he no longer conduct, but the effects of his stroke rendered him unable to perform many of the most basic physical functions, to the consequent embarrassment of even his most intimate friends and colleagues who had endured frequent other embarrassments of a different nature from this rather uncouth individual. Serge Radamski befriended him where others had lost patience, and formed a small choir in New York to encourage him to exercise at least that arm whose usefulness remained to him. And it was in New York that Klemperer learned, with immense patience, that deeper significance of music which can only be revealed to those who have endured and survived the fires of physical and spiritual torment. In 1947, after the end of the Second World War, he re-turned to Europe and to the scene of youthful aspiration—Prague—where he remained for three years, until the age of sixty-five. Then, at an age when most people are grateful to be able to retire, he began to appear in this country for the first time, at first as the guest and then—after Karajan's abdication at the end of the Philharmonia's tour to America in 1955—as musical director of the Philharmonia Orchestra.

Today we think of Otto Klemperer primarily in the context of the music of Beethoven, but as early as 1927 the Royal Philharmonic Society had had the opportunity of engaging his services as a Beethoven conductor, but had been compelled to renounce them because Klemperer had insisted on a pro-gramme which should consist solely of the Third and Fifth Symphonies—a programme whose uncompromising fare, from the hands of a conductor who was then quite unknown in this country, that illustrious society felt unable, or unwilling, to digest. They could not have known that, thirty years later, Klemperer's would be a name to conjure with, and that the alliance of the Beethoven Third and Fifth Symphonies under his presidency would be ample guarantee of a sold-out Festival Hall weeks in advance.

The Philharmonic Society had been incorporated under Royal Charter in November 1812, and its role in the destinies of British music-making con-tinued to be one of predominance. From the date of the society's inception a hundred years earlier, concerts had been given in the Argyll Rooms, on the corner of Argyll Street and Oxford Street, moving in 1819 to the New Argyll

Rooms on the corner of Little Argyll Street and Regent Street, thence in 1830 to the King's Theatre, Haymarket, and three years later to the Hanover Square Rooms which were to be the society's headquarters for the next thirty-five years. These were moved in 1869 to St. James's Hall, Piccadilly, and in 1894 to the Queen's Hall, where they remained until its destruction by enemy action in 1941.

The pre-eminence of the society's position was not seriously challenged until 1904 when, on 4 June of that year, the London Symphony Orchestra was founded with Hans Richter as its permanent conductor, now dividing his duties with the Hallé Orchestra in Manchester. On Richter's return to Germany in 1911 the London Symphony Orchestra appointed Artur Nikisch as *their* musical director, and it was with Nikisch that the orchestra toured Canada and the United States in May of the following year. Nikisch had appeared with the Philharmonic Society for the first time in 1908—an appearance which was repeated in the course of the following three seasons, when his prior commitment with the London Symphony (not to mention those of Berlin and Leipzig) precluded his further activity with that institution. But by this time the fortunes of the society had entered a new phase of prosperity, and one whose connection with the name of Beecham is not entirely remote. For it was Thomas Beecham, who had originally appeared at one of the society's concerts in December 1910, who now came to its rescue four years later, conducting five of the seven concerts, and in the following season—1915–16—appearing as its sole conductor and making substantial donations to the society's dwindling funds from his own private fortune. This arrangement continued for the next two seasons when, as the result of an exceedingly ill-advised letter from four of the society's directors under the chairmanship of Thomas Dunhill in July 1918, Beecham resigned and the reins were gathered back once more into the society's tight and despotic hands—though they naïvely believed that they were acting in the best interests of "democracy", a euphemistic term for their shareholders. Nor did Beecham reappear under the society's aegis for the next ten years—until 22 March, 1928—when he received the society's Gold Medal. The fact that a radio choir had made its debut at one of the society's concerts four months previously presaged new crises for the society, which were to materialise in the form of the BBC Symphony Orchestra in 1930. One may draw the inference, if one so wishes, that the society—who must by this time have had wind of the BBC's plans—desired to placate Sir Thomas in the only manner in which they could hope to be successful, and well ahead of the event which, in March 1928, already looked uncomfortably near. Beecham, too, knew full well of the BBC's plans, and in September 1928 was able to publish ambitious plans of his own for the formation of a Royal Philharmonic Orchestra which was to give twenty concerts annually under the aegis of the society—but without financial liability to them—besides fifty more at the Albert Hall and in the London suburbs and the provinces, and forty recording sessions with the Columbia recording company. These plans did not materialise, and following the inauguration of the BBC Symphony Orchestra under the musical directorship of Adrian Boult, Beecham countered with the formation of his own orchestra—the London Philharmonic—which gave its first concert on 7 October, 1932, under the auspices of the Royal Philharmonic Society. At the third concert of the 1932–33 season, on 10 November, Beecham had as his soloist in the Tchaikowsky Piano Concerto the twenty-eight-year-old Vladimir Horowitz, and committed the inexcusable breach of professional etiquette of declaring publicly that Horowitz did not know the work, where he himself had patently missed the notoriously treacherous woodwind entry after the first-movement cadenza. This was in marked contrast to Hans Richter who, after missing an analogous entry in the scherzo interlude of the slow movement in a performance of the same work with the Hallé Orchestra in 1910, and with Wilhelm Backhaus—then aged twenty-six—as his soloist, had had the grace publicly to acknowledge his own mistake to the entire audience at the conclusion of the concerto.

This is not to call in question Beecham's artistry, that it should have been guilty of a technical error which, however professionally inexcusable, anyone could commit and most of us have—Beecham perhaps more often than most. Rather is it a reflection on his intellectual honesty and professional integrity in refusing to admit his own error, and of impugning the artistry of a colleague in consequence, and as such it becomes a reflection which is ineradicable. For a lapse of artistic integrity, like any other form of integrity, be it never so momentary, must reflect unequivocally on our assessment of the man and his entire work: and Beecham's conduct in the Horowitz incident cannot be accounted a whit better than that of Malcolm Sargent, who left Aleksandr Helman to finish the performance of the Rachmaninoff Third Concerto entirely on his own, claiming that he could not follow him, and effectively preventing the orchestra from doing so either. Such flagrant sabotage of a performance is unforgivable, and merits no further attention to the artist in question.

But the attitude of the Royal Philharmonic Society who, in 1946, after high-handedly refusing the offer of Beecham's services on his return from the United States, took such grave exception to his founding the Royal Philharmonic Orchestra which he had once had occasion to offer them, displayed—if not a comparable breach of professional etiquette, then a superlative ingratitude to one who had served them well, if not always wisely, in artistic and plain economic terms. In his command of immense personal wealth, Sir Thomas Beecham has been likened to Serge Koussevitsky, and the comparison drawn between their respective successes as the new patrons of music. Beecham's achievement is manifestly less than that of Koussevitsky— partly by reason of our national disposition to disparagement, and partly by reason of Beecham's inability to match the stamina of Koussevitsky, and it may be argued that this was necessarily so in that Beecham had never enjoyed that opportunity to command identical and superlative forces which was Koussevitsky's for twenty-five years. One might further argue that if the Royal Philharmonic or any other society had accorded, or been in a position to accord, or been wholeheartedly disposed to accord, that opportunity to Beecham or any other comparable British conductor we might enjoy today that reputation as an enlightened musical nation which America enjoys largely as a result of Koussevitsky's activities with the Boston Symphony Orchestra. But one may state quite categorically that neither the orchestra of the Royal Philharmonic Society, nor the London Philharmonic, nor the Royal Philharmonic, can be mentioned in the same breath as the Boston Symphony Orchestra, and that we as a nation are woefully slow to learn. Our conviction that nobody can teach us anything is one which is shared by at least one member of the New York Philharmonic, and that is one reason why that orchestra cannot vie with the Boston Symphony Orchestra either. Omniscience is accorded to few and but rarely, and never at the same identical moment to a hundred and one orchestral musicians of whatever their individual artistic stature. But this has been to digress, and to overlook a number of distinguished British conductors who came into prominence between the two world wars, and whose dictum might have been that of Erich Kleiber: "Routine and improvisation are the two mortal enemies of art".

Sir Hamilton Harty, who was born in Hillsborough, Ireland, on 4 December, 1879, and Sir John Barbirolli, who was born in London on 2 December, 1899, both shared service as the permanent conductors of the Hallé Orchestra—Harty from 1920 until 1933, and Barbirolli from 1944 until the present day. The Hallé Concerts Society had been formed in 1857 to finance and manage the concerts which Sir Charles Hallé founded in the same year, and the Hallé Orchestra is therefore the oldest established orchestra in Great Britain. Hallé left an enviable musical legacy in Manchester, which the city corporation has subsequently, consistently and conspicuously betrayed. Richter assumed control of the orchestra in 1899, in succession to Frederick Cowen who had come to Manchester in 1888—following his resignation from the Philharmonic Society—to assist Hallé in his final years. Richter resigned from the Hallé in 1911 and returned to Germany, and following a season of guest conductors in 1911–12, Michael Balling, a German conductor from Heidingsfeld, was appointed at Richter's recommendation and served with the Hallé until the outbreak of war. Manchester's musical public was of predominantly German extraction, and the musical life of the city suffered greatly in the 1914–18 War in consequence. It was not until 1920 that Hamilton Harty was engaged to reconstitute it—which he succeeded in doing and in a remarkably short space of time had restored the former glory which it had enjoyed under Richter, Cowen and Hallé himself.

Conducting had not in fact been the chosen profession of Hamilton Harty, who had gained the reputation of a brilliant accompanist and gifted composer in his youth, and he was forty-one when—after a début with the London Symphony Orchestra—he assumed control of the Hallé Orchestra in 1920. A dispute with the city corporation over conditions in the orchestra led to his resignation thirteen years later, in 1933, but he continued to make frequent appearances with orchestras in London and the provinces until his death on 19 February, 1941, in Brighton, whither he had retired to devote the greater part of his time to composition. During the twenty or so years of his activity as a conductor he had displayed that admixture of whimsy and penetration so essential to his Irish temperament, and that accomplished musicianship which is content with revealing new secrets from conventional repertoire rather than making a fetish of discovering new works. The programme for one of his concerts with the Royal Philharmonic Society on 1 May, 1924, is revealing for the supreme honesty and native ebullience of his outlook—Berlioz's *Royal Hunt and Storm*, Schubert's Great C major Symphony, and Strauss's *Ein Heldenleben*—three works which must depend for their success on innate artistry alone.

Albert Coates, who was born in St. Petersburg on 23 April, 1882, was the son of an English businessman living at the time in Russia. He was educated at the Royal Naval College in Dartmouth, but turned to music and entered the Leipzig Conservatoire in 1902—perhaps the first English conductor to sense that an English conservatoire training could offer him little of professional consequence. He studied conducting in Leipzig under Artur Nikisch— anticipating Adrian Boult by ten years—and became a coach at the Leipzig Opera. In 1906, at the age of twenty-four, he became first conductor at Barmen-Elberfeld—now anticipating Erich Kleiber's occupancy of the same post thirteen years later—and thence to the more important houses in Dresden in 1908, under Schuch, and Mannheim in 1910. He made his London debut in 1910 with the Queen's Hall orchestra, and returned to Russia in 1911 to become permanent conductor of the St. Petersburg Opera at the Marynskaya Theatre for the next five years. In 1913 he made his debut at Covent Garden, and from 1916 to 1919—when the aftermath of the revolution necessitated his flight from Russia in the face of extreme opposition—worked as first conductor of the Bolshoi Theatre in Moscow. On his return to England he became a regular conductor with the London Symphony Orchestra, and also appeared with the orchestra of the Royal Philharmonic Society on frequent occasions, introducing Scriabin's *Poème Divine* on 20 November, 1919 and Beethoven's Ninth Symphony on 26 February, 1920, in collaboration with Charles Kennedy Scott, who had just formed the Philharmonic Choir. (Kennedy Scott's next appearance, in the capacity of sole conductor, was at the next Philharmonic Society concert, and in November of that year he shared the programme with Hamilton Harty, who was making his Philharmonic Society debut.)

Coates had meanwhile accepted engagements with Beecham's opera company at Covent Garden, and in 1920 made his American début as guest conductor of the New York Symphony, at the invitation of Walter Damrosch. In 1923 he became conductor of the Rochester Philharmonic for two seasons, and also appeared with the New York Philharmonic both in the course of its winter season and at Lewisohn Stadium in the summer. At the age of sixty-three, still largely unrecognised in his own country, Coates emigrated to South Africa to become conductor of the Cape Town Municipal Orchestra until his death on 11 December, 1953.

Eugene Goossens, who was born in London on 26 May, 1893, of Belgian parentage, follows the pattern of Albert Coates in his inacceptance of this country as providing the professional stimulus *sui generis* for the conductor of potential distinction. His studies were divided between Bruges, Liverpool and London, and centred in his youth on composition and the violin—which he played, from 1911 to 1915, under Sir Henry Wood in his Queen's Hall orchestra. In 1915, at the age of twenty-two, Goossens became Beecham's assistant, and during the 1921–22 season conducted the Russian ballet and opera at Covent Garden. In 1923 he joined Coates in America as assistant conductor of the Rochester Philharmonic, becoming its principal conductor when Coates returned to England two years later. Goossens remained in Rochester until 1931, when he became principal conductor of the Cincinnati orchestra until 1946, meantime appearing as guest-conductor with the Philadelphia Orchestra, the New York Philharmonic, and the Berlin Philharmonic, in addition to his début with the Royal Philharmonic Society on 22 February, 1923—which had included a performance of *Le Sacre du Printemps*—and but three further concerts with that society between 1923 and 1946. In 1947 he accepted an invitation from the ABC Orchestra in Sydney,

Australia, and carried on largely pioneer work in that country until his return to England in 1956, where he was accorded the occasional guest appearance— including a memorable performance of *Le Sacre du Printemps* with the London Symphony Orchestra in 1960—but was chiefly active in the iron-curtain countries. He died in London on 13 June, 1962, at the age of sixty-nine.

The youngest member of this quartet of conductors is Sir John Barbirolli, whose name has been associated with the Hallé Concerts Society since the reconstitution of its orchestra in May 1944. Barbirolli made his London début as a solo 'cellist with the Queen's Hall orchestra under Sir Henry Wood in 1910, at the age of ten, and studied both with his father and at the Royal Academy of Music. In 1919 he formed his own chamber orchestra, which led to his appointment as a conductor of the British National Opera Company. In 1927 he became an assistant conductor at the Royal Opera House, Covent Garden, while continuing to hold the posts of permanent conductor with both the BBC Scottish Orchestra and the Leeds Symphony Orchestra, as well as fulfilling guest engagements with the London Symphony Orchestra. His début with the orchestra of the Royal Philharmonic Society took place on 30 March, 1930, with Casals as soloist in the Schumann 'Cello Concerto. Following Harty's resignation from the Hallé Orchestra in 1933, Barbirolli shared guest engagements in Manchester with Albert Coates, Edward Elgar, Clemens Krauss, Pierre Monteux, and Georg Szell, amongst others, and in 1936 received the invitation of a guest engagement with the New York Philharmonic, and in the following year entered a three-year contract with that orchestra in the capacity of musical director. He returned to England shortly after the outbreak of war, where the Manchester corporation could no longer claim the predominance of a German musical public as an excuse for the inactivity of the Hallé Orchestra. Nor did Barbirolli find the rest of England conspicuously ready to welcome him with open arms, for a musical monopoly had been established which was being jealously guarded, and it was not until 9 October, 1943, that he was accorded another concert with the Royal Philharmonic Society. On 26 May of the following year, Barbirolli brought a reconstituted Hallé Orchestra to London for its first concert under the Philharmonic Society's auspices, and during the following seasons the society's concerts were shared between five orchestras—the BBC Symphony Orchestra under Sir Adrian Boult, the London Symphony under George Weldon, the Liverpool Philharmonic under Malcolm Sargent, the Hallé under John Barbirolli, and the London Philharmonic under Basil Cameron, thereby breaking the monopoly of the last-named orchestra which had been held since its inception, at the instance of Sir Thomas Beecham, in 1932.

With the coming of an uneasy peace in 1945, Britain was to corner the European musical market in recording with which her continental neighbours were as yet unable to compete, and the perfection of recording techniques—which had by the early 'thirties and the advent of electrical recording already achieved an astonishingly high standard—now made the exploitation of the long-playing gramophone record, with all its attendant commercial implications, only a matter of time.

I   Hans von Bülow, from a painting by Franz von Lenbach

II   Richard Strauss, from a drawing by Edward Grützer

III   Gustav Mahler, from caricatures by Otto Boehler

IV   Artur Nikisch with the Boston Symphony Orchestra. A photograph taken in 1891

V   Erich Kleiber

VI   Bruno Walter, Arturo Toscanini, Erich Kleiber, Otto Klemperer and Wilhelm
Furtwängler. A photograph taken at the Italian Embassy in Berlin, 1929

II   Willem Mengelberg

VIII   Arturo Toscanini

IX   Wilhelm Furtwängler

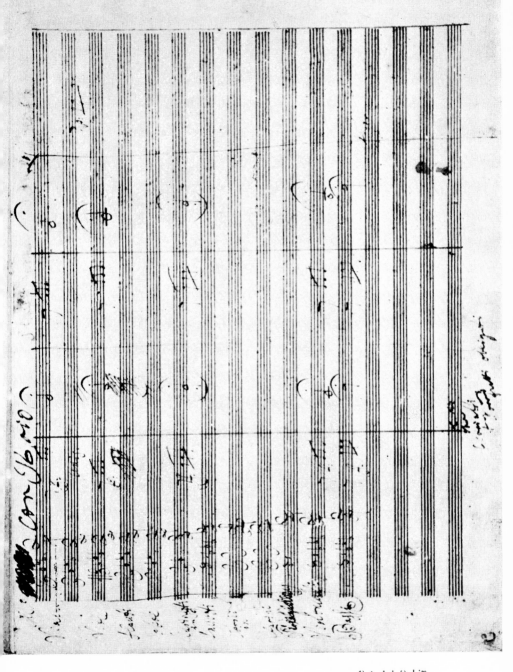

X The first page of the autograph score of Beethoven's Fifth Symphony. In addition to the interpolated bar, there is the cryptic footnote: *flauti, oboi, clarinetti, fagotti, corni, tutti obligatti*

XI   A page from the manuscript of *The Fourth of July*, by Charles Ives. The passage
—in common with many others from the composer's other works—is one which
requires two conductors

XII   The climax of the symphonic epilogue from Act III of *Wozzeck* by Alban Berg, showing the structure of a twelve-tone chord above a firm tonality of D minor

XIII   Leopold Stokowski with the Leipzig Gewandhaus Orchestra in 1959

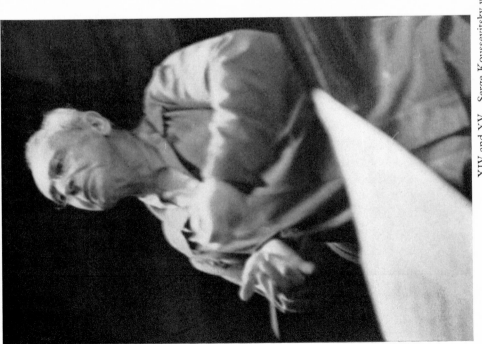

XIV and XV   Serge Koussevitsky with the Boston Symphony Orchestra in 1950

XVI and XVII   Charles Munch with the Boston Symphony Orchestra in 1956

XIX Herbert von Karajan

XVIII Georg Szell

XXI   Dimitri Mitropoulos

XX   Leonard Bernstein

Chapter 13

HERBERT VON KARAJAN AND GEORG SZELL

Behrens drew out a fat magic tome, turned the heavy leaves, and chose a paper envelope which showed a coloured label through a round hole on the front. He set the disc on the turntable, set it in motion, waited until it had gathered speed, and then carefully set the fine steel point on the edge of the record. There was a low rasping sound. He lowered the lid, and simultaneously a blast of music came from the open doors at the front, from between the slats of the blind, from the box as a whole in fact—a hubbub of instruments bearing the lively, bustling, insistent melody: the contagious opening bars of an Offenbach overture.

They listened, their lips parted in smiles. They could hardly believe their ears at the purity of colour and fidelity of reproduction of the woodwind. A solo violin began its whimsical prelude, bowing, plucking, the saccharine shifts from one position to another—all were clearly audible. It struck up the melody of the waltz, *Ach, ich habe sie verloren!*, the orchestra providing a light and graceful accompaniment—and it was captivating to hear the way it was taken up by the ensemble and repeated as a resounding *tutti*. Of course, it was hardly like a real orchestra playing in the room. The volume of sound, though not to any extent distorted, had suffered a diminution of perspective. If we may draw a simile from the visual field, it was as though we were looking at a painting through the wrong end of an opera-glass, seeing it as remote and diminutive, though with all its luminous precision of drawing and colour. The vivid and consummate piece was reproduced in all the richness of its light-hearted invention. The finish was abandon itself, a galop with a drolly hesitant beginning, which was built up into a shameless *can-can*, calling up visions of skirts flying, knees tossing and opera hats waved in the air, and seeming never to reach the end of its intoxicating revelry. But at last the mechanism stopped of its own accord. It was over. There was enthusiastic applause.

This excerpt from the final chapter of Thomas Mann's *Der Zauberberg*[1] refers to the installation of a Polyhymnia gramophone for the benefit of the patients

[1] Thomas Mann: *Der Zauberberg*, S. Fischer Verlag, 1924.

—Hans Castorp among their number—at Dr. Behrens's clinic in the Swiss mountains. The year is not specified, though it must have been earlier than 1912, for there is a later reference to the sinking of the *Titanic*. The writer implores us to realise that this

> was not that paltry box with a handle to it, a turntable and shaft atop and a shapeless brass funnel attached, which used to be set up outside country inns to gratify the ears of the rude with its nasal braying... With that antediluvian mechanism it had nothing in common. You lifted a prettily bevelled lid, which was automatically supported by a brass rail attached to the inside, and there above the slightly depressed surface there was a turntable, covered in green cloth, with a nickelled rim and a nickel peg on which you fitted the hole at the centre of the hard rubber record ...

Nor was *Orpheus in the Underworld* the only record, for there were twelve volumes containing twelve records each—many of them double-sided. *Il Barbiere* and *La Traviata*, *Tales of Hoffman*, *Faust*, *Don Giovanni*, *Aïda* and *Carmen* were among the recordings mentioned—and more surprising, Debussy's *Prélude à l'après-midi d'un faune*. While vocal and instrumental reproduction is revealed as having been astonishingly faithful, the reproduction of the piano sounded "thin and cold, like a spinet".

Although there would be every reason for according Thomas Mann poetic licence in respect of the complete accuracy of his account, his knowledge of things musical is known to have been far too penetrating, and the whole section is far too well-documented and exhaustive for there to be very much doubt that it is quite as authentic historically speaking as it is musically. There could have been no valid artistic reason why he should have introduced the subject at so late a juncture in his novel if it had not been. Even in the years immediately prior to the 1914–18 war the recording was of course by no means new. The wax cylinder recording had been more or less perfected by Edison about 1888, and the voices of Queen Victoria, Florence Nightingale and Gladstone were among others preserved. Brahms is reputed to have played one of his works on one of the cylinders in Vienna in 1889, and Adelina Patti to have made several records in America in 1890. But the persistent rumour that the voice of Jenny Lind is preserved on record is a myth. These early records were all unique copies made by the artist in question to gratify a personal whim, and it was not until a method was devised to duplicate records in bulk that the gramophone began to play any significant role in the dissemination of good music. The disc-recording was patented in 1896, and five years later the Gramophone and Typewriter Company was formed in London.

It was not until 1903 that America began to show interest in recording, the Victor Company having imported a number of matrices from Europe, and in April the Columbia Company replied with a series of "Celebrity" recordings of Edouard de Reske, Marcella Sembrich, Ernestine Schumann-Heink, Antonio Scotti and Suzanne Adams. Melba followed in 1904, and between 1905 and 1907 the Odeon Company in Berlin released thirty-four records of Lilli Lehmann. By 1910 there was hardly a singer of repute who had not made records, and Joseph Joachim, Eugène Ysaÿe, Mischa Elman, Fritz Kreisler, Jan Kubelik, Efrem Zimbalist, Raoul Pugno, Grieg, Paderewski and de Pachmann were among the instrumentalists who had embraced the new medium. The orchestral field was lagging behind, partly for acoustic and partly for economic reasons, and it is the more surprising to read of Hans Castorp's listening, *circa* 1911, to so (then) exotic a work as *L'après-midi d'un faune*, though Mann was too thorough-going a scholar to have misled us when there must have been any number of other "mood" pieces which would have served his purpose. In 1913 Artur Nikisch made his famous recording of the complete Beethoven Fifth with the Berlin Philharmonic, and four years later the Chicago Symphony under Stock, the Cincinnati Symphony under Ernst Kunwald, and the New York Philharmonic under Stransky followed suit with excerpts from Beethoven and Wagner for Columbia. In 1918 the Boston Symphony recorded some Wagner and Tchaikowsky excerpts for Victor, and in 1919 Leopold Stokowski and the Philadelphia Orchestra made their appearance with two Hungarian Dances by Brahms.

These were however—with the exception of the Beethoven Fifth—sample offerings to a very wide public who, with the advent of radio in the early 'twenties, were almost permanently lost to the record industry. It took many years for the publicity paladins responsible for sales promotion to grasp the elementary fact that there was a far larger market which remained unexplored, and whose demands were not quantitative but qualitative. With the advent of an initial refinement of electro-acoustical recording, a wealth of classical repertoire was bequeathed to this minority public.

The early electric recordings made in the late 'twenties and early 'thirties were of a remarkably high standard, as is invariably the case when a new and valuable market is being explored by artists of integrity rather than academics of engineering. The Viennese pianist Alfred Brendel had this to say in 1964:

> I am still waiting for the "experts" to explain to me why the piano-tone of Cortot or Edwin Fischer was more faithfully reproduced on their "historic" recordings of the early 'thirties than on any of the

post-war recordings. One had the impression of sitting in a comfortable seat in a good hall, and could perceive a *timbre* that was quite personal. The listener to very many Hi-Fi recordings, on the other hand, has the unexpected sensation of sitting inside the piano or on top of it, or of being perilously suspended somewhere underneath the roof.[2]

The faithful reproduction of the sound of the piano has been a perennial and notorious problem for the recording engineer—*vide* Behrens's audience of a piano which sounded "thin and cold, like a spinet". But it is a problem which has now extended to the orchestral and operatic world as well. Willem Mengelberg's recording of *Ein Heldenleben*, made in 1930, is incomparably better than Beecham's version of the same work with the Royal Philharmonic, made twenty years later. Leaving aside the purely musical aspects of the two versions, and their qualities as recordings *per se*, the reason for this is that the recording engineers used the limited facilities at their disposal in 1930 more artistically than their colleagues of twenty years later, with vastly improved facilities. The much vaunted—and derided—recording of *Salome* by Georg Solti was made with a superlative cast, a superlative orchestra, with superlative equipment, and under superlative conditions. Nor can I agree with those who maintain that the ultra-high-fidelity three-dimensional stereophonic sound makes a caricature of Strauss's opera in bringing an artificial clarity to bear which would not have been apparent or even audible in the opera house—the xylophone solos in the *Dance of the Seven Veils*, for example. It is completely legitimate for the gramophone record to capture clarity in all its aspects and wherever it finds it, and in these days when recorded sound has ceased to be a substitute for live sound, it is its ultimate *raison d'être*. But the recording is not omnipotent, nor will it ever be so, for there are by final analysis only two dimensions which it can capture: the vertical aspect of the page of score, expressed in frequency range, and the depth of the score, expressed in the bringing of various contours of sound into relief at given moments in the musical discourse. The third dimension—the horizontal progress of the music—is the only factor which has remained constant in recording techniques because it is the one factor over which, by final analysis, the recording engineer has no control (apart from the artificially induced *crescendo* or *diminuendo*, over which the less said the better). It is the one dimension which must remain, as it always has done, in the hands of the executive artist, and it is fair comment on the calibre of that artist if he allow himself to be overruled, however tacitly, by extra-musical considerations and extra-musical pressures on his rightful domain. The only quality which is

[2] Alfred Brendel: *Phono*, 8th year, No. 6, Vienna.

ultimately lacking in Georg Solti's recording of *Salome*, and which makes it sound so contrived and artificial, is the quality of musical co-ordination and leadership which he alone could have given and of which his recording engineers, for musical as well as extra-musical considerations, have demonstrably deprived him.

The immediate post-war scene, both in Britain and America, was one of indescribable activity, not only the recording industry, but the film industry as well, providing an outlet of ever-increasing dimensions for the market of musical talent. A new generation for whom the privations of war had revealed the miracle of music for the first time was no longer prepared to view it as that polite social pastime which it had been for their elders, and the final concerts of the war in every part of the western world had been the occasions for a deep musical communion of youth. With the coming of peace, the recording industry underwent a state of siege.

To meet this demand Sir Thomas Beecham formed the Royal Philharmonic Orchestra in 1946: Walter Legge, chief recording engineer for EMI, replied with the formation of the Philharmonia Orchestra, comprising the best elements of the musical profession, many of whom had just been released from the armed forces. Under the direct aegis of EMI, the Philharmonia could enjoy the unprecedented luxury of recording more or less at *their* leisure, and *their* early recordings—up until 1952, and the universal prevalence of the long-playing record—are a monument to a perfection of both playing and recording.

Herbert von Karajan had become the Philharmonia's musical director in 1948—a post which he held until 1955—and was able to employ the months which preceded the orchestra's début at the Royal Albert Hall in bringing its playing to a level of virtuosity which has never again been equalled. Karajan's early recordings of Balakirev (Symphony in C), Bartók (Music for Strings, Percussion and Celesta), Beethoven (Symphony No. 7), Brahms (Symphony No. 1), Handel-Harty (*Water Music*), Mozart (*Haffner* Symphony and E flat Divertimento, K.334), Sibelius (Symphonies No. 4, 5 and 7, and *Tapiola*), Strauss (*Till Eulenspiegel* and *Don Juan*), and Tchaikowsky (Symphonies No. 4 and 5) were all but the training-ground—accomplished with a meticulousness in rehearsal which provoked despair among many members of the orchestra—for their later concert performances, and in particular the prelude for the Philharmonia's spectacularly successful tour to France and Austria in the early months of 1952.

Karajan was born in Salzburg on 5 April, 1908, the younger son of a doctor of Greek extraction, whose family had been settled in Austria for two and a half centuries. At the age of eighteen he entered the *Kapellmeisterschule* of the Vienna Music Academy, now—in the absence of Clemens Krauss, whose commitments in Frankfurt had made it no longer possible to commute with Vienna—in the nominal hands of Alexander Wunderer, one of the directors of the Vienna Philharmonic. The students were however left very much to their own devices, and on 17 December, 1928, Karajan made his conducting début with the orchestra of the Vienna Music Academy in the overture to *William Tell*. Three weeks later came his "professional" début with the orchestra of the Salzburg Mozarteum, in a programme which included Strauss's *Don Juan* and Tchaikowsky's Fifth Symphony. On 2 March, 1929, after six weeks of intensive rehearsal, he made his operatic début at the Ulm Stadttheater—the oldest theatre in Germany—with the *Marriage of Figaro*, and on 14 March his engagement as *Opernkapellmeister* until the end of the 1929–30 season was confirmed by the intendant, Erwin Dietrich.

> At that time Ulm was a theatre which received a subsidy of only 60,000 DM a year [says Karajan]. This meant that the ensemble were either complete beginners or people who had already sung themselves out. They wouldn't have been able to pay anyone else. I started with 80 DM a month, and ended up after five years with 120 DM. The orchestra consisted of seventeen players for operetta, augmented to twenty-six for grand opera. There were sixteen chorus members. The proscenium width was seven and a half metres—the size of a large room ... When I set out for Ulm I had no idea what "provincial theatre" could mean ... I arrived in the morning and saw *Lohengrin* announced for the afternoon, and naturally made a point of going to it. At the sight of the orchestra I could hardly believe my eyes. And that was only the start of it. The playing was unspeakably bad. Instead of four trumpets for the trumpet-call in *Lohengrin*, there was only one. And when he had finished on-stage, he came back and sat down in the orchestra pit again, still in his costume ...[3]

Nevertheless, Karajan stayed in Ulm for five years, and only left when Dietrich terminated his contract, explaining much later that he had done so because he thought that Karajan would never leave—and knew that the twenty-five-year-old was destined for greater things. In April 1934 Karajan made his way to Berlin, and remained out of work until the autumn, apart from leading the conducting class in Salzburg during the summer at the instigation of a far-sighted American. When he had left Ulm, the local critic wrote:

> Karajan's *Meistersinger, Lohengrin, Tannhäuser, Fidelio, Rosenkavalier, Arabella, Don Giovanni, Marriage of Figaro, Trovatore, Rigoletto*

[3] Ernst Haoussermann: *Karajan*, C. Bertelsmann Verlag, Gütersloh, 1968.

and the brilliant performance of *Merry Wives of Windsor* deserve highest praise ... Also his achievement with the symphony concerts ... among other things he gave us Beethoven's Third, *Death and Transfiguration, Till Eulenspiegel,* the Mozart D minor Concerto—with Karajan as a brilliant soloist—and Debussy's *l'aprés-midi d'un faune.* A particular achievement was his organisation of an orchestra of ninety for the final concert—a Strauss evening with *Don Juan,* the orchestral songs, and *Heldenleben,* which remain unforgettable ...[4]

On 18 September, 1934, Karajan made his début in Aachen, on the Dutch and Belgian border. Hans Swarowsky, first conductor at Aachen, had been offered a similar post under Paul Pella in Hamburg and had asked to be released, and Edgar Gross, who had taken over as intendant in Aachen in June, found himself looking for a new first conductor to work under the general musical director, Peter Raabe. Karajan's first opera in Aachen was *Fidelio,* followed on 23 October by *Walküre,* and he now had an orchestra of seventy, augmented to ninety for symphony concerts, and a chorus of three hundred. There had been initial antipathy to him from the orchestra, who would have preferred someone quieter and more experienced. But the administration was an enlightened one which foresaw Karajan's potentialities, and when Karlsruhe made him some tempting offers it took action to keep Karajan in Aachen, and Peter Raabe, now sixty-two, was "promoted" to president of the Reichsmusikkammer in succession to Richard Strauss. On 12 April, 1935, at the age of just twenty-seven, Karajan became the youngest general musical director in Germany. Three days earlier, the mayor of Aachen asked him to go and see him. There was one more formality to be dealt with, it seemed. Karajan was not a member of the Nazi Party. According to the District Leader of the Party, he could not hold a post of this importance without being a Party Member. And so Karajan became a Party Member.

Three years later, on 26 July, 1938, Karajan married Elmy Holgerloef, the small blonde first soprano of the Stadttheater operetta, and this marked the beginning of Karajan's first negotiations with Berlin. Clemens Krauss, who had succeeded Kleiber at the Staatsoper in January 1935, became intendant and general musical director in Munich in 1936, and Heinz Tietjen, intendant of the Berlin Staatsoper, was left without a single conductor of importance. In a letter written on 25 December, 1966, Tietjen claims that he brought Karajan to Berlin in 1936, but this cannot be true, for their first exchange of letters through Dr. Prittwitz was only in the spring of 1938. Tietjen invited Karajan to come and conduct Wagner-Régeny's *Bürger von*

[4] Ibid.

Calais, offering him a first-class cast. Since this was a completely unknown work, Karajan asked to be allowed to conduct *Fidelio, Tristan* and *Meistersinger* as well. After a complex and amusing exchange of letters, he finally made his Berlin debut with *Fidelio* on 30 September, 1938—just over fifteen years after Kleiber's Berlin début with the same work. *Tristan* followed on 31 October, and a new production of *Zauberflöte* on 18 December. On 28 January, 1939, the *Bürger von Calais* received its première. Tietjen sought to secure Karajan's services on a permanent basis, but he was determined to maintain his headquarters in Aachen where, by 1939, he had managed to mount a performance of *Götterdämmerung.* Karajan succeeded in keeping a foot in both camps until March 1941 when the final breach with Aachen came, and Paul van Kempen, conductor of the Dresden Philharmonic, was appointed in his place. On 10 April, 1941, the Berlin Staatsoper was hit by incendiary bombs and burnt down, but it was rebuilt again within an incredibly short space of time. Karajan, who had been with the State Opera company in Rome, and was now in Cervinia, read that Furtwängler had returned to the Staatsoper to conduct its official re-opening. Tietjen had once told him: "One thing you can take for sure. If Furtwängler ever comes through the door of the Staatsoper, I shall go out by another one", and on his return to Berlin Karajan went to see him. Tietjen prevaricated, spoke of high-level politics which he would not expect Karajan to be able to understand, that it had to be, and so on. Two weeks later Karajan received his call-up papers which had originated from the Prussian Home Office.

Karajan elected to join the Air Force, but was told that he was too old to be a fighter pilot. On the eve of his call-up he paid a farewell visit to Tietjen, who refused to see him, and a final visit to his dentist. The dentist's daughter happened to be Goebbels's private secretary, his case received special and urgent attention, and Karajan was released from his military obligations. But the doors of the Staatsoper were now closed to him, and he was left with only his six annual concerts with the Staatskapelle. His first marriage had by this time broken up, and his second wife was Anita Gütermann who, according to the Nuremberg Race Tribunal was one-quarter Jewish—a fact which was hardly calculated to have endeared Karajan to the Nazi authorities. With the total destruction of the State Opera in 1944, even the six concerts with the Staatskapelle were lost, and Karajan—having incurred Hitler's personal opprobrium during a performance of *Meistersinger* in 1940—was not accorded permission to conduct elsewhere. Shortly before the end of the war, Karajan received an invitation to conduct in Milan, and received a visa to go there. The Karajans arrived in Milan to find the Axis armies in full flight. The concerts did not materialise, and they were now stranded in Italy until the intendant in Trieste heard of their plight, and invited Karajan to give some concerts there. He was driven to Trieste by an English army major. Finally, on 18 January, 1946, he gave his first concert with the Vienna Philharmonic in Vienna, in the teeth of the Russian military authorities. When a second Karajan concert was announced six weeks later, the Russians placed a military cordon round the Musikvereinsaal, which lay in the Russian zone of Vienna, and prevented anyone from entering. Karajan had not been through the formalities of de-nazification. Nor was he given formal permission to conduct again in public until October 1947—three months before Furtwängler—and he spent the actual performances of *Figaro* and *Rosenkavalier* at the 1946 Salzburg Festival sitting in the prompt-box while Felix Prohaska and Hans Swarowsky conducted.

In 1948 Karajan was reinstated in the capacity of conductor at the Salzburg Festival, conducting *Marriage of Figaro* and *Orphée et Euridice*, while Furtwängler conducted *Fidelio* and some of the concerts. 1948 also saw the beginning of his association with the Philharmonia Orchestra in London—where Walter Legge had initiated negotiations for Karajan in 1946—his appointment as director of the Gesellschaft der Musikfreunde, which prompted Furtwängler's immediate resignation—and the start of a six-year association with the Vienna Symphony Orchestra which quickly came to vie with the Philharmonic. On 28 December 1948, Karajan conducted the Salzburg production of *Figaro* at La Scala and was appointed musical director of the German season there, while Victor de Sabata, a colleague from Berlin days, remained general musical director for the Italian repertoire. In 1951, Karajan conducted *Meistersinger* and the second *Ring* cycle at Bayreuth, Knappertsbusch conducting *Parsifal* and the first *Ring*, and Furtwängler Beethoven's Ninth.

On 30 November, 1954, Furtwängler died in the Ebersteinburg clinic in Baden-Baden, and the Berlin Philharmonic immediately cabled Karajan, who was in Italy, inviting him to become his successor. There was also a delegation from the Vienna Philharmonic, but Karajan declined their invitation—perhaps not without some secret amusement—on the grounds that it was not, as the Berlin Philharmonic's had been, a *cri de coeur*. For the Berlin Philharmonic had already been committed for the past year to a forthcoming tour of the United States in March 1955. On 1 December, 1954, Claudia Cassidy, notorious for her successful efforts at unseating Rafael Kubelik and a number of other conductors, wrote in the *Chicago Daily Tribune*:

> Music lost a giant when Wilhelm Furtwängler died. His was the noblest Beethoven I have known, the most revealing Bruckner, in the realm of Mozart the most truly magical *Magic Flute*. Ironical

that Chicago was to have heard such an artist for the first time at
three Allied Artists with the Berlin Philharmonic, booked for March
in Orchestra Hall. For it was "artists", some of them worthy of the
word without quotation marks, whose refusal to appear under his
direction caused Furtwängler's withdrawal as guest conductor of the
Chicago Symphony Orchestra for what must have been eight incredible weeks in the season of 1949–50.

My first inkling of that boycott came in a secret telephone call
from a pianist of the highest rank, obviously under pressure and
asking what to do. What did I know of Furtwängler's political
record? Nothing, I said. I know what interests me. He is a great
conductor. Even recordings prove that. A week or two later the
boycott burst into print, the orchestra board got nervous, and
Furtwängler withdrew.

How great the loss, how curious the cause, I knew more about
when the summer of 1949 took me to Salzburg. I saw the tall, quiet
man about whom so much controversy raged, the man so revered
that at a Sunday morning concert those who could not buy tickets for
the Festspielhaus waited outside until the doors were opened at the
end of the performance, then crowded in, just to applaud. I knew,
because I heard it, that he understood and communicated the glory
of music. His *Fidelio* was light to banish darkness and truth to shame
the lie.

Because of Claire Dux, now Mrs. Hans von der Marwitz, we met
quietly, over coffee. No questions were put. But he made up his mind
in my favour. He said: "Is there anything I can tell you that you
would like to know?" So we met and talked for hours, finding an
interpreter unnecessary, and official documents underscored what
I already knew, for I am Irish enough to put faith in such a face, and
such music. The *Tribune* printed that interview, a long one, Sunday
4 September, 1949. Later, a letter from his villa in Clarens, Switzerland, thanked the *Tribune* for stating his case.

It was for me the simple, tragic case of a man in high position who
felt that his place was with his people. "It would have been much
easier to emigrate", he told me, "but there had to be a spiritual
center of integrity for all the good and real Germans who had to stay
behind. I felt that a really great work of music was a stronger and
more essential contradiction to the spirit of Buchenwald and Auschwitz than words could be."

Rembering the *Fidelio*, the matchless Beethoven Ninth with which
he re-opened Bayreuth in 1951, I knew that he believed this to be
true, and that many Germans and Austrians took strength from his
conviction. Though Berlin-born, he was a Salzburg, not a Bayreuth,
man. He found Bayreuth, comparatively, stiff and cold. But although
I always heard him with the Vienna Philharmonic, which he loved,
he told me: "The Berlin Philharmonic is my right arm." It will be
welcome if it comes without him, this Berlin Philharmonic due here

on March 11, 12 and 13. The likely replacement is a famous conductor, Herbert von Karajan . . .

That he was to be something more than a replacement, subsequent history has shown, and on the occasion of the Berlin Philharmonic's opening concert at Carnegie Hall, Howard Taubman was moved to write: "He may well be the finest conductor in Europe, as his admirers claim. For the moment, let it be said that he is an extraordinarily gifted one"—a testimony which received nation-wide confirmation during the Philharmonia's tour in the autumn of the same year. Over the Philharmonia Orchestra, the consensus of American press opinion was equally unanimous: "Without question, the finest orchestra in Europe". In November 1958, Karajan was accorded the distinction of two guest appearances with the New York Philharmonic, and the *New York Herald Tribune* wrote:

Herr von Karajan really is one of the greatest conductors of our time. Maybe he inclines to elegance and extravagance, but what matters is the fact that he can convey his artistic intentions to a strange orchestra. It seems to me that once an orchestra has got used to his somewhat unusual and flamboyant beat, he can do what he likes with them. It is very seldom that we have heard such capacity for musical expression, and we hope that there will be many more opportunities for us to see and hear him making music with us.

This was not to be, for these two concerts are the only instance of Karajan's conducting an American orchestra on American soil. There is in every American a quality of political immaturity and political intransigence which equally afflicts the country's musical life, and the most obvious retort to a universal—if also immature—cry of "Go home Yankee" was that made by a member of the Carnegie Hall audience at Karajan's American début with the Berlin Philharmonic in 1955—"Go home Nazi". Like Furtwängler before him, Karajan has always been politically suspect in some quarters of American musical life. But unlike Furtwängler, he has never had the slightest ambition to confine his musical activities to America, and has long since attained recognition at not only the international, but the supranational level. Yet there remains in Karajan's make-up something of the Brutus, for it was he who recalled the soloists for the Vienna performance of Verdi's *Requiem* under Erich Kleiber five days ahead of schedule, ostensibly so that he could have more rehearsal time for his own performance of *Zauberflöte* at La Scala. Karajan had given the Verdi *Requiem* in Vienna the previous year, with excellent soloists from La Scala, and Kleiber's performances of the work on 23 and 24 November, 1955, would therefore have a heightened interest which

Karajan was evidently not prepared to permit. In the event, Kleiber gave the performances with an assiduously rehearsed scratch ensemble, which included the American mezzo-soprano Jean Madeira who had just made her début at the Vienna State Opera. And he made the only mistake which I have ever seen him make—one whose elementary brazenness of miscueing a choral entry a Beecham and still less a Sargent would never have allowed themselves to commit in so mercilessly exposed a fashion, and one which, I have little doubt, contributed to Kleiber's death only nine weeks later, on 27 January, 1956, the bi-centenary of Mozart's birth. His obituary appeared the following day even in the ship's newspaper of the America-bound *Queen Elizabeth*, but there was no mention of his death in a single Viennese newspaper.

The Vienna State Opera had combined the reopening of their rebuilt *Opernhaus am Ring* with the signing of the Austrian peace treaty, and the gala opening, with Beethoven's *Fidelio*, took place on 5 November, 1955, under the new general musical director, Karl Böhm, before a distinguished audience including all Europe's heads of state—but no musicians, of course. The second performance was of *Meistersinger*, under Karajan, the third *Rosenkavalier* under Knappertsbusch, and the fourth *Aïda* under Rafael Kubelik, who had become general musical director of the Royal Opera House, Covent Garden, once it had become patently clear that Kleiber would never accept the post. On 28 February, 1956, on his return from an American tour, Karl Böhm announced to a press conference that he was not prepared to sacrifice an international career for the sake of the Vienna Opera, and tendered his resignation. It was not immediately accepted, but it was obvious that, of all avaliable successors, Herbert von Karajan was the most suitable candidate—and the most popular. He was neither able nor prepared to accept the major commitment implicit in the term "general musical director", and the term "artistic director" was coined. Karajan signed the contract as artistic director of the Vienna State Opera on 14 June, 1956, and announced his plans for engaging a wide array of the world's leading conductors. The political machinations and recriminations which led to his initial resignation after four years, and final resignation after six, have tended to overshadow the magnitude of Karajan's achievement at the Vienna Opera. They are dealt with in all their proliferation in Ernst Haouessermann's biography of Karajan, from which Dr. Egon Hilbert emerges as a typical and supreme specimen of Viennese double-dealing and artistic betrayal.

In 1955, Karajan had written, *à propos* the problems of interpretation:

Clearly it is impossible to convey the spirit of a work of art by means of notation alone . . . What exactly is *forte* and what is *piano*? Is *piano* half *forte*, or a third, or an eighth? What sonic power do they represent? And even if it were possible to measure them, what is their effect in different halls? Does Beethoven tell us how many decibels this or that passage from the Ninth should have? And how long should the echo of a chord last to give the desired length to the whole? It is clear that these questions are dead ends. We must try and establish new standards which are independent of such specific scales of values.

In the course of fourteen seasons with the Berlin Philharmonic, Karajan's incredible ear would seem to have achieved precisely this. There is now no longer an echo of the Furtwängler tone for which the orchestra had been celebrated, and Karajan's approach—if it can be said to have a model at all—is now nearer that of Artur Nikisch in the warmth and opulence of its sound and the extensive employment of *rubato*. At the age of sixty, one can no longer look for any radical change in artistic outlook and temperament, and Karajan at sixty presents us with a perspective which we must deem to be final. But it is not a particularly endearing one, and it is significant that Herbert von Karajan and Georg Szell should have exchanged orchestras in Lucerne in the summer of 1967, Szell conducting the Berlin Philharmonic and Karajan conducting the Cleveland—for both are the perfectionists of an art which we can admire as long as it remains suffused with a vestige of human compassion.

Georg Szell was born in Budapest on 7 June, 1897, and appeared in Germany and England as a pianist at the age of eleven. At the recommendation of Richard Strauss, he succeeded Klemperer as first conductor in Strasbourg in 1917, at the age of twenty, and in 1919 became second conductor—at Klemperer's recommendation—of the Deutsches Landestheater in Prague. In 1921 he became second conductor in Darmstadt—a position vacated by Erich Kleiber two years earlier—and in 1922 first conductor in Düsseldorf, in direct succession to Kleiber. From 1924 until 1929 he worked as first conductor under Kleiber at the Berlin State Opera, and returned to Prague as general musical director of the German Theatre at the age of thirty-two. The German occupation of Czechoslovakia led to his flight, first to Britain, where be became conductor of the Scottish National Orchestra, and then to America where, since 1942, he became guest conductor of all the major American symphony orchestras, including the New York Philharmonic. His appointment to the Cleveland Orchestra in 1946, at the age of forty-nine, was in succession to Erich Leinsdorf, who had gone to the Rochester Philharmonic.

The Cleveland Orchestra had been founded in 1918 under the auspices of the Cleveland Musical Arts Association, and its first concert given in

December of that year under Nikolai Sokoloff, who continued to lead the orchestra until 1933. On 11 December, 1928, Mr. and Mrs. J. L. Severance announced that they would donate $1 million towards the construction of a new hall for the orchestra, and on Mrs. Severance's death her husband doubled the gift as a tribute to her memory. The first concert in Severance Hall took place under Sokoloff on 5 February, 1931. Artur Rodzinski succeeded him in 1933 and remained at the head of the Cleveland Orchestra until 1943, when he assumed the musical directorship of the New York Philharmonic, and was succeeded by Erich Leinsdorf.

The impact of Georg Szell was one which was quickly felt in Cleveland, for he is a musician to whom all compromise is utterly alien. The orchestra trustees were quick to realise with what stature of man they were dealing, and accorded him supreme powers. Numerous dismissals followed, with the normal kind of reaction from the American musician, who is not prepared to suffer such things in complete silence, and found his own position threatened in consequence, for Szell will tolerate insubordination no more than he will tolerate compromise. He began to play on the Cleveland Orchestra, like Hans von Bülow before him, as on the piano—but unlike Bülow, with a complete disregard for the other colours of the musical spectrum save those of the black and white presented by the keys of the piano, and uniformity of tone and ensemble became his obsession. There is a story, which is probably apocryphal, about an instrument factory in Cleveland which had evolved an extremely serviceable violin made of plastic. Szell was approached, displayed keen interest, and ordered a complete section of violins, violas, 'cellos and basses—which of course involved the factory in question in a great deal of work. Months later the instruments were produced, and a special rehearsal of the orchestra's string section was called. His obsession for uniformity might now at long last be satisfied, and Szell was beside himself with pleasurable anticipation. But it was not to be. The musicians of the orchestra, who had spent tens of years learning to adjust to one another in every minutia of tone, timbre, intonation and ensemble—and on largely disparate instruments—could now produce from a set of instruments which were identical in their every property only a conglomeracy of sound, the enormity of whose disparity was only too obvious even to the most untutored ear.

Whether or not the story is authentic, the inferences are inescapable. The string glissandos (figs. 173 and 175) from the Second Suite of *Daphnis and Chloe*, produced with such magic by Karajan, have no musical significance for Szell, and he therefore dispenses with them:

Ex. 45

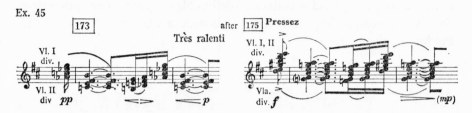

He will concede that the famous flute run (fig. 158)—which every American flute section from Boston to Philadelphia has rehearsed together to make the individual notes of the septuplets equal to the sixteenth-notes which precede them—is "a good idea, but of course impracticable", and cannot understand why his maintenance of strict-tempo at this point should pose difficulties for his own flute section:

Ex. 46

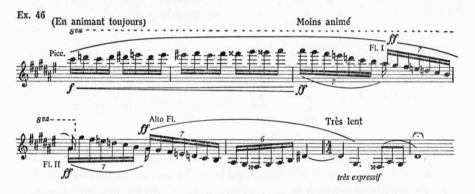

He is at pains to elucidate the two-bar phrasing of the trombone ensemble during the 6/4 interlude in the finale of Brahms's Fourth, and destroys thereby the continuity of the whole. He will object to the traditional cut-off at the beginning of the waltz in the overture to *Fledermaus* on the grounds that it is not in the text, but will ignore the text at the beginning of Beethoven's Fifth on the grounds that the timpani part, in the later return in *tutti*, will be impracticable—unaware that Kleiber, under whom he spent five years in Berlin, has already furnished an overwhelmingly eloquent solution to this problem. The up-beat to the *Andante* of Mozart's G minor Symphony K.550 becomes artificial through his literal observance of the text, and has nothing of the magic of a Munch or a Kleiber. But one is persuaded that Szell is not impelled by textual considerations at this juncture—Mozart's bowings are often incomplete—but rather by his own fastidious instinct which embraces the logic (a supremely cold logic) of the *Urfassung*. For his reading does furnish a logic of its own which must result in a completely different phrasing

of the entire passage and is eminently defensible on any grounds other than
those of the compassion which the symphony as a whole may be deemed to
exude:

Ex. 47 Andante

But for all his dispassionate objectivity, there is about Szell a quality of the
intellectual which is very engaging, and he will on occasion permit himself a
certain dry humour which betrays a sharp sense of wit. On one such occasion
a pupil had raised the point, *à propos* the solo recitatives in Lalo's *Symphonie
Espagnole*, that it was possible to give the orchestral entries, in actual practice,
"rather too early". Without hesitation Szell replied: "Then that is already too
late". The pupil on that occasion was also his assistant concertmaster,
Brusilov, who had been entrusted with the solo of the Lalo on many occasions. "Tell me", asked Szell, "do you find it easier to conduct or play the
violin?" "Oh, the violin!" replied Brusilov. "That's funny", replied Szell,
"I've always found it easier to conduct". But where he will have no compunction about doubling up the percussion forces—modest forces, in the
score—in the scaffold-scene from *Till Eulenspiegel* to the point of extreme
vulgarity, he will betray acute embarrassment in Bartók's Concerto for
Orchestra if the "interruption" in the *Serenata Interrota* is in any way overdone
—which it assuredly must be, for it is out of the question to make the glissando
from the low B on the bass trombone anything other than blatantly vulgar,
and this vulgarity must in consequence imbue the whole passage. In truth,

Szell is a little frightened of works which are in any way unfamiliar to him, for he will not readily venture onto ground where he must inevitably expose himself as feeling unsure in the eyes of his orchestra. But having thus ventured, he will not hesitate to invite them to learn from him—even to the point of giving them individual lessons—for the instinct to impart knowledge, where he does not become impatient, is remarkably strong.

Georg Szell is an uncompromising figure, motivated by a wilfulness of purpose which informs his inspired moments as much as it destroys the magic of those which are less inspired—and this is as he would wish, one feels, for the sentiment of inspiration is one to which he is unlikely to subscribe. If he is able to generate a white heat in the finale of Brahms's Third Symphony, or to infuse the Dvořák *Slavonic Dances* with incomparable artistry and supreme magic, then this is as much the product of his own will as is the acute unhappiness which he generates among the weaker reeds of his own orchestra. Even his display of *bonhomie* on those occasions of social necessity so dear to the American matron is inclined to be contrived—and rather transparently so —and one has the impression that he is acting a part to which he could bring greater conviction and sincerity.

Conviction and sincerity, however, are very much a part of the make-up of Herbert von Karajan, who is clearly quite sincerely convinced by everything which he undertakes. Szell is unlikely to admit any flaw in his armour to anyone but himself, but Karajan will openly admit his mistakes to younger and inferior colleagues, and is in fact only concerned with his shortcomings, and not at all with his successes. He has the faculty of putting people at their ease, under all circumstances, and I recall going to see him in 1961 in connection with my own career—and not without some feeling of trepidation. I experienced the sense of immediate equanimity which everyone feels in his presence, and in the course of the subsequent conversation learned that Karajan would not know how to go about sight-reading *Rosenkavalier* either. Or so he said. But this faculty also has a public manifestation. During a recording session of *Till Eulenspiel* with the Philharmonia in 1951 which had embraced the solo violin entry many times over, Manoug Parikian produced a split-second of faulty intonation on his high E flat in the course of a "take" which gave the promise, at long last, of being perfect. There was an audible groan from the whole orchestra. Karajan remained silent for a moment, and then began to go through the elaborate pantomime of standing on a chair, looking for a suitable beam in the roof of Kingsway Hall, throwing an imaginary rope over the beam and catching its end, tying a noose in it, and finally proffering it to Parikian *à la Eulenspiel*, and with the blandest of smiles. The orchestra, which had been watching this ingenious dumb-show with growing interest—and to the point where the occasion for its introduction had long since been forgotten—exploded in gales of laughter, the tension of the moment was released, and Parikian—who had been visibly annoyed with himself over his blemished E flat—once more returned to his studied self-composure.

Under portents so patently benign it is therefore the more alarming to have to read others which presage little but ill. His more discerning critics have long been aware of an element of over-breeding in Karajan's musical nature which, for all that it can produce the uttermost ravishment of sound in a score like *Daphnis and Chloe*, threatened to undermine the sturdier works of the symphonic and operatic repertoire with its insidious influence. And so it was that, in the Beethoven cycle which constituted the programme of the Berlin Philharmonic's tour in 1961, the evidence of a more ascetic approach was the more to be welcomed—although a carping Hans Keller, on loan from the BBC, could find little more than a missed flute-entry in the Scherzo of the *Eroica* at which to scoff, and was clearly blind (or deaf) to the fact that this might have been symptomatic of a crucial stage in even Karajan's development.

Over-refinement may be suited to Mozart, whose proximity to the Gods makes absolute perfection a mandatory virtue, and it is here that Karajan is manifestly successful where Furtwängler had, on occasion, failed so conspicuously. It is true that Furtwängler gave a stupendous performance of *Don Giovanni* in Salzburg in 1954, and had produced many a performance of the G minor Symphony—the outer movements played at prodigious speed—which brought out the lines of the architecture like burnished filigree. But the spirit of *commedia* so essential to Mozart remained foreign to him, and his Mozart performances were a little loveless in consequence. Kleiber, on the other hand, possessed the ultimate key to Mozart, which resided in the fact that he was a greater human being than either Furtwangler or Karajan, and it is a supreme irony of fate that, on the day of his death and the bi-centenary of Mozart's birth, Kleiber was one of the very few conductors in the world who was not destined to raise his baton in the cause of Mozart—or at all. That, I am sure, was what killed him, for his was no lingering illness. He was struck down at one blow. But the extreme of cultivation which is imperative to Mozart is not suited to Beethoven or Bartók—and still less to Berlioz—where the surging impulse of the music brooks no refining element which is not innate in its very structure, and Karajan's tremendous performance of Beethoven's Ninth with the Philharmonia in the early months of 1949 was the more to be marvelled at. Brahms, too, finds an illustrious interpreter in Karajan—as in his performances of the First Symphony with the Philharmonia at the Festival Hall in 1952, and later in Vienna, and of the Second Symphony with the Berlin Philharmonic in Berlin in 1957. But the symphonies by Beethoven—apart from the Ninth, whose very stature seems to bring out the best qualities in almost every conductor—share with the music of Bartók a quality of rhythmic intensity and driving inevitability which any amount of sheer sound will fail to ignite. This is a quality which has consistently evaded Karajan, and a shortcoming of which he is probably only too well aware.

These are none the less sins of commission rather than omission which need not cause undue concern if it were not for the fact that they are symptomatic—not of a phase in Karajan's development which, at sixty, is now unlikely to experience any further extensive progress—but of an arrest in that development, a sense of complacency and a betrayal of his musical *raison d'être*. This was especially evident in his performance at the Festival Hall on 11 May, 1967, of Berlioz's *Symphonie Fantastique*—an eccentric reading which recalled both the mannerism and the splendour of Artur Nikisch, and an eccentric reading of a work which is, by its very nature, eccentric. But there are moments where the voice of Berlioz becomes unequivocal, where it betrays an identity and a unity with the voices of Beethoven and of Bartók, and where the operatic principle of always holding something in reserve—so eloquently displayed in Karajan's performances of Strauss opera, or in his memorable reading of *Tod und Verklärung* with the Philharmonia on 1 April, 1960—is of no further avail. Berlioz, for all the plasticity of his writing, cries out for a treatment which is unscrupulously brutal and uncompromisingly direct, and that Karajan should have been unwilling or unable to furnish such a treatment I find infinitely more disturbing than his fantastic dream of a fantastic opera company, universally dispensing opera studied from fantastic tape-recordings. His performance of the *Fantastic Symphony* was not even fantastically polite, but smugly self-satisfied.

Chapter 14

ST. PETERSBURG REBORN: THE LENINGRAD PHILHARMONIC

In September 1960 the Leningrad Philharmonic Orchestra visited London as part of their first tour of western Europe, and in the course of their two concerts of Russian music—together with Britten's *Variations on a Theme by Purcell*—aroused scenes of unforgettable enthusiasm. They came together with their two conductors—the tall and austere Jevgeni Mravinski and the bald and ever-smiling Rozhdestvensky—and their soloist, the master-'cellist Rostropovitch. Their second London concert opened with a dazzling performance of the overture to Glinka's *Ruslan and Lyudmila,* in which the critics were in agreement that the second subject had acquired, in its very speed, a new dimension of extended phrasing which allowed of its being "sung in one breath" for the first time in their experience. And it closed with a performance of the Fifth Symphony by Tchaikowsky, the main tempo of whose finale echoed the tempo of the Glinka overture, and sent the critics scurrying to their scores to see if Tchaikowsky had not in fact prescribed a sequence of down-bows at the *Allegro Vivace.* (Nor had he in fact done so, for the down-bows in the manuscript are—according to Mravinski—in another hand, and presumably that of Artur Nikisch, who resurrected the work after its unsuccessful Moscow première under the composer's direction.) It was not, however, the excellence of the conductors, nor the mastery of Rostropovitch in the Shostakovitch 'Cello Concerto, nor yet the superlative artistry of the whole orchestra which evoked such a heartfelt and spontaneous response from a Festival Hall which had been sold out since the day of the concert's announcement. Rather was it the feeling that some sentient spirit of St. Petersburg had been resurrected, and with it the shades of the Philharmonic Society, the Marynskaya Theatre and the Conservatoire, the ghosts of Vieuxtemps, Wieniawski and Auer, of Leschetitzky, Bülow and Liszt, of Siloti, Safonov and the "Five", of Glinka, Prokofieff, Rachmaninoff, Shostakovitch and Tchaikowsky himself.

St. Petersburg—whose name had been changed at the beginning of the First World War to Petrograd, and under Soviet rule to Leningrad—has always preserved an autonomy in relations to the arts which is still jealously guarded to the present day. Her Philharmonic Society was founded in 1802, and the first complete performance of Beethoven's *Missa Solemnis* was given under its auspices in 1824. The Imperial Opera, founded during the reign of Peter the Great, had functioned in the Marynskaya Theatre since 1827. The St. Petersburg Conservatoire had opened under its founder and director, Anton Rubinstein, in 1862. But the history of Russian music—whose origins are generally attributed to Dargomyzjsky and Glinka, and associated with the première of *Ivan Susasin* (*A Life for the Tsar*) at the Imperial Opera on 9 December, 1836—are in reality much older, and bear witness to the fruits of royal patronage so abundantly dispensed by Russia in common with other countries of western and central Europe of the eighteenth century. Nor are these origins quite so Italianate as is commonly supposed, for while Russian and Italian opera share common ground in the immediacy and intensity of their appeal to the emotions, there is little evidence in Russian opera of those extremes of absurdity which are all too often apparent in that of Italy. The Venetian composer, Catterino Cavos, who emigrated to Russia in 1797, wrote an earlier version of *Ivan Susasin* in 1815, and this has given currency to the supposition that Russian opera was born out of the Italian idiom. But although Cavos's opera enjoyed immense though brief popularity, its significance lay not in the fact that he employed the same text as Glinka was to use twenty-one years later, but in its total absorption of an idiom which was already specifically Russian.

Russian music of the eighteenth and nineteenth centuries was centred overwhelmingly in St. Petersburg, and its history is one of gradually increasing freedom from northern European influences, and particularly those of Germany. French influences were never strongly marked, musically speaking, and the political implications of Moscow in 1812 had repercussions which were scarcely felt at all in the Imperial city. The last Italian influences were from Giovanni Giornovici—a violinist born in Palermo of Polish parentage, and who moved from Hamburg to St. Petersburg in 1802 to become a founder-member of the Philharmonic Society—and Clementi, who visited Russia frequently from 1802 until his final return to London six years later. In 1804 Clementi brought with him a young Irishman by the name of John Field, who decided to settle in St. Petersburg and gave piano-lessons until shortly before his death in 1837—among others to Michael Ivanovitch Glinka. In 1832 Karl Romberg, a native of St. Petersburg, became first 'cellist of the Philharmonic Society, with Weschbilowitch as his partner, in a 'cello section which also included Cyprian Romberg, his second cousin and also a member of the famous Mannheim family of instrumentalists. In 1836

Ossip Petrov—a Russian bass who had been with the Imperial Opera since 1830, and possessed the prodigious range of B flat below the bass clef to F sharp above—created the role of Ivan Susasin in Glinka's opera. In 1838 Adolf von Henselt, Bülow's first teacher, inherited Field's practice in St. Petersburg and extended it to include the capacity of court pianist and private teacher to the Imperial Family, and later inspector of music for the Imperial Schools for girls. In 1842 and 1846 Franz Liszt played in St. Petersburg, and Berlioz had his first unqualified success there, in 1847, in the dual capacity of composer and conductor. Henri Vieuxtemps had been appointed Court violinist in 1846, and in the season of 1852–53 Ferdinand Hiller was guest conductor of the Philharmonic Society. Theodor Leschetitzky, meanwhile, had in 1852 become professor of piano at the St. Petersburg School of Music—ten years later to become the Conservatoire under Anton Rubinstein —and remained teaching in St. Petersburg until 1878, having among his pupils Frank Merrick, who was to win the Diploma of Honour at the Rubinstein Competition in St. Petersburg in 1910 and who now, at eighty-two, is the last surviving pupil of Leschetitzky. In 1855 Vera Victorovna Timanova, a former pupil of Liszt, Tausig and Rubinstein, settled in St. Petersburg to give piano classes.

Henri Vieuxtemps had been succeeded as Court violinist in 1860 by Henri Wieniawski, who became professor of violin at the St. Petersburg Conservatoire in 1862, and was in turn succeeded in 1869 by Leopold Auer— a former pupil of Joseph Joachim, who was to hold the post continuously until 1917. Auer, to whom Tchaikowsky was to dedicate his Violin Concerto, and who gave its first performance, produced in the course of his forty-eight years at the head of the Conservatoire's violin department an astonishing array of distinguished violinists including Jascha Heifetz, Efrem Zimbalist, Mischa Elman, Nathan Milstein, Michel Piastro (concertmaster of the New York Philharmonic from 1931 to 1943), and the English violinist Isolde Menges, who made her London début in 1913.

Meanwhile, Count Matvei Yurievitch Wielhorsky—a former pupil of Romberg—had, on his death in 1863, bequeathed his Stradivarius 'cello to Karl Davidov who, at the age of twenty-four, had become principal 'cellist of the Philharmonic and professor of 'cello at the Conservatoire in the previous year, and was destined to become its principal in 1876, in succession to Nikolai Zaremba. The year 1863 also marks the publication of a music catalogue of the Imperial Library by Prince Nikolai Yussupov, a former pupil of Vieuxtemps, under the supervision of Vladimir Stassov, who had been its music librarian since 1857—the year of birth, in Leamington Spa, of Rosa Newmarch, who was to become his pupil forty years later. (It was Vladimir

Stassov who wrote the libretto to Borodin's *Prince Igor*, first produced at the Imperial Opera in St. Petersburg on 23 October, 1890). In 1864 Julius Melgunov, a protégé of Henselt and Anton Rubinstein, made his début at the age of eighteen with the St. Petersburg Philharmonic.

In 1866 Nicholas Rubinstein—brother of Anton and like him a pianist, composer and conductor—founded the Moscow Conservatoire and invited Tchaikowsky to leave St. Petersburg and come to Moscow as professor of composition. Sergei Ivanovitch Taneiev, nephew of the St. Petersburg composer Alexander, now became one of Tchaikowsky's pupils at the Moscow Conservatoire, and was a pianist of consequence, who gave the Moscow première of the Brahms D minor Concerto in 1875, at the age of nineteen. Meanwhile St. Petersburg had, between 1855 and 1862, acquired a national movement in music in the form of the "Five", headed by Balakirev, who was to gather round him within the course of the next seven years the figures of Cui, Moussorgsky, Rimsky-Korsakov and Borodin, and under whose influence Tchaikowsky must inevitably have fallen had it not been for Nicholas Rubinstein's invitation for him to come to Moscow. And to Moscow, in 1868, came Karl Klindworth as the emissary of Liszt, whose pupil he had been—together with Hans von Bülow—in 1852. In 1869 Klindworth made the piano reduction of Wagner's *Walküre* in Moscow, Hans Pfitzner was born there, and the French baritone Victor Maurel—disenchanted with the Paris Opéra where he had made his début two years earlier as De Nevers in *Les Huguenots*—made his début in St. Petersburg.

In 1877 Anatol Liadov graduated from the St. Petersburg Conservatoire, and in the following year was appointed a teacher there, holding a similar post at the Imperial Chapel. As the first outstanding pupil of Rimsky-Korsakov, Liadov represented the first example of a second-generation Russian composer whose death in 1914 was justly mourned—and significantly so by Koussevitsky and Rachmaninoff. In 1882 Rachmaninoff, then aged nine, moved with his mother to St. Petersburg where he was to spend the next three years before going to Nicolas Zverev in Moscow, and Angelo Neumann's travelling Wagnerian Opera Company appeared there under Anton Seidl's direction. Two years later Sergei Liapunov was appointed assistant conductor of the St. Petersburg Philharmonic, at the age of twenty-five, and in 1885 Bülow made his St. Petersburg début as conductor of a series of concerts with the Philharmonic—Klindworth having assumed direction of the Berlin Philharmonic in 1882, which was to be Bülow's subsequent appointment. In 1886 Liberius Sacchetti, a former pupil in the 'cello class of Karl Davidov, was appointed the Conservatoire's first professor in aesthetics, and in 1895 became Stassov's assistant librarian at the Imperial Library. In 1887 Tchai-kowsky, inspired by Bülow's example of two years earlier, made his début as conductor of the St. Petersburg Philharmonic, and the following year Alexander Vinogradsky, a former pupil of the Conservatoire, became director of the Kiev branch of the Imperial Russian Music Society. Nikolai Tutkow-sky, a native of Kiev who had been professor of piano at the St. Petersburg Conservatoire from 1881 to 1890, and professor of music history there from 1888, returned to Kiev in 1893 to found a school of music at which Vladimir Horowitz was to become a pupil in 1910, at the age of six. The year 1888 also saw the Moscow début, at the age of nine, of Mark Hambourg with—incredibly—the Tchaikowsky B flat minor Concerto. The following year, Angelo Neumann's Wagnerian company returned once again to Moscow and St. Petersburg, now under the direction of Karl Muck, and the Lithuanian violinist Emil Mlynarski, former pupil of Leopold Auer and future father-in-law to Artur Rubinstein, made his début with the St. Petersburg Phil-harmonic. In 1897 Mlynarski became assistant conductor of the Warsaw Opera, conductor of the Warsaw Philharmonic in 1901, conductor of the St. Petersburg Philharmonic from 1904 to 1909, and conductor of the Scottish National Orchestra in 1911, returning to Warsaw in 1919 and be-coming professor of conducting at the Curtis Institute in Philadelphia and conductor of the Philadelphia Grand Opera in 1929.

Meanwhile, Ferruccio Busoni had become professor of piano at the Moscow Conservatoire in 1890, travelling thence to America to occupy the same position at the New England Conservatory in Boston from 1891 to 1894. Kallinikov had become conductor of Italian opera at the Marynskaya Theatre in 1893, and in the same year Antonio Scotti, a native of Naples, made his début there, and the opera *The Power of Love*, by the twenty-three-year-old Peter Schenk, received its première. In 1898 Count Alexander Scheremetiev, who had founded his own orchestra in St. Petersburg six years earlier, introduced a series of concerts at popular prices, sharing the baton with Vladimirov. In 1902 Scheremetiev became intendant of the Marynskaya Theatre, and in 1914 conducted the Russian première of *Parsifal*. Meanwhile Smolensky had become conductor of the St. Petersburg Philharmonic in 1901, to be succeeded two years later by Alexander Siloti. In 1908 the operatic soprano Maria Kutzenova made her début at the Marynskaya Theatre, followed in 1910 by Lydia Lipovska in the role of Gilda.

Diaghilev had meanwhile progressed from a dilatory student of law and dilettante reviewer of art to professional impresario, and in 1909 launched his *Ballets Russes* in Paris, under the direction of Nicholas Tcherepnin and with Pierre Monteux as his assistant. The year 1908 had witnessed the wedding, on 17 June, of Rimsky-Korsakov's daughter to Maximilian Steinberg—former pupil and future director of the St. Petersburg Conservatoire, and the teacher of Shostakovitch who, in 1908, was aged two. For this wedding, the twenty-six-year-old Stravinsky had written *Feu d'Artifice* as his Op. 4, and which followed his Symphony in E flat, Op. 1 (premièred by the St. Petersburg Philharmonic on 22 January, 1908) and *Le Faune et la Bergère*, Op. 2, for mezzo-soprano and orchestra (premièred by the Philharmonic on 29 February, 1908). His *Scherzo Fantastique*, Op. 3, received its St. Petersburg première on 6 February, 1909.

In 1909 the Imperial Russian Music Society in St. Petersburg, alarmed by deficits and the competition of Siloti's Philharmonic, appointed Serge Koussevitsky—then aged thirty-six—as their musical director for one season, and in 1910 Vassili Safonov—aged fifty-eight—returned to St. Petersburg to assume musical directorship of the Society. Safonov, who was born in Itsyursk in 1852, had been a pupil of Leschetitsky at the St. Petersburg Conservatoire and had made a distinguished career for himself as a concert pianist, making his St. Petersburg début in 1880, and subsequently touring extensively with the 'cellist, Karl Davidov. From 1889 he had been director of the Moscow Conservatoire, and this date marks his Moscow début, at the age of forty-seven, as a conductor—and a conductor who, moreover, conducted without baton. From this time, his rise had been meteoric, and he returned to St. Petersburg in 1910 after three years as musical director of the New York Philharmonic. On 30 April, 1911, Jascha Heifetz, then aged ten, made his St. Petersburg début.

By this time the revolutionary spirit was abroad in earnest—not only politically, but musically as well. On 29 May, 1913, Pierre Monteux, then thirty-eight, gave in Paris the historic first performance of the ballet *Le Sacre du Printemps* by the twenty-nine-year-old Stravinsky, and released the loudest single musical explosion which the world had ever been called upon to witness. Vyshnegradtsky, a pupil of twenty at the St. Petersburg Conservatoire, was experimenting with quarter-tone music, and Prokofieff, at twenty-three a pupil of Liadov for composition (and a former pupil of Rimsky-Korsakov, who had died in 1908) and of Tcherepnin for conducting, was working on his *Scythian Suite* which was to receive its St. Petersburg première under his direction on 29 January, 1916. The Moscow première of the *Scythian Suite* had been scheduled for December 1916, and Leonid Sabaneiev reviewed the first Moscow performance of the work in his newspaper, *News of the Season*, on 26 December:

> At a current Koussevitsky concert, one of the main attractions was the first [Moscow] performance of the *Scythian Suite* by a young

composer, Prokofieff, under his own direction. If one is to say that it
is bad, that it is cacophony, that a person with a differentiated audi-
tory sense cannot listen to it, the reply would be, "But this is a barbaric suite", and the critic would have to retreat in shame. So I shall
not criticize this suite—quite the contrary I shall say that this is
magnificent barbaric music, the world's best barbaric music. But if
I am asked whether this music gives me pleasure, or an artistic
sensation, or produces an impression in me which is profound, I
must say categorically "No". The composer himself conducted with
barbaric abandon.

The only fault in this review lay not in its tone, nor in the opinion which it
expressed, but in its monumental irrelevance, for the performance in question
had never taken place. In his reply, Prokofieff wrote:

> In the preliminary programmes of the Moscow Symphony
> Concerts, it was announced that my *Scythian Suite* was to be per-
> formed under the composer's direction on 12 December. In view
> of the impossibility in time of war of assembling the augmented
> orchestra which the work requires, the performance was can-
> celled . . .[1]

By 1919 Russia was in the hands of the Bolsheviks, and the Soviet
Union had been proclaimed. St. Petersburg, having become Petrograd at the
outbreak of the First World War, was now rechristened Leningrad. Alexander
Siloti had resigned from the Philharmonic, and made his way in due course
to America to become professor of piano at the Juilliard School of Music in
New York from 1924 until 1942. Arthur Lourié, a native of St. Petersburg
and a student of music at its Conservatoire, became the new People's Com-
missar for Music in the department of education. In 1922 he too left Russia
for Paris, and left France for New York in 1940. Issay Dobrowen had become
conductor of the Bolshoi Theatre in Moscow, leaving for Dresden in 1923,
and for America in 1932. Alexander Glazounov, who had become director of
the St. Petersburg Conservatoire in 1909, and had initiated the Philharmonic
concerts as a regular feature of the musical life of St. Petersburg in 1882—
conducting the ill-fated première of Rachmaninoff's First Symphony on
15 March, 1897[2]—now succeeded Siloti as permanent musical director of
the Leningrad Philharmonic in the auditorium of the ancient Hall of the

---

[1] Sabaneiev's review and Prokofieff's reply appear in Nicolas Slonimsky: *Music Since
1900*: Norton, New York, 1937.
[2] Rachmaninoff later decided that Glazounov was incompetent as a conductor—a view
finding vindication in the eloquent performance of a highly original work which exists on the
recording of the First Symphony by the Leningrad under Kurt Sanderling. The low esteem
in which Glazounov held Rachmaninoff's music in general may be gathered from the fact
that he left the manuscript of his Fourth Concerto in a Paris taxi-cab in 1930.

Nobility, where its concerts had taken place since the society's inception in 1802. On 15 June, 1928, Glazounov left Russia for Paris, where he settled until his death on 31 March, 1936. He made his American début on 29 November, 1929, with the Detroit Symphony Orchestra which had been founded in 1914, and since 1917 conducted by Ossip Gabrilowitsch—a native of St. Petersburg and former pupil of Anton Rubinstein and Theodor Leschetitzky, who died in Detroit in 1935. Grigori Kazatchenko was appointed conductor of the Marynskaya Theatre in 1922—the year which also saw the formation, in Moscow, of the *Pervyi Symfonitchesky Ansamble*, a conductor-less orchestra which gave its first concert under the leadership of Zeitlin, Koussevitsky's former concertmaster, on 13 February, 1922. The orchestra was still active in 1929 when it visited America for the first time with the pianist Paul Stassevitch—a former pupil of Josef Lhévinne—as soloist, but it was disbanded shortly afterwards.

The *Pervyi Symfonitchesky Ansamble*—Persymfans for short—had originally been formed with the principle of equality, so dear to the spirit of communism, very deliberately in mind. Socialist sensibility could not suffer the concept of absolute power concentrated in the hands of an autocratic conductor, and the conductor's responsibilities automatically devolved on the concertmaster, Zeitlin, who was later to comment: "Of course, we don't really mind playing under a conductor—as long as he's good enough"—a sentiment shared by concertmasters and orchestral players in general the world over. Outwardly, the presence of a conductor must seem superfluous to any orchestra of first-rate pretensions, were it not for the fact that his absence would lead to automatic anarchy unless the concertmaster—or some other musician—were to take charge of the proceedings, and in so doing effectively assume the role of conductor. For the performance which the public hears is, by definition, a finished one—or should be so—and implies the existence of prior rehearsal and of a dominant personality who is in every way qualified to undertake those rehearsals. In this country, where neither conductor or orchestra are normally very well disposed to rehearsal, there is perhaps less of a case for a permanent conductor, whose musical function inevitably tends to be superfluous in that players have the misguided impression that they know it all already. It is of course those players who know most who accede most readily to the necessary principle of a conductor, and those who know least are are most ready to question it—like their respective counterparts among the audience.

In Russia, doctrinaire socialism was swift to take its effect after the revolution, and freedom of musical expression—not always an unqualified advantage—was temporarily stifled. The Soviet obsession in regard to "bourgeois culture" was to lead in due course to the production of works whose orientation was unfeignedly nationalist and specifically Soviet— Andrei Pastchenko's *Eagles in Revolt*, premièred at the Marynskaya on 7 November, 1925, Shaporin's *On the Field of Kulikovo* and *The Battle for the Russian Land*, Arutunyan's *Cantata about the Fatherland*, Zhukovsky's *Glory to Thee, My Country*, and Khachaturian's *Poem for Stalin*. On 12 May, 1926, the First Symphony by the nineteen-year-old Shostakovitch received its first performance under Glazounov and the Leningrad Philharmonic and won immediate acclaim. But it was to be eleven years before Shostakovitch could regain the favour of the official party line, and which he finally accomplished with the première of his Fifth Symphony. In 1927 Glazounov resigned his position at the head of the Leningrad Philharmonic, and was succeeded by Nikolai Malko—a former student of Tcherepnin at the St. Petersburg Conservatoire and of Felix Mottl in Munich. And in 1929, at the age of forty-five, Boris Asafiev, a native of St. Petersburg whose opera *The Flames of Paris* was to receive its première at the Marynskaya on 23 June, 1932, came out with a defence of Stravinsky which is remarkable for the degree of autonomy of expression which it preserves:

> Stravinsky is a representative of European urban musical culture, a daring constructor and a master strong in the knowledge of his craft. In his work there is not a trace of emotionalising dilettantism, abstract academicism or philosophising erotic individualism [sic] . . . With all the depths of his soul Stravinsky is attached to the great Russian melodies, to the folk and peasant art, both vocal and instrumental . . . If anyone does not wish to learn from Stravinsky's mastery and thinks he can get by in music with the technique of the epoch of pre-aviation, pre-automobile and—for some—pre-railroad, if the virile rhythms of his music say nothing to him and his idiom of speech appears demoralising, then there is no use quarrelling—the final word must be left to posterity. Every work of a great artist is always to some extent a protest and reaction against the philistinism of his epoch . . . Musical form is the summation of a complicated process of crystallisation in our consciousness of the combined elements of sound. The material, by its own characteristics, determines the form, but the choice and arrangement of the component elements is the task of the composer's intelligence. In the final analysis, form is the concrete expression of the composer's conception. Contemporary music gravitates ever more unmistakably towards investigation of the *processes* which must govern musical form, and at the same time towards an analysis of the role of the intellectual factor in musical creation . . . With *Pétrouchka* Stravinsky definitely became himself, and the whole contemporary generation of musicians followed after him. Everyone who wished to avoid becoming a "living corpse"

understood that a great event had taken place, that Russian music had really made a new and unheard-of conquest. Stravinsky here felt for the first time, as nowhere previously, the elements of festivity, of the streets and of mass movement. He revealed the peculiarities, the ringing qualities, and the brilliance of native instrumental idioms (*intonatsiya*). He disclosed the energy of the diatonic Russian melodies to its full extent and completeness. He established mode as a free and original principle, and not as something undeveloped and subordinate to major and minor key, introduced merely for the sake of stylisation or archaic colour. He was not afraid to give artistic form to tunes which are familiar to everyone, and to preserve in them everything characteristic and vitally concrete. He demonstrated that reality should not be dressed up for the sake of rules which have outlived their usefulness, but that on the contrary one should proceed from living musical practice, from the everyday musical language of city and village, from the idiom and rhythm which are the product of experience, created by a way of life, and consolidated over a period of generations. It is the direct and conscious choice created by life which should enrich the composer's consciousness . . . With *Oedipus Rex* Stravinsky confidently enters a phase of post-individualist creation, striving to express the content of a universally significant ancient tragedy through the simplest sound-formulae, through broadly based socialised lines and rhythms, through an idiom which constitutes new selections and new combinations from the classical and popular phases of European operatic language, outside the framework of the nationalist and the romantic, and mainly from the experience of the oratorio forms of the eighteenth century . . . On the social-artistic plane *Oedipus Rex* is an experiment in entering the region of supra-individualistic aesthetics, and a step towards the exit from the blind alley of subjective searchings, no matter how profound their beauty, or how valuable their conquest of an idiom which might influence the further evolution of music.[3]

A "direct and conscious choice" is here somewhat at variance with the underlying spirit of Greek tragedy manifest in Sophocles's original, and whose operatic version by Stravinsky and Cocteau had received its first performance at the Kroll Theatre in Berlin under Otto Klemperer on 25 February, 1928—the year before the publication of Asafiev's book. For the essence of classical tragedy lies in its very inevitability, its complete abrogation of choice—an essence best expressed musically in the supremely romantic language of *Tristan* and the *Ring*—and is a concept which had a profound appeal for the romantic movement as a whole. At this distance of time its clothing in the exotic garb of romanticism must seem at odds with the romantic but austere principles of Hellerian atonement which best define Olympian inevitability,

[3] Boris Asafiev: *Kniga o Stravinskom*, Leningrad, 1929.

but it is the essence of tragedy which is in question, and not its substance.

For all the overloading and self-consciousness of Asafiev's language, he reveals a penetration into the substance of Stravinsky's music which merits study, and a freedom of expression which the western world would have but hardly credited from a Russian author in the late 'twenties—a time when Stravinsky's music evoked even more violent reactions from the official organs of Soviet culture than they did immediately after the Second World War. Twenty-two years after the publication of Asafiev's book, Stravinsky, now an American citizen, received the Gold Medal of the American National Institute of Arts, in recognition of his "great services in the realm of musical culture", and with especial reference to *Pétrouchka*, *Les Noces* and *Le Sacre du Printemps*—which must have caused the sixty-nine-year-old composer some momentary distress, for in 1951 he was about to embark on that adventure into serialism from which no successful composer has ever returned. Anticipating this award, Ivan Nestiev wrote an article in *Izvestiya* on 7 January, 1951, entitled *Dollarovna Kakofoniya* "Dollar Cacophony" in which he spoke of the "complete spiritual emptiness" of "this homeless cosmopolitan", recalling Vassili Gorodinski's similar sentiments in his book, *The Music of Spiritual Poverty*:

> As in other fields of bourgeois science, the "learned" decadents provide the dead philosophic-aesthetic systems with new and artificial arguments, restoring Pythagorean conceptions, renovating the musical aesthetics of Kant and Schopenhauer with Freudian mystical means, providing a base for the formalistic speculations of modernist composers, implanting the loathsome amoralism of a Jean-Paul Sartre or an André Gide, or that English troubadour of mud and swinishness, Aldous Huxley—who, by the way, has for long manifested a special and specific interest in music—proclaiming betrayal as valour and preaching an infamous homeless cosmopolitanism. Such is the shameless "ideology" of international rascals and black treason . . .[4]

The Soviet party line, which had long espoused the principle of permissiveness, had by now transferred its affections to an emphasis on the principle of the "home"—sentiments which were shortly to find an extravagant echo among the older generation of a western world on the violence of their reaction to the growing promiscuity of the younger generation. But in Russia, this was symptomatic of yet another "ideology" which was incapable of original or coherent thought, and could only derive its principles from the

---

[4] V. Gorodinski: *Muzykha dukhovnoi nischety*, Moscow–Leningrad, 1950.

naïve promulgations of its leaders. This being so, it was with the more amazement that the western musical world began to learn of the position of especial privilege which the musician in Soviet Russia enjoyed. Contrary to popular superstition, freedom of movement had never been restricted for the Russian musician, who was allowed to emigrate if he so wished—and if he subsequently earned the opprobrium of his native country, this was no more than that which other nations have accorded their expatriate musicians.

Music is an international language, or should be so, and Glazounov, Koussevitsky and Prokofieff are among many other distinguished Russian musicians who left Russia at one time or another after the revolution. Prokofieff left in 1918, but returned to settle in Moscow in 1934, and for the rest of his life wrote without any noticeable diminishment in his creative faculties, though attempts have been made to show that he was unduly inhibited by the Kremlin—especially in reference to his 'Cello Symphony, which received its first performance with the Moscow Philharmonic on 26 November, 1938. But it is a moot point whether official criticism emanating from "ideological" sources is in any way more invidious or pernicious than that of Leonid Sabaneiev in 1916, or that of any other critic hired to represent—whether wittingly or not—the necessarily partisan views of his newspaper. The power of the "free" press in largely determining the futures of young British and American artists—whether in terms of adulation or of condemnation—is out of all proportion to the paltriness of the fees which the critics themselves receive for a review whose necessary immediacy must preclude any pretence at considered or responsible opinion, and out of all proportion to the qualifications of most critics to criticise in any case. The critics in general have fostered more bad and suspect talent than they have attempted to promote good and wholesome, but whereas the artist must bow his head to an unfavourable review—and generally does so with a good grace—any attempt by the artist to take the critics to task is met by their spontaneous and universal howl. And for all that they ridicule the doctrinaire criticism of Soviet Socialism, I am not persuaded that theirs is any the lesser evil.

After the war—and more particularly after the descent of the Iron Curtain—news from Russia became slow to reach the west, and sparse in its content. Rumour became rife of the lavish conditions which the Russian artist enjoyed by comparison with his more humble comrades—a rumour which was amply endorsed after the artists themselves began to filter through to western Europe and America. It became apparent that not only were they themselves accorded every luxury, but that a system of musical education had been evolved which ensured that no student of potential should lack either the means or the teaching—with especial emphasis on the teaching, which was carried out by duly qualified experts. And if the appearance of the Leningrad Philharmonic in 1960 were any criterion, the reports were not exaggerated. Recordings began to filter through to the west in the early 'fifties, and in 1956 a whole series of recordings by the Leningrad Philharmonic, recorded in East Berlin, came onto the American market. They were—appropriately enough— exclusively of Russian music, and ranged from the Fifth and Sixth Symphonies by Tchaikowsky, the First and Second Symphonies by Rachmaninoff, to the First Concertos by Rachmaninoff and Prokofieff respectively, with Sviatoslav Richter as soloist.

Following my return from America in November 1957, I heard the Leningrad Philharmonic in Berlin for myself, playing under their assistant conductor, Kurt Sanderling, a native of Germany who had clearly absorbed the essences of Russian music-making. The orchestral sound—particularly of the woodwind—was slightly archaic, the oboes sounding rather like cors anglais, and the brass being accorded a vibrato which was startling to one unaccustomed to its sound, but not unattractive. The instruments themselves date back to pre-revolutionary days when this had been the St. Petersburg Philharmonic, and the woodwinds therefore give an accurate sound-picture of what their tone properties must have been at the turn of the century in every musical country in the world—allowing for the fractional discrepancies of differing makes of instrument and individual styles of playing. As new instruments have been acquired, the individual players have been at pains to preserve this quality of tone, which can be one of exquisite nostalgia in the hands of a great artist—like the first clarinetist, who played his great theme from the slow movement of the Rachmaninoff Second Symphony with wistful and consummate mastery. Nor was this theme cut where it returns later in the movement in the first violins, who matched the clarinet's every nuance and rubato with like freedom of breath and expression, and there is no truth whatever in Eugene Ormandy's assertion that Rachmaninoff himself authorised the cut. (The only cut which he did authorise, according to members of the Philadelphia Orchestra who visited England in 1949, were the three bars before fig. 73 in the finale—and then only with a bad grace.) But the practice of cutting the clarinet theme at its return in the violins has an origin of which Ormandy himself is probably unaware, and which goes back to the last days of the great Philadelphia clarinetist, Maclaine. Maclaine was already mortally ill when a performance of the Second Symphony was announced—perhaps for his benefit, for the slow movement solo is one of the most hauntingly beautiful in the whole repertoire:

Ex. 48

a tempo (Adagio)

Clarinet 1 in A

Solo

In rehearsal Maclaine had insisted on playing the solo—which is also physic-ally extremely exhausting, calling for prodigious breath-control—and in the performance, the whole orchestra, acutely conscious that he would never play again, cut with one accord the reprise of the melody as a last, and significantly silent, tribute to a superlative artist. This is the kind of spon-taneous gesture of which the language of music is especially capable, and Maclaine was quick to understand its implications. He died during the night, and thence arose the tradition of making a cut at the reprise—a tradition which held a certain significance so long as the memory of Maclaine's playing per-sisted in the imagination of the Philadelphia Orchestra and its public.

In his performance of the symphony with the Philadelphia Orchestra at Harringay Arena in the spring of 1949, Ormandy made a number of other cuts which, although less objectionable in themselves, nevertheless distorted an overall sense of phrase-structure which Sanderling and the Leningrad Philharmonic were at pains to preserve in their Berlin performance eight years later. The opening of the first *Allegro Moderato*—a four-bar accom-paniment figure which Ormandy arbitrarily cut to two—has an organic function in the pattern of four-bar phrasing which it generates, and it acquired under Sanderling a barely perceptible but uniformly graded *decrescendo*, incomparably phrased, as was the ensuing violin phrase which

K

displayed an innate sense of *rubato* and had clearly been carefully assimilated
by the whole violin section:

Ex. 49

The 'cello passage beginning at fig. 10 and the great passage after fig. 17, with
its powerful violin syncopes and tumultuous horn-writing—for which Sanderling used eight horns, although only four were in evidence at the London
concerts three years later—were executed with a burning conviction and a like
comprehension of the fuller significance of *rubato*. The Scherzo was a veritable study in precision and controlled temperament which put all save the
great American orchestras to shame, and the fugato at the *Meno Mosso* after
fig. 31, and the March (12 bars after fig. 35), had to be heard to be believed.
Sanderling had made one cut in the first movement—bars 5 to 12 after
fig. 19—and in the finale he made five more, apart from that which Rachmaninoff had authorised: the ninth bar after fig. 61 to the ninth bar after
fig. 62, the fifth to the eighth bar after fig. 68, thirteen bars after fig. 68 to
fig. 69, fig. 82 to the fifth bar of fig. 84, and the four bars before fig. 85. But
they were appreciably more convincing than those which Ormandy had made
in 1949. The whole concert under Sanderling—which had included a performance of the overture to *Freischütz* in the best traditions of Wagner, and
an astonishing account of the Scriabin Piano Concerto with Emil Gilels as
soloist—boded well for the Leningrad Philharmonic's title as the world's
greatest orchestra, and Sanderling's title as the world's greatest conductor—
a title which Rachmaninoff had accorded to Leopold Stokowski.

It was therefore with a sense of profound disappointment that I learned that Kurt Sanderling was not to accompany the Leningrad Philharmonic on their visit to London in 1960, and that Rozhdestvensky was to come in his place. Ever since Van Cliburn's famous cable to Khrushchev, requesting that Rozhdestvensky be released to accompany him in London, he has become an increasingly familiar and popular figure in this country. But his account of the Rachmaninoff Third Symphony was appreciably more superficial than Sanderling's account of the Second had been—and it may well be that it is a more superficial work, in which case it must surely lend itself the more readily to the rescuing hands of a conductor of distinction. There was little in Rozhdestvensky's interpretation of the work—which concluded the Leningrad Philharmonic's first London concert—which I could find it in me to admire, and there was the same total absence of light and shade and the same cloying texture which had identified a performance of the work by the Philadelphia Orchestra under Ormandy at the Academy of Music in Philadelphia in 1956. Mercifully, Rozhdestvensky did not employ Ormandy's Hollywood tactics with the work, which had consisted in seizing upon every dynamic nuance and exaggerating it out of all proportion. But either Rozhdestvensky, or the string section of the Leningrad orchestra, did not seem to have acquired the trick of their Philadelphia colleagues, in the passage for unison first and second violins beginning at the second bar before fig. 37, of taking the eighth-note D at the second bar of fig. 37 as an harmonic from the D string, and playing the rest of the phrase entirely on the A string—a device which Rachmaninoff employed in his own recording of the work:

Ex. 50

Charles Foley Inc., New York, N.Y., Copyright proprietors.

In Rozhdestvensky's performance there was the same monotonous droning of the ostinato triplets at the *Poco Meno Mosso* after fig. 13 which had characterised Ormandy's 1956 performance. The woodwinds and strings had not been transposed at fig. 17 in accordance with Rachmaninoff's directions— manifest in his own recording—and there was the same absence of transparency of line in the fugue of the finale, and the same circus ending to a work whose finish is notoriously difficult to handle, and cannot be handled at all at

breakneck speed. The first flute of the Leningrad orchestra could not manage
the solo at the *Allegretto* after fig. 110 with the same flexible mastery of
Kincaid in the Rachmaninoff recording—but it is doubtful whether anyone
could, save Doriot Anthony Dwyer of the Boston Symphony Orchestra:

Ex. 51

The second London concert, under Yevgeni Mravinski, was another
matter altogether, and in their performance of Tchaikowsky's Fifth Symphony
the Leningrad Philharmonic came into their own in a dual sense. "They
played", wrote Edmund Tracey in the *Sunday Times*, "with a conviction born
of absolute belief in the work," and brought to it, not that degenerate and
hackneyed playing which typifies its usual performance, but a spirit of regeneration and renewal which was utterly compelling. As Mravinski was at
pains to point out after the performance, the successive down-bows at the

beginning of the finale's *Allegro* are not in Tchaikowsky's own hand—but even if they had been, the performance was of such conviction to have rendered such a marking superfluous. Elsewhere, there was nothing in Mravinski's performance which was as variance with Tchaikowsky's text, and yet the work as an entirety acquired an integrity of dimension which was wholly new to the London audience. From the very first chord there could have been no doubt that this was a Russian orchestra, and the sombre opening for unison clarinets was treated with a leisurely and meticulous attention to detail. The brooding intensity of the opening *Andante* was carefully preserved—in accordance both with the actuality of Tchaikowsky's markings, and the sentiments which lie behind them—and it was this leisured quality of the introduction, allowing ample room for the individual phrases to make their effect, which set the tone for the ensuing movement, and the work as a whole. The *Allegro* began like a half-smile—"a smile on the face of a child who has been crying for a long time" as Kleiber had said *à propos* the second subject of the first movement of the Unfinished Symphony, adding (with characteristic recognition of the professional musician's embarrassment in the face of an emotional proposition): "*Sul tasto, vibrato, pianissimo*". But here the smile was that of an adult to whom a ray of hope has been offered, and the all-important accompaniment was accordingly played at the point, *senza vibrato*, and *ppp*—in accordance with the text—which allowed the superimposition of a wistful smile from the first clarinet and first bassoon:

Ex. 52

The great string tune at bar 170 was again allowed ample room to breathe, with a fine control of *rubato*, leading to the first and formidable climax at bar

194—a climax which was yet sensible of the fact that this was by no means the ultimate climax of the movement, let alone of the whole work:

Ex. 53

In the slow movement it was again the attention devoted to the introduction which impressed, and which set the tone for the movement as a whole. The opening string chords, evoking the spirit of a cathedral choir of the Russian Orthodox Church, provided a luminous framework for the solo horn entry at bar 8. The horn in turn generated that marvellous woodwind counterpoint which is so characteristic of Tchaikowsky's writing—bars 101 to 126 from the first movement of the *Pathétique*, and bars 38 to 70 from its finale are among countless other examples in his writing. But since they offer no semblance to the generally accepted and acceptable principles of academic counterpoint they are consistently ignored in the standard critical assessments of Tchaikowsky. The oboe phrase at bar 24, reminiscent of the 'cello solo in Act II of *The Sleeping Beauty*, and so utterly different from it in every aspect of its expression, now came as a supremely logical fulfilment of the horn solo, and its subsequent appearance *con noblezza* assumed a significance and a justification at the hands of the musical representatives of the Russian proletariat which had consistently evaded a supposedly more nobility-conscious western world. Unlike the *Sleeping Beauty* solo, whose expression must be relaxed and free-breathing—for it comes at the very beginning of Aurora's most exacting *pas de deux*—the *con noblezza* string passage compels an utterance of vibrant intensity and controlled passion whose sense of exaltation is only matched in the *Sleeping Beauty* solo at the point where the entire 'cello section has joined the soloist:

Ex. 54 (i)

Second subject, slow movement, Fifth Symphony

(ii)

Grand Adage from Act II, Sleeping Beauty

(iii)
Ibid

(iv)

Second subject, slow movement, Fifth Symphony

The Waltz, again, afforded surprises, for the opening tempo was deceptively innocuous, and the sixteenth-note figures became a *tour de force* by virtue of the fact that they were consistently subordinated to the underlying waltz-rhythm. But it was the finale which presented the biggest revelation of all. Once again the leisurely introduction, and once again the meticulous attention to every detail and every nuance of expression—including the very first bass notes:

Ex. 55

The concluding phrases of the introduction became a conscious preparation
for what was to come, and anticipated bars 274 to 295 from the body of the
movement. But one was totally unprepared for the sheer tempo of the
Allegro Vivace, which entered precipitately over a timpani roll which was yet
to reach its climax, and had in fact only reached *mf*—Tchaikowsky's text—
causing an audible gasp of amazement:

Ex. 56

But once again the tempo was eminently logical, and its logic became demon-
strable with the arrival of the second subject at bar 128, making every other
performance of the work sound turgid and vapid. The tempo was further
advanced for the great trumpet passage beginning at bar 214, and the quasi-
inversion of the second subject in the basses at bar 234, *fff*, was accompanied
by strenuous playing in the upper strings:

Ex. 57

Ex. 57 *(continued)*

Thence a gradual relaxation of the tempo—from bar 274 to 295, already mentioned—only served to heighten the surprise of the explosive return to *tempo primo* at bar 296, a passage whose employment of double-counterpoint at the octave serves to underpin its whole structure:

Ex. 58

Ex. 58 (continued)

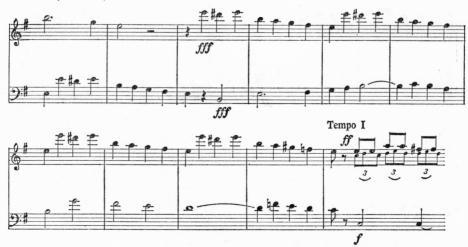

Nikisch described the *fermata* on the dominant at bar 471 as a point where "anything can happen", and it seems unnecessary to add that the audience on this occasion indulged in no precipitate applause, for this was the Festival Hall on a Friday night and not the Albert Hall on a Sunday afternoon. Stokowski, in his performance of the Tchaikowsky Fifth with the London Symphony Orchestra six years later, cut the next two bars (as had been his life-long habit), for in their character of introductory bars to the return of the motto' theme they can conjure up the alarming cliché of a Gilbert and Sullivan Grand Finale. Nor is Stokowski alone in this practice, which a number of other conductors have emulated—without, needless to say, his talent for going to the heart of the matter and seizing the motto theme with both of his expressive hands. Mravinski—in this performance, at all events—compromised by playing only one bar of the introduction, and the triumphal return of the motto theme was accorded a stupendously eloquent counterpoint of trumpet playing. At the final climax at the half-bar of bar 502, Stokowski introduced a cymbal-clash—a practice which is both questionable and defensible, for it is the ultimate climax of the work, and it is perfectly legitimate to underline it. Once again, he is not alone in a practice which nevertheless owes its origin to him, but which can become less convincing in the hands of imitators. The Leningrad Philharmonic must have been familar with it, for Stokowski had introduced it to them on his tour of Eastern Europe in the spring of 1959, when his concerts with the Leningradskaya had evoked sensational acclaim, and the vast overflow audience had had to be equipped with loudspeakers and television screens. But at their September concert in London, Mravinski evidently felt that his orchestra was capable of deriving this final climax unaided, and the music sped thence to a brilliant conclusion, with no faltering over the 6/4 passage (*Molto meno mosso, ffff*) which recalls the main theme from the first movement, and is a notorious stumbling block.

The personal evidence of three concerts under three different conductors, even when corroborated by a substantial body of critical opinion, would seem scant enough reason for eulogy if it had not been for the actual and overwhelming evidence of the orchestra itself. But this was sufficient testimony that it must, reasonably, have witnessed a tradition and a cultural heritage of a richness and continuity perhaps unrivalled anywhere in Europe—a heritage which spoke of the existence of cultural reserves which had amply withstood the successive influences of the revolution of 1905 (which had occasioned Rimsky-Korsakov's dismissal from the St. Petersburg Conservatoire), of the First World War, of the February and October revolutions of 1917, and of Soviet Socialism itself. For there is no other orchestra which has survived the political implications of three successive changes of name within its long history.

Chapter 15

CHARLES MUNCH AND THE BERKSHIRE
MUSIC FESTIVAL

In September 1949 Charles Munch succeeded Serge Koussevitsky as conductor of the Boston Symphony Orchestra, and with it to a unique heritage. For during the course of his twenty-five seasons at the head of the Boston orchestra Koussevitsky had not only welded them into a unity which had made them the world's greatest orchestra, but he had come to represent for the people of Boston and of America as a whole an entire mystique, a virtuoso *par excellence* who embraced a formidable and catholic repertoire and a *grand seigneur par excellence* who was also an enlightened educator, one who came to personify that specific quality of Americanism which he had contrived to resist for so long, and which is embodied in the words *in pluribus unam*.

In his book on Serge Koussevitsky, Hugo Leichtentritt has written:

> In discussing Koussevitsky as an artist, one comes to a matter that is of special interest to the concert hall public though perhaps not to the professional musician—a matter that can be summed up in the words "public appearance". The professional musician knows that a conductor's principal work with the orchestra is done at rehearsals and that the public concert is, so to speak, a clean copy of an essay fully drafted in advance and corrected in all details. The public, however, believes that the conductor's manner of wielding his baton and his personal appearance and action at the desk electrify the men in some mysterious way and are primarily responsible for the impression the listener receives. There are different types of conductors as they appear before the public: some are handsome, elegantly dressed, carefully groomed men, intent on impressing the audience—and especially the ladies—by their *mondaine* aspect. In their style of conducting, too, they stress elegance, beauty of motion, carefully avoiding any aberration in the opposite direction. In his younger years, Artur Nikisch was the unsurpassable example of this type. Others, unpretentious in their appearance, trust more in the power of their musicianship than in their showmanship. Of this type, Karl Muck was perhaps the most accomplished representative: with a minimum of agitated motion he obtained all the desired effects, a

glance of his eyes and the expression on his face sufficed. Still others act a theatrical part at their desk, gesticulating profusely and violently, transmitting the emotion of the musical score to the orchestra and to the public by their own bodily reaction, mindful of the fact that the concert hall public not only wants to hear the music but also likes a spectacle. Were the conductor to be made invisible to the public as in Wagner's Bayreuth Theater, a great attraction for many people would be lost.

Koussevitsky in a way is a composite example of all these types, assembling various traits with good taste and rejecting gross ex-aggerations. A man of the world in his distinguished appearance, he yet manifests to everyone that he is still more an artist, passionately intent on his cultural mission. As an advocate for the great art of music, he pleads to the large jury filling the concert hall. Outbursts of passion are restricted to a few, decisive movements, but when they arrive, at their proper place, their effect is irresistible. He also has repose, grace, simplicity, quiet humour, and artless gaiety at his command, and all the intermediate expressions on the emotional scale. His manner at the desk is not designed to draw attention to himself but to underline the character of the music, and to encourage his players in giving their best on the spur of the moment.

Finally it may be attempted to define Koussevitsky's position in the small élite of conductors of the very first rank. This exalted class is a small one—in the author's opinion including Toscanini, Bruno Walter and Wilhelm Furtwängler as well as Koussevitsky—with Georg Szell, Otto Klemperer, Erich Kleiber, Rodzinski, Mitro-poulos, and two or three others as younger aspirants to highest honours in the reserve. It would be presumptuous to attempt balancing in detail their respective merits and excellences, each one of them having individual greatness. Yet it may not be unjust to assert that of all conductors Koussevitsky is the most universal and cosmopolitan, not only because of his great art but also by reason of the exception-ally independent position he occupies at the head of the Boston Symphony Orchestra. Toscanini, for all his eminent mastery, does not have much interest in American music, preferring Italian symphonic scores, generally considered the less valuable part of the musical productions of Italy, with its centre of gravity in opera. Bruno Walter has not had enough independence in America to show the full extent of his powers; he is expected to perform mainly the Vienna classics, Mozart, Haydn, Beethoven, Schubert and Brahms, with a little Bruckner and Mahler mixed in occasionally—not because his American public demands it, but because of his well-known love of these masters. Furtwängler's eminent art is an almost unknown quantity in this country, and likely to remain so for political reasons.

Koussevitsky's manifold activities, his international affiliations, and his authority in a multitude of fields are at present unique in

America; altogether they represent the maximum of active power
and influence ever accorded to a musician in this country.[1]

For Charles Munch, accession to a throne on which Koussevitsky had for
so long enjoyed undisputed rule was hazardous in the extreme, and he
assumed the place of honour with caution. He did not have a twenty-five-
year accumulation of convinced admirers, and had first to prove himself—not
in terms of isolated guest engagements, which he had already enjoyed on
previous occasions, but over the course of an entire season and with the
knowledge that this would be but the first of many victories to be gained
before the conservative public of Boston could be finally won over. But little
by little, by dint of supreme tact and the exercise of that art of diplomacy
which is the birthright only of the Frenchman, Munch succeeded in establishing a bridgehead, deploying his musical forces, and introducing new musical
principles and—above all—a new sound to the orchestra. With the wisdom
of hindsight it is now possible to observe that Munch's thirteen years of
office in Boston constituted a spectacular victory: *s'il n'existait pas—Munch—
il faudrait l'inventer.*

Charles Munch was born on 26 September, 1891, in Strasbourg, in the
province of Alsace, which lay at that time on German soil. His father was
organist of the Wilhelmsdom in Strasbourg, and brother of Eugene, Albert
Schweitzer's first teacher, and was regarded as the likely incumbent of the
Strasbourg Conservatoire and Municipal Orchestra when Franz Stockhausen
retired in 1907. But the two posts were filled the following year by Hans
Pfitzner, who became general musical director of the Strasbourg Municipal
Opera in 1910 as well. It was Pfitzner who supervised Charles Munch's
studies at the conservatoire where his first study was that of the violin, with
which instrument he made his first public appearance as soloist in 1912. On
the eve of his twenty-first birthday, Munch left for Paris to study with
Lucien Capet, first violinist of the Capet Quartet, but with the outbreak of
war he was—as a native of Alsace—drafted into the German army which
Klemperer, six years his senior and now assistant to Hans Pfitzner at the
Strasbourg Opera, was successful in evading. Munch was sent to the front,
where he was wounded, and returned after the war to a Strasbourg which,
under the terms of the peace treaty, had been awarded to France. He became
assistant concertmaster of the Municipal Orchestra under Guy Ropartz, for
symphonic repertoire, and Paul Bastide, for opera, and in 1922 was accorded
extended leave of absence to audition for the post of concertmaster of the
Leipzig Gewandhaus Orchestra under Wilhelm Furtwängler, who had just
succeeded Nikisch on the latter's death. In 1929, Furtwängler was succeeded

[1] Hugo Leichtentritt: *Serge Koussevitsky*, Harvard University Press, 1947.

by Walter, but although Munch was still concertmaster of the Leipzig orchestra, it is significant that neither he nor Walter makes any reference to the other in their respective biographies.[2] Munch, who had retained his French citizenship since 1918 when Strasbourg had once more become French territory, was with the rise of German nationalism now faced with the prospect of losing it again if he should wish to stay in Germany, and in 1932 he made a choice which was to prove doubly historic. He left Germany, and abandoned his career as a violinist. Thenceforward, he was to be a conductor.

It is never without the utmost difficulty that an orchestral player succeeds in making the leap from the platform to the podium—particularly those who have exercised their profession in the former capacity for any substantial length of time, and Munch was now almost forty-three. It is true that Hamilton Harty had been forty-five and Vassili Safonov forty-seven before they embarked on their respective careers as conductors, but they had both been pianists—Harty a distinguished accompanist and Safonov a fully-fledged concert pianist. Frederick Stock is the only other violinist of long service who became a conductor of distinction, but he began this latter career at thirty-one—albeit among his own colleagues, which must always be a disadvantage. For Munch at least this last problem did not exist, for his name was entirely unknown in Paris where he now sought his destiny. But the habits of a concertmaster—and especially in so distinguished a post as that which Munch had just abandoned—die hard, for there is in every successful concertmaster that quality of dedication which must yet retain an element of submission. His position is doubly exposed, for he must represent the conductor's will on the one hand, and be seen to represent it, and must represent the corporate will of his colleagues on the other. When, at the end of the Philharmonia tour of America in November 1955, a member of the orchestra was misguided enough to pick a quarrel in public with Herbert von Karajan, it was on their concertmaster, Manoug Parikian, that the heaviest burden fell, and he handled the situation with innate tact. The orchestral player in question was of course summarily dismissed—and rightly so, for an exchange of personalities between orchestra and conductor on the rehearsal platform is intolerable from any point of view. But whereas Karajan forthwith washed his hands of the Philharmonia after this their final American concert—in Symphony Hall, Boston, curiously enough—Parikian felt it incumbent upon him also to tender his resignation, and the Philharmonia was thus the poorer for three musicians of distinction within their own clearly defined fields of

<hr/>

[2] Bruno Walter: *Theme and Variations*: trans. by J. Galston: Alfred A. Knopf, New York 1946; Hamish Hamilton, London, 1947. Charles Munch: *Je suis chef d'orchestre*, Editions Conquistador, Paris, 1954. Issued in English as *I am a Conductor*, trans. L. Burkat, O.U.P., 1955.

activity. Clearly Munch had never had to experience this kind of situation, for such insubordination would have been unthinkable in so professional an orchestra as that of the Leipzig Gewandhaus. But there is, particularly in Germany, a tendency of the concertmaster not only to submission but even to obsequiousness, and that Munch should have been free of any such proclivity is sufficient testimony of his qualities.

Assembling all his financial resources, Munch placed his stake on the Straram Orchestra, which in 1932 enjoyed a world reputation as a champion of contemporary music, and engaged them for his historic Paris début on 1 November, 1932. He describes this concert with characteristic modesty:

> I cannot honestly say that I conducted the orchestra for I was fully occupied with allaying the fear that paralysed me. I walked on to the stage with the feeling that I was floating through a heavy fog. My legs felt no weight. I was a stranger to the laws of gravity. I floated through a dream-world where all was *not* rosy, and I conducted like an automaton. My sympathetic audience mistook my panic for inspiration. Do not ask me whether it was a good concert. I saw nothing and heard nothing. I left the hall as one leaves hospital after a long illness.

Self-criticism notwithstanding, Munch's second concert was with the Orchestre Lamoureux, and achieved the enthusiastic and prophetic review:

> In watching and listening to him, I was moved to predict that Munch is one of those who, with a special kind of galvanic power, knows how to maintain and increase the musical life of a great city.

Munch rapidly became a *succés fou*, in demand all over Paris and all over France, and in the course of time formed his own orchestra, the Paris Philharmonic, with whom he conducted a vast range of contemporary music, including the concerts of the ISCM. His activities were extended to London, Vienna, Prague and Budapest, and in 1937, a bare five years after he had taken up the baton for the first time, he was appointed musical director of l'Orchestre de la Société des Concerts du Conservatoire in succession to Philippe Gaubert, who had held the post for nineteen years. For any French musician, this represented the pinnacle of achievement, and Munch set to work at once to resurrect the orchestra from those standards of pedestrian routine into which it had fallen under his predecessor. During the occupation of France he remained at the head of the orchestra, his substantial earnings being contributed to the French Resistance, and his country house being used as a vital link in the chain of escape for Allied air-crews and refugees from Germany. On 5 December, 1940 he conducted a performance of the Berlioz

Requiem which had been written in memory of the war-dead of 115 years earlier, and had received its first performance in December 1837.

After the war, Munch gradually withdrew from his activity with the Paris Conservatoire Orchestra, whose restraints and obligations had been his daily lot for eight years. He appeared at the Prague and Edinburgh Festivals in 1947, and was among the first to record for the new high-fidelity equipment. In 1948 he made his third visit to the United States within the space of two years, taking with him the French National Radio Orchestra on a transcontinental tour. And following this tour, the trustees of the Boston Symphony Orchestra announced that Koussevitsky would be retiring at the end of the 1948–49 season, and that Charles Munch would be his successor.

Apart from his activities at Symphony Hall, Koussevitsky had, since the summer of 1936, been musical director of the Berkshire Festival, which from the summer of 1940 included the Berkshire Music Center. The Berkshire Hills lie in western Massachusetts, a comfortable two-hour drive from Boston, and it had been in 1934 that Henry Hadley had conceived and put into operation the plan for a "Symphonic Festival", which was held that first summer on the estate of Interlaken, near Stockbridge, and for which sixty-five members of the New York Philharmonic were engaged for a series of three concerts in late August. In the autumn of 1934 the festival was incorporated as a non-profit-making organisation—qualifying automatically for tax exemption in America—and in 1935 a further three concerts were given on the Interlaken estate, with an enlarged orchestra recruited from among the principal orchestras of the Eastern states, and one of the concerts marking the début of the Berkshire Musical Association chorus of 200 voices. Notwithstanding an average attendance of 3,000 there were deficits, which were taken up by the festival guarantors, and at the conclusion of the season it was decided to engage the Boston Symphony Orchestra under Koussevitsky for the following summer's trio of concerts, which were given early in August at Holmwood, the estate of Mrs. Margaret Emerson. This time attendance averaged 5,000 at each concert and the festival was a resounding success, in consequence of which Mrs. Gorham Brooks offered her estate at Tanglewood as the Festival's permanent home. A cloud-burst in 1937, during the course of one of the concerts, revealed the inadequacy of the tent which had been built to hold 5,000 people, and led to the raising of $80,000 for the purpose of constructing a permanent music-shed, which was put in hand in March 1938. The shed was designed by the Finnish architect Eliel Saarinen, in collaboration with Richard Fay, professor of acoustics at the Massachusetts Institute of Technology, and was inaugurated at the first concert of the 1938 season, on 4 August.

Attendance had meanwhile risen from nine thousand for three concerts in 1934 and thirty-eight thousand for six concerts in 1938 to ninety-five thousand for nine concerts in 1941. With America's entry into the war, and the consequent rationing of petrol, the festival—which is virtually inaccessible without a car—was suspended after the summer of 1942, but reinstated at Koussevitsky's urgent plea, and on a smaller scale in 1944, with a festival of Mozart, followed in the summer of 1945 by a festival of Bach and Mozart. The Berkshire Music Center, which had opened in 1940 and included among its students a young man from Boston named Leonard Bernstein, was closed after the summer of 1942 for the duration, for military service was claiming a great majority of its potential students. And its activities were not resumed until 1946, when it furnished the training-ground over a period of eight weeks of intensive study for the young talent which was by then issuing from the services in ever-increasing numbers, and which included future orchestral players and conductors of all the major American orchestras.

The Berkshire Music Center was America's version of the Salzburg Mozarteum or the Accademia Chigiana in Siena—a summer-school offering master-classes in every branch of professional music-making, but with a sense of purpose which the Mozarteum had never achieved, and of which it would never have been capable. In 1938, Koussevitsky had drawn up plans for the Center, which had originally been conceived in Russia in 1911, and in his address to the trustees of the Boston Symphony Orchestra had said:

> The United States of America can and are destined to have such a Center . . . American freedom is the best soil for it. American financial resources will make it eventually possible. Rapid growth of American culture dictates its necessity as an historical mission and perennial contribution of America to human art and culture . . .

The weight of Koussevitsky's progressive ideas, and the magnitude of his personality, were perhaps best expressed by the music critic of the *New York Herald Tribune* in a review which he sent to his paper from Tanglewood on 10 August, 1942, after a concert by the student orchestra under Koussevitsky's direction:

> By the results which he has achieved with a student orchestra exactly five weeks old, this conductor must be accounted as one of the greatest cultural figures of our time . . . Never yet have I heard such a thrilling concert as that of last night. First of all, it had the spark that can come only from youth—the enthusiasm and receptivity of young players, who have their careers before them and have not slipped into the deadening ways of routine, and the eternal youth of a conductor whose flame for music has never burned low . . .

The concert, which had included Howard Hanson's Third Symphony, as well as the Mozart two-piano concerto, K. 365, and the Fourth Symphony by Brahms, was followed four days later by the American public première—again with the student orchestra—of Shostakovitch's Seventh Symphony at a concert in aid of Russian War Relief given before a distinguished audience. Toscanini had given the radio première of the work with the NBC Orchestra, and Koussevitsky now followed it with its first public performance in America, and became an ardent proponent of Shostakovitch's art. His broadly democratic attitude, which was apparent not only in the *apologia* which he wrote for the Information Bulletin of the Russian Embassy in Washington on 10 August, 1942—three days before the first public performance—but also on countless other occasions, must have come as a shock to those people who were only familiar with the elegant and sophisticated Koussevitsky. To them, his autocracy was the antithesis of democracy as they understood it, and they could not conceive that a spirit of genuine democracy is one of the enlightened autocrat's first principles.

But when, in 1949, Charles Munch assumed the mantle of the Boston Symphony Orchestra, the activities of the Berkshire Festival—and particularly those of its Music Center—remained in Koussevitsky's experienced hands by a common consent whose wisdom Munch was the first to acknowledge and enjoin. And when, after Koussevitsky's death in 1951, Munch's activities at Symphony Hall were supplemented by his succession as musical director to the Berkshire Festival and its Music Center, his impact was slow to make itself felt—as, indeed, it had been in Boston. The heritage of Tanglewood was vast and manifold, and Munch was well advised to move here, as in Boston, with infinite caution—nor was he accorded any effective alternative.

> Music is an art which expresses the inexpressible. It rises far above what words can mean or the intelligence define. Its domain is the imponderable and impalpable land of the unconscious. Man's right to speak this language is for me the most precious gift that has been bestowed upon us. And we have no right to misuse it ... Let no one be astonished then that I consider my work a priesthood, not a profession. It is not too strong a word. And like all sacred callings, that of the conductor supposes a total self-renunciation and a profound humility.

Munch's words are eloquent of two characteristics of the man himself, and of the excessive difficulty which many people experience in their attempt to provide him with a convenient label. For they evoke at the same time the very nature and purpose of music, in simple language of unusual beauty, and pose the ultimate problem of all music-making—the necessary pre-supposition

of a vast reserve of artistic means. And in his unassuming modesty as a professional musician, Munch gives us no help, but rather expects us to arrive at
our verdict of him on the evidence of the music which he has made for us
alone. But he does give us an occasional clue. On the very last page of an
autobiography which is distinguished for its brevity, Munch says:

> It is not too bad to read in the papers from time to time that one
> is a blockhead, but if the gentlemen of the press feel free to say
> that what we are doing is terrible, they might at least take the trouble
> to let us know how they can tell.

This displays, for all its outward *bonhomie*, that inward and supreme conviction which is the hallmark of every great artist, but it also reveals Munch's
penchant for spontaneous wit—a wit exemplified at Tanglewood on one
occasion after a performance of *Harold in Italy*, when he took his bow together with the solo violist, Joseph de Pasquale, who had been playing from
music. Unlike Munch, who was a large man, de Pasquale is slight of stature,
and found that he was hidden from the public, every time he tried to take his
bow, by the music stand which stood uncompromisingly in his way. Munch,
who might have resorted simply to removing the offending stand, chose
rather to lower it, so that de Pasquale might enjoy an unobstructed view of his
applauding public, and they of him—a trivial but endearing incident, and one
which revealed a piquant personality behind the sublime honesty of his
Gallic exterior.

Such incidents serve to remind us, not only that Munch was extremely
human (if also extremely shy, like so many other great conductors) but that he
was on occasion also a superlative showman—a factor which one is all too easily
inclined to overlook in that it is the one quality which we might least have
suspected in him. In fact, when we come to examine Munch's art more
closely, we discern an innate showmanship which is evident not only in the
unashamedly extrovert works of Berlioz, Strauss or Ravel, but even in such
works as the *Eroica* and Beethoven's Ninth, or Mozart's *Jupiter* or the symphonies by Brahms and Schubert. That *Daphnis et Chloé* or the *Symphonie
Fantastique* or the overture to *Le Corsair* should lend themselves to a display
of dazzling bravura is not perhaps surprising. But one finds in Munch a
continual tendency to evoke the brilliant touch, always accomplished with
lightning legerdemain, and which will bring a welcome brightness to tarnished
trumpets in the final coda of the *Jupiter*, or drive the three horns which he
employed for the famous phrase from the Funeral March of the *Eroica* up to
their top C with uncompromising energy. Nor was there any compromise in
Munch's use of horns in the Scherzo of the Ninth Symphony, or in the white

heat which he could generate from the very beginning of the First Symphony by Brahms, or in the coda of the first movement of his Fourth Symphony—not, as with Georg Szell, as the deliberate and calculated end-product of an express will, but with the dazzling brilliance of spontaneous combustion. His readings of French music, and in particular that of Berlioz, Ravel and Debussy, were of course famous—and justly so—but it was the music of Beethoven and Brahms which owed its greater indebtedness to his art. His performances of the Third, Sixth and Seventh Symphonies by Beethoven, and of the First and Fourth by Brahms, were among the ultimate pinnacles of music-making—nor can the recording quite capture them for, as in everything else, Munch's performances of these works were never identical. I have heard three performances of the Brahms Fourth from Munch—one at Tanglewood, and two at Symphony Hall—and in each he adopted different tempi and chose to bring out the saliency of different features of the work. Yet the total effect of the three performances was indisputably that of Munch, showing how utterly futile it is to attempt to assess any individual interpretation in terms of tempo or even of nuance. Not only is there manifestly no uniform tempo which is suited to every conductor, but there was for Munch himself no single tempo which suited him on every occasion. Nor, in the case of Munch, would one have wished it otherwise, for it enabled him to bring to each and every work at each and every successive performance a specific quality of excitement which was infectious, and which kept his players sitting on the edge of their chairs, grinning like a bunch of schoolboys every time they succeeded in matching their own virtuosity against his. Munch's Paris performance of the *Eroica* with the French National Orchestra in 1953 was utterly different from the performance which I heard him give, three years later, in a gymnasium in Schenectady. The first performance was extremely fast, almost up to Beethoven's metronome markings, and the second comparatively slow. But each bore the indelible stamp of Charles Munch, demonstrating yet again the extent to which the conductor's personality may influence his interpretation of the same work. For there was in neither performance of the *Eroica*, nor in the three performances of the Brahms's Fourth, any evidence whatsoever of a tendency to wilfulness, or to a striving after effect for its own sake, or at any price—nothing, in short, to which Stravinsky might have been able to take exception. And in Munch's Tanglewood première of the *Canticum Sacrum* in 1957, Stravinsky would have found an ideal interpretation.

Munch has been criticised by American colleagues on frequent occasions for his alleged indifference to American music, a cause so ardently espoused by his illustrious predecessor. During his first five seasons with the Boston

Symphony Orchestra, Munch performed thirty works by composers of American citizenship, as compared with sixteen works by contemporary composers of other nationalities. Nor were they all premières—far from it— for the American first performance was not an objective after which Munch's temperament clamoured instinctively. But in allowing a significant place on his programmes to such music as he adjudged worthy of merit, he performed a service to American music in which his predecessor—in common with many other American conductors—had singularly failed, the composer's right to have his music performed more than once. It is however the name of Walter Piston by which Munch's service to American music is chiefly remembered, and if Piston had, over his long years of association with the Boston Symphony, evolved a style which was peculiarly suited to the virtuoso instinct of that orchestra, it is equally certain that the works which he wrote during the thirteen years of Munch's incumbency betray an ever-increasing identity with those qualities in Munch which Piston's shrewd eye had been able to observe. The essential whimsy of the scherzo from his Sixth Symphony, for example, or the Gallic panache of his Viola Concerto—written for William Primrose—both envisaged their ultimate resolution in the indistinguishable unity which Charles Munch and the Boston Symphony had now become for them.

Yet it must inevitably be for his readings of French music with the Boston Symphony Orchestra that the name of Charles Munch will survive. These extend from Berlioz's Op. 1 to Honegger's Fifth Symphony and beyond, and embrace the manifold treasures of Debussy and Ravel and their contemporaries. His performance of Honegger's Symphony *Di Tre Ré* in August 1956 was one of overwhelming mastery and blazing conviction, and that of the complete *Daphnis et Chloé* an experience which I do not expect to hear repeated. And it was here that the superlative playing of the Boston Symphony Orchestra was allowed free rein. It goes without saying that the orchestra was complete in every department, with fourfold wind everywhere in evidence. But not only was the percussion section complete as to numbers —it was also complete as to instruments, and to quality of instruments. The cymbals were of Turkish brass—for the Turkish manufacturer who held the monopoly of his secret had been an immigrant to Boston in the nineteenth century, and his alchemy is retained in his family to the present day. (The final cymbal stroke from Debussy's *Fêtes*, for example, had been a miracle of sensitivity.) The antique cymbals, eight in number, were genuine antique cymbals, requiring eight players—not just one, improvising with a glockenspiel—and of immaculate pitch and temperament. The triangles, six in number, ranged from pure silver to rarest platinum, and were chosen with infinite care for the musical context. There were three pairs of castanets, ranging from black ivory to cherry-wood. The wind-machine, in performance, held a quality of pitch that could be exactly and infinitely graded. The players of the more conventional percussion instruments—snare-drum, tenor-drum, bass-drum, tambourine, tambour de basque—were, needless to say, all virtuosi of their instruments, fulfilling their respective functions with very extrovert *élan*. Among the brass, the rapid articulation of the four trumpets at fig. 96, and the slur one bar before fig. 204, were accomplished with a precision of ensemble which had only been acquired by dint of long and assiduous sectional rehearsal under Roger Voisin, their principal trumpet:

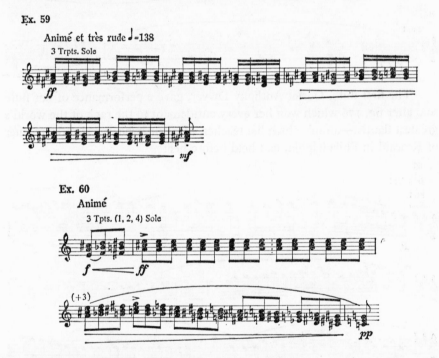

The first horn, James Stagliano, did not perhaps have the technical equipment of Dennis Brain, but was the superior artist, and his treacherous top Cs after figs. 44 and 48 were attained without difficulty or strain:

The first oboe, Ralph Gomberg, took his opening top F and G at fig. 2 with an accomplished ease and self-assurance, and played the 9/8 passage beginning at fig. 170 without support from his second—a practice common to many other great virtuosi of the oboe, and one which has become *de rigueur* in most American orchestras:

Ex. 62

The first flute, Doriot Anthony Dwyer, gave a performance of her flute solo after fig. 176 which won her every entitlement to the rank of the world's greatest flautist—a rank which her teacher, Mariano, who was also the teacher of Kincaid in Philadelphia, had held before her:

Ex. 63

Ex. 63 (*continued*)

The cor anglais, Louis Speyer, and the concertmaster, Richard Burgin, were no longer of a quality wholly consistent with such an astonishing array of talent, but were adequate to an extent where Munch was clearly unwilling to dispense with their services—and it is in such a situation that the conductor must make every attempt, even out of deference to a fundamental spirit of compassion, to make do with the resources at his disposal, for at the moment where music must dispense with the services of artists who still have a valid contribution to make it becomes something inhuman. But the string section as a whole, from the double-basses who had inherited a two-fold tradition from Koussevitsky, to the violins who had inherited a two-fold tradition from Munch, was veriest perfection, unsurpassed and unsurpassable—even by the string section of the Philadelphia Orchestra. (Heaven only knows how many million dollars-worth of instruments there are wrapped up in the respective string sections of the Boston and Philadelphia orchestras, but the figure must be astronomical.)

The chorus of the New England Conservatory completed the picture which presented itself to Munch and an audience stretching away across the Music Shed and spilling out in its thousands onto the abundant lawns of the Tanglewood estate, from where the quietest *pianissimo* was clearly audible. And to Munch fell the ultimate responsibility for creating a performance which was as moving as it was memorable, and this he did—not with any display of seductive fervour or immaculate restraint—but with the subtlest sense of *culture érotique, erotisches Kultur*, a phrase whose literal translation into English becomes as nonsensical as it does suspect.

In the autumn of 1956, the Boston Symphony Orchestra under Charles Munch had made an extensive tour of Europe, which had taken them as far as Leningrad and Moscow, and it was after their first concert in Paris that Munch was presented, in the name of France, with the now famous pair of bells which supplement an otherwise not very numerous percussion section in the *Symphonie Fantastique*. Once again, I was to hear three performances of the work: the first—and fastest—with the student orchestra at Tanglewood in the summer of 1956, the second with the Boston Symphony at Symphony Hall on their return from Europe, and the third with the same orchestra the following summer at Tanglewood again. And once again all three performances were different, and utterly different from the performance by the Berlin Philharmonic under Karajan which I was destined to hear ten years later.

There were of course the obvious discrepancies. The first *crescendo* was handled with varying degrees of intensity and insistency. The delightful figure which caps the thrice-recurring violin phrase in the Waltz was treated on each occasion with a slight variation of emphasis. The tempi of the March were all different. But the quality which all three performances shared in common was that of subliminal passion—perhaps, for all its inaccuracy, the best translation of *culture érotique*—and which bore the now indistinguishable signature of Berlioz and Munch alike. The phrasing of the very opening wind chords, which are then exchanged for the subtler texture of the first violins, was on each successive occasion more marvellous than the last. The Mozartian grace which informs this first page of score—and which eluded Karajan, for all his Mozartian sensibility—acquired a unity of expression despite, and perhaps because of, its three palpably different readings. For the one quality which all great music shares in common is its innate resilience, allowing of every shade and degree of interpretation, and indeed demanding it—not as something deliberate or contrived, though it may not be improvised —but as something which compels the artist to make music for its own sake and for the moment itself, without reference to anything which he may have done last week or may do next, or consideration for the fact that the performance will be taking place in Berlin or Boston or Beirut. This is the condition which makes assiduous rehearsal with even the most experienced orchestra vital and mandatory, for without the opportunity for daily artistic renewal and regeneration performances must perforce become routine. On the other hand, the moment such resilience becomes the obedient vehicle of improvisation, all is lost, for the performance must degenerate into the conscious awareness that one is improvising—or, still worse, the complete unawareness that one is so doing. There must be no consciousness that the performance is anything other than unique to itself, self-evident, self-explanatory, and self-sufficient, and this demands a conscious awareness which is directed specifically—and to the exclusion of all else—to the performance and the rehearsals which have led up to that performance.

These were qualities in which Munch excelled, and the overall impression which I retain, with astonishing vividness, of his three performances of the *Symphonie Fantastique* is one of widely varying emphasis, but consistent symmetry, in each. The performances were, if you will, complementary to one another, furnishing three facets of the same whole, yet preserving intuitively the individual integrity of each as a separate and disparate entity.

Of course the three performances shared many more features in common than they displayed discrepancies, but their common origin was not preconceived as a conscious and deliberate act, and consciousness was total and all-excluding only within the framework of each individual performance. One could of course remark the discrepancies and compare them—a practice as prone to odium as remarking and comparing their similarities, "die jeder Esel hören kann", to quote Brahms's famous retort, when people remarked on the similarity of the great tune in the finale of his C minor Symphony to that in Beethoven's Ninth. The one quality which was superabundantly in evidence on all three occasions, and which in many ways characterises Munch's art, was the employment of *rubato*—especially noticeable at the climax of the first *crescendo*:

Ex. 64

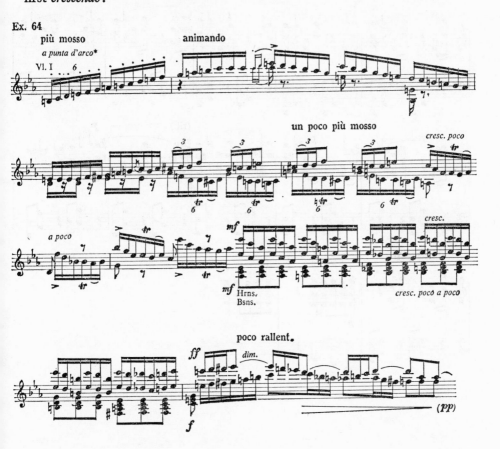

* The practice of orchestral spiccato was unknown to Berlioz: an artificial spiccato, 'a punta d'arco'—i.e. at the point of the bow—is known to some solo players today, but it is only practicable at very much greater speed. All orchestras today play the passage quite simply 'spiccato.'

And again, after the three-fold *fermata* leading to *cresc e poco pressante* twenty-three bars later:

Ex. 65

Or again, from the fifth bar of the final movement, *Songe d'un nuit du Sabbat*:

Ex. 66

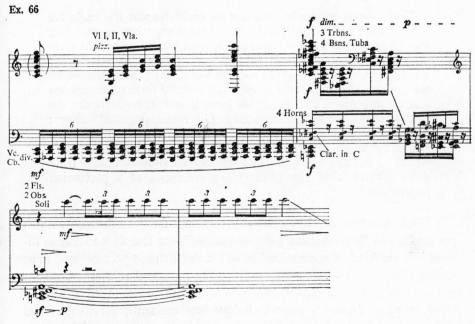

The use of *rubato* by the professional conductor presupposes the command of a flexible and businesslike baton-technique, complete freedom in which—unless he has an inborn flair—is perhaps the hardest thing for him to acquire. Furtwängler is sufficient evidence of this, and Parikian has said of Furtwängler:

> ... I entirely disagree with those who maintain that his beat was uncertain or unclear. I know more than one story about this aspect of Furtwängler's conducting technique ("Start playing when his stick reaches the third button of his waistcoat", etc., etc). But I always found his beat firm and eloquent. On one occasion he sensed that the strings would have liked a firmer up-beat. He stopped and explained, rather impatiently, that he could, if he wanted to, give a perfectly clear up-beat—and showed it to us. "But" he said, "that is not the effect I want." Another important point: even when you let your attention wander away from the beat for a moment, you always returned to it and found it where you expected it to be ...[3]

In his book, *A Composer's World*, Paul Hindemith painted a picture of the conductor which was very different to that of Parikian, though he shared

[3] Daniel Gillis: *Furtwängler Recalled*: Meredith Press, New York, 1965.

with Parikian and most orchestral players the naïve conviction that a baton-technique is easily acquired:

> There was a time when leading an orchestra was the exclusive task of men with a universal musical wisdom, when outstanding musicianship and great musical and human idealism were the foremost requirements . . . In an era that leaves little opportunity in the individual's life for the application and display of overt despotism, the demonstration of some refined and stylized form of oppression seems imperative . . . Identifying himself with these activities the listener enjoys the perfect abreaction of his own suppressed feelings: he now swings the teacher's cane, the dignitary's mace, the general's sword, the king's sceptre, the sorcerer's wand, and the slave-driver's whip . . . But the acquisition of a serviceable baton-technique is no more difficult than the rudimentary command of a percussion instrument.[4]

Hindemith here displays a palpable contempt for the refinements which are implicit in "a serviceable baton-technique"—or else an uncommon insight into the kind of apprenticeship which the virtuoso percussionist must undergo before he acquires even a rudimentary command of his instrument—rudimentary in virtuoso terms, that is to say. Cane, mace, sword or sceptre, wand or whip, Munch's baton-technique was eminently serviceable, and showed a greater awareness of its supreme virtues than one might expect from one who had also been a former concertmaster. It was certainly clearer than that of Furtwängler, but retained all the more positive and subtle qualities of the former conductor of the Gewandhaus Orchestra under whom he served for seven years. He would, for example, use his baton like a diviner's rod, searching out a particular colour or texture from the orchestra with importunate fervour and evident amusement at the players' discomfiture—especially during his rehearsals of the *Symphonie Fantastique* with the student orchestra at Tanglewood. This was particularly noticeable in the twenty-one bars which follow the second-time bar, which were executed as a continuous *stringendo*, and where he seemed to be reaching his long arms right inside the orchestra, with an expression of silent and Homeric laughter on his face for the specific benefit of the woodwinds:

[4] Paul Hindemith: *A Composer's World*, Harvard University Press, 1953.

Ex. 67

This was also reminiscent of Munch's tactics in the closing pages of the first movement of the *Eroica* in his Schenectady performance, where the principal

subject finds its apotheosis against increasingly insistent scale-passages which
ultimately embrace the entire orchestra. The deceptively slow tempo—by
comparison with his Paris performance of the work—meant that the woodwind section, in particular, was called upon to give ever-increasing clarity
to the articulation of the scale-passages—always more uncomfortable at a
slower rather than a faster tempo—and to Munch's evident enjoyment, for he
knew that his orchestra would rise to the challenge:

Ex. 68

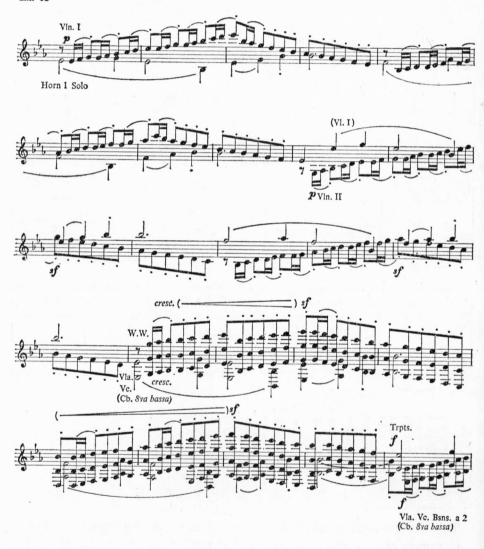

* Beethoven scores these written C's (on the B♭ trumpet) at the octave below, since this was a dangerously high
   register for the first trumpet in his day, and incapable of a good tone, especially in *forte*. It is universally played
   in the above version nowadays, although the dynamic marking of *forte* is almost always exceeded - usually by
   conductors who are intent on creating a sensation, or by those who are unable to control their forces, (which is
   often the same thing).

I do not know how much of his technique had been acquired from the example
of Furtwängler, who must in turn have inherited much that was important to
him from the tradition of Nikisch during his own eight years with the Gewandhaus orchestra. Munch spoke but rarely of Furtwängler—and rarely of
Nikisch, who had been the possessor of perhaps the greatest baton-technique
of all time. But the spontaneous *rubato* (and the contrived *rubato* sounds
hideous), for all that it may *sound* improvised, comes only as the fruit of long
experience or infallible intuition, and never as the fruit of instinct, whose
virtues are essentially chaste and bear no fruit. True spontaneity demands a
lightning sense of foreknowledge which is able to take split-second decisions—
on the basis of intuition or experience, but never with conscious reference to
them. It is the technical and artistic proposition of "How?" rather than the
intellectual one of "Why?"

The *March to the Scaffold* which forms the fourth movement of the
Symphonie Fantastique affords little opportunity for *rubato*, for it is of the five
movements of the work the most direct, and its rhythm is inexorable. The
subdued thunder of the opening triplets in the timpani is written out in full,
and the strings enter in great loping strides, to be joined by a counterpoint of
four bassoons which are very largely in unison—and sounded so under the
leadership of the Boston Symphony's principal bassoonist, Sherman Walt,
who had achieved a miraculous unity of ensemble and texture. The movement
passes like some grotesquely distorted spectre of the *Sanctus* from the B
minor Mass, the descending scale in the strings and then the brass being
ultimately answered by its inversion into an ascending scale, and the Lutheran
spirit of the witch-hunt is never far below its surface. Since Strauss had been
an eminent exponent of Berlioz's music, besides revising his treatise on
instrumentation and bringing it up to date—for Berlioz had committed a
number of gaffes, including his ignorance of the existence of the five-string
bass—we must infer that his E flat clarinet solo in *Till Eulenspiegel* is a conscious
echo of the clarinet solo at the end of the Berlioz march. But the strangulated

cry of Till as he dangles from the end of a rope—as Manoug Parikian will have cause to remember—has none of the summary impact and dreadful realism of the severed head which falls to the ground with an audible thud in the *March to the Scaffold*, to be answered by a shout of approval from the rest of the orchestra with their sustained major chords.

Munch here finished the movement with despatch, to kill any impulse to applause which the audience might have felt—a principle which found its reversal in his performances of the Fourth Symphony by Brahms, where the final chord of E minor at the end of the first movement was prolonged to the point where even the most uninitiated listener in his audience could not have supposed that this was the end of the symphony. Those who will think these observations naïve have clearly never heard a good performance by Munch, which can arouse the enthusiasm of orchestra and audience to the point where they overcome the impulse to indulge a spontaneous—if silent—cheer only with the greatest difficulty. Munch, like the canny professional he was, had no illusions about his quality as an artist, and was fully aware of the impulse he was capable of generating in his listeners which, if accorded whole-hearted indulgence, would have been unfortunate, and if accorded only partial in-dulgence would have had the effect of a *coitus interruptus*. In his summary dismissal of the final chord of the *March to the Scaffold*, he shared a practice which is common to a host of other great conductors—and to some who are less great. It is a legitimate trick, which compels the listener to store away that particular experience for the time being and until the end of the performance, when it will be automatically recalled. But in prolonging a *fortissimo* chord to the point where its function is entirely unambiguous, Munch was doing something else again.

Brahms wrote on one occasion of Joachim's playing of his own cadenza to the Violin Concerto, and of how the audience's applause carried over right into the fabric of the coda—and what a coda! But he wrote with evident enthusiasm, and it is clear that the audience of his day had none of our inhibitions—if also none of our education. I have no patience with the person who will scowl disapprovingly at spontaneous applause at the end of the first movement of the Tchaikowsky Piano Concerto, for example. It is an un-ashamed showpiece, the soft string pizzicati which open the second movement must compel any conceivable conductor to wait until the applause has sub-sided, and if the performance of the first movement has been spectacular to a degree, the audience should be permitted to indulge its natural impulse. But here the creative hand of the enlightened educator, instead of imposing an unfeeling restraint, can ease their burden for them by allowing their natural impulse the opportunity to expend itself entirely, and without interruption of the musical discourse or of their concentration upon it. Whether such tactics as Munch displayed in the final chord of the first movement of the Brahms symphony could be applied to the final chord of the first movement of the Tchaikowsky concerto, I have not had the occasion to discover for myself. But their respective codas are analogous, and although the Brahms is by far the greater and more profound work, there is the same apotheosis of excitement in both.

Munch could bring the same measure of showmanship to bear alike when he was conducting from memory—which was his normal practice, and one which he extended to the première of Piston's Sixth Symphony—or from score, and this is remarkable. To give a performance which is complete in its every detail, and to maintain that directness of contact with the orchestra which is essential to that performance with the score sitting in front of you, is prodigiously difficult. Klemperer can do it, and scoffs at "memory-conductors" to such an extent that one must begin to suspect that he is unable to commit a score to memory—surely one of the easiest of the conductor's tasks, just as the acquisition of an immaculate stick-technique is one of the most difficult. Dimitri Mitropoulos could do it, and gave a performance of the *Symphonie Fantastique* from score in Rochester in 1957 which was the finest—from score—I have ever heard. But I know of no one else who had this faculty, other than Charles Munch, and his was superlative. There are, in fact, very many reasons why this should present difficulties—apart from the superficial one that the practice of score-reading in public is normally confined to those who are not as yet familiar with the notes. But everything militates against its success at the highest level. One would not expect even the most inexperienced actor to come on stage with a copy of the play in his hands, though the experienced solo actor may create a *tour de force* from the practice on intimate and isolated occasions. No one would accept seriously—today—even the most distinguished soloist who came onto the recital or concert platform with the music in his hands, unless he had already established a reputation for himself as someone who was perfectly capable of committing it to memory. And the practice will always arouse the subconscious fear in the orchestra that the conductor does not really know the work—a question which would be quite unambiguous to them were the conductor to dispense with the score. I have seen some catastrophic errors committed in the name of slavish attention to the score in performance—too closely for comfort on one occasion—and although soloists tend to become nervous if a conductor suggests that his score might be dispensable, their confidence is swiftly restored when once he is able to convince them of a genuine mastery.

I recall an incident at the Albert Hall some eighteen years ago, when the orchestra had been the Royal Philharmonic, the soloist Alfred Cortot—already an old man—and the conductor one of our most famous, with a programme which opened with the Unfinished Symphony by Schubert. In a spirit of indulgent concession to "popular taste", he conducted the symphony —which he must have known backwards and inside-out—"from memory", with the result that the performance was tedious beyond endurance and the unwonted absence of the conductor's stand a source of acute discomfort to him. In the second movement of the Chopin E minor Concerto—the conductor's stand having now been replaced—Cortot suffered a memory lapse, a not infrequent occurrence in his last years. The conductor, now uncomfortable for a different reason, offered him his own score, which Cortot graciously declined. The plentiful Albert Hall audience, meanwhile, had displayed a massive unembarrassment, and were waiting patiently, and a little curiously, for Cortot to resume—which, after a few moments' reflection, he did—but not at the place where he had stopped. The concerto was not at that time very familiar to the orchestra—though one might argue that it *should* have been— and there was clearly discernible consternation among its ranks. The first clarinet, Jack Brymer, was the first to pick up a familiar landmark, the concert-master Oscar Lampe followed him, and one by one the remainder of the orchestra joined in, leaving the conductor beating time perfunctorily and turning the pages of his score helplessly back and forth until the end of the movement, in the vain attempt to recover his place in a work which, likewise, he *must* have known backwards and inside-out—even if the orchestra did not.

It is pertinent to remark that, where the printed notes of the score have lost any very substantial significance for its conductor, then he had by all means better dispense with it. And if its absence cause him the embarrassment of unfamiliarity, then he had by all means better familiarise himself with the practice of conducting from memory, for it is precisely and only then that the printed notes will re-acquire their significance. When Charles Munch conducted a work which was wholly familiar to him from score—and he would never permit himself to conduct a work which was unfamiliar to him from score or at all, save in dire emergency—he did so for the very reason that the printed notes had *not* lost their significance for him, but were on the contrary constantly renewing their significance under his inquisitive eyes. His exemplary baton-technique came on such occasions to the fore, the left hand was dispensed with *à la* Strauss, and the audience became the privileged *assistance* at his private workshop. It is an experience which is utterly fascinating, for it contains the ultimate essences of purest music-making.

Always careful of his own health, like Furtwängler and Kleiber, Munch held nothing but contempt for those conductors who were careless in this respect. "Imagine having to conduct for three hours at a time when you are suffering from stomach-ache or a cold in the head", he said. His admiration for Erich Kleiber, one year his senior, who once had had to conduct a performance of *Walküre* at the Rome Opera House while suffering from acute fibrositis in his right arm, and simply dispensed with it and used his left, was wholehearted: and when Kleiber died in January 1956, he mourned his death sincerely, for here had been an artist after his own heart. Now, in his seventy-eighth year, the musical world has lost Charles Munch, and a whole musical epoch is all but spent.

Chapter 16

THE NBC SYMPHONY AND THE NEW YORK PHILHARMONIC:
TOSCANINI, RODZINSKI, MITROPOULOS AND BERNSTEIN

In November 1930, Edward Robinson wrote in the *American Mercury*:

> Toscanini has the single, phenomenal capacity for maintaining a persistent tempo with the mechanical rigidity of a metronome. This has the decided effect of ruining an orchestra which achieved real greatness under Willem Mengelberg, for it forces the men into a strait-jacket of precision, and eliminates all spontaneity and expression in performance. By way of substitution for these wholly admirable qualities, Toscanini's only demand is that the notes must be clear, in tune, and observant of any expression marks that happen to be present. Beyond that he asks nothing—and, I may add, gets it.

Seven years later, on Christmas Night 1937, Toscanini conducted the newly-formed NBC Orchestra in a concert whose programme included Vivaldi, the Mozart G minor Symphony, K.550, and the Brahms C minor Symphony. Seventeen years later still, at the age of eighty-seven, he gave his final concert with that orchestra, which was forthwith disbanded for want—in the absence of the public allure which Toscanini's name by now commanded—of an available sponsor to take over the series of programmes. The programme for the last concert had consisted of two works: the Prelude and Liebestod from *Tristan*—replaced at the last moment by the Overture and Venusberg Music from *Tannhäuser*, since Toscanini's memory had begun to play him tricks—and the Prelude to *Meistersinger*. But his memory for the Venusberg music was little better, and near its close it faltered and was finally lost altogether. This possibility had been foreseen, however, and the panic-stricken NBC engineers rapidly substituted Toscanini's recording of the Brahms C minor, made seventeen years earlier, only to have to fade it out shortly after it had started because Toscanini had now embarked on the Prelude to *Meistersinger*. The prelude moved in a series of fits and starts to a finish from which Toscanini was excluded, for he dropped his baton and walked unsteadily from the platform before the final chords, which were literally screamed from an orchestra which had been stricken to its very soul by the futility of the spectacle.

So much is historical fact, bearing witness to the pathetic dénouement of a prodigiously gifted artist who was, in the estimation of many, the greatest conductor the world has ever known. But for all its pathos, the spectacle is not in itself very significant. What is significant is the extent to which his seventeen-year tenure of office with the NBC had pandered—for all Toscanini's alleged horror of publicity and hatred of the press—to the worst instincts of Madison Avenue, the more so because the influence had been largely invisible, Studio 8H in Radio City offering only strictly limited accommodation to a carefully-invited audience. True, there had been the tour of Central and South America in 1940, as the NBC's reply to Stokowski's All-American Youth Orchestra which had toured the same territory earlier in the year, and the immensely successful transcontinental tour in 1950 which had, however, been in the nature of a "whistle-stop", affording most of its audiences but a ninety-minute glimpse of an orchestra which was otherwise known to them only through the medium of radio. Apart from this, the NBC Orchestra's had been a mission of stealth, reaching tenuously out over the air before the days of high-fidelity FM equipment, from an atrocious recording studio whose acoustics left everything to be desired.

One may ask then how the Toscanini legend was accomplished, for the influence of his seven years at the Metropolitan and ten years with the New York Philharmonic had not extended far beyond the Eastern States, inter-larded since 1932 with occasional visits to Philadelphia, but with his summer holidays spent consistently at the Villa Diurni in Milan or on his private island on Lake Maggiore. Then, too, there had been Toscanini's morbid superstition of publicity in all its manifold guises, which had however made the paladins of the press the more curious, and had whetted their appetites to do battle in Toscanini's cause. But what could they unearth which was not directly related to his making of music—a worthy, but not exactly news-worthy, pastime?

They could unearth his political obsessions, which furnished copy eminently suited to the instinctual palate of American democracy—a palate which would have been outraged by the flavour of Toscanini's behaviour in the private world of the recording studio. Because of his intolerance of Fascism, born of earlier association with a party whose embrace of the liberal ideal he now saw to have been betrayed, he would use the Fascist label to impugn everything and everyone who incurred his displeasure. Furtwängler, Krauss, Karajan, Böhm, Abendroth, even Munch—all became for him "Nazis", "porci", "assassini", "imbecili fascisti". The international press which had been only too ready to ascribe political motives to the Milan incident of 1926, or the Bologna incident of 1929, now sensed political overtones in Toscanini's behaviour in Bayreuth in 1931, in Salzburg in 1937, and in his cancellation of concerts in London in 1947, and it is only surprising that politics have not been found at the root of the Metropolitan affair in 1915, the Buenos Aires affair in 1904, or La Scala affair in 1903. He would fulminate, with every justification, against the strutting turkey of his own spurious Caesar Mussolini—blind to the fact that he had also become a tyrant who was to be humoured, diverted, placated, tolerated, and contained. Toscanini's espousal of the Jewish cause had led him to make his much-publicised second visit to Palestine in 1937, on the eve of the Austrian *Anschluss* with Germany. But this afforded small comfort to those Jews who were already exposed to the abominations of Auschwitz, Belsen and Buchenwald, and whose plight such musicians as Furtwängler could at least alleviate to some extent, for in their qualified espousal of the Nazi cause they occupied a position of privilege which enabled them to arrange the flight from Germany of countless victims of Nazi persecution, besides pricking the conscience of the German people through the medium of their music-making.

Direct and uncompromising opposition to the forces of malignity can never be as effective as the insidious and benign influence within its ranks—though the gesture will always enjoin the enthusiastic acclaim of the free world. But such publicity, and all publicity, was anathema to Toscanini, so that his fanatical intransigence in political matters can have only been motivated by humanitarian instinct, by a deep and abiding sense of compassion which must belie his ruthless eradication of all expressive sentiment in his music-making. His self-identification with the common causes of humanity fostered a dualism in Toscanini's nature whose manifestation is by no means unique, and presented to the public at large the image of a champion of democratic principles on the one hand, and of an unmitigated prima donna to his intimates on the other, giving currency to the myth that common standards of morality are not to be applied to the true artist, who must be a law unto himself, and can do no wrong. This dichotomy in Toscanini's personality led to an inevitable waywardness in his readings, and a process of change which was not however a process of development.

In his book on Toscanini, Robert Marsh claims to see three clearly defined stages of development in Toscanini's readings of German repertoire, and of Wagner in particular:

> First, the "ancestral" performance, that is, the earliest Toscanini performance of a German work, based upon his assimilation of the reading of German conductors; secondly, the "transitional" per-

formance, in which Toscanini's *bel canto* manner has replaced some of the German style, and rhetorical devices have been subdued; third, the "singing" performance, in which German influences have disappeared, and Toscanini has re-conceived the work in terms of little or no rhetoric[1].

Mr. Marsh's book is a refreshingly serious and well-documented study of a conductor whose importance is not in dispute, but I beg leave to say that his assertions in this extract are arrant nonsense, and demonstrably so. Toscanini's first contact, at the age of forty-one, with a conductor of stature from the German-speaking world was with Gustav Mahler at the Metropolitan in 1908. Mahler was hardly typical of a German school of conductors, and their encounter was not in any case very extensive, nor did any significant Germanic elements remain on the staff of the Metropolitan Opera after Mahler's departure to the Philharmonic. On the contrary, where they were not native American, they were all imported from Italy. The next opportunity which Toscanini had of "assimilating the reading of German conductors" was with the New York Philharmonic in 1926, when he was fifty-nine, and when he shared an engagement as guest conductor with Wilhelm Furtwängler—an opportunity repeated on the occasion of the Philharmonic's tour of Europe in 1929, which of course included Germany and Austria. In the following summer, and again briefly in the summer of 1931, he was working at Bayreuth with Karl Muck and Furtwängler—but hardly any longer consciously "assimilating the reading of German [or any other] conductors". Nor, after 1933, was he to visit Germany again. So much for the "ancestral" perform-ance. In his second assertion, Mr. Marsh refers to the emergence of a *"bel canto* manner", and to the subduing of "rhetorical devices", and if we are to understand his sequence as containing an element of chronological signific-ance, we are dealing with Toscanini's years of maturity—broadly speaking, the first thirty years of this century, and certainly in good time for the advent of recording techniques in any appreciable degree of refinement. If we take his recordings of the Beethoven First and Sixth Symphonies, made with the BBC Symphony Orchestra at the Queen's Hall in 1937, as being to some extent representative of a period already past—and presumably refined upon—there is no evidence of any very significant decrease in the use of rhetorical device, nor of the emergence of a personal, or any other, *"bel canto* manner". The recordings are certainly better than those which emanated shortly afterwards from Studio 8H in New York, but they are mannered beyond endurance and employ continual and exaggerated *sforzati* which are

---

[1] Robert C. Marsh: *Toscanini and the Art of Performance*, Allen & Unwin, London, 1955; Lippincotte, Philadelphia, 1956.

out of context and out of style—as in the following example from the *Pastoral* Symphony, where he arbitrarily and senselessly imposes an insensitive *sforzato* on the text:

Ex. 69·

Bel canto—literally "fine singing", which implies purity of tone and free but controlled use of the breath—is here, as everywhere else, constricted into an impoverishment of tone and an exaggeration of intensity which are once again out of style and out of context. The features of Beethoven are burned beyond recognition, exposing an underlying bone-structure which is scorched and inhuman—"die Schönheit tragend ein gebranntes Gesicht". Nor is his recording of *Zauberflöte*, made in the same year at the same hall and with the same orchestra, noticeably better, and one can find fugitive solace only in the fact that his recording of the Mozart G minor, made at Studio 8H in 1938 and completed the following year, is infinitely worse.

We should here stop to reflect why Toscanini ever elected to record in such a studio at all. An ear which was so sensitive to sound as to experience acute discomfort at the Boston Symphony Orchestra's A—which, at 445 vibrations a second, is one vibration above the normal tuning—must presumably have been affected by even a fractional deviation in sound quality, and Toscanini should have been fully equal to consigning Studio 8H summarily to the devil, and refusing to work there (as many another conductor had done). But, on the contrary, he continued to work there with every evidence of pleasure and satisfaction, and when Samuel Chotzinoff, who was now working with the NBC, was commissioned to tell him that the NBC authorities had decided to move the studio to new premises, he flew into a rage. One can only suppose that its alleged properties of pure, naked and unadulterated sound—real enough for the acoustician, perhaps—struck some congenial chord in Toscanini's nature, and made him stone deaf to the quite dreadful things which he was perpetrating there in the name of music.

Toscanini had made his reputation, during his youth at the Teatro Reale in Turin and La Scala, Milan, as an opera conductor who forbade encores and enjoined the strictest observance of the composer's text. This was at a time when opera singing, especially in Italy, had sunk to the level of vaudeville, and opera singers would indulge in lavish cadenzas without compunction, and without regard for whether they were in keeping with the character of the role which they were playing. Encores were demanded by the public as their divine prerogative, and singers displayed a divine prerogative of their own in succumbing to the public's wishes with the minimum of appropriate diffidence, so that the sequence of the opera—if it could ever have claimed to have had one—was lost beyond recall. And the incongruity of the practice was self-apparent in Figaro's encore—at the public's insistence and with the singer's complaisance—in the Covent Garden production of *Nozze di Figaro* in 1952 under Erich Kleiber, who had conceived the work in terms of an overall integrity. Where such terms apply, as in Mozart and Verdi, or—obviously—Wagner and Puccini, the encore has no place. But the great bulk of Italian opera is incongruous enough in itself, the sequence of scenes very often arbitrarily contrived so as to provide a great voice with every opportunity for an encore, and the integrity of the work as a whole not to be measured in terms of continuity of action. The cadenza, too, has an appropriate place, where it bears an immediate reference to the character of the role which is being portrayed, and Rossini would have shared the general public's dismay at Toscanini's strictures, which were quantitive rather than qualitative. Toscanini would have been unequivocal in his disdain of a voice like that of Alessandro Bonci—his junior by three years—who could bring superlative expression to the use of *rubato* in a piece like the Cavatina from *El Capitan*, for example, where his top C sharp was allowed to linger with infinite and consummate artistry. In Rossini's *Barbiere*, a comparison is available in the two recorded versions by Conchita Supervia—under the direct influence of Toscanini—and Maria Callas of *Una voce poco fa*. The former version is faultless, save that the abundant personality of Rosina herself is never permitted to come through. The Callas version is also faultless, cadenzas are indulged freely but with constant regard for the character of her role, and it is extremely significant that the senseless little *fermata* at bar 20 of the *Allegro* is avoided with exquisite taste. It is the quality of Callas's singing which is here impressive—not the quantity of notes which her cadenzas display, and which are never "out of character". Although Toscanini's influence in the Italy of the 'nineties was a timely reminder to an art which had been increasingly exposed to malpractices, his continued influence became pestilential to the Italian public, for he was clearly saying the "wrong thing" for the "right reason"—a reason whose logic had already been borne home to the more discriminating among them.

But music is not simply a progress of isolated resonances—however rich or immaculate these resonances may be—and the absence of such qualities from Toscanini's performances might therefore be forgiven, for the primary function of music is to provide an articulate sequence in a horizontal (and not a vertical) sense. Here the absurdity of Mr. Marsh's third contention becomes patent, for we are dealing now with performances which were made at the very height of Toscanini's fame, and of repertoire—German repertoire—which had for him become an obsession. Between 1936 and his death, there were countless versions of Siegfried's Rhine Journey from *Götterdämmerung*—of which no less than four found their way on to commercial recordings—and heaven alone knows how many public performances. They become successively faster in each performance—which, bearing in mind his notoriously slow readings of Wagner (consistently slower than any known reading from the "German school of conductors", Knappertsbusch included), must imply that he was progressively attempting to assimilate a German style, whether consciously or no. As to rhetoric, they become unalloyed bombast from start to finish—a hysterical *carabinieri* band finish of Toscanini's own invention—employing that inflated rhetoric which we associate with the grosser excesses of banality of which the German temperament is sometimes capable. Since the recording which I have heard—sufficiently often to have conceived an unqualified distaste for it—was presumably issued with Toscanini's blessing and as the best which was available from four different versions, I can only assume that it had qualities for Toscanini in the recording studio which are not evident on the turntable. But of the "singing performance" there is no trace. Every phrase which might conceivably lend itself to the expression of song is confined to the strait-jacket (to borrow Mr. Robinson's words) with metronomic rigidity, and the overall Wagnerian *melos* treasonably betrayed. It is certainly a "re-conception", and a most unhappy one.

It is fortunate, therefore, that there remains the sparse evidence of an occasional performance and an occasional recording which is wholly convincing. Toscanini had an especial sympathy for the music of Debussy, and his performances of *La Mer* could be electrifying—and very beautiful. So could those of Elgar's *Introduction and Allegro* and the *Enigma Variations*, and the Samuel Barber *Adagio for Strings* which he performed for the first time with the NBC Orchestra on 25 November, 1938, and recorded with them shortly afterwards. Embracing rather than rejecting a specifically German approach to the music, he gave memorable performances of the four Brahms symphonies, together with the Haydn Variations and the *Tragic* Overture, with the Philharmonia Orchestra at the Festival Hall on 29 September and 31 October, 1952—the last performances of these works (save for the Third Symphony and the *Tragic* Overture with the NBC the following November) which he was to give anywhere.

The finale of the Philharmonia's performance of the First Symphony had been marred by an unfortunate slip on the part of one of the members of the brass section, who lost his job in consequence. That he should have been nervous is perhaps understandable, as we shall presently see. But that he should have allowed his nervousness to inhibit his playing would have been unforgivable, had there not been a history to the incident. The player in question had taken part, some months previously, in a performance by the Philharmonia of the fifth *Concerto for Orchestra* by Goffredo Petrassi at the BBC Maida Vale studios, and had been reprimanded in rehearsal by the conductor, Hermann Scherchen, for playing an exposed entry one bar too early. Verbal comparison of part with score revealed an apparent error in the part, which was duly corrected—but the reputation of the player was already compromised in the eyes of his colleagues, for it is one of the oldest excuses in the profession for an orchestral-player to complain that there is a mistake in his part whenever he is guilty of one of his own. Visual consultation of the control-copy of the score—a photostat of the manuscript which was sitting on the conductor's desk—revealed however that the original part *did* correspond with the score, which Scherchen had evidently misread and miscued. This would have been understandable enough had not Scherchen continued in his insistence that the player had made a mistake, which in the light of later discovery implied either that Scherchen really *was* unable to read a score—unthinkable in Scherchen's case—or that he had been prepared to sacrifice the composer's quite unambiguous manuscript on the altar of his own reputation, *vis-à-vis* the orchestra, as an immaculate score-reader.

The incident was unfortunate in that it was immediately recalled after the Toscanini performance, but without reference to Scherchen's artistic dishonesty, to which few of the orchestra had been privy. Having incurred the opprobrium of his colleagues and the profession as a whole ("there's the fellow who made a mistake in one of Toscanini's concerts"), he was compelled to leave the country, and went to Canada. This was hardly Toscanini's fault, of course, but it is eloquent of the inflated reputation which he enjoyed, and which presupposes that any orchestral player who was guilty of such an error under *his* baton must *of course* be dismissed.

The terror in which Toscanini was held, by brass sections in particular, was especially manifest on the occasion of his concert-performance of *La Bohème* with the NBC Orchestra in February 1946. In the final bars of Act

IV there was a fractional anticipation by the brass, who were duly arraigned in Toscanini's dressing-room—whither he had abruptly retired even before the soloists had started to take their calls, and abandoned himself to elemental rage. Chotzinoff's account continues:

> Screaming and roaring incomprehensible things, he tore at his clothing and upset every moveable object that yielded to his inspired strength. His piano and a large desk resisted all efforts at dislodgement, and in exasperation he kicked them repeatedly with such fury that I feared for his legs. After minutes of fulmination and wreakage he suddenly desisted and said: "Send me the *porci*. I wish to speak with them." The erring players had not dared to leave the hall. There were nine of them, and I led them into the Maestro's room, where they took up an uneasy position in a line against a wall, their faces pale, their heads down. The Maestro walked up and down like a sergeant inspecting his squad, glaring at each with hatred and contempt. At length he said with bitter sincerity: "I hide my head in shame. After what happened tonight, my life is finished. For me it is impossible to look in the face of *anybody*. *I* can live no more. But *you*—"and he pointed at the man at the head of the dejected line— "you will sleep with your wife tonight as though *nothing* had happened. I know *you!*" [2]

The Toscanini myth was unfortunate in that it eclipsed all other Italian colleagues—not only in the eyes of a credulous world, but in those of his native Italy as well. The conventional history of Italian interpretative art since the turn of the century is one of those opera houses—and only those— under Toscanini's stormy and fleeting direction, and takes little or no account of his many and conspicuous contemporaries and rivals, chief among whom was the late Victor de Sabata. For the Italian temperament worships nothing so adoringly as the *prima donna*, of whose arts Toscanini was the exceptional and pre-eminent exponent. He combined the jealousy of Furtwängler and the vanity of Koussevitsky with the musical insensitivity of neither, and over a period of twenty-seven years successfully turned the musical life of New York over to the tender mercies of commercial exploitation, and created of her musicians arrogant and swashbuckling caricatures of themselves. His musical legacy is sparse, for the much-vaunted Toscanini recordings are largely shallow and of no enduring worth, and the few memorable performances which he gave—for his instincts were too professional to be ignorant of the art of rising to the occasion—too high a price to pay for a man who seemed bent on the very destruction of music in his insistence that it serve his will, and be compelled to sing instead of being allowed to sing.

[2] Samuel Chotzinoff: *Toscanini: An Intimate Portrait*, Alfred A. Knopf, New York, 1953.

Having endured the loss of Toscanini in 1936, the New York Philharmonic had found a replacement—and not a conspicuously happy one, under the circumstances—in John (later Sir John) Barbirolli. The Toscanini cult had been damaging insofar as it necessarily placed his inevitable successor in an invidious position, for not every European conductor was as anxious as Furtwängler to come to America, and few indeed could have contemplated the musical directorship of the New York Philharmonic with anything but the gravest of misgivings. The case of Mitropoulos was to show just how disreputable the corporate behaviour of this orchestra could be, and in the light of later knowledge it is astonishing that Barbirolli contrived to survive for so long.

The 1941–42 centenary season opened without a permanent conductor for the first time since Safonov's appointment in 1906. Instead, a series of nine guest conductors was announced—including Toscanini, who was now in his fourth year with the NBC—and the practice continued during the 1942–43 season. In 1943 Artur Rodzinski, who had been responsible for training the NBC Orchestra in readiness for Toscanini, was appointed the new musical director. Since becoming assistant to Stokowski with the Philadelphia Orchestra in 1926, at the age of thirty-two, this Dalmatian conductor had served at the head of the Los Angeles Symphony from 1929 to 1933—when he was succeeded by Otto Klemperer—and since 1933 with the Cleveland Orchestra, with whom he gave the American première of Shostakovitch's *Lady Macbeth of Mtzensk* in 1935. He had, moreover, the unique reputation of having survived Toscanini's attempts to dislodge him from his temporary post with the NBC for many months, and of having emerged from the battle unscathed and with professional opinion very much on his side. Rodzinski was, too, already familiar with the Philharmonic, having appeared as a guest conductor during Barbirolli's first season, and he began his duties by dismissing fifteen players, including Michel Piastro, the concertmaster, before his very first rehearsal—to the subsequent dismay of James C. Petrillo, president of the American Federation of Musicians, who was successful in having five members reinstated and thereby making Rodzinski's position impossible. Nevertheless, the rebuilding of the orchestra proceeded to the apparently entire satisfaction of the public and the critics, and his abrupt resignation in the middle of the 1946–47 season came the more as a surprise. In his letter of resignation, Rodzinski alleged crass invasion of his directorial responsibilities by the management, who remained significantly silent. The Chicago Symphony, which had been harassed for four years by the critics of Désiré Defauw—Frederick Stock's successor—quickly extended Rodzinski a contract, and the Philharmonic were once again without a permanent conductor.

They were to remain without one for the next two years, during which the inevitable and reprehensible practice of guest conductors was restored, and it became increasingly clear to management and public alike that there was a world dearth of conductors—at least of conductors for the New York Philharmonic. Bruno Walter was at the Metropolitan Opera, and although he could be enticed away for an occasional guest appearance, he was unwilling to accept a permanent engagement. Nor was Leopold Stokowski, who had been enjoying free-lance activity since 1938, and was not prepared to commit himself to a permanent post either—until, in 1955, he was finally persuaded to accept the responsibility for building the Houston Symphony Orchestra. Stokowski did, however, accept the New York Philharmonic's proposition for him to share the 1949–50 season with Dimitri Mitropoulos, and the following season Mitropoulos became their permanent conductor.

Mitropoulos—originally Dimitrios Dimitropoulos—had been born in Athens on 18 February, 1896, of a family which was profoundly religious. Two of his uncles were priests in the Greek Orthodox Church, and when Asia Minor was invaded by the Turks in 1921, his father was arrested for his work on behalf of the two million refugees from Smyrna, and died in his prison cell. Mitropoulos began studying with Armand Marsick, the Belgian conductor of the Athens Symphony Orchestra, at the age of twelve, and eleven years later his opera *Sister Beatrice* was performed at the Athens Conservatoire before an audience which included Camille Saint-Saëns, who carried a glowing account of it back with him to Paris. This aroused a sense of responsibility in the city of Athens, who provided funds for their talented son to study with the Belgian composer, Paul Gilson, in Brussels, and two years later with Ferruccio Busoni, to whom the Weimar Government had awarded, in 1920, the chair of composition in Berlin. Busoni, however, was less impressed by Mitropoulos as a composer than as a pianist, and for the next two years the young man enjoyed the benefit of private tuition from a master of that instrument. In 1923, at Busoni's recommendation, he joined the Berlin State Opera under Erich Kleiber in the capacity of *répétiteur*. Kleiber, however, was quick to recognise Mitropoulos's especial talents, and very soon had him conducting. Two years later, at the age of twenty-nine, and now at Kleiber's recommendation, he was appointed conductor of the Athens Symphony Orchestra, and returned in May 1930 as conductor of the Berlin Philharmonic, with Egon Petri as soloist in the Third Piano Concerto by Prokofieff.

Shortly before the performance, Petri was taken ill, and Mitropoulos proposed, to a dubious but desperate management, taking his place in the dual role of conductor and pianist—a practice which Hans von Bülow had initiated in Berlin with the Brahms D minor Concerto. The management had no choice but to accept, and the performance was a sensation, for Mitropoulos knew the solo part from memory as well. Not since Bülow himself had the Berlin public witnessed such a feat, and the critics were quick to seize their opportunity. But Mitropoulos remained loyal to the Athens Symphony Orchestra until 1932, when he finally accepted a contract with the Orchestre Lamoureux in Paris where he repeated the Berlin experiment at his first concert. (This was the orchestra with whom Charles Munch was destined to make his second public appearance as a conductor in December of the same year.) In 1936, Koussevitsky invited him to Boston as guest conductor of the Boston Symphony, an invitation which was extended again the following year when it was combined with one from Minneapolis, where Mitropoulos made his début on 29 January, 1937. His appointment as permanent conductor of the Minneapolis was confirmed as from the autumn of 1937, and the following year he received the invitation of a guest engagement with the newly-formed NBC Symphony, when he was to suffer the unpardonable indignity of Toscanini's constant interference in the course of rehearsal—the common fate of countless other conductors. In 1940 Mitropoulos appeared as a guest conductor with the New York Philharmonic—now under the musical directorship of Barbirolli—and in 1945 and 1946 he appeared at the summer seasons of the Philadelphia Orchestra in Robin Hood Dell.

In the Autumn of 1955, the New York Philharmonic made their first tour of Europe in sixteen years, and gave—among countless others—two concerts in Vienna. Dimitri Mitropoulos, now in his sixth season as their full musical director, gave performances of the Third Symphony by Schumann and the Second by Brahms, the *Reformation* Symphony by Mendelssohn and the Tenth by Shostakovitch, which—for this writer at least—amply supported the reputation which he had made for himself in the United States. The Viennese, as usual, were grudging in their praise—as they had been in 1952, when the Philharmonia Orchestra had visited Vienna under Herbert von Karajan, and when Manoug Parikian had been compelled to uphold the orchestra's reputation, at an impromptu gathering in the Hochhaus restaurant after one of the concerts, by playing a completely impromptu *Zigeunerwaisen* on a fiddle borrowed from the resident Maestro and under the critical eyes of Willy Boskowsky, concertmaster of the Vienna Philharmonic. After the first concert—which had opened with an electrifying account of the overture to *Forza del Destino* (to which Michael Gielen, future general musical director of the Stockholm Opera, had succinctly remarked: "Toscanini hätte anwesend sollen"), and closed with a swaggering account of the Brahms Second, in which the cruel top D of the first trombone in the coda had rung out with tone as big as a house—the public's and critics' reaction was cautious. "It was a very *large* orchestra . . ." (Mitropoulos had used a standard full orchestra, together with five horns, whereas most American orchestras carry eight horns —and there had been eight, I seem to remember, in a performance of *Don Juan* at the Albert Hall by the Philharmonia under Alceo Galliera in 1948.) "It was "inauthentic" to allow a "fifth" horn to take over from the first . . ." (It is standard orchestral practice to have a sub-principal horn to take over from the principal, in order to allow him to rest after an exhausting solo— and to prepare for the next.) The press were, however, unanimous in their opinion that the orchestra was too loud, and as an encore to the second concert Mitropoulos decided to show the Viennese public how quietly the New York Philharmonic could play when they wanted too. Unfortunately he chose a piece which that public could hardly be expected to have known, although it is very well known in America—the Rachmaninoff *Vocalise*, in his own orchestral transcription—and the point was somewhat lost. The almost inaudible whisper of the opening, in a full section of thirty-two violins, was only matched by the incredible *ppp* at the climax of the final phrase, which seemed to hang on the top C sharp for an eternity—and recalled the voice of Bonci in the same register. The oboe solo which precedes it—played by Gomberg, brother of the Boston Gomberg—was matchless artistry. As an encore to the first concert, Mitropoulos had produced the final movement from *The Three-Cornered Hat* by de Falla, and I was particularly impressed by the short snare-drum roll, involving a prodigious *crescendo* from a very young percussion-player—but this was before I visited America and heard for myself the incredibly virtuoso playing of even the simplest percussion instruments in that country. But some untidy playing by the first clarinet near the opening of the Schumann Third Symphony was disturbing, and could not—with all charity—be entirely attributed to the effects of a long and arduous tour, for it betrayed an arrant carelessness from a player who was demonstrably too fine an artist to be guiltless, slight though the blemish was.

Mitropoulos was quite evidently a showman, in the highest and most literal sense of the word. From the very first bars of *Forza del Destino*, with their pungent brass chords, one had the sensation of being invited to take part in the performance, and he would address himself to the various sections of the orchestra long before their respective entries. Clearly, this was not for the orchestra's benefit—nor was it for that of the public in the sense that they might have construed it as being a desire on Mitropoulos' part to draw attention to himself. Far from wishing to draw attention to himself, he wanted to draw *our* attention to the various sections of *his* orchestra, and in the process succeeding in making the articulate progress of the Verdi text transparently clear. But he did not accord this treatment to the Rachmaninoff *Vocalise*, for

example, where it would have been inappropriate. Other aspects of his performances were, perhaps, less convincing—and particularly the ending to the
Brahms symphony, which was built up into a climax of size and sound
entirely out of style. But of this the Viennese were less critical, and when, at
the end of the second concert, Mitropoulos blew the audience a kiss, they
were prepared to forgive everything. "Wie war das *schön!*"

Mitropoulos had been guest conductor of the Maggio Musicale in
Florence in 1953, where, among other things, he had given a performance
of the First Symphony by Mahler—which was accordingly programmed the
following summer at the Accademia Chigiana in Siena, at which the Florence
orchestra habitually played at that time. As a student of Paul van Kempen,
who had charge of the Maggio Musicale Orchestra at Siena, I was given the
opportunity of conducting the symphony in public, and it became apparent
at first hand what nature of musician Mitropoulos was, and this in turn
revealed to me the full stature of Mahler. Every nuance which I could have
wished for was there for the taking—together with many others which, in my
wildest imaginings, I had never dreamed of at that time. Van Kempen was,
moreover, a devout Mahlerian, having been a pupil of Mengelberg, which
gave the two-fold sensation of trespassing on another's property. The performance was, I think, magnificent, but I assuredly had little hand in it, and
it was the hand of Mitropoulos which guided my own. Van Kempen's own
concert with the Florence orchestra had included the overture to Tchaikowsky's *Romeo and Juliet*, and he contrived to make the final chords, which had
seemed so inappropriate to Tchaikowsky's contemporaries, sound as though
a series of elemental and grief-stricken sobs of Romeo for his Juliet—thus
revealing the sureness of Tchaikowsky's instinct, as Mengelberg had done
before him:

Ex. 70

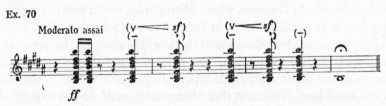

In 1954 Mitropoulos, in addition to his duties with the New York
Philharmonic, assumed the musical directorship of the Metropolitan Opera
in succession to Bruno Walter, and from this time date his astonishing performances, and subsequent recording—so vastly superior, musically speaking,
to the current version by Pierre Boulez—of *Wozzeck*. *Wozzeck* had received
its American première under Stokowski in 1931 at the Academy of Music in
Philadelphia, which serves the dual function of concert hall and opera house,

and where he had given the American premières of the stage version of *Le Sacre du Printemps* and Schoenberg's *Die glückliche Hand* the previous year, and was to give the première of Stravinsky's *Mavra* in 1934. At the first rehearsal for the recording of *Wozzeck* in 1954, Mitropoulos had already committed the score to memory, explaining to the incredulous orchestra and assembled soloists: "You have to practice, so I have done some homework too"—a sentiment which might well have been inverted by any other conductor.

Mitropoulos's memory was of course legendary, and extended far beyond the orbit of *Wozzeck* into the *avant-garde* domain of the Musica Viva concerts in Munich which had been organised until his death by Karl Amadeus Hartmann. Kleiber had appeared at one of these concerts in 1955, and had given the first performance of Hartmann's Fifth Symphony, together with the three excerpts from *Wozzeck* and *Due Pezzi* by Dallapiccola—all from memory also—and establishing, I would think conclusively, that memory and talent are directly related. Klemperer might demur, although Mitropoulos *did* conduct from score on occasion—as did Kleiber, witness his Berlin performance of the *Four Last Songs* by Richard Strauss—which must presumably mean that they knew how to read a score. But this is not to suggest that a conductor who can go through an opera performance of *Fidelio*, turning the pages of the score back and forth the while, and apparently oblivious of stage, orchestra, and audience, has not every right to expect that everyone shall know what he is doing, or that he may not simply have lost his place.

It was discouraging therefore to visit Carnegie Hall in the early months of 1956 and find that the first-clarinet's slip in the Schumann Third Symphony a few months earlier had not been attributable to accident, and that it really was symptomatic of a condition in the orchestra as a whole over which Mitropoulos no longer exercised any control. The rehearsal began with Ravel's *Alborada del Grazioso*, where Mitropoulos was at pains to explain that it was perfectly possible—and, in fact, clearer—to beat the first and third bars (and analogous bars throughout the work) in *three*, but his remarks were treated with studied inattention. The point was too simple to grasp for an orchestra of this calibre, just as Mitropoulos's prepared entries at the concerts in Vienna had been. The most that Mitropoulos could do was to suggest that if they did not like it, there was a colleague of his in Cleveland who would be only too happy to come and conduct them—a colleague, moreover, who could no more accept a beat of three in the basic 6/8 of *Alborada del Grazioso* than he could in the analogous passage in the *Andante* of Mozart's G minor Symphony:

Ex. 71
(i)
Assez vif

(ii)

The point is rudimentary, and to suggest that beating three in the first and third bars of *Alborada del Grazioso*, or the analogous bars from the Mozart symphony, is destroying the underlying syncopation must be to ignore the purpose of that syncopation. There is ground for ambiguity in the Ravel, since these are pizzicato chords, but the Mozart is quite unambiguous —as is self-evident from the text. The sense of syncopation in the bar itself, isolated from the context of the passage as a whole, is *of course* destroyed—but that very destruction sets up a chain-reaction in the bars which follow and (in the case of the Mozart) precede it. The orchestral player who will reply that this is splitting hairs and complicating matters unnecessarily is he who will attack the composer's use of variable metre—employed since *Le Sacre du Printemps* and *Pétrouchka*—and complain that it would be far simpler to read if the composer had written it all in common time and just marked in the accents, fondly imagining that the functions of accent and bar-line are synonymous. Nor can one accede to Berlioz's contention that the visual aspect plays a decisive part, and that the audience will gather the implications of a syncopation far more readily if they see the conductor consciously conducting against it. On the contrary, they will gather its implications instantaneously if they see him conducting *with* the syncopation—always providing that it is an isolated instance, and not one which establishes its own pattern like the famous cross-rhythm in the finale of the Schumann Piano Concerto:

Ex. 72

From the spring of 1956 it became increasingly clear to everyone that Dimitri Mitropoulos was, in the words of Aaron Copland, "a lost cause", and he

shared his duties in the 1957–58 with a co-conductor before retiring altogether, and dying two years later, on 2 November, 1960, at the age of sixty-
four, a broken man. And it was not the public, nor the critics—though
B. H. Haggin had been particularly brutal in his reviews—but the New York
Philharmonic itself which had broken him.

Individually, the members of the Philharmonic are typical New Yorkers
—brash, genial, generous, kind to their children, and with that sizeable chip
on their shoulders which is common to so many members of their profession,
of all nationalities. And like so many members of their profession, of all
nationalities, they are mostly disappointed soloists, who regard their daily
round with the Philharmonic as so much time wasted doing something which
they never really wanted to do anyway. Or so they say—for in New York the
artist's one unforgiveable sin is to display enthusiasm and dedication for his
work. Sometimes, in performance, the New York Philharmonic will play like
a very great orchestra indeed, so much so that when one witnesses the free-
for-all which constitutes their rehearsals, one wonders why on earth they ever
bother to rehearse at all—not that they ever do bother, very much. The co-
conductor in question, who was shortly to assume full command of the
Philharmonic, was none other than Leonard Bernstein, whose rise to the
directorship of the orchestra at the age of thirty-nine had—by American
standards—been meteoric, though it would have been nothing unusual in
pre-war Europe (or pre-war America, for that matter). For the image of the
conductor as a person who is all-powerful and little short of a dictator is in-
consistent with the concept of democracy so dear to the heart of the American,
and in accepting the principle of the conductor they had hitherto made the
unconscious stipulation of requiring him to be by all means foreign, preferably
Hungarian—or from some other European country whose only claim to fame
was one of picturesqueness—and as eccentric as possible. Bernstein was not
only the youngest conductor of the Philharmonic in its long history, but he
was also its first American-born musical director since Theodore Thomas.
All America—the whole musical world, in fact—was agog to see what he
would accomplish in his new position of authority.

Leonard Bernstein had been born in Lawrence, Massachusetts, on 15
August, 1918, of a family of Russian extraction. His early musical training
was achieved in the face of acute parental opposition, and while his father
was prepared to send him to Harvard University, he made it quite clear that
piano lessons under Heinrich Gebhart must be at his son's own responsibility.
Mitropoulos, ironically enough, was the first person to encourage him to take
up conducting, after he had graduated from Harvard *magnum cum laude* in
1938, and he enrolled the following year at the Curtis Institute in Philadelphia

under Fritz Reiner—former musical director of the Dresden State Opera, and later to succeed Kubelik in Chicago—for conducting, Randall Thompson for composition, and Isabella Vengerova for piano. (Bernstein had in fact elected to study piano with Rudolf Serkin who, with exquisite tact, had suggested that "he would be happier under Miss Vengerova".) For the next three summers he attended Koussevitsky's conducting classes at Tanglewood, where the Berkshire Music Center had opened, at Koussevitsky's initiative, in 1940—Bernstein's first summer there. He left Curtis in the summer of 1941, and the following year found him transcribing jazz improvisations for the New York publishers, Harms-Remick, at $25 a week. During the summer of 1943—the Berkshire Music Center being now closed—Koussevitsky invited Bernstein to come up to Stockbridge, his home near Tanglewood, to illustrate on the piano a lecture which he was giving in aid of the local Red Cross. Three days later Bernstein found himself the new assistant conductor to Koussevitsky's Stockbridge neighbour, Artur Rodzinski, who had just been appointed musical director of the New York Philharmonic.

On Sunday, 14 November, 1943, Bruno Walter—who was to have appeared as guest conductor of the Philharmonic—fell ill, and Rodzinski insisted that Bernstein be allowed to substitute for him. It was, of course, a unique opportunity for Bernstein, and he made the most of it. And it was an occasion which appealed immensely to a nation whose parochial instinct is unleavened by scepticism—"A shoe-string catch in center field. Make it and you're a hero. Muff it and you're a dope. He made it", reported the New York *Daily News*. But to show exceptional talent on an isolated occasion, when a whole nation is wishing you well, is not necessarily indicative of reserves of stamina, and it was now up to Bernstein to consolidate the overnight sensation which he had caused. The opportunity to do so came barely a month later when Howard Barlow—a conductor with none of the drawing-power of a Walter or a Rodzinski—was compelled, again through illness, to cancel a guest engagement with the Philharmonic, and Bernstein again substituted. The Philharmonic, in particular, were no longer disposed to allow Bernstein the benefit of any doubt which may have existed in their minds the previous month, and were, on the contrary, only too prepared to give him as hard a time as possible. But the concert was an outstanding success. On 28 and 30 January, 1944, Fritz Reiner—who had just become the conductor of the Pittsburgh Symphony—invited Bernstein to come and conduct his own *Jeremiah* Symphony, whose performance Bernstein repeated with the Boston Symphony Orchestra in Boston on 18 and 19 February. At the end of March Rodzinski offered him three dates with the Philharmonic, with authority to choose his own programmes, which included the *Jeremiah* Symphony with Jennie Tourel as soprano soloist. In April he conducted the première of his ballet, *Fancy Free*, and in May he received the Music Critics' Award for the *Jeremiah* Symphony.

After his first sensational season, Bernstein was in demand all over America—but only as a guest conductor, and the Rochester Philharmonic was among other orchestras which turned down his application for a permanent post, awarding it instead to Erich Leinsdorf—later to become permanent conductor of the Boston Symphony in succession to Charles Munch. The Broadway première of his *On the Town* on 28 December, 1944, was to bring in a share of $100,000 for Bernstein when it was later made into a film, and this enabled him to take over the New York City Symphony in 1945—a post which is honorary, and had been occupied by Leopold Stokowski the previous year. In the spring of 1946, the war now being over, Bernstein came to Europe for the first time, conducting the Czech Philharmonic in Prague and later the London Philharmonic in London. His ballet *Fancy Free* received its Covent Garden première and a second ballet, *Facsimile*, its Metropolitan première in October. By now Bernstein was writing a second symphony, *The Age of Anxiety*, based on the poem by W. H. Auden, for piano and orchestra, which was composed over a period of two years of extensive touring which took him as far afield as Tel-Aviv, and completed on a tour of the Pittsburgh orchestra which Bernstein had taken over from Reiner while the latter was in Europe. The Second Symphony received its first performance with the Boston Symphony Orchestra under Koussevitsky on 8 April, 1949—Koussevitsky's last season as director of the orchestra—with the composer as soloist. On Koussevitsky's death, two years later, Bernstein assumed control of his conducting class at Tanglewood until 1955, when his place was taken by another former Koussevitsky pupil, Eleazar de Carvalho, later conductor of the St. Louis Symphony. A one-act opera, *Trouble in Tahiti*, received its first performance at the Brandeis Arts Festival in June 1952, and in November 1953 Bernstein made his début at La Scala in a revival of Cherubini's *Medea*, which provoked savage comment from the European press, but did not prevent his being invited back for a dozen or more reappearances before his appointment to the New York Philharmonic. *Candide* appeared in 1956, *West Side Story* in 1957, and the Third Symphony, *Kaddish*, in 1963.

Bernstein, now fifty-one, has completed twelve seasons at the head of the New York Philharmonic, and has announced his retirement, with Pierre Boulez from Cleveland as his heir. Twelve seasons are enough to reveal even the most elusive aspects of any conductor or any orchestra, and it cannot be said that our final assessment of either is altogether complimentary. But whatever criticisms—and they are many—may be levelled against Bernstein's extraordinary antics on the podium, and equally extraordinary tactics in rehearsal, he is a figure whom it is impossible to ignore. His performances of the Fifth Symphonies of Shostakovitch and Sibelius, of *Le Sacre du Printemps*, and of the Mahler Eighth at the Albert Hall—all with the London Symphony Orchestra within the last two years, and at the initiative of their ex-manager, Fleischmann—have revealed a preoccupation and an obsession with the musical substance which is entirely compelling, for although there may be other ways of achieving the same end, it remains beyond dispute that Bernstein fulfils the prime and imperative function of any conductor in bringing the music abundantly to life. As for the New York Philharmonic, their playing under Leonard Bernstein shows greater inner composure than it did under Mitropoulos, who was perhaps a necessary sacrifice to the caprice of what is— potentially—one of the world's great orchestras. It has been given to Bernstein to redeem that sacrifice, just as it fell to Mitropoulos to redeem the ten-year sacrifice of the Philharmonic itself to the whims and tantrums of Toscanini.

Chapter 17

THE POWER GAME

It is reasonable to suppose that the retirements of Georg Szell, who is seventy-one, and of Eugene Ormandy, who is sixty-nine, must also be only a matter of time—though both are still extremely active men, and it would be equally reasonable to suppose that they will continue in their present positions for many years to come. Szell, who was born in Budapest on 7 June, 1897, has been musical director of the Cleveland Orchestra since January 1946, with twenty-three seasons to his credit. Ormandy, born in the same Hungarian city on 18 November, 1899, has been musical director of the Philadelphia Orchestra since September 1938, and with thirty seasons to his credit his tenure has been the longest in America since that of Frederick Stock in Chicago. (Nor is Ormandy quite such a musical charlatan as this book would appear to have painted him, for although the sound which he produces from the Philadelphia Orchestra is diabolically out of style and out of context in almost everything on which he lays his hands, his performances reveal, in their overall sense, a consistently high standard of orchestral playing which is entirely unknown in Britain.) Erich Leinsdorf, who succeeded Charles Munch at the head of the Boston Symphony Orchestra in 1962, has himself been superseded by William Steinberg who now divides his time between Boston and Pittsburgh. And the Chicago Symphony, after only four years under Jean Martinon, engaged the guest services of Carlo Maria Giulini and Georg Solti for the 1968-69 season.

Together with the New York Philharmonic, this makes five major American orchestras whose managements are searching, in varying degrees of earnest, for suitable successors to their present incumbents. Nor is the European picture very much more encouraging, for while the Berlin Philharmonic have Herbert von Karajan—who, at sixty, is also musical director of the Salzburg Festival and of La Scala, Milan—and the Leningrad Philharmonic have Yevgeni Mravinski and Kurt Sanderling, the only other European conductors of comparable stature are Otto Klemperer and Carlo Maria Giulini, the respective musical and co-musical directors of the New Philharmonia. Klemperer's function, at eighty-three, is now little more than nominal, while that of Giulini, at fifty-one, is now virtually non-existent by reason of the pressure of his work on the Continent which, combined with the absence of a very robust constitution, has led the Philharmonia to seek, with increasing insistence, the services of Rafael Frühbeck de Burgos. The ministrations of Václav Neumann with the Leipzig Gewandhaus Orchestra are not conspicuously happy, for he is not really a conductor at all, and the Vienna Philharmonic have been effectively without a musical director since Furtwängler's death in 1954. Only the Amsterdam Concertgebouw would seem to have found, in the thirty-eight-year-old Bernard Haitink, a potential successor to that orchestra's great tradition which—apart from Willem Kes, its conductor for the first seven years of its existence—has beheld only two other permanent conductors: Willem Mengelberg, from 1895 to 1938, and Eduard van Beinum, who became Mengelberg's assistant in 1932, and succeeded him in 1938 until his own premature death early in 1958.

The young conductor has to start somewhere, and there resides behind the relative reputations of every second and third-line orchestra any amount of talent which is there for the asking, if only the managements of our major orchestras would be prepared to abandon their present policy of regarding prospective candidates in the light of a "popularity poll"—to use Adlai Stevenson's words in the American election campaign in 1956. There was a time when the recommendation of a distinguished musician carried sufficient weight and conviction to ensure the election of a young conductor to a responsible post—responsible, that is to say, in terms of his immediate environment, and where his talents could be allowed to mature in their own good time. The history of conducting holds countless instances of the personal testimonial which was effective because there was no necessity to aim higher at that juncture of the young artist's career, which could develop freely and naturally and at its own speed—and often a spectacular speed, for there were at that time few extra-musical considerations which could impede its progress. But with the increasing encroachment of mass-media this has ceased to be effectively true, for the minds of public and management alike have become jaundiced with the obsession that everything must be weighed in the balance, every factor taken into consideration, every conceivable form of statistical analysis applied, before they can feel prepared to take a decision which, even then, is no less fallible than the convinced testimony of the distinguished musician had been in the past—and may indeed be very much more so. And even the distinguished musician himself is now much more prone to the vicissitudes of mass-media, for his recommendation will now be tempered by self-consciousness, and a consideration of the implications of "public relations"—an activity which should be the concern of managements alone.

It is no longer possible to hold an implicit belief in the potential of a young artist: there must be tangible evidence, for all to see, as well.

The delicate and sensitive structure which had enabled every conductor from Bülow to Karajan to achieve the first rung in the ladder of their subsequent climb to fame has been destroyed—and it is the public relations "image" of those qualities which the potential conductor is nowadays allegedly required to possess which has destroyed it. No longer is the artist's opinion of a younger colleague of any importance and if it is sought at all, it is only that it may be weighed against other and supposedly weightier considerations—where it must inevitably be found wanting. The *Time* issue of 19 January, 1968, carried a feature article on nearly a dozen young conductors between the ages of thirty-four and forty-one, claiming that "the conductor's profession bears as little resemblance to what it was fifty years ago as does the life of an astronaut to a World-War I pilot's". This may be very true, but its truth lies not in the fact that the conductor has changed—though he tends to be somewhat more travelled—but in the fact that the public has had its image of him forcibly changed by courtesy of such magazines as *Time*. Nor have the conductors in question had very much say in the matter.

At Tanglewood in the summer of 1956, I was invited to meet John D. Rockefeller III, to discuss with him the plans for a music school at the Lincoln Center—then only a project still on the drawing-board. It was proposed to inaugurate a school which, with the finest teachers and the finest facilities, would cater for the needs of the finest young musicians in the land. There seemed little point in arguing that the finest teachers might already be committed elsewhere, and that the finest young musicians *ipso facto* might not feel the necessity of further academic training—apart from the fact that the Berkshire Music Center was already fulfilling all three conditions already—and it bore home the folly of attempting arbitrarily to create anything at all from a soil as resistant to growth as that of Manhattan musical life. The nourishment which that soil could afford was brief, and could support the life of any flower through a progress of spectacular growth and ignominious death —like the death, two years earlier, of the NBC Orchestra, whose members had been arbitrarily recruited as being "the finest in the land". The following extract from the writing of Paul Henry Lang sums up the point:

> Here then is the America teeming with hundreds of symphony orchestras, with thousands of glee clubs and choral societies, with composers-in-residence and string quartets on campus—yet an America which enters this period of the 20th century without a single radio symphony orchestra and with a TV opera theatre that becomes more anemic from year to year, for want of a sponsor.

Here is the America with five hundred or more FM Good Music stations that play nothing but recordings from Gesualdo to Stockhausen—yet when asked to pay $25 for the broadcasting of a full-length contemporary opera, hurriedly take it off the air.

Here is the America with the most up-to-date, the most expensive, the most futuristic electronic musical device, the RCA Synthesiser at Columbia University—yet with a copyright law whose basic thoughts were codified under the reign of Queen Anne in 1709, retaining provisions clumsily applied to LPs, stereophonic tapes, television, juke boxes, written into the law in 1909 before any of these and many other modern devices were ever thought of, and never changed.

Here is the America with hundreds of opera workshops, but with 350 of its excellent native singers gainfully employed in the professional opera houses of Europe.

And here is the America that, through a public outcry of heartwarming intensity, shocked even a state legislature and a city council and stopped the bulldozers at the very threshold of Carnegie Hall —the America that, at this moment, is erecting in the Lincoln Center for the Performing Arts the largest and most ambitious combination of cultural edifices in modern times.

A symbol, we take it, of a bright future and of great and wonderful things to come.[1]

Any system which can admit the principle of the guest conductor as a standard feature of orchestral and opera house practice is to be roundly condemned, and although managements, in their lack of enterprise, have brought this tyranny largely on themselves, they are not entirely to blame. Nor are a public who, in their docile acceptance of the practice, have been equally conditioned in their predictable reactions to the power of the printed word, elegantly couched in the advance-publicity brochures which are pushed through their letter-boxes. And still less are an orchestra whose members, in the absence of a permanent conductor who fulfils their collective ideal, must inevitably tend to prefer itinerant diversion to indigent pedestrianism. Ultimately to blame are the conductors themselves, for in embracing such a principle they are committing themselves, their orchestras and their art to protracted and inescapable suicide. In our own capital the practice has become pernicious, and is yearly becoming more so. Apart from Colin Davis— since 1967 musical director of the BBC Symphony Orchestra—our London orchestras have neither permanent musical directors, nor permanent associate conductors, nor even permanent assistant conductors, whose actual function is anything more than nominal or, at best, extremely spasmodic. The situation on the continent of Europe—with many and notable exceptions—is scarcely

[1] P. H. Lang: *One Hundred Years of Music in America*, G. Schirmer, New York, 1961.

better, and in attempting to fulfil a host of guest-engagements abroad, their own "resident" musical directors are undermining the artistic life of their own orchestras and communities. With sickening facility, *Time* magazine analyses the effect, without troubling to diagnose the root cause:

> And the conductors? There are not enough good ones to go round. Now that most of them jet off to play musical podiums with the world's far-flung orchestras, they scarcely have time to guide the artistic policy of their own ensembles, plan the programs, select the soloists, learn new works, rehearse and perform—let alone address fund-raising luncheons of the ladies' clubs. The best of today's conductors are thus tired, ageing, or both . . .

It is clear that if the conductor can no longer have time to devote himself to the artistic policy of his orchestra, the burden of this responsibility must devolve upon the shoulders of the next most qualified individual—the man on the spot—and it is ironic that those individuals best qualified to do this are residents of the very cities where their services are rendered gratuitous by the presence of permanent and resident musical directors. At the Performing Right Society's annual luncheon in 1967, Lord Goodman spoke of "the dearth in this country of managements and artistic directors who were in any way equipped to dictate an effective policy for our orchestras"—not by virtue of inexperience, or lack of potential, but by the unwillingness of individual boards of directors, impresarios, orchestras, conductors, and managements themselves to see such authority placed in the hands of a single individual. In consequence, our national instinct for "muddling through", for "losing every battle save the last", has been allowed to prevail, at least three eminently qualified artistic directors in recent years have been compelled to resign (or have given the whole orchestra notice), and a misguided sense of democracy which must always defer to the lowest common factor has become a tyranny which bids fair to strangle the musical life of our capital. The managements of our provincial orchestras, on the other hand, show an enlightenment which is in strong contrast to those of London, in having successively maintained both artistic and musical directors in happy conjunction this many a year—in the case of the Hallé, for twenty-three years. The January 1968 issue of *Time* continues, unalarmed:

> In short, conducting is increasingly becoming a field for younger, more vibrant men—all the more so because of the overriding example of Leonard Bernstein. His projection and box-office appeal have made him as much a model for conductors in his era as Toscanini was in his, although, as Bernstein nears 50, even he is slackening his frenetic pace somewhat. In this image-conscious culture, every orchestra wants its conductor to have some of Bernstein's in-

calculable personality force—what Conductor Charles Munch calls
the "magic emanation" that can lift a conductor's performance
above the mere exercise of knowledge and professional skill . . .

Bernstein's initial success had been at the instigation of Artur Rodzinski, and
with the close connivance of Serge Koussevitsky—two musicians whose distinction yet carried insufficient weight for their combined recommendations
(together with a third, from Fritz Reiner) to be of any effect on managements
who had become besotted by the image of Toscanini. It had therefore required the catalyst of a spectacular début with a spectacular orchestra—an
opportunity which has been accorded to but few. Yet overnight it prescribed
the pattern for success. Mitropoulos—Bernstein's predecessor with the New
York Philharmonic—had of course enjoyed a comparable success with the
Berlin Philharmonic in 1930, in his last-minute substitution for Egon Petri,
and the history of music-making is rich in such anecdotes of the spectacular
début, of which that of Colin Davis with the Philharmonia, in a concert-
performance of *Don Giovanni* in 1959, is perhaps the most recent in this
benighted country. But the spectacular début is no substitute for spectacular
artistry, whose manifestation is more frequently the fruit of other and quite
different creative impulses. Such artistry must always embrace a prepared-
ness to take the fullest advantage of every opportunity, however trivial, and
this had been the secret of Toscanini's success. Yet it must also embrace the
prior conviction of a qualified sponsor of that artistry, and it is pertinent to
enquire into the less spectacular fates of some of Bernstein's—and Davis'—
contemporaries.

These represent a generation which was, in one way or another, directly
involved in the 1939–45 War and its immediate after-effects. One of the very
few benign symptoms of the war itself had been the universal renaissance of
an interest in the creative arts, and in music in particular—an interest whose
requirements had been amply met, if not always happily fulfilled, by a generation of conductors who were no longer eligible for national service. The war
itself had, too, afforded notable opportunities to younger conductors who, like
Bernstein, were exempt from military service on medical grounds. But its
general effect was to engender the conflicting spirits of impatience and apathy,
philosophical acceptance and despair, in those musicians whom its catastrophe engulfed. The war over, a spirit of musical opportunism became rife,
and a younger generation of conductors could take shelter behind the excuse
that its elbows were not sharp enough to enter the general mêlée, or that the
war itself had interfered with their musical studies—nor was this very much
less than true, for a further effect of the war had been to promote in them a
spirit of caution and sensitivity not conspicuously evident in their elders.

But in the course of time, new conductors began to emerge, Guido Cantelli and Wolfgang Sawallisch among their number. Cantelli's premature death in an air-crash on 24 November, 1956, at the age of thirty-six, was universally mourned, for in his concerts with the Philharmonia in particular he displayed a youthfulness and extreme of sensitivity which, as a protégé of Toscanini, were at considerable variance with the methods and results of that *Maestro*. Cantelli's sense of pitch and timbre swiftly became proverbial, and I recall the infinite care with which, in 1952, he sought an exact gradation of *crescendo* and *diminuendo* from a single tam-tam stroke at a rehearsal of Busoni's *Sarabande and Cortège* at EMI Studios, for a performance at the Festival Hall the following day—and his subsequent dismay when the well-meaning percussion-player responded: "That's all right, Mr. Cantelli. We'll have a great big one tomorrow." (And this invited inevitable comparison, four years later, with the immaculately equipped percussion section of the Boston Symphony Orchestra, and the anxiety of its members to submit their instruments—and the music—to exhaustive enquiry *before* rehearsal.) In the overture to *Romeo and Juliet*, Cantelli applied his critical ear to the chording of the opening woodwind passage, experimenting with the change from Tchaikowsky's original text to a dovetailing of the clarinet and bassoon parts. The experiment continued, with much allusion to the original and back, and concluded with the collapse over his music stand of a sobbing Cantelli, crying: "Ho sbagliato . . . Ho sbagliato . . . I was wrong!"—for this had been a matter of veritable life and death for him. And it afforded the equally poignant picture of such hardened artists as the late Messrs. Jack Thurston and Jack Alexandra patting him on the shoulder and attempting to console him.

But elsewhere the post-war harvest in the field of conducting had not been so abundant, and since this could not reasonably be attributed to any very substantial decline in potential, its cause lay necessarily at other doors. These doors had remained effectively shut to the free world since 1933, in the case of Germany, and 1938, in the case of Austria. In Leipzig—whose traditions had nurtured the talents of Sullivan, Coates and Boult, from this country—they still remain closed for a western world, but those to the musical traditions of western Germany and Austria have been reopened for more than twenty years, and plentiful evidence of new talent began to emerge from them in the early 'fifties. Vienna, as anxious to speed the youthful and parting guest on his way as she is ever reluctant to give harbour to native genius, has been especially prolific, and the *Kapellmeisterschule* of her Music Academy (until 1952 under the direction of Clemens Krauss, and since then in the able hands of Hans Swarowsky) has adorned the talents of a notable contingent of young artists—among them André Vandernoot, present conductor of the Brussels Radio Orchestra and musical director of the Theatre de la Monnaie, Claudio Abbado, present assistant-conductor of La Scala, and Zubin Mehta, present conductor of the Los Angeles Philharmonic, whom *Time* quotes as saying:

> Go to the young conductors who are not making it and you will hear how we shouldn't push ourselves or sell ourselves, how they don't have the right connections or the right opportunities. But to make your way in a conducting career, you not only have to have opportunities, you have to make them a success.

Success is not everywhere to be measured, however, in terms of Apollonian good looks and musical fluency within a very restricted range of showpieces, though in its worldly acquisition they are useful and perhaps necessary adjuncts to it. The young conductor has every right to push himself and sell himself providing that his prospective clientèle are as convinced as he is of the artistic value and viability of the article which he is pushing and selling—and know how to appreciate it. We may be assured that the article is both valuable and viable in the case of Mr. Mehta himself, since his services are clearly everywhere in demand, but though his reasoning is admirable, he is impatient of the wrong things. For neither is success to be measured in quantitive terms, and there can be greater satisfaction and sense of artistic fulfilment in realising the solution to the problem of an isolated phrase of music in the solitude of one's room at the age of seventy than in finding a whole city at one's feet at the age of twenty-five. The enduring bond which unites all artists worthy of the name is one which recognises and acknowledges the fundamental seriousness and sanctity of their calling, which is prepared to involve itself only in such experiences as further musical ends, and which can survive all the false prophets of a musical Baal. This does not mean the public display of the garb of humility, although there have in all conscience been enough conductors only too willing to don one publicly. But it does mean the humility of a Kleiber or a Furtwängler or a Karajan or a Munch, of a Stokowski or a Koussevitsky or a Szell, a Strauss or a Mahler or a Nikisch, of being able and willing to come to terms with one's art and with oneself in the privacy of one's own room—a humility which would astonish orchestra and public and critics alike, could they but be privy to it.

One must therefore reserve judgement upon the younger generation, according them every licence to make their mistakes and to learn from them in the privacy of the rehearsal-room, but otherwise to confine oneself to reading portents which are not wholly encouraging. I find it disturbing that Thomas Schippers, in his concert with the New York Philharmonic in

M

December 1967, should have so failed in his duties to the soloist, Abbey Simon, in his accompaniment of the Rachmaninoff Third Piano Concerto—a work specifically written for America and which Gustav Mahler, at its New York Philharmonic première in 1909, had incidentally taken the trouble to commit to memory. I find it disturbing that Lorin Maazel, in his concert with the London Symphony Orchestra in 1965, should have so failed the soloist, Vladimir Ashkenazy, in his accompaniment of the Brahms Second Concerto—because he *had* committed it to memory—and, at a concert with the Vienna Philharmonic, for all his prodigious equipment, should have given (and later recorded) a performance of the *Hamlet* Overture by Tchaikowsky which was bereft of all trace of definable or indefinable temperament. I find it disturbing that Claudio Abbado, in his performance in 1967 of the *Italian* Symphony by Mendelssohn, should have occasioned the London Symphony Orchestra to stumble and to blunder in a work necessarily more familiar to them than it had been to the Berlin Philharmonic under Furtwängler and Kleiber, and Mendelssohn himself, at their own respective ages of thirty-three—an age when any conductor should be able to reveal more enduring qualities. In all four instances the critics, out of deference to their established reputations, abjured from a castigation which they would have mercilessly accorded any unknown conductor. Such is the power of the printed word to deceive even the critics.

Although individual judgements will differ, we have none the less an absolute criterion on which to base our assessment of the great conductors of the past, and of the older generation of conductors of the present day, and this is inextricably bound up with their length of service at the head of their respective orchestras—twenty-three seasons with the Cleveland in the case of Georg Szell, twenty-four with the Hallé in the case of Sir John Barbirolli, twenty-five with the Boston Symphony in the case of Koussevitsky, twenty-six and thirty with the Philadelphia in the cases of Stokowski and Ormandy respectively, twenty-seven and thirty-four with the Berlin Philharmonic in the cases of Nikisch and Furtwängler, thirty-eight with the Chicago Symphony in the case of Frederick Stock, and forty-three with the Amsterdam Concertgebouw in the case of Willem Mengelberg. The respective merits of these orchestras, viewed as a continuum, enable us to gauge with some accuracy the respective merits of their conductors, and if the Hallé Orchestra is clearly no longer as good, let us say, as the Philharmonia or the London Symphony, player for player, this is not to suggest that Otto Klemperer or Carlo Maria Giulini or Istvan Kertesz are necessarily better conductors than Barbirolli, for they have not been associated with these orchestras for so long a period of time, and their contact with them ranges, as has already been said, from the spasmodic to the purely nominal. Barbirolli has sought to invest in the capital of the Hallé Orchestra instead of living off it, as some conductors of other orchestras have done, and one can only say that if the Philharmonia or the London Symphony or any of the other London orchestras should choose to invest in the services of a permanent musical director of the potential of Sir John Barbirolli, and over a period of twenty-four seasons, they would become very much better orchestras than they already are. But a direct comparison of the Hallé with the Cleveland Orchestra enables us to say something about the respective merits of Barbirolli and Szell.

With the younger generation, however, no such criteria exist, and any such assessment must inevitably be speculative. It will be interesting to see, for example, whether Colin Davis will survive at the head of the BBC Symphony for as long as, or longer than, Bernstein has survived at the head of the New York Philharmonic, and whether he can translate what is potentially the finest—though as yet faceless—orchestra in this country into terms more enduring than those of the New York Philharmonic which has remained one of the potentially finest orchestras in America for the last sixty years (apart from its years of association with Mengelberg, when it became not only a fine but a great orchestra). For the prolonged term of office is necessarily indicative of the stamina of the conductor in question, and in the case of the great orchestra, or that which achieves greatness under a single conductor—like the Concertgebouw under Mengelberg, or the Philadelphia under Stokowski—the question of stamina becomes one of mutual concern to both conductor and orchestra. No great orchestra will tolerate indefinitely the ministrations of a conductor who has shown himself conclusively to be anything less than one hundred per cent professional over a period of ten or fifteen years, and that the Amsterdam, Chicago, Berlin, Philadelphia, Boston, Hallé and Cleveland orchestras should have continued to re-engage their musical directors for far longer periods of time is conclusive evidence of their respective conductors' professional qualifications *per se*. This implies the constant renewal of the substance of music-making, and the conductor's daily rededication of his art to its service—qualities which, in the hand of an artist of lesser stature, would inevitably degenerate at some juncture into idle and unproductive routine.

The question of the opera house is more complex, for here there is a necessary interplay and conflict of temperament at a level to which the orchestra and public are not privy, and length of tenure is neither an absolute criterion nor an infallible guide. Nevertheless, Kleiber's twelve seasons as general musical director of the Berlin State Opera, and twenty-nine seasons of association with the Teatro Colón in Buenos Aires must constitute a record—not in terms of tenure, which has been exceeded on occasion, but in terms of the standards of performance attained. These standards must, by the very nature of the operatic medium, be ephemeral—and this is perhaps their most enduring quality, for each and every performance must be conceived and executed as something existing in its own right, and for its own sake alone. This constant rivalry between the essence and the substance of music-making, between the craft of conception and the art of realisation, between the pursuit of an intellectual absolute and the acceptance of intelligent compromise, is the very stuff of which the great musical experience is made—the imperishable quality of an interpretative art which constantly asks the question, not of "Why?", but of "How?".

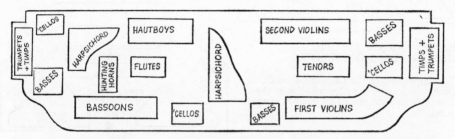

Ex. 1: PLAN OF DRESDEN OPERA ORCHESTRA UNDER JOSEPH ADOLPH HASSE

The Dresden Opera Orchestra as described by Jean-Jacques Rousseau. Hasse had become first Kapellmeister in 1731, and made the first major operatic innovation of taking his place on the further side—nearest the audience—of the orchestra pit, with the orchestra grouped in front of him, the second violins, violas, flutes and oboes with their backs to the stage. Hitherto, the whole orchestra had faced the stage, the "violin-conductor" at their head being compelled to divide his attention between the stage and the orchestra behind him. This was a practice which persisted in some opera houses—notably the Bolshoi in Moscow—until the early years of the present century. Weber, arriving in Dresden in 1817, introduced the following further innovations within the orchestra itself:

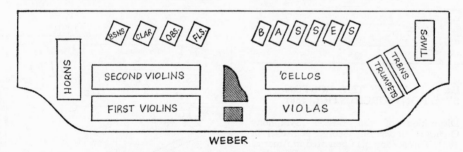

WEBER

Ex. 2: PLAN OF WEBER'S ORCHESTRA AT DRESDEN

M*

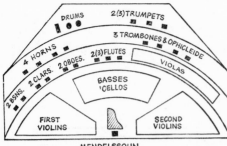

Ex. 3: PLAN OF LEIPZIG GEWANDHAUS ORCHESTRA

The disposition of the Leipzig Gewandhaus Orchestra under Felix Mendelssohn in 1835. The orchestra was placed on steeply terraced risers.

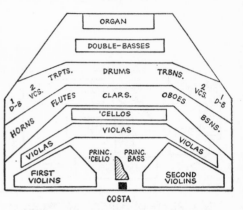

Ex. 4: PLAN OF THE LONDON PHILHARMONIC SOCIETY ORCHESTRA

The disposition of the London Philharmonic Society Orchestra under Sir Michael Costa in 1846. The absurdly complex arrangement reduced definition to the minimum, and incurred Wagner's strongest censure.

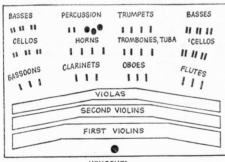

Ex. 5: PLAN OF THE BOSTON SYMPHONY ORCHESTRA, 1881

Disposition of the Boston Symphony Orchestra under Sir George Henschel in 1881. This seating plan persisted in America until 1900, and was adopted by Theodore Thomas in New York and Chicago, and Anton Seidl in New York.

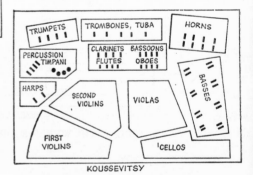

Ex. 6: PLAN OF THE BOSTON SYMPHONY ORCHESTRA, 1925

Disposition of the Boston Symphony Orchestra under Serge Koussevitsky in 1925. This seating plan became the standard for all American and many European orchestras.

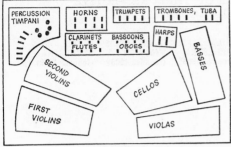

MUNCH

Ex. 7: PLAN OF THE BOSTON SYMPHONY ORCHESTRA, 1951

Charles Munch introduced the above seating plan to the Boston Symphony in 1951, which has the advantage of placing the violas nearest the audience, where they can be most clearly heard, and of establishing a direct contact between the 'cello and bass sections. It is a principle which is employed by Sir John Barbirolli and a number of other conductors—the author included.

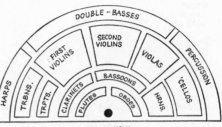

STOKOWSKI

Ex. 8: PLAN OF THE PHILADELPHIA ORCHESTRA, 1932

A 1932 experiment with the seating of the Philadelphia Orchestra under Leopold Stokowski. The concert platform of the Academy of Music in Philadelphia is backed by a shell which—in theory—served to act as a resonator to the entire string section placed close to its reflecting walls. The definition and tone-quality of the individual wind players, brought nearer to the audience, was also improved. The experiment was abandoned in the face of heated prejudice from the public, the critics, and the musicians themselves, but a number of its salient features were revived at a recent performance of Birtwistle's *Nomos*—at the composer's specification—in a Promenade Concert at the Royal Albert Hall.

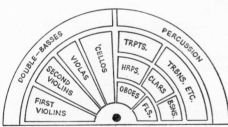

STOKOWSKI

Ex. 9: CURRENT STOKOWSKI SEATING PLAN

The "classic" Stokowski seating plan. The division of the whole body of strings to the left and winds to the right leads to greatly improved ensemble in—and within—every section, and to a broad antiphonal effect between the string and wind choirs. The principal elements of the string quartet and the wind quartet are brought together at the front of the platform, and several lines of communication opened to the more distant desks of the orchestra. It has been employed by other orchestras—the most recent being the Beirut Symphony Orchestra—with unvarying success.

TABLE OF SIX MAJOR AMERICAN ORCHESTRAS
WITH THE TERMS OF OFFICE OF THEIR RESPECTIVE
PERMANENT CONDUCTORS

NEW YORK PHILHARMONIC (founded 1842)	BOSTON SYMPHONY (founded 1881)	CHICAGO SYMPHONY (founded 1891)	PHILADELPHIA ORCHESTRA (founded 1900)	MINNEAPOLIS SYMPHONY (founded 1903)	CLEVELAND ORCHESTRA (founded 1918)
Hill, Timm, Loder, etc. (1842–49)					
Eisfeld, Bergmann, etc. (1849–65)					
Bergmann (1865–76)					
L. Damrosch (1876–77)					
Thomas (1877–91)	Henschel (1881–84)				
Seidl (1891–93)	Gericke (1884–89)				
	Nikisch (1889–93)				
	Paur (1893–98)	Thomas (1891–1905)			
Paur (1898–1902)	Gericke (1898–1906)				
W. Damrosch (1902–03)			Scheel (1900–07)		
Guests (1903–06)		Stock (1905–43)		Oberhoffer (1903–22)	
Safonoff (1906–09)	Muck (1906–08)		Pohlig (1907–12)		
Mahler (1909–11)	Fiedler (1908–12)				
Stransky (1911–21)	Muck (1912–18)		Stokowski (1912–38)		
	Rabaud (1918–19)				Sokoloff (1918–33)
Mengelberg (1921–30)	Monteux (1919–24)			Guests (1922–23)	
	Koussevitsky (1924–49)			Verbrugghen (1923–31)	
Toscanini (1930–36)				Ormandy (1931–36)	Rodzinski (1933–43)
Barbirolli (1936–41)				Guests (1936–37)	
Guests (1941–43)			Ormandy (1938 to present)	Mitropoulos (1937–49)	
Rodzinski (1943–47)		Defauw (1943–47)			Leinsdorf (1943–44)

NEW YORK PHILHARMONIC (founded 1842)	BOSTON SYMPHONY (founded 1881)	CHICAGO SYMPHONY (founded 1891)	PHILADELPHIA ORCHESTRA (founded 1900)	MINNEAPOLIS SYMPHONY (founded 1903)	CLEVELAND ORCHESTRA (founded 1918)
Guests (1947–49)		Rodzinski (1947–48)			Guests (1944–46)
Stokowski-Mitropoulos (1949–50)	Munch (1949–62)	Guests (1948–50)		Dorati (1948–58)	Szell (1946 to present)
Mitropoulos (1950–58)		Kubelik (1950–55)			
Bernstein (1958–68)		Reiner (1955–62)		Samuels (1958–59)	
	Leinsdorf (1962–69)	Guests (1962–64)		Scrodetchevsky (1959 to present)	
	Steinberg (present musical dir.)	Martinon (1964–68)			

The following list is intended only as a guide, and makes neither the claim nor the attempt to be in any way exhaustive. Its purpose is to show a number of recordings which are actually in existence, and to serve as a commentary on the recording medium as a whole by revealing facets which might be less readily visible in a more complete version. Its selection of a team of eleven conductors has been governed by a number of factors, the most important being geographical, and it does not include the names of those conductors—Karajan, Szell, Fricsay, Giulini, Cantelli, Bernstein, Mitropoulos, Ormandy —whose recording reputations have been made largely since the war, and more particularly since the advent of the long-playing record, since this could only serve to duplicate information which is already available elsewhere. Nor does it include the names of many distinguished conductors—Leo Blech, Karl Muck, Hans Knappertsbusch, Victor de Sabata, Fritz Reiner, Ernest Ansermet, Carl Schuricht—whose names have found, more by accident than design, only passing mention in the body of the text. If there is a tenable reason for these omissions—both from the text, and from the following discography—it is that they had only an incidental influence on the continuing traditions of the five great centres of Berlin, Vienna, Amsterdam, Boston and Philadelphia. Toscanini has also been omitted, for the same reason, and because several fully documented discographies are already in existence.

The great majority of the undermentioned recordings was made between the two world wars, and the listings continue over to include the earlier post-war LPs where this is relevant. The five acoustic recordings by Artur Nikisch have been included for historical reasons. The paucity of "first recorded versions" must suggest that the medium of recording in the earlier years of electrical recording had little appeal to the conductor of distinction, and that the immense musical repertoire received the majority of its maiden recordings at the hands of conductors whose names are virtually unknown today. Leo Blech and Hans Knappertsbusch are notable exceptions, and were responsible for the first recorded versions with the Berlin State Opera Orchestra of a substantial portion of the repertoire. The following list reveals a high proportion of "lollipops"—popular pieces served by their

interpreters as masterly aperitifs to their more substantial work in the opera house and concert hall.

The discography shows the overwhelming musico-political importance of Berlin until the mid 'thirties. Nikisch had recorded the Beethoven Fifth with the Berlin Philharmonic in 1913, and following the war—from his appointment to the Berlin State Opera in 1923—Kleiber dominates the Berlin musical scene with a spectacular range of recordings, while the contributions of Klemperer, Walter and—most surprisingly—Furtwängler are meagre indeed when one considers the extent to which they dominate the immediate post-war years. Kleiber divided his pre-war recording work between the Berlin State Opera and the Berlin Philharmonic until 1934, after which he shared the fate of Klemperer in being absent from the recording field until 1948. Walter's Berlin recordings are confined to four with the Berlin State Opera Orchestra—until his resignation from the Charlottenburg Opera in 1929—and two with the Berlin Philharmonic in 1930. The serial numbers of Furtwängler's earlier recordings with the Berlin Philharmonic show that his entry was tentative, and in fact includes only seven recordings—one of which is a duplication—before Hitler came to power in 1933.

The emphasis then moves to Vienna, with a number of recordings by Weingartner during the 'thirties—interspersed with others made with various London orchestras and two with the Paris Conservatoire Orchestra—Kleiber's four recordings of 1934, eleven by Walter, including the complete first act of *Walküre*, the Mahler Ninth and the *Song of the Earth*, and fourteen pre-war recordings by Clemens Krauss. Mengelberg's recording is confined to three orchestras—three late recordings again with the Berlin Philharmonic, eleven early recordings with the New York Philharmonic, including the first recorded version of *Heldenleben*, and the remainder (an impressive remainder) with his own orchestra, the Amsterdam Concertgebouw, with whom he later re-recorded *Heldenleben*.

The geographical emphasis moves now to America, and to Stokowski's astonishing legacy of recordings with the Philadelphia Orchestra, of which the first "serious" one is the Franck Symphony made in 1927. Behind the anonymity of the numerous operatic "excerpts" lies the hand of an enlightened educator whose highly skilled symphonic "syntheses" brought the medium of opera within the reach of a public whose only operatic experiences had been the largely humdrum repertoire of the Metropolitan Opera and the Chicago Opera Company of the late 'twenties and early 'thirties. The same may be said of his transcriptions of Bach, which masterfully preserve the native spirit of the originals to an audience who might otherwise have been frightened away. Stokowski's first recorded versions include Schoenberg's *Gurrelieder* of 1938—a monumental undertaking for a recording company at that time—Scriabin's *Poème de l'Extase* and *Prometheus* of the same year, and the first complete *Le Sacre du Printemps* in 1929 on four "78" discs as compared with the composer's six, although it is Stokowski who keeps the more faithfully to Stravinsky's metronome markings.

Finally, the Boston Symphony, to whom Koussevitsky remained faithful throughout his recording career—apart from three recordings made on a visit to London in 1932—reveals a certain preponderance of Russian repertoire, and of Prokofieff in particular. Charles Munch's pre-war recordings, understandably enough, had all been with French orchestras, and chiefly with the Paris Conservatoire Orchestra. There are four post-war recordings with the London Philharmonic, one with the Amsterdam Concertgebouw, and two with the New York Philharmonic before he succeeded Koussevitsky in Boston. Thereafter, he displayed an extremely catholic repertoire, although his recordings of French music show a natural preponderance, while those of Berlioz put every living conductor to shame.

Information for this discography has been drawn from a number of sources, and notably R. D. Darrell's *Gramophone Shop Encyclopædia of Recorded Music* (New York, 1936). I should like to take the opportunity of thanking the Librarian of the B.B.C. Record Archives, Mr. Patrick Saul of the British Institute of Recorded Sound, the Editors of *The Gramophone*, and the Curator of the British Museum for the facilities which they have provided. The sequences of serial numbers are not to be taken as the actual recording sequence, as a comparison between alternative serial numbers (e.g. HMV and Victrola) will readily show. In the case of American orchestras, it might have been more logical to have followed the sequence of American rather than European serial numbers, but this would have been to enter a realm of expertise which few have mastered and about which no one agrees.

D.H.M.W.

LIST OF ABBREVIATIONS

AmCol	American Columbia (U.S.A.)	Pat	Pathé (France)
AmVox	American Vox (U.S.A.)	Phil	Philips (Holland)
AusT	Austrian Telefunken (Austria)	Poly	Polydor: Deutsche Grammophon
Br	Brunswick (Britain & U.S.A.)		(Germany)
Cap	Capitol (U.S.A.)	RCA	RCA Victor (U.S.A.)
Col	Columbia (Europe)	T	Telefunken (Europe)
CBS	Columbia Broadcasting System	T/U	Telefunken & Ultraphon
	(U.S.A.)	U	Ultraphon (Czechoslovakia)
Decca	Decca (Europe): London (U.S.A.)	Vic	Victrola (U.S.A.)
Elec	Electrola (Germany)	V/K	Vox/Kristall (Europe)
HMV	His Master's Voice (Europe)	Vox	Vox (Europe)
OisL	Oiseau Lyre	*frv*	*first recorded version*
Parlo	Parlophone (Europe)	★	*pre-electrical (acoustic) recording*

★ All series numbers in *italics* are 10 inch (25 cm) discs.

Serial numbers with the suffix "S" denote a single-sided record at the end of the set to which they refer.

ACO	Amsterdam Concertgebouw Orchestra	NYP	New York Philharmonic Orchestra
		OLa	Orchestre Lamoureux
AYO	American Youth Orchestra	PCO	Orchestre de la Societé des Concerts
ASO	American Symphony Orchestra		du Conservatoire de Paris
Bas	Basel Symphony Orchestra	PhO	Philadelphia Orchestra
Bav	Bavarian State Opera Orchestra	POr	Philharmonia Orchestra, London
BBC	B.B.C. Symphony Orchestra	PPM	Paris Pro Musica Orchestra
BPO	Berlin Philharmonic Orchestra	PPO	Paris Philharmonic Orchestra
BRO	Belgian Radio Orchestra	RPS	Orchestra of the Royal Philharmonic
BSO	Boston Symphony Orchestra		Society, London
BSt	Berlin State Opera Orchestra		(*precursor to the London Philharmonic*
CPO	Czech Philharmonic Orchestra		*Orchestra*)
FNR	French National Radio Orchestra	Tiv	Tivoli Orchestra
LFO	Lucerne Festival Orchestra		(*used in the recording of the 1926 film*
LPO	London Philharmonic Orchestra		*version of Rosenkavalier*)
LSO	London Symphony Orchestra	VPO	Vienna Philharmonic (and State
MFO	Mozart Festival Orchestra, Salzburg		Opera) Orchestra
NBC	N.B.C. Symphony Orchestra	VSO	Vienna Symphony Orchestra
NYC	New York City Symphony Orchestra		

ARTUR NIKISCH

HMV.D8/92	BPO	Beethoven: Symphony No. 5, Op. 67 (frv)*
HMV.D814	LSO	Beethoven: Ov. Egmont, Op. 84*
HMV.D815/6	LSO	Mozart: Ov. Le Nozze di Figaro, K 492*
		Liszt: Hungarian Rhapsody No. 1 (14) in F minor*
HMV.D817	LSO	Weber: Ov. Freischütz, Op. 77*
HMV.D818	LSO	Weber: Ov. Oberon*

RICHARD STRAUSS

HMV.040869	Bav	Strauss: Ov. Ariadne auf Naxos, Op. 60*
HMV.D1096 (Vic. 9282)	Tiv	Strauss: Trio & Duet Act III, Rosenkavalier, Op. 59 (Barbara Kemp, Delia Reinhart, Hedwig von Debička)
Poly.27320/4 (Br.90319/23)	BSt	Strauss: Don Quixote, Op. 35 (Mainardi, 'cello)
Poly.66826 (Br.90255)	BSt	Mozart: Ov. Zauberflöte, K 620
Poly.66814/7 (Br.90172/5)	BSt	Beethoven: Symphony No. 5, Op. 67
Poly.66827 (Br.90088)	BSt	Strauss: Dance of the Seven Veils, Salome, Op. 54
Poly.66828	BPO	Weber: Ov. Euryanthe
Poly.66887/8 (Br.90044/5)	BSt	Strauss: Till Eulenspiegel, Op. 28
Poly.66902/3 (Br.90046/7)	BSt	Strauss: Don Juan, Op. 20
Poly.67599/600	Bav	Strauss: Festmusik
Poly.67756/60	Bav	Strauss: Helden-leben, Op. 40
Poly.67800/4	Bav	Strauss: Don Quixote, Op. 35 (Otto Uhl, 'cello)
Poly.69833/5	BSt	Mozart: Symphony No. 39, K 543
Poly.69840/4 (Br.25000/4)	BSt	Strauss: Helden-leben, Op. 40
Poly.69845/8	BSt	Mozart: Symphony No. 41, K 551
Poly.69849/51	BSt	Strauss: Tod und Verklarung, Op. 24

N

Poly.69854	BSt	Strauss: Waltzes from Act II, Rosenkavalier, Op. 59
Poly.69867	BSt	Strauss: Interlude from Intermezzo, Op. 72
Poly.69868	BSt	Strauss: Waltz scene from Inter-mezzo, Op. 72
Poly.95392/6 (Br.90130/4)	BSt	Strauss: Suite, Le Bourgeois Gentilhomme, Op. 60
Poly.95442/5 (Br.90082/5)	BSt	Mozart: Symphony No. 40, K 550
		Schubert: Ov. Die Zwillingsbrüder, D 647
HMV.DB5662/75	Bav	Strauss: Alpensin-fonie, Op. 64 (frv)

ERICH KLEIBER

V/K.08034	BSt	Wagner: Prelude, Meistersinger*
V/K.08296/7	BSt	Wagner: Ov. Fliegende Holländer*
V/K?	BSt	Strauss: Don Juan, Op. 20*
Parlo.E10954: 11017/8	BSt	Stravinsky: L'Oiseau de Feu (1919 Suite) (frv)
		Dvořák: Slavonic Dance, Op. 72 No. 8 (frv)
Parlo.E11248	BSt	Schubert: Allegretto & Menuetto, Symphony No. 3, D 200 (frv)
U.E193	?BSt	J. Strauss I: Waltz, Sorgenbrecher, Op. 230 (frv)
T/U.E461	BSt	Saint-Saëns: Danse Macabre, Op. 40
HMV.D1448/50 (Vic. 9438/40)	BSt	Mozart: Symphony No. 39, K543
HMV.D1807 (T.SK1215)	BPO	Berlioz: Hungarian March, Damnation de Faust, Op. 24
		Rezniček: Ov. Donna Diana
Poly.66532	BSt	Mozart: German Dances, K 600 Nos. 2, 5 K 602 No. 3 (frv), K 605 No. 3
Poly.66552	BSt	J. Strauss II: Ov. Fledermaus
Poly.66556	BSt	Nicolai: Ov. Merry Wives of Windsor

Catalogue		Work	Catalogue		Work
Poly.66596/7	BSt	Rossini: Ov. *William Tell*	T.E961 (U.EP781)	BPO	Beethoven: Ov. *Egmont*, Op. 84
Poly.66598 (HMV.EJ360)	BSt	Schubert: Entr'acte III, Ballet Music, *Rosamunde*, D 797	T/U.E963	BPO	J. Strauss II: Waltz, *An der schönen, blauen Donau*, Op. 314
Poly.66652/3 (Br.90086/7)	BSt	Smetana: *Vltava (Ma Vlast)* Dvořák; Slavonic Dance, OP. 46 No. 1	T/U.E964 (U.EP873)	BPO	J. Strauss II: *Kaiser-Waltzer*, Op. 467
Poly.66674 (Decca.CA8197)	BSt	Berlioz: Ov. *Carnaval Romain*, Op. 9	T/U.E988 (U.EP875)	BPO	Weber/Berlioz: *Aufforderung zum Tanz*, Op. 65
Poly.66717/9	BPO	Schubert: Symphony No. 8, D 759	T/U.E1017 (U.EP1017)	BPO	Smetana: Ov. *Bartered Bride*
Poly.66729 (Br.90106)	BSt	Mozart: Ov. *Idomeneo*, K 366 German Dances, K571 No 6, K600 No 3 (*frv*)	T.E1052	BPO	Dvořák: Wedding Dance, *Waldtaube*, Op. 110 Janaček: *Lasské-Tänze*, No. 1
			T.E1154	BPO	Liszt: *Tarantella*
Poly.66730	BSt	Mozart: German Dances, K509 No. 6, K571 No. 4 (*frv*) K600 No. 4, K605 No. 2 (*frv*)	T.E1156 (U.EP1195)	BPO	J. Strauss II: *Acceleration Waltz*, Op. 234
			T.SK1205 (U.FP963)	BPO	Stravinsky: *Feux d' Artifice*, Op. 4 (*frv*) Rezniček: Ov. *Donna Diana*
Poly.66731	BPO	Mendelssohn: Scherzo, *Midsummer Night's Dream*, Op. 61 No. 1	T.E1206 (U.EP978)	BPO	J. Strauss II: Ov. *Wein, Weib und Gesang*, Op. 333
			T.E1232 (U.EP1055)	BPO	Weber: Ov. *Preciosa*
Poly.66850	BPO	Mendelssohn: Nocturne, Wedding March, *Midsummer Night's Dream*, Op. 61 Nos. 7, 9	T.E1233 (U.EP1176)	BPO	J. Strauss II: Ov. *1,001 Nächte*, Op. 346
			T.SK1295 (U.GP1075)	BPO	Beethoven: Allegretto, Symphony No. 8, Op. 93
Poly.66905/8 (Br.90140/3)	BSt	Beethoven: Symphony No. 2, Op. 36 (*frv*)	T.E1322 (U.EP1128)	BPO	Suppé: Ov. *Light Cavalry*
Poly.66909/13 (Br.90150/4)	BPO	Dvořák: Symphony No. 9 (5), Op. 95	T.E1406 (U.EP1201)	BPO	Tchaikowsky: *Capriccio Italien*, Op. 45
T.E463/4 (U.EP328/9)	BPO	Bach: Organ Prelude & Fugue in E flat (*St. Ann*) orch. Schoenberg	T.E1422	BPO	Josef Strauss: Waltz, *Dorfschwalben aus Österreich*, Op. 164
T.E532/3	BPO	Berlioz: Ov. *Benvenuto Cellini*, Op. 23 Hungarian March, *Damnation de Faust*, Op. 24	T.E1491 (U.EP1242)	BPO	J. Strauss II: Ov. *Zigeunerbaron*
			T.E1536	BPO	J. Strauss II: Ov. *Fledermaus*
T/U.E612	BPO	Wagner: Funeral Music, *Götterdämmerung*	T.E1669/70	BPO	Mozart: Serenade in G, K 525 (*Eine kleine Nachtmusik*)
T/U.E651/2	BPO	Strauss: *Till Eulenspiegel*, Op. 28	T.E1688	BPO	Strauss: Waltzes, Act II, *Rosenkavalier*, Op. 59
T/E653 (U.EP127)	BPO	Beethoven: Ov. *Coriolan*, Op. 62	T.E1713	BPO	Nicolai: Ov. *Merry Wives of Windsor*
T.E808 (U.EP346)	BPO	Berlioz: Waltz, *Symphonie Fantastique*, Op. 14	T.E1777/9	BPO	Schubert: Symphony No. 8, D759
T/U.E844 (U.EP697)	BPO	Gluck: Ov. *Iphigénie en Aulide*	HMV.C1676 (HMV.EH219)	VPO	J. Strauss II: Waltz, *Du und du*, Op. 367

HMV.C1685 (HMV.EH323)	VPO	Josef Strauss: Waltz, *Dorfsch- walben aus Öster- reich*, Op. 164
HMV.C1686/8 (HMV.AN274/6)	VPO	Mozart: Sym- phony No. 38, K 504
HMV.C1697	VPO	J. Strauss II: Waltz, *Künstler- leben*, Op. 316
T.E2022/3	CPO	Liszt: *Les Préludes*
T/U.E2041/2	CPO	Bizet: Ov., Entr'acte I, II, III, *Carmen*
T.E2485/8	BRO	Beethoven: Symphony No. 2, Op. 36
Decca.K1824/8	LPO	Beethoven: Symphony No. 6, Op. 68
Decca.K1989	LPO	Dvořák: Ov. *Carnaval*, Op. 92
Decca.AK2272/6	PCO	Tchaikowsky: Symphony No. 4, Op. 36
Decca.AX383/9 (Decca.LXT2546)	ACO	Beethoven: Symphony No. 3, Op. 55
Decca.AX406/10 (Decca.LXT2547)	ACO	Beethoven: Symphony No. 7, Op. 92
Decca.AX448/50	LPO	Mozart: Symphony No. 40, K 550 Handel: Overture *Berenice*
Decca.LXT2725/6	VPO	Beethoven: Symphony No. 9, Op. 125 (Gueden, Wagner, Dermota, Weber, Singverein d. Gesellschaft der Musikfreunde)
Decca.LXT2954/7	VPO	Strauss: *Rosen- kavalier*, Op. 59— —complete— (Gueden, Jurinac, Reining, Weber, Vienna State Opera Chorus)
Decca.SXL2087/90	VPO	Mozart: *Le Nozze di Figaro*, K. 492 —complete— (Gueden, della Casa, Danco, Poell, Siepi, Vienna State Opera Chorus)
Decca.LXT5359	ACO	Beethoven: Symphony No. 6, Op. 68
Decca.LXT5370	PCO	Tchaikowsky: Symphony No. 6, Op. 74
Decca.LXT5388	ACO	Beethoven: Sym- phony No. 5, Op. 67

OTTO KLEMPERER

HMV.E476/7 (HMV.EW27/8)	BSt	Wagner: Prelude, *Tristan & Isolde*
HMV.D1663 (HMV.EJ276)	BSt	Strauss: Dance of the Seven Veils, *Salome*, Op. 54
HMV.D1853/4	BSt	Brahms: Academic Festival Overture, Op. 80
Parlo.E10807/12	BSt	Brahms: Symphony No. 1, Op. 68
Parlo.E10925/6	BSt	Strauss: *Till Eulenspiegel*, Op. 28
Parlo.E10935	BSt	Offenbach: Ov. *La belle Hélène*
Parlo.E11051/2	BSt	Strauss: *Don Juan*, Op. 20
Poly.66599 (Decca.CA8091)	BSt	Beethoven: Ov. *Coriolan*, Op. 62
Poly.66601/2	BSt	Beethoven: Ov. *Leonora No. 3*, Op. 72a
Poly.66603	BSt	Mendelssohn: Ov. *Midsummer Night's Dream*, Op. 21
Poly.66629	BSt	Weber: Ov. *Euryanthe*
Poly.566209/23	PPM	Bach: Brandenburg Concerti 1–6
Poly.566224/5	PPM	Mozart: Serenade in G, K 525 (*Eine kleine Nachtmusik*)
Poly.566329/31	PPM	Mozart: Symphony No. 36, K 425
Poly.566345/6	PPM	Mozart: Symphony No. 25, K 183
AmVox.PL6800	OLa	Schubert: Sym- phony No. 4, D 417
AmVox.PL6930	VSO	Bruckner: Sym- phony No. 4
AmVox.PL6960	VSO	Beethoven: Symphony No. 6, Op. 68
AmVox.PL6992/3	VSO	Beethoven: *Missa Solemnis*, Op. 123 (Steingrüber, Schüthoff, Majkut, Weiner, Vienna Music Academy Chorus)
AmVox.PL7000	VSO	Mahler: *Das Lied von der Erde* (Cavelti, Dermota)

WILHELM FURTWÄNGLER

Poly.35013 (Br.90402)	BPO	Mozart: Ovs. *Entführung aus dem Serail*, K 384, Ov. *Le Nozze di Figaro*, K 492

Poly.35028 (Decca.CA8218)	BPO	Rossini: Ov. *Barbiere di Siviglia*	HMV.DB6574/9S	LFO	Beethoven: Violin Concerto, Op. 61 (Menuhin)
Poly.66925/6 (Br.90137/8)	BPO	Bach: Air, Suite No. 3 in D	HMV.DB6625	VPO	Beethoven: Ov. *Coriolan*, Op. 62
		Mendelssohn: Ov. *Midsummer Night's Dream*, Op. 21	HMV.DB6634/9S	VPO	Brahms: Symphony No. 1, Op. 68
Poly.66935/6 (Br.90050)	BPO	Bach: Air, Suite No. 3 tn D	HMV.DB6707/11	VPO	Mozart: Wind Serenade in B flat, K 361
		Schubert: Ballet Music, *Rosamunde*, D 797	HMV.DB6792/4S	POr	Wagner: Immolation scene *Götterdämmerung*
Poly.67054 (Br.93251: Decca.CA8173)	BPO	Wagner: Funeral Music, *Götterdämmerung*			(Flagstadt)
			HMV.DB6916/7	VPO	Wagner: Siegfried Idyll
Poly.67055 (Br.90250: Decca.CA8170)	BPO	Beethoven: Ov. *Egmont*, Op. 84	HMV.DB6932/4	VPO	Brahms: Variations on a Theme by Haydn, Op. 56a
Poly.67156/8	BPO	Mozart: Serenade in G, K 525 (*Eine kliene Nachtmusik*)			Hungarian Dances, No. 1 in G minor, No. 3 in F
Poly.90190	BPO	Brahms: Hungarian Dances, No. 1 in G minor,	HMV.DB6941	VPO	Mendelssohn: Ov. *Hebrides*
		No. 3 in F	HMV.DB6946	VPO	Wagner: Funeral Music, *Götterdämmerung*
Poly.95410/1 (Decca.CA8053/4)	BPO	Strauss: *Till Eulenspiegel*, Op. 28			
		Berlioz: Hungarian March, *Damnation de Faust*, Op. 24	HMV.DB6997/9	VPO	Mozart: Symphony No. 40, K 550
Poly.95417/8 (Br.90161/2: Decca.CA8013/4)	BPO	Bach: Brandenburg Concerto No. 3 in G	HMV.DB21000/4S	LFO	Brahms: Violin Concerto, Op. 77 (Menuhin)
		Schubert: Entr'acte III, *Rosamunde*, D 797	HMV.DB21099/103	VPO	Schubert: Symphony No. 8, D 759
			HMV.ALP1030/5	POr	Wagner: *Tristan & Isolde*—complete—
Poly.95427 (Br.90188: Decca.CA8055)	BPO	Rossini: Ov. *La Gazza Ladra*			(Flagstadt Schwarzkopf), Theborn, Suthaus, F-Dieskau
Poly.95458 (Decca.CA8098)	BPO	Schubert: Entr'acte III, Ballet Music, *Rosamunde*, D 797	HMV.DB21315/9 (HMV.ALP1051)	POr	Greindl) Beethoven: Piano Concerto No. 5, Op. 73 (Fischer)
T.SK3230/2	BPO	Bruckner: *Adagio*, Symphony No. 7 in E major	HMV.ALP1130/2	VPO	Beethoven: *Fidelio*, Op. 72—complete —(Mödl, Jurinac,
T.SK3266	BPO	Gluck: Ov. *Alceste*			Windgassen,
HMV.DB3328/32 (Vic.11000/4)	BPO	Beethoven: Symphony No. 5, Op. 67			Schock, Vienna State Opera Chorus)
HMV.DB3419/20 (Vic.14934/5)	BPO	Wagner: Prelude and Liebestod, *Tristan & Isolde*	HMV.DGM18015/6	BPO	Schubert: Symphony No. 9, D 944
HMV.DB3345/7 (Vic.15219/21)	BPO	Wagner: Prelude and Good Friday Music, *Parsifal*			Haydn: Symphony No. 88 in G
HMV.DB4609/14 (Vic.15395/400)	BPO	Tchaikowsky: Symphony No. 6, Op. 74	HMV.LPM18854	BPO	Bruckner: Symphony No. 9 in D minor
Elec.E90994	BPO	Brahms: Symphony No. 3, Op. 90			
Elec.E90995	BPO	Brahms: Symphony No. 4, Op. 98	FELIX WEINGARTNER		
Decca.K1875/9	LPO	Brahms: Symphony No. 2, Op. 73	Col.8856/7	Bas	Weber: Ov. *Freischütz*, Op. 77

Col.9887/90 (AmCol.67671/4D)	RPS	Mendelssohn: Symphony No. 3, Op. 56
Col.L1775/82	LSO	Beethoven: Symphony No. 9, Op. 125 (Licette, Brunskill, Eisdell, Williams, LSO Chorus)
Col.L1808/13	LSO	Berlioz: *Symphonie Fantastique*, Op. 14
Col.L1893/7	RPS	Beethoven: Symphony No. 6, Op. 68
Col.L1898/902	RPS	Beethoven: Symphony No. 7, Op. 92
Col.L1903/5	RPS	Beethoven: Symphony No. 8, Op. 93
Col.L2086	RPS	J. Strauss II: *Acceleration Waltz*, Op. 234
Col.L2145/9	RPS	Brahms: Symphony No. 1, Op. 68
Col.DX266	RPS	J. Strauss II: Waltz, *Frühlingsstimmen*, Op. 410
Col.DX516/9 (AmCol.68078/81D)	LPO	Beethoven: Symphony No. 5, Op. 67
Col.LX40	RPS	Josef Strauss: Waltz, *Sphärenklänge*, Op. 235
Col.LX133 (AmCol.50315D)	LPO	J. Strauss II: Waltz, *1,001 Nächte* Op. 346
Col.LX274/7 (AmCol.68217/20D)	LPO	Beethoven: Symphony No. 4, Op. 60 Ov. *Prometheus*, Op. 43
Col.LX413/20 (AmCol.68357/64D)	VPO	Beethoven: Symphony No. 9, Op. 125 (Helletsgrüber, Anday, Maikl, Mayr, Vienna State Opera Chorus)
Col.LX484/8 (AmCol.67298/302D)	VPO	Beethoven: Symphony No. 7, Op. 92
Col.LX532/7	VPO	Beethoven: Symphony No. 3, Op. 55
Col.LX563/5	VPO	Beethoven: Symphony No. 8, Op. 93
Col. LX677/9	VPO	Beethoven: Symphony No. 1, Op. 21 Ov. *Egmont*, Op. 84
Col.LX705/9	LSO	Brahms: Symphony No. 4, Op. 98
Col.LX712/3	LSO	Beethoven: Ov. *Leonora No. 2*, Op. 72a
Col.LX725/8	VPO	Beethoven: Symphony No. 2, Op. 36
Col.LX744/5	LPO	Brahms: Variations on a Theme by Haydn, Op. 56a
Col.LX748/51	LPO	Brahms: Symphony No. 3, Op. 90
Col.LX784	LPO	Beethoven: Ov. *Fidelio*, Op. 72a
Col.LX789/91	PCO	Liszt: Concerto No. 1 in E flat (Sauer)
Col.LX811/2	LPO	Beethoven: Ov. *Zur Weihe des Hauses*, Op. 124
Col.LX833/7	LSO	Brahms: Symphony No. 1, Op. 68
Col.LX854/5	LSO	Mozart: Serenade in G, K 525 (*Eine kleine Nachtmusik*)
Col.LX860/1	VPO	Wagner: Ov. *Rienzi*
Col.LX862/4	PCO	Liszt: Concerto No. 2 in A major (Sauer)
Col.LX877/8	LSO	Liszt: *Les Préludes*
Col.LX881/3	LPO	Mozart: Symphony No. 39, K 543
Col.LX886	LSO	Brahms: Academic Festival Overture, Op. 80
Col.LX890	LPO	Weber/Weingartner: *Aufforderung zum Tanz*, Op. 65
Col.LX897/8	LPO	Liszt: Mephisto Waltz Beethoven: Ov. *Die Ruinen von Athen*, Op. 113
Col.LX899/903	LSO	Brahms: Symphony No. 2, Op. 73

BRUNO WALTER

Poly.66073	BSt	Cherubini: Ov. *The Water-Carrier*
Col.L1744/5	RPS	Wagner: Prelude & Act I Transformation Scene, *Parsifal*
Col.L1961/2	RPS	Wagner: Ov. *Fliegende Holländer* Prelude, Act III, *Lohengrin*
Col.L2067/8	RPS	Strauss: *Don Juan*, Op. 20
Col.L2209/12 (AmCol.67526/9D)	MFO	Schumann: Symphony No. 4, Op. 120
Col.L2270	BSt	J. Strauss II: Waltz, *Wiener Blut*, Op. 354
Col.L2311 (AmCol.9080D)	BSt	J. Strauss II: Ov. *Fledermaus*

Col.DX31/3 (AmCol.68109/11D)	BSt	Mozart: Symphony No. 40, K 550
Col.LX28 (AmCol.9081M)	BPO	J. Strauss II: Waltz *Rosen aus dem Süden*, Op. 388
Col.LX39 (AmCol.67814D)	BPO	Strauss: Dance of the Seven Veils, *Salome*, Op. 54
Col.ROX165/71	VPO	Mahler: *Das Lied von der Erde* (Thorborg, Kullmann) (*frv*)
HMV.DB2253/7 (Vic.11734/8)	BBC	Brahms: Symphony No. 4, Op. 98
HMV.DB2258/60 (Vic.11775/7)	BBC	Mozart: Symphony No. 39, K 543
HMV.DB2261 (Vic.11809)	BBC	Beethoven: Ov. *Fidelio*, Op. 72a
HMV.DB2636/43 (Vic.8932/9)	VPO	Wagner: Act I, *Walküre* (complete) (Lehmann, Melchior, List)
HMV.DB2885/6 (Vic.11958/9)	VPO	Beethoven: Ov. *Leonora No. 3*, Op. 72a Ov. *Die Ruinen von Athen*, Op. 113
HMV.DB2937/9	VPO	Schubert: Symphony No. 8, D 759
HMV.DB3051/5 (Vic. 36349/53)	VPO	Beethoven: Symphony No. 6 Op. 68
HMV.DB3075/6 (Vic.12060/1)	VPO	Mozart: Serenade in G major, K 525 (*Eine kleine Nachtmusik*)
HMV.DB3112/4 (Vic.12239/41)	VPO	Mozart: Symphony No. 38, K 504
HMV.DB3273/6 (Vic.12151/4)	VPO	Mozart: Concerto in D minor, K 466 (Walter)
HMV.DB3277/81 (Vic.12264/8)	VPO	Brahms: Symphony No. 1, Op. 68
HMV.DB3394 (Vic.12190)	VPO	Brahms: Academic Festival Overture, Op. 80
HMV.DB3428/30 (Vic.12467/70)	VPO	Mozart: Symphony No. 41, K 551
HMV.DB3554	PCO	Weber: Ov. *Freischütz*, Op. 77
HMV.DB3613/22	VPO	Mahler: Symphony No. 9 in D minor (*frv*)
HMV.DB3852/7 (Vic.12692/7)	PCO	Berlioz: *Symphonie Fantastique*, Op. 14
Col.LZX207/10 (AmCol.11749/52D)	NYP	Beethoven: Symphony No. 5, Op. 67
Col.LZX230/3 (AmCol.11581/4D)	NYP	Schumann: Symphony No. 3, Op. 97
AmBCol.11896/8D	NYP	Beethoven: Symphony No. 8, Op. 93

Col.LX949/54 (AmCol.1034)	NYP	Mahler: Symphony No. 4 in G major (Halban)
Col.LX963/7 (AmCol.12399/403)	PhO	Beethoven: Symphony No. 6, Op. 68
Col.LX1077/8 (AmCol.12128/9D)	NYP	Samuel Barber: Symphony No. 1, Op. 9 (*frv*)
AmCol.12639/42D	PhO	Schubert: Symphony No. 8, D 759
Col.LX1204/7 (AmCol.12924/7D)	NYP	Beethoven: Symphony No. 1, Op. 21
Col.LCX8019/26 (AmCol.12666/73D)	NYP	Mahler: Symphony No. 5 in C sharp minor
AmCol.33CX1077	NYP	Beethoven: Symphony No. 5, Op. 67
AmCol.33CX1082	NYP	Mozart: Symphony No. 41, K 551
AmCol.ML5303/4	NYP	Mahler: Symphony No. 2 in C minor (Cundari, Forrester, Westminster Choir)
Col.LXT1365	NYP	Dvořák: Symphony No. 8(4), Op. 88

CLEMENS KRAUSS

HMV.E539/41 (Vic.4189/91)	VPO	Haydn: Symphony No. 88 in G
HMV.EG1628 (HMV.B3149)	VPO	J. Strauss II: Perpetuum Mobile, Op. 257 *Annen-Polka*, Op. 117
HMV.L968 (HMV.AN377)	VPO	J. Strauss II: Ov. *Fledermaus*
HMV.C2026/9 (HMV.AN577/80)	VPO	Brahms: Symphony No. 3, Op. 90
HMV.C2030/3 (Vic.11256/9)	VPO	Beethoven: Symphony No. 2, Op. 36
HMV.C2034/7 (Vic.9917/20)	VPO	Strauss: Suite, *Le Bourgeois Gentilhomme*, Op. 60
HMV.EH484 (Vic.9990)	VPO	J. Strauss II: Waltz, *1,001 Nachte*, Op. 346
HMV.C2194 (Vic.11142)	VPO	Mozart: Ov. *Entführung aus dem Serail*, K 384 Ov. *Le Nozze di Figaro*, K 492
HMV.C2195 (HMV.AN667)	VPO	Josef Strauss: Waltz, *Sphärenklänge*, Op. 235
HMV.C2233 (HMV.AN724)	VPO	Mozart: Ov. *Cosi fan Tutte*, K 588 Schubert:

Ballet Music,
Rosamunde, D 797

HMV.C2339 (HMV.AN727)	VPO	J. Strauss II: Waltz, *Liebeslieder*, Op. 114
AusT.Elo3o/15	VPO	Schubert: Symphony No. 9, D 944
T.SK3139/40	VPO	Strauss: *Till Eulenspiegel*, Op. 28
T.SK3199	VPO	Strauss: Dance of the Seven Veils, *Salome*, Op. 54
Decca.K1726	LSO	Brahms: Academic Festival Overture, Op. 80
Decca.K2107/8	LSO	Brahms: Variations on a Theme by Haydn, Op. 56a
Decca.AK2245/6	LPO	Wagner: Prelude and Liebestod, *Tristan & Isolde*
Decca.K23097/100	VPO	Strauss. *Also sprach Zarathustra*, Op. 30
Decca.K23112/22 (Decca.LXT2550/1)	VPO	J. Strauss II: *Fledermaus*—complete—(Lipp, Gueden, Wagner, Dermota, Patzak, Poehl)
Decca.K28364/5	VPO	Strauss: *Till Eulenspiegel*, Op. 28
Decca.K28366/7	VPO	Strauss: *Don Juan*, Op. 20
Decca.LXT2863/4	VPO	Strauss: *Salome*, Op. 54—complete

WILLEM MENGELBERG

Vic.1486	NYP	Mozart: Ov. *Zauberflöte*, K 620
HMV.E548/9	NYP	Handel: Suite, *Alceste*
HMV.D1704 (Vic.7006)	NYP	Saint-Saëns: *Le Rouet d'Omphale*, Op. 31
HMV.D1711/15 (Vic.6982/6)	NYP	Strauss: *Heldenleben*, Op. 40 (*frv*)
HMV.D1716	NYP	Mendelssohn: War March of the Priests, *Athalie*, Op. 74 / Meyerbeer: Coronation March, Act IV, *Prophete*
HMV.D1385	NYP	Rossini: Ov. *Barbiere di Siviglia*
HMV.D1867/70 (Vic.7211/4)	NYP	Beethoven: Symphony No. 1, Op. 21
HMV.D1908 (Vic.7436)	NYP	Beethoven: Ov. *Egmont*, Op. 84
Br.50072	NYP	Tchaikowsky: *Marche Slave*, Op. 31

HMV.D1988/9 (Vic.7483/4)	NYP	J.C. Bach: Sinfonia in B flat / J.S. Bach: Air, Suite No. 3 in D (arr. Mahler)
HMV.DB1599/605 (Vic.7439/44)	NYP	Beethoven: Symphony No. 3, Op. 55
Col.9560S	ACO	Mendelssohn: Scherzo, *Midsummer Night's Dream*, Op. 61, No. 1
Col.DX6S	ACO	Bizet: Adagietto, Suite No. 1, *L'Arlésienne*
Col.DHX20/24	ACO	Beethoven: Violin Concerto, Op. 61 (Zimmermann)
Col.D41003	ACO	Tchaikowsky: Waltz, String Serenade, Op. 48 / Mendelssohn: Scherzo, *Midsummer Night's Dream*, Op. 61, No. 1
Col.L1798	ACO	Mahler: Adagietto, Symphony No. 5 in C minor (*frv*)
Col.L1810	ACO	Berlioz: Hungarian March, Danse des Sylphes, *Damnation de Faust*, Op. 24
Col.L1948	ACO	Wagner: Prelude, Act I, *Lohengrin*
Col.L1972/3	ACO	Cherubini: Ov. *Anacreon* / Beethoven: Allegretto, Symphony No. 8, Op. 93
Col.L2047	ACO	J. C. Bach: Sinfonia in B flat
Col.L2176/82	ACO	Tchaikowsky: Symphony No. 5, Op. 64 / Waltz, String Serenade, Op. 48
Col.L2312/3	ACO	Weber: Ov. *Oberon* / Mendelssohn: Scherzo, *Midsummer Night's Dream*, Op. 61, No. 1
Col.L2362/3	ACO	Liszt: *Les Préludes*
Col.L2366/70	ACO	Tchaikowsky: Symphony No. 4, Op. 36
Col.LX48/9 (AmCol.67890/1D)	ACO	Ravel: *Bolero*
Col.LX55/6 (Am.Col.67868/9D)	ACO	Tchaikowsky: Ov. *Romeo & Juliet*
Col.LX58/9 (AmCol.67893/4D)	ACO	Brahms: Academic Festival Overture, Op. 80

Col.LX59 (AmCol.67894D)		Allegretto, Symphony No. 1, Op. 68
Col.LX129/30 (AmCol.67987/8D)	ACO	Beethoven: Ov. *Leonora No. 3*, Op. 72a
		Turkish March, *Die Ruinen von Athen*, Op. 113
Col.LX134/6 (AmCol.68013/5D)	ACO	Bach: Suite No. 2 in B minor
Col.LX154 (AmCol.68042D)	ACO	Weber: Ov. *Freischütz*, Op. 77
Col.LX157 (AmCol.68069D)	ACO	Weber: Ov. *Euryanthe*
Col.LX159 (AmCol.50345D)	ACO	Suppé: Ov. *Poet & Peasant* (Maria Loevensohm, 'cello)
Col.LX160 (AmCol.68055D)	ACO	Beethoven: Ov. *Leonora No. 1*, Op. 138
Col.LX161 (AmCol.68048D)	ACO	Beethoven: Ov. *Egmont*, Op. 84
Col.LX167 (AmCol.68049)	ACO	Beethoven: Ov. *Coriolan*, Op. 62
Col.LX170/1 (AmCol.68082/3)	ACO	Wagner: Ov. *Tannhäuser*
Col.LX220/3 (AmCol.68103/6D)	ACO	Brahms: Symphony No. 3, Op. 90
Col.LX240 (AmCol.9076M)	ACO	J. Strauss II: *Perpetuum Mobile*, Op. 257
Decca.K771	ACO	Gluck: Ov. *Alceste*
T.SK2210/3	ACO	Beethoven: Symphony No. 5, Op. 67
T.SK2214/8	ACO	Tchaikowsky: Symphony No. 6, Op. 74
T.SK2424/8	ACO	Beethoven: Symphony No. 6, Op. 68
T.SK2489	ACO	Berlioz: Ov. *Carnaval Romain*, Op. 9
T.SK2743/4	ACO	Strauss: *Don Juan*, Op. 20
T.SK2760/2	ACO	Beethoven: Symphony No. 8, Op. 93
T.SK2770/2	ACO	Beethoven: Symphony No. 1, Op. 21
T.SK2773/7	ACO	Brahms: Symphony No. 4, Op. 98
T.SK2794/7	ACO	Beethoven: Symphony No. 4, Op. 60

T.SK2901/3	ACO	Tchaikowsky: Serenade for Strings, Op. 48
T.SK2955	ACO	Debussy. *Prélude á l'après-midi d'un Faune*
T.SK3075/9	ACO	Brahms: Symphony No. 2, Op. 73
T.SK3081/1	ACO	Tchaikowsky: Ov. *1812*
T.SK2092/5	BPO	Tchaikowsky: Piano Concerto No. 1, Op. 23 (Conrad Hansen)
T.SK3145/9	ACO	Franck: Symphony in D minor
T.SK3181/5	ACO	Strauss: *Heldenleben*, Op. 40
T.SK3190/4	ACO	Dvořák: Symphony No. 9(5), Op. 95
T.SK3244	ACO	Schubert: *Marche Militaire* No. 1 in D, D 733
T.SK3744/5	ACO	Wagenaar: Ov. *Cyrano de Bergerac*
T.LT7006	ACO	Beethoven: Symphony No. 3, Op. 5
T.LGX66032	ACO	Strauss: *Tod und Verklärung*, Op. 24
Phil.GL6689	ACO	Schubert: Symphony No. 8. D 759[1] Beethoven: Symphony No. 5, Op. 67[1]
Phil.WO9903L	ACO	Beethoven: Symphony No. 6, Op. 68[2]
Phil.WO9904L	ACO	Beethoven: Symphony No. 7. Op. 92[2]
Phil.WO9907L	ACO	Brahms: Symphony No. 1, Op. 68[3]
Phil.WO9908L	ACO	Franck: Symphony in D minor[3] Strauss: *Don Juan*, Op. 20[3]
Phil.WO9909L	ACO	Schubert: Symphony No. 9, D 944[4]
T.HT3	BPO	Tchaikowsky: Symphony No. 6, Op. 74
T.HT4	BPO	Tchaikowsky: Symphony No. 5, Op. 64

[1] *Transcription of Broadcasts: 1939/40.*
[2] *Transcription of Broadcast: April 1940.*
[3] *Transcription of Broadcast: October 1940.*
[4] *Transcription of Broadcast: December 1940.*

LEOPOLD STOKOWSKI

Vic.645	PhO	Wagner: Magic Fire Music, *Walküre**
HMV.E507 (Vic.1309)	PhO	Debussy: Fêtes, *Nocturnes* No. 2
Vic.1312	PhO	Schubert: Ballet Music, Act III, *Rosamunde*, D 797 *Moment Musical*, Op. 94, No. 2 (arr. Stokowski)
Vic.1675	PhO	Brahms: Hungarian Dance No. 1 in G minor (arr. Stokowski) Glière: Dance, *The Red Poppy*
Vic.1720	PhO	Brahms: Menuetto, Serenade, Op. 11
HMV.D1046 (Vic,6513)	PhO	Tchaikowsky: *Marche Slave*, Op. 31
HMV.D1121 (Vic. 6505)	PhO	Saint–Saëns: *Danse Macabre*, Op. 40
HMV.D1214/6 (Vic.6615/7)	PhO	Tchaikowsky: Suite, *Casse-Noisette*, Op. 71a
HMV.D1218 (Vic.6584)	PhO	J. Strauss II: Waltz, *An der schönen, blauen Donau*, Op. 314 Waltz: *G'schichten aus dem Wiener Wald*, Op. 325
HMV.D1226/7 (Vic.6624/5)	PhO	Wagner: Ov. *Rienzi* Finale, Act III, *Götterdämmerung*
HMV.D1285 (Vic.6643)	PhO	Weber/Stokowski: *Aufforderung zum Tanz*, Op. 65
HMV.D1296 (Vic.6652)	PhO	Liszt: Hungarian Rhapsody No. 2 (orch. Müller-Berghaus)
HMV.D1404/8S (Vic.6726/30S)	PhO	Franck: Symphony in D minor
HMV.D1427	PhO	Stravinsky: Dance of the Firebird, *L'Oiseau de Feu*
HMV.D1428 (Vic.6751)	PhO	Bach: Toccata & Fugue in D minor (orch. Müller-Berghaus)
HMV.D1436/40 (Vic.6738/42)	PhO	Rimsky-Korsakoff: *Scheherazade*
HMV.D1463 (Vic.6791)	PhO	Wagner: Prelude, Act I, *Lohengrin*
HMV.D1464 (Vic.6786)	PhO	Bach/Stokowski: Prelude in E flat minor, Bk. I Chorale-Prelude, "Ich ruf' zu Dir"
HMV.D1499/1503 (Vic.6658/62)	PhO	Brahms: Symphony No. 1, Op. 68
HMV.D1618 (Vic.6873)	PhO	Bizet: *Carmen* —excerpts
HMV.D1639/43 (Vic.6670/4)	PhO	Beethoven: Symphony No. 7, Op. 92
Vic.6995/7	PhO	Tchaikowsky: Ov. *Romeo & Juliet* Falla: Danza española, *La vida breve*
HMV.D1676/7 (Vic.7018/9)	PhO	Rimsky-Korsakov: Ov. *Russian Easter Festival*
HMV.D1702/3 (Vic.7090/1)	PhO	Bach/Stokowski: Organ Passacaglia & Fugue in C minor
HMV.D1708/10 (Vic.7087/9)	PhO	Bach: Brandenburg Concerto No. 2 in F Bach/Stokowski: Chorale-Prelude, "Wir glauben all' an einem Gott"
HMV.D1739/40 (Vic.6949/50)	PhO	Tchaikowsky: *Capriccio Italien*, Op. 45
HMV.D1786 (Vic.6696)	PhO	Debussy: *Prélude à l'après-midi d'un Faune*
HMV.D1769/73 (Vic.6962/6)	PhO	Brahms: Symphony No. 3, Op. 90
HMV.D1801/3 (Vic.7124/6)	PhO	Bizet: Suite No. 1, *L'Arlésienne*
HMV.D1807 (Vic.6823)	PhO	Berlioz: Hungarian March, *Damnation de Faust*, Op. 24 Saint-Saëns: Bacchanale, *Samson et Dalila*
HMV.D1877/82 (Vic.7277/82)	PhO	Brahms: Symphony No. 2, Op. 73
HMV.D1893/7 (Vic.6565/9)	PhO	Dvořák: Symphony No. 9(5), Op. 95
HMV.D1905/7 (Vic. 7262/4)	PhO	Wagner: Ov. and Venusberg Music, *Tannhäuser*
HMV.D1919/22 (Vic.7231/3)	PhO	Stravinsky: *Sacre du Printemps* (*frv*)
HMV.D1935/6 (Vic.7259/60)	PhO	Strauss: Dance of the Seven Veils, *Salome*, Op. 54 Eichem: Japanese Nocturne (*frv*)
HMV.D1997 (Vic.7380)	PhO	Sibelius: *Swan of Tuonela*, Op. 22, No. 3
(cond. Rachmaninoff)		
HMV.D2011/3 (Vic.2719/21)	PhO	Rachmaninoff: *Island of the Dead*, Op. 29 *Vocalise*, Op. 22, No. 3 (orch. Rachmaninoff)

HMV.DA1291 (Vic.1584)	PhO	Wagner: Prelude, Act III, *Meistersinger*	HMV.DB2272/3 (Vic.8617/8)	PhO	Wagner: Act III, *Parsifal*—excerpts
HMV.DB1333/7 (Vic.8148/52)	PhO	Rachmaninoff: Concerto No. 2, Op. 18 (Rachmaninoff)	HMV.DB2274 (Vic.8496)	PhO	Bach/Stokowski: "Nun kommt der Heiden Heiland" "Komm, süsser Tod"
HMV.DA1556	PhO	Handel/Stokowski: Overture in D minor	HMV.DB324/6) (Vic.8288/90)	PhO	Strauss: *Tod und Verklärung*, Op. 24
HMV.DB1584 (Vic.7412)	PhO	Sibelius: *Finlandia*, Op. 26, No. 7	HMV.DB2327/34 (Vic.8424/32)	PhO	Beethoven: Symphony No. 9, Op. 125—in English—
HMV.DB1614 (Vic.7453)	PhO	Debussy: Nuages, *Nocturnes* No. 1			(Davis, Carhart, Betts, Loewenthal, Philadelphia Chorus)
HMV.DA1634	PhO	Debussy: Clair de Lune, *Suite Bergamasque*			
HMV.DB1642/3 (Vic.7455/6)	PhO	Debussy: Danses Sacrées, Danses Profanes (Edna Phillips, chromatic harp) Thomas: Gavotte, *Mignon*	HMV.DB2367/8 (Vic.8282/3)	PhO	Ravel: *Rapsodie Espagnole*
			HMV.DB2426/8 (Vic.8553/5)	PhO	Rachmaninoff: Rhapsody on a Theme by Paganini, Op. 43 (Rachmaninoff)
HMV.DB1663/4 (Vic.7499/500)	PhO	Tchaikowsky: Ov. *1812*, Op. 49	HMV.DB2451/3	PhO	Bach/Stokowski: Chaconne, Solo Vln. Sonata No. 4 Luther/Stokowski: Chorale, "Ein' feste Burg"
HMV.DB1706/7 (Vic.7515/6)	PhO	Scriabin: *Poème del'Extase*, Op. 54 (*frv*)			
HMV.DB1708/9 (Vic.7517/8)	PhO	Scriabin: *Prometheus*, Op. 60 (*frv*)			
HMV.DA1742	PhO	Debussy: Fêtes, *Nocturnes* No. 2	HMV.ED818/20 (Vic.8492/6)	PhO	Bach/Stokowski: Chaconne, Solo Vln. Sonata No. 4 Chorale-Prelude, "Nun kommt der Heiden Heiland" Adagio, Organ Toccata, Adagio & Fugue in C major Siciliano, Solo Vln. Sonata No. 4 "Komm, süsser Tod" Sarabande, English Suite No. 3
HMV.DB1769/82 (Vic.7524/37)	PhO	Schoenberg: *Gurrelieder*—complete —(*frv*) (Vreeland, Bampton, Althouse, Betts, Robofski, de Loache, Philadelphia Chorus)			
HMV.DB1789 (Vic.7553)	PhO	Bach/Stokowski: Chorale-Prelude, "Aus der Tiefe ruf' ich' Dir"			
HMV.DB1793/7 (Vic.6929/33)	PhO	Tchaikowsky: Symphony No. 4, Op. 36	HMV.DB2470/3 (Vic.8542/5)	PhO	Wagner: *Walküre* —excerpts— Lawrence Tibbet)
HMV.DB1911/14 (Vic.7621/4)	PhO	Wagner: *Tristan & Isolde*—excerpts	HMV.2522/7 (Vic.8698/703)	PhO	Rimsky-Korsakov: *Scheherazade*
HMV.DB1976/8 (Vic.7796/8)	PhO	Wagner: *Rheingold* —excerpts	HMV.DB2543/7 (Vic.8737/41)	PhO	Dvořák: Symphony No. 9(5), Op. 95
Vic.7825/9	PhO	Brahms: Symphony No. 4, Op. 98	HMV.DB2548/53 (Vic.8589/94)	PhO	Tchaikowsky: Symphony No. 5, Op. 64
HMV.DB2126/30 (Vic.7843/7)	PhO	Wagner: *Götterdämmerung*— excerpts—(Agnes Davis)	HMV.DB2572	PhO	Bach: Toccata & Fugue in D minor
HMV.DB2203/7 (Vic.7884/8)	PhO	Shostakovitch: Symphony No. 1, Op. 10 (*frv*) Tchaikowsky: *Chant sans paroles*, Op. 40. No. 6 (arr. Stokowski)	Vic.8764	PhO	Bach/Stokowski: "Es ist vollbracht", *St. John Passion*
			HMV.DB2874/8 (Vic.8971/5)	PhO	Brahms: Symphony No. 1, Op. 68
			HMV.DB2882/4 (Vic.8926/8)	PhO	Stravinsky: *L'Oiseau de Feu*

HMV.DB2884 (Vic.8928)		Shostakovitch/ Stokowski: Prelude in E flat minor
HMV.DB3226/31S (Vic.8959/64S)	PhO	Franck: Symphony in D minor
HMV.DB3232/3 (Vic.15169/70)	PhO	Borodin: Polovtsian Dances, *Prince Igor*
HMV.DB3254/5 (Vic.15313/4)	PhO	Wagner: Prelude, Act III, *Tannhäuser* Bach/Stokowski: Chorale-Prelude, "Ich ruf' zu Dir"
HMV.DB3269/72 (Vic.14728/31)	PhO	Wagner: Prelude and Good Friday Music, *Parsifal*
HMV.DB3511/4 (Vic.15467/70)	PhO	Stravinsky: *Pétrouchka*
HMV.DB3533/4 (Vic.17501/2)	PhO	Dukas: *L'Apprenti Sorcier* Rimsky-Korsakov: Prelude, Act III, *Ivan the Terrible*
HMV.DB3596 (Vic.15814)	PhO	Debussy: Nuages, *Nocturnes* No. 1
HMV.DB3699 (Vic.15189)	PhO	Weber/Stokowski: *Aufforderung zum Tanz*, Op. 65
HMV.DB3775/7 (Vic.15310/2)	PhO	Wagner: Overture & Venusberg Music, *Tannhäuser* (Philadelphia Chorus)
HMV.DB3821 (Vic.15423)	PhO	J. Strauss II: *An der schönen, blauen Donau*, Op. 314 *G'schichten aus dem Wiener Wald*, Op. 325
HMV.DB3847/51S	PhO	Shostakovitch: Symphony No. 1, Op. 10
HMV.DB3942 (Vic.15800)	PhO	Wagner: Magic Fire Music, *Walküre*
HMV.DB3991/6 (Vic.15737/42)	PhO	Shostakovitch: Symphony No. 5, Op. 47
HMV.DB5714/5S (Vic. 15815/6S)	PhO	Debussy: Sirènes, *Nocturnes* No. 3 (Philadelphia Chor.)
Vic.15813/6S (*cond.* Rachmaninoff)	PhO	Debussy: *Nocturnes* —complete
HMV.DB5780/4S (Vic.17426/30S)	PhO	Rachmaninoff: Symphony No. 3, Op. 44
HMV.DB5827/30 (Vic.17414/7)	PhO	Moussorgsky/ Stokowski: *Pictures at an Exhibition*
Vic.18391/5	PhO	Shostakovitch: Symphony No. 6, Op. 53 (*frv*)
AmCol.11349/54D	AYO	Dvořák: Symphony No. 9(5), Op. 95
AmCol.11522/4D	AYO	Stravinsky: *L'Oiseau de Feu*
AmCol.11553/8D	AYO	Brahms: Symphony No. 1, Op. 68
AmCol.11675/7D	AYO	Schubert: Symphony No. 8, D 759
AmCol.11805/8D	AYO	Moussorgsky/ Stokowski: *Pictures at an Exhibition*
Vic.11-8100/4	NBC	Tchaikowsky: Symphony No. 4, Op. 36
Vic.11-8423/5	NBC	Stravinsky: *L'Oiseau de Feu*
Vic.11-9011/5	NYC	Beethoven: Symphony No. 6, Op. 68
AmCol.12938/40D	NYP	Tchaikowsky: *Francesca da Rimini*, Op. 32 Sibelius: *The Maiden with the Roses*, Op. 54, No. 3
AmCol.ML2140	NYP	Schoenberg: Lied der Waldtaube, *Gurrelieder* (Lipton)
AmCol.ML2153	NYP	Wagner: Ov. *Rienzi* Prelude, Act I, *Lohengrin*
AmCol.ML4273	NYP	Wagner: Siegfried's Rhine Journey & Funeral Music, *Götterdämmerung*
Br.AXA4520	ASO	Dawson: Negro Folk Symphony
CBS.Srbg72403	ASO	Ives: Symphony No. 4 (*frv*)
CBS.Srbg72483	ASO	Beethoven: Piano Concerto No. 5, Op. 73 (Gould)
CBS.S72643	ASO	Ives: *Robert Browning* Overture (*frv*)

SERGE KOUSSEVITSKY

HMV.D1735/7 (Vic.7058/60)	BSO	Haydn: Symphony No. 94 in G
HMV.D1774 (Vic.6903)	BSO	J. Strauss II: Waltz *Frühlingsstimmen*, Op. 410 *Wiener Blut*, Op. 354
HMV.D1826/7 (Vic.7143/4)	BSO	Ravel: Suite No. 2, *Daphnis & Chloé*
HMV.1857/8 (Vic.7196/7)	BSO	Prokofieff: Symphony No. 1, Op. 25 (*Classical*) (*frv*)

HMV.1858 (Vic.7197) — March & Scherzo Love of 3 Oranges

HMV.D1859/60 (Vic.7251/2) BSO — Ravel: Bolero Satie: Gymnopædie No. 1 (orch. Debussy)

HMV.D1923/7 (Vic.7294/8) BSO — Tchaikowsky: Symphony No. 6, Op. 74

HMV.D2089/93 (Vic.6939/43) BSO — Beethoven: Symphony No. 6, Op. 68

HMV.D2094/6 (Vic.6998/7000) BSO — Stravinsky: Petrouschka Apollon & Terpsichore, Apollon Musagète

Vic.7370/1 BSO — Ravel: Ma Mère l'Oye

HMV.DB1541/2 (Vic.7413/4) BSO — Ravel: La Valse Debussy/Ravel: Danse

HMV.DB1890/3 (Vic.7372/5) BSO — Moussorgsky/ Ravel: Pictures at an Exhibition Debussy/Ravel: Sarabande

HMV.DB1983/6 (Vic.12113/6) BBC — Sibelius: Symphony No. 7, Op. 105 (Sibelius Society, Vol. II)

HMV.DB2238/42 (Vic.8508/12) LPO — Beethoven: Symphony No. 5, Op. 67 Haydn: Finale, Symphony No. 88 in G

HMV.DB2346/51 (Vic.8668/73) LPO — Beethoven: Symphony No. 3, Op. 55

HMV.DB2599/604S (Vic.8721/6S) BSO — Sibelius: Symphony No. 2, Op. 43

HMV.DB2605/7 (Vic.8889/91) BSO — Mendelssohn: Symphony No. 4, Op. 90

HMV.DB2616/20S (Vic.8619/23S) BSO — Strauss: Also sprach Zarathustra, Op. 30 (frv)

HMV.DB2899/903 (Vic.12-0972/6) BSO — Tchaikowsky: Symphony No. 4, Op. 36 Waltz, String Serenade, Op. 48

HMV.DB2984/5 (Vic.18409/10) BSO — Liszt: Mephisto Waltz Schubert: Ballet Music, Rosamunde, D 797

HMV.DB3009/10 BSO — Berlioz: Minuet, Presto, Waltz, Damnation de Faust, Handel: Larghetto, Concerto Grosso No. 12

HMV.10040/2 (Vic.14117/9) BSO — Schubert: Symphony No. 8, D 759

HMV.DB3125/7 (Vic.15304/6) BSO — Haydn: Symphony No. 102 in B flat

HMV.DB3165/7 (Vic.14353/5) BSO — Tchaikowsky: Ov. Romeo & Juliet Sibelius: The Maiden with the Roses, Op.54, No. 3

HMV.DB3168/71 BSO — Sibelius: Symphony No. 5, Op. 82 The Maiden with the Roses, Op. 54, No. 3

Vic.15019/23 BSO — Sibelius: Symphony No. 5, Op. 82 Pohjola's Daughter, Op. 49

HMV.DB3172/4 (Vic.14257/9) BSO — Beethoven: Symphony No. 8, Op. 93

HMV.DB3210 (Vic. 14577) BSO — Fauré: Elégie (Bedetti, 'cello)

HMV.DB3260 (Vic.14415) BSO — Moussorgsky: Prelude, Khowantschina

HMV.DB3604/6 (Vic.14907/9) BSO — Prokofieff: Violin Concerto No. 2, Op. 63 (Heifetz)

HMV.DB3655/7 (Vic.14948/50) BSO — Prokofieff: Suite, Lieutenant Kije, Op. 60 March & Scherzo, Love of 3 Oranges, Op. 33a

HMV.DB3668/9 (Vic.18527/8) BSO — Vivaldi/Siloti: Concerto Grosso, Op. 3, No. 11 Grieg: Last Spring, Op. 34, No. 2

HMV.DB3812/3 (Vic.15363/4) BSO — Copland: El Salón Mexico (frv) Stravinsky: Song of the Volga Boatmen

HMV.DB3900/02 (Vic.15442/4) BSO — Prokofieff: Peter and the Wolf, Op. 67

HMV.DB3919/22S (Vic.15771/4S) BSO — Beethoven: Symphony No. 2, Op. 36

HMV.DB3923/5 (Vic.15851/3) BSO — Debussy: La Mer

HMV.DB3943/4 (Vic.15418/9) BSO — C.P.E. Bach: Concerto in D major

HMV.DB3983/6 (Vic.15895/8) BSO — Schumann: Symphony No. 1, Op. 38

HMV.DB5722/3 BSO — Sibelius: Pohjola's Daughter, Op. 49 Prokofieff: March & Scherzo, Love of 3 Oranges, Op. 33a

HMV.DB5738/42 (Vic.15626/30)	BSO	Brahms: Violin Concerto, Op. 77 (Heifetz)
HMV.DB5957/8 (Vic.18063/4)	BSO	Mozart: Symphony No. 29, K. 201
HMV.DB5959/61S (Vic.18065/7S)	BSO	Mozart: Symphony No. 34, K. 338
HMV.DB5992/3 (Vic.18310/1)	BSO	Sibelius: *Tapiola*, Op. 112
HMV.DB6025/7	BSO	Debussy: *La Mer*
HMV.DB6137/8 (Vic.15885/6)	BSO	Roy Harris: Symphony No. 3 (*frv*)
HMV.DB6239/40 (Vic.11-9496/7)	BSO	Ravel: Suite No. 2, *Daphnis & Chloé*
HMV.DB6261/5 (Vic.11-8751/5)	BSO	Berlioz: *Harold in Italy*, Op. 16 (Primrose)
HMV.DB6286/7 (Vic.11-8991/2)	BSO	Strauss: *Till Eulenspiegel*, Op. 82
HMV.DB6455/6 (Vic.11-9156/7)	BSO	Bach: Brandenburg Concerto No. 3 in G Prelude, Solo Vln. Sonata No. 6 (arr. Pick-Mangiagalli)
HMV.DB6457/8 (Vic.11-9158/9)	BSO	Bach: Brandenburg Concerto No. 4 in G (Laurent, Madsen, Bergin)
HMV.DB6660/4 (Vic.11-9433/7)	BSO	Prokofieff: Symphony No. 5, Op. 100
HMV.DB6699 (Vic.11-9729)	BSO	Ravel: *Pavane pour une Infante défunte*
HMV.DB6736 (Vic.11-9363)	BSO	Mozart: Symphony No. 26, K. 184
HMV.DB6764/5 (Vic.11-9538/9)	BSO	Bach: Brandenburg Concerto No. 2 in F (Voisin, Laurent Gillet, Burgin)
HMV.DB6928/9 (Vic.12-0790/1)	BSO	Strauss: *Don Juan*, Op. 20
HMV.DB9256/8 (Vic.11-9082/4)	BSO	Schubert: Symphony No. 8, D. 759
Vic.12-0273/5	BSO	Schubert: Symphony No. 5, D. 485
HMV.ED235/46 (Vic.17816/27)	BSO	Beethoven: *Missa Solennis*, Op. 123 (Vreeland, Kaskas, Priebe, Cordon, Harvard Glee Club, Radcliffe Choral Society)
Vic.11-8957/9	BSO	Rachmaninoff: *Island of the Dead*, Op. 29 *Vocalise*, Op. 34, No. 4
Vic.11-9008	BSO	Berlioz: Ov. *Carnaval Romain*, Op. 9
Vic.11-9583/5	BSO	Bach: Suite No. 2 in B minor (Laurent)

Vic.11-9634/6	BSO	Shostakovitch: Symphony No. 9, Op. 90 (*frv*)
Vic.12-0050/7	BSO	Beethoven: Symphony No. 9, Op. 125 (Yeend, Alberts, Lloyd, Pease, Berkshire Festival Chorus)
Vic.LM1021	BSO	Beethoven: Symphony No. 5, Op. 67
Vic.LM1025	BSO	Brahms: Symphony No. 3, Op. 90
Vic.LM1051	BSO	Brahms: Symphony No. 1, Op. 68
Vic.LM1063	BSO	Bach: Brandenburg Concerto No. 1 in F/No. 6 in B flat
Vic.LM1141	BSO	Mozart: Symphony No. 39, K. 543
Vic.LM1145	BSO	Beethoven: Symphony No. 3, Op. 55

CHARLES MUNCH

OisL.93	?PPO	Mozart: Adagio & Fugue in C minor, K. 546
HMV.DB2577/9 (Vic.14424/6)	?OLa	Saint-Saens: Concerto No. 4, Op. 44 (Cortot)
Pat.PDT49/50	PCO	Liszt: Concerto No. 1 in E flat (Benvenuti)
HMV.DB3885/6 (Vic.15749/50)	PCO	Ravel: Concerto for the Left Hand (Cortot) (?*frv*)
HMV.W165/8	PCO	Ravel: *La Valse*; *Pavane pour une Infante défunte*
HMV.W1524/7S	PCO	Mozart: Concerto in D minor, K 466 (Doyen)
HMV.W1600/2	PCO	Honegger: Symphony No. 2 (*frv*)
Decca.X204/5	PPO	Ravel: Concerto for the Left Hand (Blancard)
Decca.K1584/6	PCO	Ravel: *Daphnis & Chloe*
Decca.K1587/8	PCO	Franck: *Variations Symphoniques* (Joyce)
Decca.K1637/8	PCO	Ravel: *Bolero*
Decca.K1639/42	PCO	Franck: Symphony in D minor
Decca.K1644	PCO	Fauré: *Pavane*, Op. 50 Roussel: *Petite Suite*, Op. 39

Decca.K1695	PCO	Saint-Saëns: *Le Rouet d'Omphale*, Op. 31
Decca.K1715/8	PCO	Mendelssohn: Symphony No. 5, Op. 107
Decca.K1756/7	PCO	Prokofieff: Symphony No. 1, Op. 25 (*Classical*)
Decca.K1763/5 (Decca.AX490/2)	PCO	Debussy: Ibéria, *Images III* No. 2 *Berceuse héroïque*
Decca.K2069	ACO	Saint-Saëns: *Danse Macabre*, Op. 40
Decca.AK1691/2	LPO	Roussel: *Festin de l'Araignée*, Op. 17
Decca.AK1740/1	LPO	Fauré: Prelude, Fileuse, Molto Adagio, Sicilienne, *Pelléas et Mélisande*, Op. 80
Decca.AK1781/4	LPO	Bizet: Symphony in C major (*frv*)
Decca.AK1968/73	PCO	Tchaikowsky: Symphony No. 6, Op. 74
Decca.AK2022/4	LPO	Schumann: Symphony No. 4, Op. 120
Decca.AK2055/9	ACO	Brahms: Violin Concerto, Op. 77 (Renardy)
Decca.LX305	PCO	Beethoven: Symphony No. 8, Op. 93
Decca.LXT2512	PCO	Berlioz: *Romeo & Juliet*, Op. 17 (excerpts) Royal Hunt & Storm, Act II, *Les Troyens à Carthage*
Decca.LXT2565	PCO	Ravel: Concerto in G major (Henriot)
Col.LFX595/8	PCO	Tchaikowsky: Piano Concerto No. 1, Op. 23 (Konstantinov)
Col.LFX631/3	PCO	Ravel: Concerto for the Left Hand (Février)
Col. LFX880/5	FNR	Berlioz: *Symphonie Fantastique*, Op.14
Col.LFX901/4	NYP	Saint-Saëns: Symphony No. 3, Op. 78
Col.33CX1118	NYP	D'Indy: *Symphonie sur un Chant montagnard* Franck: *Variations Symphoniques* (Casadesus)
Vic.12-1207/8	BSO	Ravel: *La Valse*
Vic.12-3078	BSO	Berlioz: Ov. *Béatrice et Bénédict*
Vic.LM41	BSO	Schubert: Symphony No. 2, D 125
Vic.LM49	BSO	Haydn: Symphony No. 104 in D
Vic.LM1032	BSO	Rachmaninoff: Concerto No. 3, Op. 30 (Janis)
Vic.LM1034	BSO	Beethoven: Symphony No. 7, Op. 92
Vic.LM1041	BSO	Debussy: *La Mer* Ravel: *Rapsodie Espagnole Ma Mère l'Oye*
Vic.LM1086	BSO	Brahms: Symphony No. 4, Op. 98
Vic.LM1100	BSO	Tchaikowsky: Symphony No. 4, Op. 36
Vic.LM1114	BSO	Beethoven: Symphony No. 9, Op. 125 (Price, Forrester, Poleri, Tozzi, New England Conservatory Chorus)
Vic.LM1162	BSO	Debussy: *Images*— complete
Vic.LM1197	BSO	Tchaikowsky: *Francesca da Rimini* Op. 32 Ov. *Romeo & Juliet*
Vic.LM1741	BSO	Ravel: *Pavane pour une Infante défunte* (Stagliano) Roussel: Suite, *Bacchus et Ariane* Honegger: Symphony No. 5 (*di tre Re*)
Vic.LM2255	BSO	Wagner: Prelude and Liebestod, *Tristan & Isolde* Immolation scene, *Götterdämmerung* (Eileen Farrell)
HMV.ALP1123	BSO	Brahms: Piano Concerto No. 2, Op. 83 (Rubinstein)
HMV.ALP1179/80	BSO	Berlioz: *Romeo & Juliet*, Op. 17— complete (Roggero, Chabay, Yi-Kwei, Harvard Glee Club, Radcliffe Choral Society)
HMV.ALP1203	BSO	Schumann: Symphony No. 1, Op. 36
HMV.ALP1211	BSO	Strauss: *Don Quixote*, Op. 35 (Piatigorsky)

HMV.ALP1225/7	BSO	Berlioz: *Damnation de Faust*, Op. 24—complete (Danco, Poleri, Singher, Harvard Glee Club, Radcliffe Choral Society)
HMV.ALP1368	BSO	Debussy: *La Demoiselle élue* (de los Angeles, Smith, Radcliffe Choral Society)
HMV.ALP1384	BSO	Berlioz: *Symphonie Fantastique*, Op. 14
HMV.ALP1415	BSO	Beethoven: Symphony No. 5, Op. 67
		Schubert: Symphony No. 8, D 759
HMV.ALP1460	BSO	Chausson: *Poème* Saint-Saens: *Introduction & Rondo Capriccioso* (David Oistrakh) Berlioz: Réverie, Capulets' Feast, Love Scene, *Romeo & Juliet*, Op. 17
RCA.LD6098-1/2	BSO	Berlioz: *Romeo & Juliet*, Op. 17—complete (Elias, Valletti, Tozzi, New England Conservatory Chorus)
RCA.RB6509	BSO	Dvořák: Symphony No. 8(4) Op. 88
RCA.RB6521	BSO	Berlioz: *Symphonie Fantastique*, Op. 14
RCA.RB6540	BSO	Debussy: *Prélude à l'après-midi d'un faune* Nuages, Fêtes, *Nocturnes* 1 & 2 *Printemps*
RCA.RB6550	BSO	Tchaikowsky: Symphony No. 6, Op. 74
RCA.RB16006	BSO	Beethoven: Symphony No. 6, Op. 68
RCA.RB16061/2	BSO	Berlioz: *L'Enfance du Christ*, Op. 25
RCA.RB16024	BSO	Elgar: Introduction & Allegro for Strings, Op. 47 Tchaikowsky: Serenade for Strings, Op. 48 Barber: Adagio for Strings, Op. 11
RCA.RB16030	BSO	Piston: Symphony No. 6 Martinu: *Fantaisies Symphoniques*
RCA.RB16074/5	BSO	Bach: Brandenburg Concerti 1–6
RCA.RB16084 (RCA.SB2009)	BSO	Berlioz: *Harold in Italy*, Op. 16 (Primrose)
RCA.RB16091 (RCA.SB2025)	BSO	Beethoven: Symphony No. 3, Op. 55
RCA.RB16177	BSO	Brahms: Symphony No. 1, Op. 68
RCA.RB16204	BSO	Tchaikowsky: Violin Concerto, Op.35 (Szeryng)
(RCA.RB16210 (RCA.SB2085)	BSO	Schubert: Symphony No. 9, D 944
RCA.RB16217 (RCA.SB2040)	BSO	Brahms: Piano Concerto No. 1, Op. 15 (Graffman)
RCA.RB16224/5 (RCA.SB2096/7)	BSO	Berlioz: *Grande Messe des Morts*, Op. 5—complete— (Simoneau, New England Conservatory Chorus)
RCA.RB16254 RCA.SB2125)	BSO	Berlioz: *Carnaval Romain*, Op. 9 *Béatrice et Bénédict Corsair*, Op. 21 *Benvenuto Cellini*, Op. 23 Royal Hunt & Storm, Act II, *Les Troyens à Carthage*
RCA.RB16255	BSO	Schumann: Symphony No. 1, Op. 38 Ov. *Manfred*, Op. 115
RCA.RB16266 (RCA.SB2137)	BSO	Ravel: *Daphnis & Chloe*—complete— (New England Conservatory Chorus)

INDEX